Data Driven e-Science

Simon C. Lin • Eric Yen

Editors

Data Driven e-Science

Use Cases and Successful Applications
of Distributed Computing Infrastructures
(ISGC 2010)

Editors

Simon C. Lin
Academia Sinica Grid Computing Centre
Sec. 3, Academia Road 128
Nankang, Taipei 115
Taiwan R.O.C.
Simon.Lin@twgrid.org

Eric Yen
Academia Sinica Grid Computing Centre
Sec. 3, Academia Road 128
Nankang, Taipei 115
Taiwan R.O.C.
Eric.Yen@twgrid.org

ISBN 978-1-4899-8247-6   ISBN 978-1-4419-8014-4 (eBook)
DOI 10.1007/978-1-4419-8014-4
Springer New York Dordrecht Heidelberg London

Printed on acid-free paper

Springer is part of Springer Science+Business Media (www.springer.com)

Preface

The International Symposium on Grid Computing 2010[1] was held at Academia Sinica in Taipei, Taiwan on 9th to 12th March 2010. A series of workshops and tutorials preceded the symposium, attracting 70 people.

The symposium programme focussed on data driven e-Science highlighting use cases and successful applications of distributed computing infrastructures in the Asia Pacific region. There was a mixture of plenary and parallel sessions as well as a poster exhibition.

The symposium attracted more than 150 participants from 27 countries spanning Asia, Europe and the Americas. The keynotes by invited speakers highlighted the impact of distributed computing infrastructures in research disciplines such as social sciences and humanities, civil protection, paediatrics and high energy physics. Having identified important use cases, further keynotes outlined plans for their long-term support and the move towards sustainable infrastructures across Asia, Europe and Latin America. Plenary sessions entitled Grid Activities in Asia Pacific surveyed the state of grid deployment across 12 Asian countries.

For the first time there was participation from Latin American colleagues which opened possibilities for cooperation between groups in Asia and Latin America the two regions on research in the domain of natural disaster mitigation, epidemic studies and drug discovery for diseases such as dengue fever and malaria.

Through the parallel sessions, the impact of distributed computing infrastructures in disciplines such as social sciences and humanities, life sciences, earth sciences, high energy physics, digital libraries and natural disaster mitigation. Operational procedures, middleware and security aspects were addressed in a dedicated sessions. A subject which has seen a growing interest is the integration of grid and clouds with a very popular series of talks to the point that we are considering renaming ISGC the International Symposium on Grids and Clouds.

A number projects, many co-funded by the European Commission, are coming to close during the first half of 2010, so the symposium provided the occasion for them to present their results and lessons learnt. At the same time a number of new projects are starting and hence can build on the result and experiences of their predecessors. A key subject that was in the minds of participants from all regions was how to ensure the long-term availability of distributed computing infrastructures for the research communities. A clear value of the symposium was that participants from different continents could compare their experiences, identifying

---

[1] http://event.twgrid.org/isgc2010

common questions and barriers to sustainability and profiting from each other experiences to develop solutions.

For the first time, the symposium was covered online in real-time by the Grid-Cast team from the GridTalk project. A running blog including summarises of specific sessions as well as video interviews with keynote speakers and personalities and photos[2].

Prof. Simon C. Lin organised an intense social programme with a gastronomic tour of Taipei culminating with a banquet for all the symposium's participants at the Howard Plaza hotel.

I would like to thank all the members of the programme committee, the participants and above all our hosts, Prof. Simon C. Lin and his excellent support team at Academia Sinica.

Dr. Bob Jones
ISGC Program Committee Chair

---

[2] http://gridtalk-project.blogspot.com/search/label/ISGC 2010

Contents

Part VI Grid Middleware and Interoperability

Alberto Forti, C. Grandi, D. Gregori, L. Li Gioi, B. Martelli,
A. Prosperini, P. P. Ricci, Elisabetta Ronchieri, V. Sapunenko,
A. Sartirana, V. Vagnoni and Riccardo Zappi

Part X Applications on Humanities and Social Sciences

Part XI Applications on Earth Sciences and Mitigation

Part XII Applications on Biomedicine and Life Sciences

Program Committee

Chair: Bob Jones
  EGEE, Switzerland

Kento Aida
National Institute of Informatics, Japan

Eileen Berman
Fermi National Accelerator Laboratory, USA

Ian Bird
CERN, Switzerland

Tobias Blanke
King's College London, UK

Kors Bos
NIKHEF, Netherlands

Atul Gurtu
TIFR, India

David Kelsey
Rutherford Appleton Laboratory, UK

Doman Kim
Chonnam National University, Republic of Korea

Hing-Yan Lee
National Grid Office, Singapore

Yannick Legre
Healthgrid, France

Tanya Levshina
Levshina Fermi National Accelerator Laboratory, USA

Simon C. Lin
Institute of Physics, Academia Sinica, Taiwan

Satoshi Matsuoka
Tokyo Institute of Technology, Japan

Ludek Matyska
CESNET, Zikova 4, Czech Republic

Klaus-Peter Mickel
Karlsruhe Institute of Technology, Germany

Reagan Moore
University of North Carolina at Chapel Hill (UNC-CH), USA

Mitsuaki Nozaki
KEK, Japan

Marco Paganoni
INFN, Italy

Ruth Pordes
Fermi National Accelerator Laboratory, USA

Peter Rice
European Bioinformatics Institute, UK

Hiroshi Sakamoto
University of Tokyo, Japan

Takashi Sasaki
KEK, Japan

Pansak Siriruchatapong
NECTEC, Thailand

Dane Skow
Argonne National Laboratory and University of Chicago, USA

Geoffrey N. Taylor
University of Melbourne, Australia

Steven Timm
Fermi National Accelerator Laboratory, USA

Sornthep Vannarat
NECTEC, Thailand

Alexander Voss
National Centre for e-Social Science, UK

Vicky White
Fermi National Accelerator Laboratory, USA

Bao-ping Yan
Chinese Academy of Science, China

Contributors

Bernie Ács
National Center for Supercomputing Applications, UIUC, USA

Emmanuel D. Aldea
Research and Development Division, Advanced Science and Technology Institute, Department of Science and Technology, UP Technology Park Complex, Philippines

Balamurali Ananthan
Tech-X Corporation, CO, USA

D. Andreotti
INFN-CNAF, Bologna, Italy

Kamron Aroonrua
National Electronics and Computer Technology Center, Thailand

Andreas Aschenbrenner
State and University Library Goettingen, Germany

Hamidi Abdul Aziz
Disaster Research Nexus, School of Civil Engineering, Engineering Campus, Universiti Sains Malaysia, Malaysia

Rey Vincent P. Babilonia
Research and Development Division, Advanced Science and Technology Institute, Department of Science and Technology, UP Technology Park Complex, Philippines

Antun Balaz
SCL, Institute of Physics Belgrade, Serbia

Amnart Bali
Director of Disaster Relief and Public Health, Thai Red Cross

Roberto Barbera
INFN Catania / Catania University, Italy

Rudiger Berlich
Karlsruhe Institute of Technology, Steinbuch Centre for Computing, Germany

Tobias Blanke
Centre for e-Research, Kings College London, UK

D. Bonacorsi
University of Bologna, Physics Department and INFN-Bologna, Italy

S. Boonya-aroonnet
Hydro and Agro Informatics Institute; Ministry of Science and Technology, Thailand

P. Busson
LLR,E. Polytechnique,Palaiseau, French

Leonardo Candela
Istituto di Scienza e Tecnologie dell'Informazione "Alessandro Faedo" -Italian National Research Council (CNR), Italy

John Casson
STFC, Rutherford Appleton Laboratory, UK

A. Cavalli
INFN-CNAF, Bologna, Italy

Subhasis Chattopadhyay
Variable Energy Cyclotron Centre, Department of Atomic Energy, Government of India, India

Zhiduan Chen
State Key Laboratory of Systematic and Evolutionary botany, Institute of Botany, Chinese Academy of Sciences, China

Royol Chitradon
Hydro and Agro Informatics Institute; Ministry of Science and Technology, Thailand

Leandro N. Ciuffo
INFN Catania, Italy / RNP, Brazil

A.S. Cofiño
Dep. of Applied Mathematics and Computer Sciences, University of Cantabria, Spain

Hélène Cordier
IN2P3/CNRS Computing Center, Lyon, France

Eli Dart
Energy Sciences Network

L. dell'Agnello
INFN-CNAF, Bologna, Italy

Marco Fargetta
INFN Catania, Italy

Enrico Fattibene
Istituto Nazionale di Fisica Nucleare CNAF, Bologna, Italy

Nils gentschen Felde
MNM-Team, Ludwig-Maximilians-Universitat Munchen, Germany

Tiziana Ferrari
Istituto Nazionale di Fisica Nucleare CNAF, Bologna, Italy

Alberto Forti
INFN-CNAF, Bologna, Italy

Stefan Freitag
Dortmund University of Technology, USA

P. Mora de Freitas
LLR,E. Polytechnique,Palaiseau, French

Sven Gabriel
Gemfony scientific

Luciano Gaido
Istituto Nazionale di Fisica Nucleare, Torino, Italy

Yanping Gao
Scientific Data Center, Computer Network Information Center, Chinese Academy of Sciences, China

Ariel Garcia
Karlsruhe Institute of Technology, Steinbuch Centre for Computing, Germany

Gabriele Garzoglio
Fermi National Accelerator Laboratory, IL, USA

Antonia Ghiselli
INFN-CNAF

L. Li Gioi
now at Laboratoire de Physique Corpusculaire (LPC), Clermont-Ferrand, France
formerly at INFN-CNAF, Bologna, Italy

John Gordon
e-Science Centre, Science and Technology Facilities Council, UK

C. Grandi
INFN-Bologna, Italy

Anders Rhod Gregersen
NDGF -Nordic DataGrid Facility and Aalborg University, Denmark

D. Gregori
INFN-CNAF, Bologna, Italy

Francois Grey
UNOSAT, CERN, Switzerland

Philippe Gros
Lund University, Div. of Experimental High Energy Physics, Sweden

Dan Gunter
Lawrence Berkeley National Laboratory

O. Gutsche
Fermilab, Chicago, USA

Patrick Harms
State and University Library Goettingen, Germany

Nattapon Harnsamut
National Electronics and Computer Technology Center, Thailand

Xing He
Scientific Data Center, Computer Network Information Center, Chinese Academy
of Sciences, China

Mark Hedges
Centre for e-Research, Kings College London, UK

P. Hennion
LLR,E. Polytechnique,Palaiseau, French

Jason Hick
National Energy Research Scientific Computing Center

Wen-Jen Hu
Department of Computer Science, Tunghai University, Taiwan

Bukhary Ikhwan Ismail
MIMOS Berhad, Malaysia

Devendran Jagadisan
MIMOS Berhad, Malaysia

Ming Jiang
e-Science Centre, Science and Technology Facilities Council, UK

M. Jouvin
LAL,U.Paris-Sud, Osay, French

Peter Kacsuk
SZTAKI, Budapest, Hungary

Mohammad Fairus Khalid
MIMOS Berhad, Malaysia

Jan Kmunicek
CESNET, Czech Republic

Hock Lye Koh
Disaster Research Nexus, School of Civil Engineering, Engineering Campus, Universiti Sains Malaysia, Malaysia

Miklos Kozlovszky
MTA SZTAKI, Budapest, Hungary

Dieter Kranzlmuller
MNM-Team, Ludwig-Maximilians-Universitat Munchen, Germany

Petr Kulhánek
National Centre for Biomolecular Research, Masaryk University, Czech Republic

Marcel Kunze
Karlsruhe Institute of Technology, Steinbuch Centre for Computing, Germany

Jason Lee
National Energy Research Scientific Computing Center

Olivier Lequeux
IN2P3/CNRS Computing Center, Lyon, France

C. Leroy
IRFU, CEA, Saclay, French

Tanya Levshina
Fermi National Accelerator Laboratory, IL, USA

Jianhui Li
Scientific Data Center, Computer Network Information Center, Chinese Academy of Sciences, China

Yong Li
Fairylake Botanical Garden, Chinese Academy of Sciences, China

Ioannis Liabotis
GRNET, Greece

Simon C. Lin
Institute of Physics, Academia Sinica, Taiwan

Xiaoguang Lin
Scientific Data Center, Computer Network Information Center, Chinese Academy of Sciences, China

Jonas Lindemann
LUNARC, Lund University, Sweden

Hongmei Liu
Fairylake Botanical Garden, Chinese Academy of Sciences, China

Yong Liu
Scientific Data Center, Computer Network Information Center, Chinese Academy
of Sciences, China

Sinikka Loikkanen
IN2P3/CNRS Computing Center, Lyon, France

Jeff Long
Lawrence Livermore National Laboratory

Cyril L'Orphelin
IN2P3/CNRS Computing Center, Lyon, France

Taksiah A. Majid
Disaster Research Nexus, School of Civil Engineering, Engineering Campus,
Universiti Sains Malaysia, Malaysia

Branko Marovic
University of Belgrade Computer Centre, Serbia

B. Martelli
INFN-CNAF, Bologna, Italy

Alberto Masoni
INFN Sezione di Cagliari, Italy

Gilles Mathieu
e-Science Centre, Science and Technology Facilities Council, UK
STFC, Rutherford Appleton Laboratory, UK

Ludek Matyska
CESNET, Zikova 4, Czech Republic

Vorawit Meesuk
HAII, Head of environmental observation and telemetry section

V. Mendoza
LPNHE, U.Paris-7, Paris, French

Zhen Meng
Scientific Data Center, Computer Network Information Center, Chinese Academy
of Sciences, China

P. Micout
IRFU, CEA, Saclay, French

Giuseppe Misurelli
Istituto Nazionale di Fisica Nucleare CNAF, Bologna, Italy

Vijaya Natarajan
Lawrence Berkeley National Laboratory

Gabriel Neagu
ICI, Bucharest, Romania

Cristina Del Cano Novales
e-Science Centre, Science and Technology Facilities Council, UK

Pasquale Pagano
Istituto di Scienza e Tecnologie dell'Informazione "Alessandro Faedo" -Italian
National Research Council (CNR), Italy

Marco Paganoni
University of Milano-Bicoca and INFN, Italy

Wolfgang Pempe
State and University Library Goettingen, Germany

M. Petitdidier
Université Versailles St-Quentin; CNRS/INSU, LATMOS-IPSL, Guyancourt –
France

Jedsada Phengsuwan
National Electronics and Computer Technology Center, Thailand

G. Philippon
LAL,U.Paris-Sud, Osay, French

Jukrapong Ponhan
National Electronics and Computer Technology Center, Thailand

S. Dal Pra
INFN-CNAF, Bologna, Italy

Ognjen Prnjat
GRNET, Greece

A. Prosperini
INFN-CNAF, Bologna, Italy

Marilyn V. Rey
Research and Development Division, Advanced Science and Technology Institute,
Department of Science and Technology, UP Technology Park Complex,
Philippines

Sylvain Reynaud
IN2P3/CNRS Computing Center, Lyon, France

P. P. Ricci
INFN-CNAF, Bologna, Italy

Massimo Rizzi
ARCEM - Associazione Italiana per la Ricerca sulle Patologie Cerebrali e del Midollo Spinale, Italy

Angus Roberts
University of Sheffield, UK

Giuseppe La Rocca
Italian National Institute of Nuclear Physics, Division of Catania, Italy
Department of Physics and Astronomy of the University of Catania, Italy

William Rogers
e-Science Centre, Science and Technology Facilities Council, UK

Elisabetta Ronchieri
INFN-CNAF, Bologna, Italy

Miroslav Ruda
CESNET, Zikova 5, Czech Republic

Naiyana Sahavechaphan
National Electronics and Computer Technology Center, Thailand

Pablo Saiz
CERN -European Organisation for Nuclear Research, Switzerland

V. Sapunenko
INFN-CNAF, Bologna, Italy

Urizza Marie L. Sarte
Research and Development Division, Advanced Science and Technology Institute, Department of Science and Technology, UP Technology Park Complex, Philippines

A. Sartirana
now at Laboratoire Leprince-Ringuer (LLR), Ecole Polytecnique, Palaiseau, France
formerly at INFN-CNAF, Bologna, Italy

Diego Scardaci
INFN Catania, Italy

F. Schaer
IRFU, CEA, Saclay, French

I. Semenjuk
LLR,E. Polytechnique,Palaiseau, French

Cevat Sener
Middle East Technical University, Ankara, Turkey

Arie Shoshani
Lawrence Berkeley National Laboratory

Alex Sim
Lawrence Berkeley National Laboratory

Vikas Singhal
Variable Energy Cyclotron Centre, Department of Atomic Energy, Government of India, India

Kathleen Smith
University of Illinois at Urbana-Champaign, USA

Wong K. Snidvongs
Member of Executive Board of Directors, HAII

Peter Solagna
Istituto Nazionale di Fisica Nucleare, Padova, Italy

Milan Sova
CESNET

Zora Strelcova
National Centre for Biomolecular Research, Masaryk University, Czech Republic

Su Yean Teh
School of Mathematical Sciences, Universiti Sains Malaysia, Malaysia

Gabor Terstyansky
Centre for Parallel Computing, University of Westminster, London, UK

Steven Timm
Fermi National Accelerator Laboratory, IL, USA

Simon Toth
CESNET, Zikova 6, Czech Republic

Alexandru Tudose
Centre for Parallel Computing, University of Westminster, London, UK

Andy Turner
University of Leeds, UK

Suriya U-ruekolan
National Electronics and Computer Technology Center, Thailand

V. Vagnoni
INFN-Bologna, Italy

Sornthep Vannarat
National Electronics and Computer Technology Center, Thailand

Pierre Veyre
IN2P3/CNRS Computing Center, Lyon, France

Alex Voss
School of Computer Science, University of St Andrews, UK

Dusan Vudragovic
SCL, Institute of Physics Belgrade, Serbia

Nanbor Wang
Tech-X Corporation, CO, USA

Johannes Watzl
MNM-Team, Ludwig-Maximilians-Universitat Munchen, Germany

Dean Williams
Lawrence Livermore National Laboratory

Stephen Winter
Centre for Parallel Computing, University of Westminster, London, UK

Chao-Tung Yang
Department of Computer Science, Tunghai University, Taiwan

Eric Yen
Academia Sinica Grid Computing Centre (ASGC), Taiwan
Department of Management Information System, National Cheng-Chi University, Taiwan

Riccardo Zappi
INFN-CNAF, Bologna, Italy

Andrey Zarochentsev
St Petersburg State University, Russia

Shouzhou Zhang
Fairylake Botanical Garden, Chinese Academy of Sciences, China

Yuanchun Zhou
Scientific Data Center, Computer Network Information Center, Chinese Academy of Sciences, China

Part I
Asia Federation Report

Asia Federation Report on International Symposium on Grid Computing (ISGC) 2010

Francois Grey[1] and Simon C. Lin[2]

1. UNOSAT, CERN, Switzerland
2. Institute of Physics, Academia Sinica, Taiwan

EXECUTIVE SUMMARY

This report provides an overview of developments in the Asia-Pacific region, based on presentations made at the International Symposium on Grid Computing 2010 (ISGC 2010), held 5-12 March at Academia Sinica, Taipei. The document includes a brief overview of the EUAsiaGrid project as well as progress reports by representatives of 13 Asian countries presented at ISGC 2010. In alphabetical order, these are: Australia, China, India, Indonesia, Japan, Malaysia, Pakistan, Philippines, Singapore, South Korea, Taiwan, Thailand and Vietnam.

As in 2009, the country reports represent a wide range of Grid technology penetration, reflecting to some extent the different countries' socio-economic levels of development. Participation in the Worldwide LHC Computing Grid (WLCG) remains a common incentive for many countries' involvement in Grid technology. For example, Pakistan has established a federated Tier-2 activity, as no single institution was adequately resourced for this.

A second driving force is the European Commission's bold initiatives to spread know-how and capacity for grid-based e-Science worldwide, based on the EGEE projects, and associated projects like EUAsiaGrid (see map below). As a result some countries of the region are even taking the lead in some EGEE-related developments. For example, South Korea's KISTI now leads development of AMGA, an official EGEE gLite middleware component for a metadata catalogue service on the grid.

A third factor that can be gleaned from these reports is the leadership that Taiwan's ASGC has shown in the region, which has enhanced bilateral collaborations between countries, and also led to multilateral initiatives driven by common challenges such as earthquake monitoring and finding cures to neglected diseases such as dengue fever.

While there is much progress to report, there is also a good deal of uncertainty looking to the future. As EUAsiaGrid comes to a close in 2010, a key question, echoed in some of the reports, is how to build on the burgeoning regional collaborations that this project has helped to create. Another element of uncertainty is how to transition from Grids to a grid/cloud hybrid world. Finally, the issue of af-

S.C. Lin and E. Yen (eds.), *Data Driven e-Science: Use Cases and Successful Applications of Distributed Computing Infrastructures (ISGC 2010)*, DOI 10.1007/978-1-4419-8014-4_1, © Springer Science+Business Media, LLC 2011

fordable high bandwidth network connectivity in the region remains a complex one, for political as well as economic reasons.

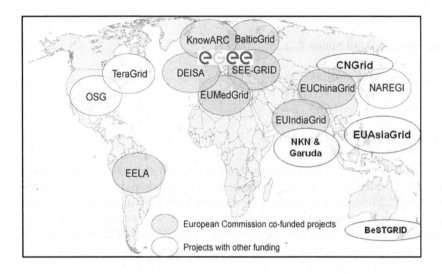

Fig. 1: EGEE-related projects (blue) and other major regional Grid initiatives.

1   EUASIAGRID OVERVIEW

EUAsiaGrid is an EU-funded project aiming to bridge a perceived gap between Europe and Asia in the area of Grid computing. The EUAsiaGrid project promotes awareness in the Asian countries of the EGEE e-Infrastructure and related European e-Infrastructure projects and supports capacity building in the region. To this end, it: (a) supports scientific communities through help with application porting and deployment; (b) provides training to further increase grid technology know-how; (c) monitors the results and gives feedback for the definition of policies. The consortium behind the project comprises 17 partners – fourteen in the Asia-Pacific region, distributed over twelve countries.

In order to develop a deeper understanding of the computing, storage, application support and training requirements, EUAsiaGrid has conducted a Requirements Survey in five different languages (English, Mandarin, Thai, Vietnamese, Malaysian). Based on the evidence collected and on the local expertise of the partner institutions in the region, the project has developed coordination and support activities to help foster the establishment of certified resources in the partner countries and to increase human capacity for local support. It has provided support for applications in areas such as high energy physics, computational chemistry, mitigation of natural disasters, bioinformatics and biomedical science and social sciences. The establishment of the EUAsia VO as a catch-all VO for the Asia-Pacific region has enabled researchers throughout the region to gain access to grid resources through a simplified process in order to increase uptake of the infrastructure.

The project has produced a number of successful instances of scientific work conducted on the infrastructure. For example, the EUAsiaGrid DC2 (Data Challenge 2) Refined Activity has focused on screening of 20,000 potential ligands for Avian Flu target proteins. EUAsiaGrid has delivered an intuitive and user-friendly productive system that enables biologists to run the simulations and to manage the results on the grid as easily as with a desktop application. In March 2009, virtual screening jobs were run consuming a total of 1,111 CPU-days under the EUAsia VO and more than 160,000 output files with a data volume of 12.8 Gigabytes were created and stored in a relational database. Based on the success of DC2, the EUAsiaGrid project has also launched the EUAsiaGrid Dengue Fever Activity. Similar activities are being prepared in other application areas such as disaster mitigation.

As many of today's scientific challenges require long-term international collaboration, it is paramount that researchers have access to a persistent, sustainable infrastructure that they can access as needed. Such an infrastructure needs to be supported so that researchers can take its operation for granted and focus on their substantive research work. In order to foster the long-term sustainability of the infrastructure the EUAsiaGrid has supported, the project has developed a roadmap that outlines the collaboration and governance structures for an Asia-Pacific Grid Initiative that will build on and expand on the work done by EUAsiaGrid.

[based on presentation by Marco Paganoni, INFN and University of Milano-Bicocca, Italy and contribution to EC Publication "Towards a Sustainable European e-Infrastructure"]

2   AUSTRALIA

The mission of the Australian Research Collaboration Service (ARCS) is to enable and enhance research through the provision of long-term eResearch support, services and tools. Core roles of ARCS include:

1. Agent for change and to promote uptake of eResearch services and tools at national level;
2. Key coordination role for national eResearch services and service providers;
3. Cooperative development & implementation of national standards & services (including international context);
4. Core activities in interoperability, collaboration and authorisation infrastructure and more recently also data storage infrastructure;
5. Development of discipline-specific tools & services.
6. Vehicle for federal government funding of eResearch services in ARCS core areas of interest;

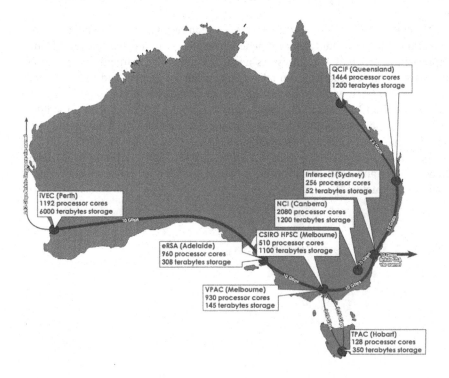

Fig. 2: Members of ARCS Services. Note figure excludes ANU and CSIRO as the figures for these are difficult to estimate.

ARCS is uniquely positioned as the entity which is the cooperative aspect of the key nationally distributed eResearch Service Providers.

ARCS Collaboration Services include:

- Video Collaboration: ARCS provides support for EVO (in collaboration with AARNET) and Access Grid technologies - including High Definition;
- Instant Messaging (IM): Jabber is flexible IM system like MSN, ICQ etc (ARCS runs an ARCS Jabber server);
- Research Oriented Web Tools: Research web-based workspaces and tools - Sakai, Drupal, Plone, Wiki, Twiki, Google Calendar, Google Apps...;
- Customer Service: End-user support is provided via telephone 1800 TOARCS (answered all business hours) & email request tracker system customer.service@arcs.org.au.

The ARCS Data Fabric is available to every Australian researcher and provides:

- Access to Data Fabric uses the AAF;
  A system to store, manage and share data currently based on iRODS (previously SRB);
- Distributed storage and access nodes;
- Some free storage to every researcher (can be extended typically at hardware cost only to arbitrary size);

The data fabric can be accessed with web interface (with Shibboleth) and webDAV and CLI tools (with SLCS); and will soon be unified with Grid/Cloud computing infrastructures.

Keys to a future successful ARCS:

1. deliver well and strongly into these core roles as required by the federal goverment;
2. development, deployment and operation of highly valued, robust, reliable & easy-to-use tools and services.

The 2008 Strategic Roadmap for Australian Research Infrastructure provided a future perspective and identified significant gaps in infrastructure provision, particularly electronic storage of research data. The result was a plan for a government funded enhanced eResearch infrastructure via a Super Science investment of $312 million for 2009-2013, with $97 million to ARCS for Data Storage and Collaboration Tools made up as:

- $35 million for ARCS Managed Core Services;
- $12 million for Research Community Projects;
- $50 million for Data Storage Infrastructure.

Concerning the ARCS Managed Core Services ($35m), the breakdown is:

- Continuous development, deployment and operation of ARCS managed core services Research Community Projects ($12m):
- Open competitive process involving national research communities to identify discipline specific services to be developed - typically ongoing operation by the research community themselves, perhaps building on core services.
- Data Storage Infrastructure ($50m):
- Consultation underway to identify data storage coinvestors and to decide on how many/which sites and how to achieve seamless interoperability.

[based on presentation by Anthony Williams, Executive Director, ARCS]

3   CHINA

In the past year, the Beijing Tier-2 Site for WLCG at the Institute of High Energy Physics, Chinese Academy of Sciences has ramped up to 1100 CPU cores, and 400TB disk storage capacities. This site has achieved a high availability in the range 98%-100%.

The analysis efficiency of the LHC detector ATLAS has been increased by a factor of 16 by introducing the FroNTier/Squid system. Frontier is a software subsystem that translates database queries into HTTP, looks up the results in a central database at CERN, and caches the results in an industry-standard HTTP proxy/caching server called Squid.

More than 85,000 jobs of CMS for LHC 2009 first collisions have been completed on the Beijing Tier-2 site in 2009, with a success rate of 95%.

The networking infrastructure used by the Tier-2 site in China is based on a TEIN3 Link to Europe: 1Gbps with timeout <170ms and the GLORIAD Link to America at 622Mbps. Data I/O per day is around 3TB.

To enhance the efficiency of software deployment, the Quattor system, an administration toolkit for optimizing resources, was improved. A customized monitoring system was developed to monitor the status of the local resources. The Tier-2 in Beijing has implemented a multi-grid job management system to facilitate job submission, query and management over different grid systems.

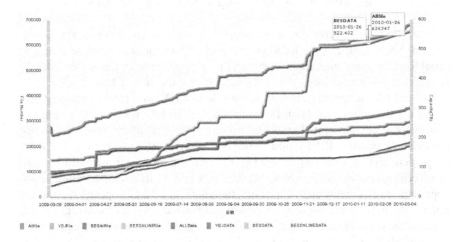

Fig. 3: Real time monitoring of CASTOR, showing rapid increase in file number and capacity handled since March 2009.

[based on presentation by Lu Wang, Computer Centre, IHEP]

4   INDIA

EUIndiaGrid has supported the improvement of the Indian network infrastructure both at National and International Level. It has also supported the establishment of the Indian National Certification Authority providing access to grids worldwide for Indian Researchers. The project has had an excellent collaboration with Indian National Grid Initiative, GARUDA, now entering phase three, and with the Department of Atomic Energy Grid Project, which focuses on WLCG.

The GARUDA project is coordinated by the Centre for Development of Advanced Computing (CDAC) and its network infrastructure was designed, set-up and operated by ERNET (Indian Education & Research Network, (http://www.eis.ernet.in/index.htm). Both CDAC and ERNET are partners in EU-IndiaGrid2 project.

The National Knowledge Network (NKN) will provide links to all the networks in India by a multi-gigabit, low-latency, OFC-based backbone. The main design consideration for NKN is to create an infrastructure that can scale and adapt to future requirements. The project's ultimate aim is to unite stakeholders in science, technology, higher education, R&D and e-governance using network speeds of tens of gigabits per second coupled with extremely low latencies.

The NKN will eventually cover over 1000 institutions directly. The initial phase of NKN, with 15 Core locations and about 57 institutes covering leading national R&D labs and educational institutes, is operational since December 2008. It is expected to connect more than 100 institutes by the end of March 2009. EU-IndiaGrid2 Indian partners have an active role in NKN with leading responsibilities in the Committee for High Performance and Grid Computing. This national framework is complemented by the transition to phase III of the TransEurasia Information Network (TEIN3) (http://www.tein3.net) which sees, for the first time the participation of India (represented by ERNET and the Department of Information Technology) to the feasibility study. NKN and TEIN3 set the premises for important developments and significant strengthening of the cooperation between Europe and India in the domain of international connectivity. This was highlighted in the context of dedicated meetings held in January 2009, with participation of representatives from EU-IndiaGrid project, DANTE, the European Commission and the Indian Government.

In addressing global research challenges, EU-IndiaGrid2 mobilises the provision of global cross-disciplinary research services by supporting specific user communities benefiting from Grid infrastructure in four strategic areas for EU-Indian user communities:

- Climate change – developing studies on South Asian climate change scenarios with a worldwide perspective
- High Energy Physics – driving EU-India collaboration in Large Hadron Collider data research
- Biology – increasing detail and scope of simulation software
- Material Sciences – testing and extension of complex applications

[Based on presentation by Alberto Masoni, INFN and on the EUIndiaGrid website]

5   INDONESIA

Research on Grids in Indonesia started around 2006, together with the development of INHERENT (Indonesia Higher Education Network). INHERENT connects more than 200 universities in Indonesia.

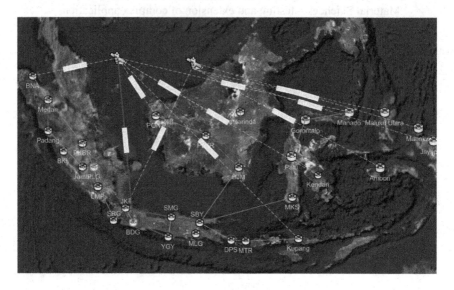

Fig. 4: INHERENT is the Indonesian national Research and Education Network which is currently connecting about 500 universities in Indonesia.

inGrid or Indonesian Grid is an infrastructure developed by the University of Indonesia using UCLA Grid Portal consisting Globus Toolkit 4 grid middleware and Gridsphere grid portlet framework. It is based on the INHERENT network. In 2008, there are two clusters connected to inGrid: one production cluster from Faculty of Computer Science, University of Indonesia and one research cluster. A range of applications available in the research cluster: Povray (3.1g); gcc; mpiB-LAST; g77; GNU Octave; GROMACS.

Some departments in Institut Teknologi Bandung (ITB) have been using cluster computing to support their Research and Education activity, including for weather prediction http://weather.geoph.itb.ac.id, and engineering physics to support data processing, design, and testing. http://computational.engineering.or.id.

In 2008 ITB joined the EUAsiaGrid Project, with the objectives of assisting regional integration to the wider Grid Infrastructure, capturing local e-Science requirements and promoting common e-Science applications, both existing and new.

The ITB Grid site was developed in collaboration with EUAsiaGrid Project and uses gLite middleware, consisting of:

- – User Interface combined with MON-Box
- – DPM/Storage Element
- – Computing Element
- – Workload Management System

Future Development includes integrating existing Cluster to Grid Infrastructure (current experiment is by Computational Engineering Lab In Engineering Physics Dept.)

In weather forecasting, the experimental application is using MODIS data from satellite images to generate weather forecast information and display it in a web page. Grid utilization to support Numerical Weather Prediction (NWP) research activity is concerned with the development of a common regional platform for NWP application in Southeast Asia. An NWP experiment is performed by implementing WRF4G (WRF for Grid) developed by University of Cantabria under EELA2 to find the most suitable downscaling strategy for NWP in South East Asia.

The result covers Indonesia and its neighbouring countries with horizontal resolution of 30 km, and covers the islands of Java, Bali, and South of Sumatera with a horizontal resolution of 10 km. Plotted parameters are 3-hourly convective rainfall, temperature at 2 m height, and surface equivalent potential temperature. The output is made available via a Google map interface, covering a few Indonesian cities twice a day.

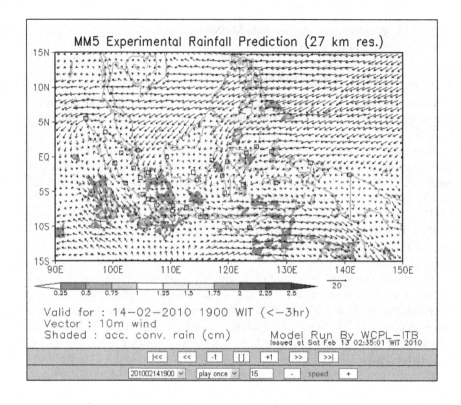

Fig. 5: Predicted rainfall over Indonesia, based on Numerical Weather Prediction.

[Based on a presentation by Basuki Suhardiman, Institut Teknologi Bandung, Indonesia]

6   JAPAN

The National Research Grid Initiative (NAREGI) Project originally started as an R&D project funded by the Ministry of Education, Culture, Sports, Science and Technology, MEXT (FY2003-FY2007) with a budget of 2bn Yen (~17M$) in FY2003. It involved a collaboration of National Labs Universities and Industry in the R&D activities. Nano-science applications were promoted. Starting in 2006, the project was redirected as a part of the Next Generation Supercomputer Development Project.

The goals of NAREGI were to develop a Grid Software System (R&D in Grid Middleware and Upper Layer) as the prototype of future grid infrastructure in scientific research in Japan and to provide a testbed to prove that a high-end grid computing environment (100+Tflop/s expected by 2007) could be practically utilized by the nano-science research community over the academic backbone network, SINET3. A further goal was to participate in international collaboration/interoperability (U.S., Europe, Asian Pacific), and to contribute to standardization activities such as OGF GIN-RG, PGI-WG etc.

NAREGI version 1 middleware was developed in FY2007, to have more flexible scheduling methods, reservation-based scheduling, coexistence with locally scheduled jobs, support of non-reservation-based scheduling, support of "bulk submission" for parameter sweep type jobs. In addition, improvement in maintainability and more systematic logging using Information Service (IS), an easier installation procedure were requirements.

NAREGI Version 1.1.4 was released in September, 2009, with version 1.1.5 to be released end of March, 2010. NAREGI Grid Middleware is being deployed to the national supercomputer centers as an important component of the Japanese Cyber Science Infrastructure Framework. A new project (RENKEI) started in FY 2008 to provide seamless access between NAREGI and the 3rd Tier resources. NAREGI is planned to provide the access and computational infrastructure for the Next Generation Supercomputer System, and is being deployed on the SINET4 upgrade to the research network planned for 2010 (see Fig. 6).

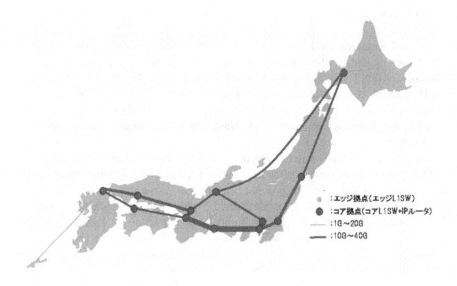

: エッジ拠点(エッジL1SW)
: コアL1SW+IPルータ)
: 1G～20G
: 10G～40G

Fig. 6: Map of the SINET4 upgrade to a 40GB backbone (green) planned for FY2010

6.1   The RENKEI Project

The RENKEI Project is a new R&D project, which started in September 2008 under the auspices of MEXT. In this project, a new light-weight grid middleware and software tool will be developed in order to provide the connection between the NAREGI Grid environment and wider research communities (3rd Tier resources).

In particular, technology for the flexible and seamless access between the national computing center level and the departmental/laboratory level resources, such as computers, storage and databases is highly emphasized. Also, this newly developed grid environment will be made interoperable with the major international grids.

One highlight of the RENKEI project in 2009 is a demonstration of interoperability conducted at the 5th IEEE eScience Conf.(Oxford UK) where job submission of the application Minem (Plasma Charge Minimization) was realized to multiple grids via HPCBP.

Other activities include development of nation-wide distributed file system technology. Research in this area involves optimal automatic placement of file replicas based on Gfarm 2.0. Development of an interoperable file catalog service between heterogeneous grid environments has also been a research topic, since current file catalog systems (LFC (EGEE gLite), MCAT (SRB), etc.) are not interoperable. Work has focused on development of standardized file catalog based on RNS (Resource Namespace Service) specifications (OGF).

KEK has played a key role in promoting interoperability between gLite and NAREGI, based on GIN and JSAGA. KEK is also investigating the use of Grid and cloud technologies to support the computing infrastructure for the Belle-II accelerator, which is the upgrade of KEKB.

6.2   The Next Generation Supercomputer Project

The Next Generation Supercomputer Project aims at the development, installation and application of an advanced high performance supercomputer system, as one of Japan's "Key Technologies of National Importance". The total budget is about 115bnYen ($1.15bn) over the period of FY2006 - FY2012

The goals of the Next Generation Supercomputer Project include:

1. development and installation of the most advanced high performance supercomputer system;
2. development and wide use of application software to utilize the supercomputer to the maximum extent;
3. provision of flexible computing environment by sharing the next generation supercomputer through connection with other supercomputers located at universities and research institutes;
4. establishment of an "Advanced Institute for Computational Science" (tentative name).

It is planned that NAREGI will provide the access and computational infrastructure for the Next Generation Supercomputer Project, and discussions are underway towards this goal.

[Based on reports by Kenichi Miura and Kento Aida, Center for Grid Research and Development, National Institute of Informatics, Takashi Sasaki, KEK]

7   MALAYSIA

The original implementation plan for the National Grid Computing Initiative (NGCI) in Malaysia, agreed in 2006, was shared, distributed computing resources to be deployed at several locations throughout the country with a similar facility to be run by a Grid Operations Centre and all sites to be connected via MYREN. In practice, an alternative approach was implemented which is more of an access to HPC services rather than a truly distributed shared resources: it focused on Grid application users with nearly no access for Grid core technology developers.

EUAsiaGrid has contributed greatly towards the next phase of Grid development and in particular gave Malaysian scientists and institutions a better understanding a truly distributed shared compute resources, and emphasize the importance of federated certificates with certificate issuance to users that must be adhered to.

Partly as a result of this, a review of NGCI activities last year, it was agreed to establish a true Grid computing ecosystem that:

1. addresses the needs of both Grid technology developers and users in various domain specific applications;
2. delivers the services of high performance computing and shared computing/storage resources locally, regionally and globally;
3. Facilitates the access of Grid computing resources for all through world-standard technology framework and best practices that are consensually agreed between the Grid service provider and the users.
4. includes cloud computing; both public and private cloud.
5. enables internationally recognized, federated and trusted security framework for Grid resource sharing among government agencies including private companies over the global network;
6. coordinates and facilitate application, review, approval, monitoring, and enforce accountability (including corrective/punitive actions) of grants by Grid R&D Expert Committee;
7. determines distribution of costs and billing on the use of the facility for both public and commercial when sharing resources;
8. introduces new scientific applications and technology components on Grid computing into local R&D;
9. establishes and expands joint research in all aspects of Grid Computing technology and grid-enabled applications locally and globally
10.   establishes research collaborations with international Grid computing organizations (such as PRAGMA, SEAGF, CGF, OGF etc);

NGCI is now able to contribute and share computing resources with partners with a federated certificate authority (ASGCCA), and work has begun to establish a Malaysia certificate authority. NGCI will follow closely EGI especially on the middleware. NGCI will promote trust and encourage sharing for example by implementing VOMS or GridShib Digital Certificates and developing policies for harmonization of Raw and Clean Data coming from various disciplines.

Future directions include extending National Grid terms of reference and roadmap to Cloud Computing, exploring Virtual Machine Managers, implementing Fat Nodes for RAM intensive computing for Gene Sequencing Analysis. MYREN Phase 2, the next phase of the Malaysian network, is being deployed and will see the inclusion of polytechnics and community colleges.

KnowledgeGRID is a strategic initiative by the Ministry of Science, Technology and Innovation spear-headed by MIMOS in close collaboration with local universities, research institutions and industry. The initiative aims to maximize the utility of high performance computing resources to accelerate research and industrial development.

KnowlegeGrid combines networked resources – desktops, servers, storage, databases, with scientific instruments, to form a massive repository of computing power to be tapped whenever and wherever it is needed most.

Research areas include AgriGRID for precision farming, BioGRID (DBrain) for dementia studies, VLSI GRID for Integrated circuit design (FRGA) for green motion controller and AutomativeGRID for fuel efficient concepts in automobiles. The 2nd KnowledgeGRID Malaysia Forum was held 26-29 October 2009.

Fig. 7: Snapshot of homepage of KnowledgeGRID Malaysia.

[based on presentations made by Suhaimi Naipis, CTO and Director, Info-Comm Development Centre and Bukhar Ikhwan Ismail, MIMOS]

8   PAKISTAN

8.1   *Progress of HEP Grid in Pakistan*

The effort to bring Pakistan on the WLCG map as a Grid Node was started in October, 2003. A Grid Technology Workshop was organized by NCP from October 20-22, 2003. The first ever test-bed was deployed during the workshop for tutorial. This test-bed consisted of 9 machines.

Today, Pakistan operates a Tier-2 Federation. No single site had enough resources and bandwidth to become a Tier 2 site so the Idea of a Tier 2 Federation was proposed based on WLCG Tiered Architecture. The National Centre for Physics (NCP) is a Regional Center for this federation. Other participating institutes were The Commission on Science and Technology for Sustainable Development in the South (COMSATS) National University of Science & Technology (NUST) Pakistan Atomic Energy Commission (PAEC1, PAEC2, PAEC3). In 2010, statistics for the Tier-2 federation are as follows: 360 CPU cores, 195TB of storage and 155 Mbps bandwidth.

For example, NCP is connected with 3 ISPs: fiber connection from Nayatel @ 10Mbps, Wireless Radio LinkDotNet@ 3.5Mbps, and Fiber Connection from HEC (PERN2) with 2Mbps internet and 155Mbps R&D link connected with TEIN3, GEANT2, and Internet2. User traffic and Grid traffic is divided among these links.

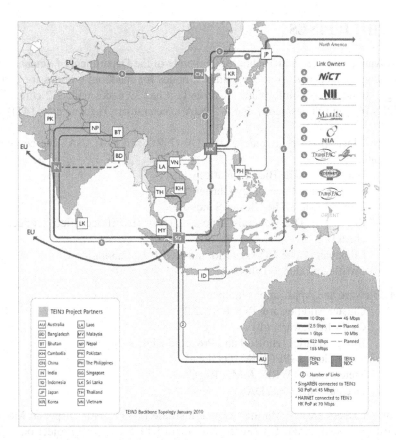

Fig. 8: TEIN3 connectivity in South and South-East Asia, showing the link between Pakistan and Singapore.

High availability and fault tolerance is achieved by installing physically re-dundant devices, running high availability protocol between redundant devices, Hot Standby Routing Protocol (HSRP), Virtual Router redundancy Protocol (VRRP), Gateway Load balancing Protocol (GLBP). As a result by March 2010 nearly 70,000 KSI2K hours of raw processing has been served by NCP-LCG2, with around 120,000 jobs executed, with similar figures for PAKGRID-LCG2.

PK-GRID-CA was the first certification authority in Pakistan, starting in 2004. It issues X.509 digital certificates, having issued over 150 certificates so far, of which over 50 are active still. There is a web portal for submitting certificate re-quests.

Despite challenges of limited bandwidth and frequent power outages, the effort to establish a Grid node in Pakistan has been successful, and Pakistan is actively contributing CPU and storage resources to the LHC community.

[based on presentation made by Sajjad Asghar, National Centre for Physics (NCP)]

9   PHILIPPINES

The Advanced Science and Technology Institute of the Department of Science and Technology (ASTI) has 16 nodes online: 2 nodes for sandbox; 6 nodes for meteorology; 8 nodes for bioinformatics. Currently it has 39 nodes with 312 cores, 2.5 TFLOPS (6 more nodes soon) and 8 FPGA accelerators. There is also 14TB of storage.

Current local partners include ADM, UP CSRC and PAGASA. The compute clusters are:
- Banyuhay – The Bioinformatics Cluster
- Unos – The Meteorology Cluster
- Dalubhasaan – The Cluster Sandbox
- Buhawi – The General-Purpose Cluster (EGEE certified production cluster)
- Liknayan – The EUAsiaGrid and EGEE Collaboration Cluster (EGEE certified production cluster)

Middleware and Applications include
- Cluster Middleware: ROCKS 5.2.2
- Grid Middleware: gLite
- Bioinformatics (BioRoll and Progeniq BioBoost)
- Seismology (SPECFEM3D Globe)
- Meteorology (WRF , MM5, RegCM)
- Oceanography (SeaDAS)

Current Users are UP Marine Science Institute (Fish Larval Dispersal Model for the Bohol Sea), PAGASA (Forecasting) and UPLB Biotech (Project on Data Warehousing for Drug Discovery). Future Users are Nimbus, Phivolcs, PAGASA (for climatology) and UP National Institute of Physics.

ASTI is a contributing member of EUAsiaGrid and institutional member of the Pacific Rim and Grid Middleware Assembly (PRAGMA). Training activities in 2009 included the Philippines Grid Computing 2009 Forum and Training-Workshop on 17-18 Nov 2009, with participants from UP-MSI, UPLB-BIOTECH, PAGASA, UP-NIP, UP-MathDept., UPM-NTHC, DLSU, IRRI.

Future plans include launching of the Philippine e-Science Grid (April 2010), Launching of ASTI's 3D Visualization Facility (April 2010), acquiring additional 6 computing nodes and 12 TB of storage space (2010), Resource Virtualization (Q1 2010), developing more FPGA applications, installing more grid based applications, continuing to advocate and promote grid technology to local universities and research communities.

Another area of focus for Grid-based research in the Philippines is disaster mitigation. A research team from the School of Science and Engineering of AdMU is collaborating with scientists at the Manila Observatory for Landslides and Flood Disaster Mitigation. The goal is to establish a grid-based database of Philippine geographical data related to landslides and floods that can be analyzed and visualized through the EUAsiaGrid infrastructure. Cellular automata and agent-based models of landslides and floods are being developed and will be used for the simulations.

Biodiversity mapping is another direction being investigated for grid-based data warehousing. In terms of biodiversity, more than 7,100 islands fall within the borders of the Philippine, identified as one of the world's biologically richest countries. The country is one of the few nations that is in its entirety, both a conservation hotspot and a megadiversity country, placing it among the top priority hotspots for global conservation.

Also in 2010, a workshop was held with the Asian Development Bank on evolutionary trade modelling and poverty alleviation. A team from AdMU is collaborating with economists from ADB to model evolutionary trade in some of the poorest regions in South East Asia, such as East India, Bangladesh, Bhutan and Nepal. The goal is to determine the impact of investments in the economic growth of the region using a geographical information system and cellular automata/agent-based modeling techniques, based on a grid infrastructure.

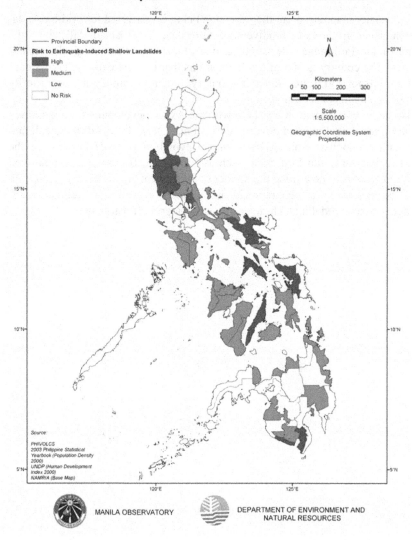

Fig. 9: Landslide and Flood disaster mitigation involves Grid-enabled data warehousing, risk assessment, monitoring and modeling and simulation.

[Based on presentations by Peter Antonio Banzon, Advanced Science and Technology Institute, and Rafael Saldana, Ateneo de Manila University]

10   SINGAPORE

Bioinformatics and computational biology are growing fields in the wake of a global digitalisation and quantitization of modern biology. The requirement for computing power increases with the volume of biological data, which is exploding due the great reduction in the cost of procedures such as genome sequencing. This translates into a growing need for computational power at the bench top and on the field, wherever biologists go, and wherever they are being trained.

An example is BioSLAX, a new live CD/DVD suite of bioinformatics tools that has been released by the resource team of the BioInformatics Center (BIC), National University of Singapore (NUS). Bootable from any PC, this CD/DVD runs the compressed SLACKWARE flavour of the LINUX operating system also known as SLAX. SLAX is becoming the live CD/DVD of choice because of its ability to modularize almost any application and plug it into the system on the fly. The system can also be installed to USB thumbdrives or directly to the PC as a regular Linux using the BioSLAX installer provided.

There are two parts to the SLAX build, the core system and the individual modules. The core system is the OS itself and basic tools, usually referred to as the 'base', while the modules are the individual utilities that a user wants to have on their system. Since these modules can be put in or removed prior to creating the CD/DVD/USB, the system is fully modular and easily customisable.

Grid-enabling of BioSlax has been achieved using United Devices UD MP agents. This builds on a campus wide cycle-harvesting grid called the TeraCampus Grid (TCG@NUS) and enables Rapid recruitment of machines with no need for user installation, as well as push or pull instances. Ongoing research focuses on embedding gLITE inside BioSlax.

In the context of EUAsiaGrid, NUS has collaborated with ASGC, Taiwan and National Yang Ming University to create a next generation BioMirror, which is a compressed set of biodatabases available since 1998 in 12 countries in the Asia-Pacific region. This includes an authorID system, DocID Depository for bioinformatics published datasets, minimum information about bioinformatics investigation MIABi standards. This collaboration has also initiated computationally intensive projects for complex diseases.

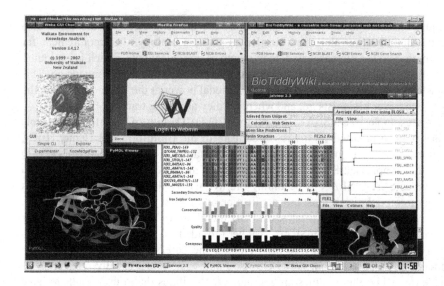

Fig. 10: Screenshot of bioinformatics teaching interface using BioSlax

[based on presentation by Tin-Wee Tan, National University of Singapore]

11 SOUTH KOREA

KISTI, the Korea Institute of Science and Technology Information, has participated in the EGEE project since 2006. Since 2007 KISTI has participated in the production grid operation, becoming an ALICE Tier2 in 2007, and contributing on that basis to the joint development of PROOF, a parallel ROOT facility. Since 2009 one full-time equivalent researcher has been devoted to PROOF development.

Currently, KISTI contributes 128 CPU cores and 30 TB storage to the ALICE distributed computing Grid, which is about 1.2% contribution to ALICE computing in the total job execution, and corresponds to processing nearly 8000 jobs per month in average.

KISTI has also been instrumental in establishing a collaborative VO with CC-IN2P3 in France in the area of Grid computing, with the objective to foster the adoption of grid technology and provide researchers in Korea and France with a production Grid Infrastructure. This has been up and running since October 2008, providing about 7,000 CPU cores and 2 TBytes of disk storage. About 50 users have joined the FKPPL VO membership.

This VO has been used for deployment of Geant4 applications, run extensively by the National Cancel Center in Korea for compute-intensive simulations relevant to cancer treatment planning as well as deployment of two-color QCD (Quantum Chromodynamics) simulations in theoretical Physics. Several thousand QCD jobs have been run on the Grid, with each job taking about 10 days.

Fig 11: In February, KISTI organized Geant4 and Grid tutorial 2010 for Korean medical physics community. About 30 participants from major hospitals in Korea took part and about 20 Grid Certificates were issued and joined the FKPPL VO.

KISTI was also involved in developing AMGA, an official EGEE gLite middleware component for a metadata catalogue service on the grid. KISTI has taken over the leadership of AMGA development since the July of 2009. AMGA 2.0 supporting the OGF WS-DAIR was successfully

released in October in 2009 in collaboration with CERN and INFN. Currently, KISTI is one of the partners of the open glite collaboration, and working with EMI, contributing to the evolution and maintenance of AMGA.

Drug screening has been a focus of Grid-related research in South Korea, through the WISDOM project. Computational methods used include pharmacophore based search and structure based docking. The requirements include 3D structure of target, databases of small molecules, a method to dock and score bound small molecules.

One example of a virtual screening challenge with grid computing concerns human intenstinal maltase. The objective is to search for an inhibitor of enzyme action which enables glucose uptake, in order to treat diabetes type 2 related to obesity. Inhibitors already exist, but the search is aimed at more potent ones with less side effects.

Starting with 454,000 chemical compounds from Chembridge, scoring based on docking score results in 3016 compounds selected. Interaction with key residues reduces the field to 2616 compounds. Focusing on key interactions and using binding models and clustering, the number can be reduced to in vitro testing of just 42 compounds.

During this filtration process, the key numbers concerning the grid-based virtual screening are:

- Total numbers of docking: 308,307
- Total size of output results: 16.3 GBytes
- Estimated duration by 1CPU: 22.4 years
- Duration of experiments: 3.2 days
- Maximum numbers of concurrent CPUs: 4700 CPUs
- Crunching Factor: 2556
- Distribution Efficiency: 54.4 %

Similar grid-enabled searches have focused on:

- Malaria. One of the crucial drug targets in malaria is plasmepsin, the aspartic proteases of the parasite plasmodium. Plasmepsin is involved in the hemoglobin degradation inside the food vacuole during the erythrocytic phase of the malaria parasite life cycle.
- SARS. The global outbreak of SARS (Severe Acute Respiratory Syndrome) in 2002 set in motion a search for an effective vaccine. 3-CL-pro (chymotrypsin-like cystein protease) is an attractive targe for development of antiviral drugs directed at SARS, since this protease is essential for the viral life cycle, there are a number of 3D structures available and preparation of the enzyme in large quantities is possible for in-vitro testing.
- H5N1. This flu strain has high fatality and resistance to available drugs such as Tamiflu. Both effective vaccination and antiviral drugs are needed. A suitable target is an inhibitor of Neuraminidase, a glycolprotein on the virion surface which releases the progeny virions from the infected cell. In vitro assay of compounds selected from in-silico screening performed at Academia Sinica.

[Based on presentations made by Hwa Ja Ryu, Chonnam National University and Soonwook Hwang, KISTI]

12 TAIWAN

The Mission of Academia Sinica Grid Computing (ASGC) is to build a sustainable research and collaboration infrastructure to support research by e-Science, on data intensive sciences and applications requiring cross disciplinary distributed collaboration.

Development of e-Science infrastructure in Taiwan is not just the result of the global e-Science collaboration (WLCG) but also occurs due to domestic support for new ways of doing science. While WLCG and EGEE usher in the petabyte-scale era, the e-Infrastructure of Taiwan has also had proved to be available for larger scale multiple sciences.

The value of adaption to new computing models and effective resource sharing has been demonstrated by user communities of high energy physics (HEP), drug discovery, long-term digital preservation and high throughput computation.

In 2010, gLite sites in Asia grew to 30 from only 5 sites in 2005, based on the support and coordination of the EGEE Asia Federation and Asia Pacific Regional Operation Centre (APROC) hosted by ASGC.

Other e-Science applications among Asia partners and with Europe and America, such as earthquake simulation, environmental change studies, computational chemistry, social sciences, and life sciences, are taking place endorsed by EUAsiaGrid and other projects.

All these efforts are driving the regional e-Infrastructure towards production quality and sustainable grids. From 2009, data centre energy saving and intelligent operation become one of key focus at ASGC. To continuously improve data management and computation for e-Science, technologies like virtualization, cloud computing and volunteer computing are under test, deployment and integration to Grid infrastructure.

Training for site administrators, e-Science application engineers, trainers and collaboration workshops with user communities were held more often, in most partner sites. In addition, ASGC is assisting more site operators joining APROC support, to take care of the regional collaboration infrastructure and to level up service quality in partnership.

In future, orchestrating users requirements to take advantage of the e-Infrastructure is the best model to grow the technology. ASGC will keep close cooperation with target user groups regionally and evolve the e-Infrastructure.

In terms of technological highlights in 2009, ASGC has promoted Grid-enabled services based on the Grid Application Platform, GAP. This has been used successfully for Grid-enabled virtual screening service for drug discovery called GVSS, which is a JAVA-based user interface developed to facilitate job submission and data management of large-scale molecular docking.

Thanks to the DIANE framework, GVSS allows submitted jobs to be split into multiple independent subtasks and run to completion; this ensures efficient utilization of the GRID resource for the massive molecular dockings empowered by Autodock3.

GVSS hides the complexity of deploying large-scale molecular docking on the GRID while provides users more flexible control over their docking jobs on the GRID. Provide on-line Avian

Flu & Dengue targets and ZINC compounds library (> 300,000). The user prepares the target/compounds gridmap files with on-line tools.

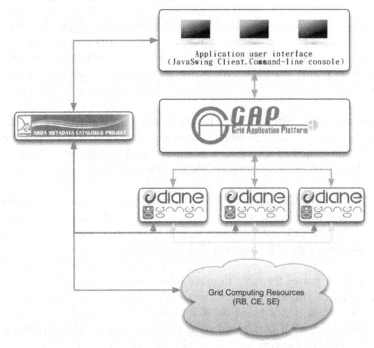

Fig.12 : Illustration of how GAP is used for GVSS

Another significant initiative led by ASGC is the Earthquake Data Center. The objective is to support both data acquisition, data services and risk analysis, as well as Earthquake Research (Earthquake data analysis). The Centre is based on a Federation of Tools and Interfaces (ANTELOP (ADPC, TW), Earthworm (TW), Wilber2, Netdc, and EIDS (Earthquake Information Distribution System). The Data Exchange Protocols used include ArcLink, ORB2ORB and others.

The participants are
- Malaysia: 5 stations
- ADPC: all 4 stations and the coming 10 more ones.
- Philippines: 1 Station (newly established in Jan.'10), more station data will be shared to IRIS and to the region.
- Taiwan: 7 stations (published to IRIS)
- Indonesia: 20 stations (indirectly through GFZ)

[based on presentations by Simon C. Lin, Eric Yen, Hsin Yen Chen & Yin Ta Wu, Academia Sinica]

13 THAILAND

Today, in Thailand, there is a need for the "National Health Information System (NHIS)" that provides the transparent and secure access to health information across geographically distributed healthcare centres.

To achieve this, several issues must be resolved altogether: (i) the diversity of health information structures among healthcare centres; (ii) the availability of health information sharing from healthcare centres; (iii) the efficient information access to at least 10,000 healthcare centres; (iv) the privacy and privilege of health information.

To implement this NHIS, we divide our work into 3 main phases starting from the healthcare centre to the information consumer perspectives. The 1st phase focuses on the application of metadata standard to enable the interoperability and usability of health information across healthcare centres.

Basically, two significant desktop tools are developed: Metadata Mapping Tool (MMT) and Metadata Conversion Tool (MCT). MMT and MCT support healthcare centres to efficiently transform their information stored in any relational databases into a standard format with a small effort.

The 2nd phase moves forwards to make information sharing possible and to provide an efficient information access to a large number of healthcare centres. This underlying work is thus based on Web Services, XML, Grid and P2P technologies. Essentially, MCT is wrapped up as a service, namely Metadata Service (MS), to accommodate the availability of information sharing.

The MS connects to a specified relational database and transforms the underlying information into a standard format. Besides MS, a Metadata Broker (MB) as a service is developed in such a way that it not only provides the linkage to a potential set of MS's but also accesses and integrates their information based upon a request. To efficiently handle information access to a large number of healthcare centers, a number of MBs along with their communication are deployed and developed.

Finally, in the 3rd phase, we plan to promote the privacy and privilege of health information with respect to roles of information consumers. To accomplish this, MBs and MS's are extended to handle the dynamic delegation of access rights, single sign on, trust relationship among multiple entities, data privacy and policy related security issues.

This underlying work is thus based on the Public Key Infrastructure (PKI) and Privilege Management Infrastructure (PMI) standards. Particularly, Role Based

Access Control (RBAC) is chosen to implement PKI. The secure health information exchange between entities at the message level relies on Web Services security standards.

Currently, we are at the end of the 1st phase. The field evaluation of MMT and MCT will be conducted soon at about 20 healthcare centres that have at least 3 different health information structures. In conclusion, our work has significantly driven the "sustainable" NHIS due to its intrinsic properties: transparency, data security, availability, extensibility and scalability.

[based on presentations Sornthep Vannarat, NECTEC, Thailand]

14 VIETNAM

The advances in biomedical computing, the abundance of biomedical and genomic data, the ubiquity of the internet and general acceptance of Grid Computing is beginning to have a big impact in various aspects of medical, biological and healthcare research and practice.

The sharing of knowledge and exchange of diagnosis between physicians can contribute to an improved standard of medical knowledge. Recently some institutions in Vietnam have set up a Grid infrastructure. By using web services technology and grid services provided by the gLite middleware, the HOPE telemedicine Platform that developed at LPC Clermont-Ferrand has been implemented on a grid site at Institute of Applied Mechanics and Informatics (IAMI) in Vietnam.

The physicians access the platform using web portal to access several distributed medical services that manage the traditional alphanumerical information such as patient personal data, diagnosis, results for analysis and investigation, medical images are stores anonymized and encrypted on the grid which their metadata are stored in the local AMGA server.

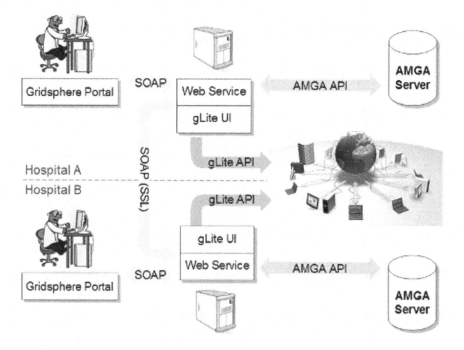

Fig.13: Shows concept of hospital open-software platform for e-Health (HOPE), with information transferred between different locations using SOAP messages over an SSL secured channel.

Currently Vietnamese researchers are also deploying the selected telemedicine applications using servers that connected to VinaREN network. IAMI has also cooperated with Pasteur Institute in HCM City to apply GVSS (GAP Virtual Screening Service) tool based on the power of Grid Computing (EUAsiaGrid) to solve docking problem (first stage in the drug discovery process) for Dengue virus.

The IFI (the Institut de la Francophonie pour l'Informatique – french-speaking Computer Science Institute) created in 2006 the MSI (Modelisation et Simulation des systems complexes) as its research team. MSI has been actively involved in EUAsiaGrid WP3 (Applications) for research, development, deployment, promotion and usage of the grid for biomedical applications. One of the objectives has been building a grid-based flu epidemic surveillance network on top of the EUAsia VO. This has involved building an information system based on AMGA which automatically synchronizes public influenza databases like NCBI with grid resources, as well as deploying a phylogenetic pipeline on the EUASIAGRID resources, and developing/adapting tools for visualization and analysis of obtained results from the pipeline. Developing a web portal for epidemiologists.

IFI is also participating actively in the proposal of CHAIN project as extension of EUAsiaGrid project. The objective would be to develop a simulation platform as an extension of the open-source GAMA platform, as a front-end for managing massive agent-based simulations based on the use of grid computing. Also, the ambition is to develop others grid-based applications in collaboration with national and international partners:

- Biomedical (LPC-IN2P3, HealthGrid, IBT-VAST)
- Earth Science (IGP-VAST, ASGC)
- Nuclear physics (IOP-VAST, IOIT-VAST, CNRS)

Finally, IFI is engaging with other national partners and with the support of the international grid community in order to propose and implemented the Vietnam NGI.

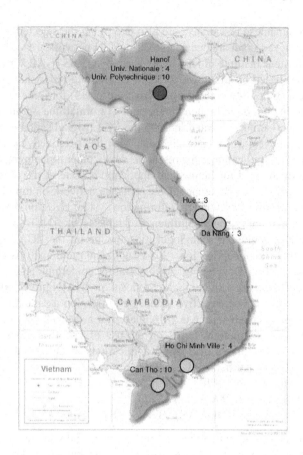

Fig.14: map indicating other centres in Vietnam that exchange researchers, Ph.D. students with IFI.

[based on presentation by Dao Van Tuyet, IAMI, Vietnamese Academy of Sciences, and Nguyen Hong Quang, IFI, Hanoi]

Part II
Keynote Speech

Roadmap for the Uptake of the e-Infrastructure in the Asia-Pacific Region

M. Paganoni

University of Milano-Bicocca and INFN, Italy

1   INTRODUCTION

Scientific research is facing today important computational challenges, as huge amount of data need processing from worldwide distributed communities. Hence data management facilities and computational infrastructures are playing an increasingly important role in science and the use of computing grids as collaborative environment for science is taking up. In the last few years Europe has pioneered the field of e-Infrastructures, by building and operating a distributed grid environment based on the gLite middleware. The EGEE [1] grid provides the framework to connect researchers worldwide, by enabling them to share resources on a large scale, with a very stable service quality.

The EUAsiaGrid [2] project, funded in the frame of the "EU Seventh Framework Program (FP7) – Research Infrastructures" has been promoting interoperation between the European and the Asian-Pacific grids, in order to meet the computing and storage needs of research communities in the Asia-Pacific region and foster e-Science collaborations with colleagues in Europe and the wider world.

In this paper the main results of the EUAsiaGrid project are presented and the roadmap towards a sustainable grid infrastructure in Asia-Pacific is outlined.

2   THE EUASIAGRID PROJECT

Altogether EUAsiaGrid involves 17 partners from four European countries (Italy, Czech Republic, France, UK) and eight countries in Asia-Pacific (Taiwan, Australia, Indonesia, Malaysia, Philippines, Singapore, Thailand, Vietnam). The project, coordinated by INFN, started on April 1st, 2008 and has come to conclusion on June 30th, 2010. EUAsiaGrid has focused on the dissemination of the knowledge about the EGEE grid infrastructure, the organization of specific training events and the support of applications.

The main objective is to identify and engage in Asia-Pacific new scientific communities that can benefit from the use of a grid-based e-Infrastructure by improving or expanding their research efforts through collaborations and new modes of research enabled by state-of-the-art grid technologies. In the past two years EUAsiaGrid has been present, with dissemination stands and public presentations, in almost one hundred national and international workshops and conferences. Different categories of users, ranging from beginners to system administrators, application experts and new trainers, have been addressed in more than 20 training events targeting Asia-Pacific region as a whole. Furthermore a catch-all virtual organization – EUAsia VO – has provided a service to user communities and is the

S.C. Lin and E. Yen (eds.), *Data Driven e-Science: Use Cases and Successful Applications of Distributed Computing Infrastructures (ISGC 2010)*, DOI 10.1007/978-1-4419-8014-4_2,
© Springer Science+Business Media, LLC 2011

current entry point for any Asia-Pacific researcher willing to investigate the grid technology. Particular care has been taken in reducing the entry barrier for new users, in order to face the high heterogeneity in grid knowledge and adoption, typical of the region.

3   APPLICATION SUPPORT BY EUASIAGRID

Asia-Pacific is not only a geographically large area, but also a very reach one in terms of scientific teams, with diverse levels of adoption of grid technologies in different countries and disciplines. The region has benefited from the participation in the LHC experiments at CERN, which has fostered since the beginning of WLCG [3] the development of a mature grid infrastructure, managed by Academia Sinica Grid Computing in Taiwan. Together with high energy physics also computational chemistry, bioinformatics and biomedical research have pioneered the use of the grid in the region.

Presently countries in Asia-Pacific are focusing on applications with direct societal and economic benefit, such as drug discovery for emerging and neglected diseases, climate and weather modelling, natural disaster mitigation and social simulations. These are the scientific communities the EUAsiaGrid project is mainly focusing on, as they are the key actors in order to build a robust, permanent and sustainable e-Infrastructure. In the rest of this paragraph a couple of examples will be given as show cases for the EUAsiaGrid role in promoting the adoption of grid technologies among these new users.

3.1   Earthquake Hazard Mitigation

Most countries in Asia-Pacific are vulnerable to earthquakes, hence Taiwan, Indonesia, Philippines, Thailand, and Vietnam have already developed their own seismic sensor station networks. In Taiwan, a seismic data center integrated with Taiwan Earthquake Center (TEC) is operational since 2006, serving as the bridge between seismic data providers, research communities and end users. More than 441,000 records of seismic events, dating from the beginning of 20th century until today, are archived with structured metadata in order to be accessible by web services and 3-D geospatial visualization interfaces.

The essence of disaster mitigation for earthquakes relies on understanding the geological structure and performing a real-time risk analysis. Even though earthquakes are not predictable, we aim at scrutinizing their potential impact, by means of 3-D seismic wave propagation analysis and simulation. This goal requires very intensive computing and fast access to both historical information and real-time data from the seismic sensor network. In perspective this activity will pave the way towards providing real time help for the organization of the rescue teams, in order to mitigate the earthquake consequences on the population.

The goal of the earthquake hazard mitigation activities [4] in the EUAsiaGrid project is the integration, over the EGEE grid infrastructure, of the sensor station network, the seismic data center and the computational analysis and simulation of seismic wave propagation. Only with this integrated approach the whole workflow can be streamlined from the research perspective, to dynamically extend the sensor network coverage and to cooperate with all partners both in the region and worldwide. Grid adoption has improved the regional networking for an efficient data collection and federation and has allowed a much faster determination of source mechanisms and rupture processes from large earthquakes.

3.2   Dengue Fever Drug Discovery

In Europe, the use of EGEE grid resources has enabled research on the development of new drugs and vaccine for diseases that are not receiving the needed attention from pharmaceutical laboratories. The WISDOM [5] initiative involving European and Asian experts has already demonstrated, for the malaria and avian flu cases, that the in silico high throughput screening is feasible on the EGEE grid infrastructure, thus reducing the time and cost of pharmaceutical development.

Similar efforts are currently propagating to other emergent and neglected diseases. The EUAsiaGrid project has concentrated on Dengue fever, a disease against which neither a vaccine nor specific antiviral therapies currently exist, which could spread in all tropical zones, both in rural and in urban areas. This molecular docking simulation is a real computing challenge, both in terms of processing time and data management. In the Dengue fever case, an exhaustive study of the NS3 protease inhibitors has required to test some 300,000 virtual compounds in a couple of months, using the equivalent of over 12 years of the processing power of a single PC. According to the binding energy, the biologists have determined the best conformation of each docking result. The 1.6% top-ranked compounds have been identified and chosen for wet lab in vitro assay processing, which is currently under way.

4   THE ROADMAP TOWARDS A SUSTAINABLE E-INFRASTRUCTURE

The EUAsiaGrid project has made a considerable effort in the analysis of the computing needs of the scientific teams in the Asia-Pacific region as well as the context in which they operate. During this survey the existing capability in the areas of networking, middleware development and standardisation, infrastructure deployment, certification and registration authorities, regional operation centres, virtual organisations as well as training, education and outreach have been thoroughly scrutinised.

Furthermore, profiting of the partners experience with creating regional grid infrastructures in Europe and in Latin America and building on the existing regional collaborations at the network level such as APAN [6], EUAsiaGrid has written a detailed document on the organisational and technical roadmap [7] to pave the way towards a persistent e-Infrastructure in Asia-Pacific.

The key point which needs addressing is the large variety of adoption of the grids between countries and disciplines. While some EUAsiaGrid partners have already laid foundations for their national e-Infrastructures, as proven by the Infocomm Development Authority mandate in Singapore and the KnowledgeGrid initiative in Malaysia, in most cases the formation of National Grid Initiatives (NGIs) is still in an embryonic state. Therefore we foresee great political difficulties in creating a structure like EGI.eu [8], based on national representation. Consequently, in the roadmap definition we opted for the APGI-Union (APGI-U), an interim structure based on membership of individual resource-providing institutions. Starting from a flexible model based on the federation of individual contributing institutions, the model contains also a set of operating principles and procedures for the APGI-U that will allow to establish this structure and to ensure that it can transform into a full APGI reality based on the membership of NGIs.

Presently a clear effort is needed on community building to bring together a wider range of stakeholders from within different research communities but also from industry, the public sector and potential funders. In order to make the e-Infrastructure sustainable, strong improvements have to be achieved in the maturity of the national grid initiatives,

On the longer term a mandatory step in order to accommodate a larger number of participating resource providers and users will be represented by the introduction of NGIs as the key entities that can coordinate activities at a national level. The presence of mature NGIs will allow to face the lack of federation and of a governance model at the international level and to steer funding arrangements and policy making

All the roadmap process in the Asia-Pacific region will profit from the fact that, thanks to the acknowledgement of world-wide e-Infrastructures as basic components of advanced research environments, the community is shifting from project-oriented funding towards a more sustainable model, as shown by the EGI.eu case. At the end of the EUAsiaGrid project the use of grid resources is gaining momentum in Asia-Pacific, with more scientific teams willing to include grids as very useful tools into their daily routine, contributing to the sustainability of the whole environment. Also, the region is involved directly in the EGI In-SPIRE [9] activities and an international JRU is part of the new collaboration that will be brought through the CHAIN project, funded by the European Commission. While there is still a long road ahead before grids become standard tools for scientific work in Asia-Pacific, the overall picture is very favourable for a fast uptake of the computing grids in the next few years.

REFERENCES

[1]   EGEE - Enabling Grids for E-sciencE, http://www.eu-egee.org/
[2]   EUAsiaGrid – Towards a common e-Science infrastructure with the European and Asian Grids, http://www.euasiagrid.eu
[3]   WLCG – World LHC Computing Grid, http://lcg.web.cern.ch/LCG/
[4]   E. Yen, S.C. Lin, and S.J. Lee et al (2009), "e-Science for Earthquake Disaster Mitigation in EUAsiaGrid", e-Infrastructure for Regional e-Science (ed. SEEGrid), pp. 211-219, ISBN: 978-975-403-510-0, 2009
[5]   WISDOM - Initiative for grid-enabled drug discovery against neglected and emergent diseases, http://wisdom.eu-egee.fr/
[6]   Asia-Pacific Advanced Network, http://www.apan.net
[7]   EUAsiaGrid Roadmap, http://www.euasiagrid.eu/roadmap
[8]   European Grid Initiative, http://www.egi.eu
[9]   EGI-InSPIRE – Towards a sustainable production grid infrastructure, http://www.egi.eu/projects/egi-inspire/

**Part III
Grid Activities in Asia Pacific**

Uptakes of e-Science in Asia

Eric Yen[1, 2] and Simon C. Lin[3]

1.Academia Sinica Grid Computing Centre (ASGC), Taiwan
2.Department of Management Information System, National Cheng-Chi University, Taiwan
3.Institute of Physics, Academia Sinica, Taiwan

1 INTRODUCTION

e-Science refers to either computationally intensive science or data intensive science that is carried out in highly distributed computing environments [1, 2]. Intuitively, incentives of the new paradigm of science are mainly due to the relentless pursuit of new science and building capacity to digest unprecedented scale of scientific data for more knowledge. Originating from the requirements of LHC collaboration, a LHC Computing Grid (LCG) system is constructed to fulfill worldwide data sharing and resource integration from early 2002 [3]. Based on LCG, the global grid-based e-Infrastructure was established very quickly in Europe, America and Asia, to support wider scientific disciplines of e-Science. Many international e-Science joint efforts on astronomy, life science, earth science, environmental changes, and humanities and social sciences are now taking advantage of the same e-Infrastructure to achieve synergy greater than sum of individuals.

In Asia, e-Science was primarily inspired by the LHC researches on unprecedented energy frontier and understanding new fundamental of the universe. Partner countries such as Japan, Korea, China, Taiwan, Australia, India and Pakistan caught up with the buildup of grid resource centers and participated in the global e-Infrastructure from 2004. Besides gLite and OSG, some other grid middleware were deployed in this region for variant purposes, for example, Globus [4], NAREGI [5], SRB [6] and ARC [7], etc. Through EGEE Asia Federation framework, ASGC conducted a generic drug screening grid application on avian flu from 2006 to reach out wider e-Science collaborations in this region and between the worldwide grid [8]. There were also GeoGrid initiative in Japan and few other high throughput computing applications employed in several countries in Asia during that time. From 2006, EUChinaGrid [9] and EUIndiaGrid [10] were funded to construct e-Infrastructure and foster e-Science applications in the two largest population countries in the world. In 2008, EUAsiaGrid [11] was commenced and the gLite-based infrastructure was soon extended to Philippine, Vietnam, Thailand, Malaysia, Singapore and Indonesia. Applications on natural disaster mitigation, drug virtual screening, bioinformatics, computational chemistry, weather simulation and climate change, and social simulation were developed teaming up closely by domain experts and Grid experts in partner countries.

S.C. Lin and E. Yen (eds.), *Data Driven e-Science: Use Cases and Successful Applications of Distributed Computing Infrastructures (ISGC 2010)*, DOI 10.1007/978-1-4419-8014-4_3, © Springer Science+Business Media, LLC 2011

Based on those successful international e-Science related collaborations in the past years, the strategic decision for huge investment from EC and US to support e-Science and e-Infrastructure in the next 10 years, and also the trend of data deluge, we envisage the adoption of high-volume data-driven science as a routine research methodology in the coming decade. The objective of this study is to establish a long-term investigation of the e-Science uptake in Asia according to specific metrics and to underpin the gaps to be bridged. Basically, internetworking, user community engagement and e-Infrastructure reliability are the most essential factors of successful e-Science collaboration. As e-Science is changing every aspect of data related activities and workflow, the study expects to discover the impact of advanced e-Science technology and track the trajectory toward the goal.

2   E-INFRASTRUCTURE STATUS AND GAPS PROBING

In June 2010, there are 30 gLite sites in production situated in 15 countries in Asia, which is 50% increase when comparing the status in end 2007 (21 production sites in 8 countries). Although the 6-times resource growth (increment from 2,047 CPU cores, 500TB disk to 12,000 Cores and 3 PB disk) is also quite impressive, the computing capacity in this region is still relative small in comparison to grid infrastructure in Europe and America.

When the e-Infrastructure is reliable and all resources are rationally provisioned, it is clear that the major driving force of e-Science uptake is the user community engagement. With highly stable LCG sites in this region, the monthly average CPU utilization gains 4 times growth between July 2007 and July 2010. Coordinated by ASGC in the framework of WLCG, EGEE and also EUAsiaGrid, ASGC already supported 30 sites in 13 countries joining the gLite-based worldwide grid collaborations. ASGC now is capable of supporting international collaborated e-Science applications by 10,000+ CPU cores, with more than 3 petabyte disk and tape storage space respectively. Maximal storage-to-storage data transmission volume reached 50 terabyte per day, with the highest rate at 9.6Gbps. In terms of daily job execution rate, till now, ASGC is able to achieve 100,000 jobs a day in 2010.

From the Grid usage statistics of Asia till end June 2010, 22 VOs were supported by Asia gLite sites and around 97.6% CPU time were used by high energy physics (HEP) applications in the past three years. Besides HEP, all other discipline collaborations were conducted by EUAsiaGrid, listed as follows in terms of resource utilization - 1.67% (332,691) CPU Hours were consumed by life science applications, 0.45% CPU time (89,371 CPU hours) was employed by earthquake disaster mitigation, 0.11% resources (21,150 CPU hours) were taken by weather simulation, and 0.09% (17,581) CPU hours were used by computational chemistry applications.

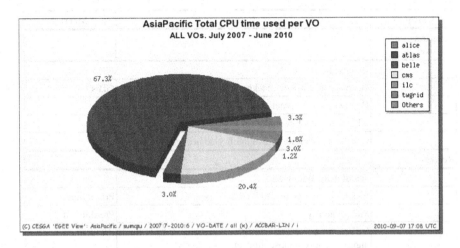

Pragmatically, to establish a long-term e-Science uptake analysis mechanism, we need to identify the metrics from basic deployment and utilization status to its impact and also policy level interactions. Below is a summary table of the major parameters to evaluate both the uptake and impact of e-Science paradigm. All the metrics need to have clearly definition and even the method of measurement should be in place beforehand. Other than those quantitative data, traditional assessment criteria such as publications, collaboration status, advantage of sharing and also efforts on sustainability should be documented as well. To reach the most complete data to be collected, the best strategy is to cover most of the measurement in the routine monitoring system of the infrastructure, which should be included in the challenge of e-Science uptake itself additionally.

Category	Items	Metrics
Infrastructure & Coverage		
	Bandwidth to NREN	GB/s
	Bandwidth of NREN backbone	GB/s
	Bandwidth to Internet	GB/s
	NREN architecture update	
	Certification authority availability domestically	
Resource		
	Middleware deployed	
	Installed capacity of CPU, Disk, Tape	Pre-defined
	Site reliability	Pre-defined
	Utilization by month and by VO, including CPU hour, number of jobs, elapse time, etc.	Pre-defined
	Data transmission rate and access statistics	Pre-defined
	Human Resource - FTE for operation	Man-month
	Usage policy	
Application Domain/VO	Need information of each application domain/VO	
	Domain, scientific problem description, type of applications, run-time resource requirements, long-term resource requirement, archive needs, type of applications (package used, computing model and computation scheme, etc), expected #users from where	Other than the plan, the real usage status has to be recorded and predefined as well.
	Sharable service/application	List or repository
	Sharable data set (with catalog and metadata)	List and URL
Policy		
	National plan and funding for e-Infrastructure or distributed computing infrastructure.	

3   EXEMPLAR APPLICATIONS

The greatest advantages of e-Science are sharing and collaboration. All useful resources should be able to share according to the requirements and computing model defined by the virtual organization. Naturally, large-scale science benefits from collaborations over distributed computing environment. With adoption of data-driven science there is an emerging need to make the research infrastructure supporting these collaborations sustainable and to support different computing models and technologies needed by respective research communities. Asia as a whole is geographically dispersed and also cultural diversified. Traditionally the region is inexperienced in regional collaboration. Even inhomogeneous Grids with limited operation experiences make regional e-Science collaboration difficult. To overcome the barriers, four principal undertakings are always implemented in the regional collaborations: 1) Tracking regional and international bandwidth progress; 2) Continuously raise awareness of e-Science and e-Infrastructure significance; 3) Technical support and sharing of daily e-Infrastructure operation and e-Science application development; 4) Facilitate regional focused e-Science applications. A number of new regional e-Science collaborations on drug discovery, natural disaster mitigation, weather simulation already in production by EUAsiaGrid. The changes by interactions between information and communication technology and scientific communities and the influence to national policy should be all attentive to the uptake study

Biomedical and bioinformatics research applications are the largest e-Science collaborations in addition to high energy physics. After several phases large scale virtual screening on avian flu over EGEE from 2006, the top ranking results are now further verified in wet lab. In EUAsiaGrid, we devoted on regional interested disease like Dengue Fever and made the GAP (Grid Application Platform) Virtual Screen Services (GVSS) to be flexible for any selected virus and compound library by users. More than 4,000 CPU-day computing resources were used for the in silico studies by NS3 protease and ZINC compound library. First 1.6% top-ranked compounds were identified and sent to wet lab in vitro assay processing. Healthy interactions among user community and Grid support group were also formed for future docking systems advancement. Philippine, Taiwan, Vietnam and South Korea joined the molecular docking process and comparison with molecular force field approach are undergoing.

Significance to leverage large-scale grid-based scientific workflows at natural disaster mitigation is straightforward, as Asia is vulnerable to compound disasters. Earthquake, storm and flood are the three most catastrophic hazards in Asia according to the studies. EUAsiaGrid focused on earthquake disaster mitigation by achieving the full process of quantitative seismic hazard assessment - a cyclic continuous-improving workflow which is essential from risk analysis and preparedness, reporting, early warning to emergency response and recovery. The collaboration is composed by Grid experts and seismologists from Taiwan, Philippine, Vietnam, Thailand, Malaysia and Indonesia. A pilot virtual research environment was also implemented based on workflow design of seismologist community to integrate the following key tasks: 1) collecting and analyzing event data; 2) understanding fault and ground motion characteristics in details; 3) facilitating accurate simulation on seismic wave; 4) assessing anticipated earthquake and potential damages by the correct seismic models and hazard maps of disaster coverage, risk and also evacuation.

Again, typhoon and tropical cyclone is one of the devastating natural disaster in Asia. International cooperation on monitoring, forecast, management experiences of disaster prevention and reduction are important. The Weather Research and Forecasting (WRF) is the most popular new generation numerical weather simulation system in this region, which is widely applied for research and real-time weather prediction and simulation. GWRF – integrating WRF to gLite has been now operational for research support at Taiwan and Malaysia with users from Philippine and Taiwan. After experimenting several typhoon cases like Morakot (2009), Parma (2009) and Conson (2010), GWRF is very stable for short interval ($\leq$ 3~4 days) forecasting, longer term and heavy output simulation ($>$ 3~4 days) is under verification. With EUAsiaGrid, it's possible to monitor and also simulate the typhoon by several different countries to achieve higher accuracy, higher resolution and faster prediction by GWRF.

4 SUMMARY

Although digital divide and collaboration culture are still issues of e-Science uptake, Asia already demonstrated energetic evolution to deploy the new e-Infrastructure and engage in regional and international collaborations. From the lessons learnt in past few years on e-Science, we are confident that regional collaboration could make very unique scientific research. Moreover, very distinctive scientific data values of e-Science application data could be further manifested. For example, earthquake data about the fault characteristics provides deeper level of earth structure ingredients with potential for other related researches and for reduction of computation cost. Drug discovery data on neglected diseases is advantageous to more knowledge discovery.

To reduce the barrier of uptake and obtain the right strategy for e-Science development, continuous monitoring of metrics routinely is indispensable. In this study, a framework of metrics is presented. We intend to keep on collect the status of Asia countries through ISGC and compare the roadmap and development path with Europe and America. More intelligent tools for data acquisition and analysis should be also fulfilled.

REFERENCES

[1]   T. Hey, A. E. Trefethen, in Grid Computing: Making the Global Infrastructure a Reality, F. Berman, G. Fox, T. Hey, Eds (Wiley, New York, 2003), pp. 809-824.
[2]   T. Hey, and A. E. Trefethen, Cyberinfrastructure for e-Science, Science, Vol. 308, pp.817-821, May 2005.
[3]   Worldwide LHC Computing Grid, http://lcg.web.cern.ch/lcg/.
[4]   The Globus Alliance, http://www.globus.org/
[5]   Japan National Research Grid Initiative (NAREGI), http://www.naregi.org/
[6]   Storage Resource Broker, http://www.sdsc.edu/srb/index.php/Main_Page
[7]   Advanced Resource Connector (ARC), http://www.nordugrid.org/middleware/
[8]   Hsin-Yen Chen, Mason Hsiung, Hurng-Chun Lee, Eric Yen, Simon C. Lin, and Ying-Ta Wu (2010), GVSS: A High Throughput Drug Discovery Service of Avian Flu and Dengue Fever for EGEE and EUAsiaGrid, Journal of Grid Computing (Accepted), 2010.
[9]   EUChinaGrid, http://www.euchinagrid.org/
[10] EU-India Grid, http://www.euindiagrid.eu/
[11] EUAsiaGrid, http://www.euasiagrid.org/

EU-IndiaGrid2 Sustainable e-Infrastructures across Europe and India

Alberto Masoni

INFN Sezione di Cagliari, Italy

Abstract   EU-IndiaGrid2 - Sustainable e-infrastructures across Europe and India - capital-ises on the results of the FP6 EU-IndiaGrid project and huge infrastructural devel-opments in India. The present article describes the main achievements of the EU-IndiaGrid project and the perspectives for EU-IndiaGrid2, which started on Janu-ary 2010 with duration of 24 months.

1   INTRODUCTION

The EU-IndiaGrid project, funded by the European Commission under the Re-search Infrastructures Programme, aimed at making available a common, interop-erable Grid infrastructure to the European and Indian Scientific Community, in order to support existing EU-Indian collaborations in eScience and promoting new ones. The EU-IndiaGrid Consortium saw the participation of Premier European and Indian Institutes with consolidated collaborations on worldwide projects. The project started on October 2006 and ended on January 2009 reporting a set of im-pressive achievements. On January 2010 started EU-IndiaGrid2 - Sustainable e-infrastructures across Europe and India - funded under the Seventh Framework Programme of the European Commission, with the target of paving the way to-wards a sustainable e-Infrastructure for the benefit of Euro-India research collabo-rations and capitalising on the success of the previous EU-IndiaGrid project.

2   THE EU-INDIAGRID PROJECT

During the period of the project activity, from October 2006 to January 2009 e-Infrastructures in India marked a considerable progress. The leading responsibili-ties of EU-IndiaGrid Indian partners and the project bridging role between Euro-pean and Indian e-Infrastructures gave to EU-IndiaGrid project the opportunity to be at the core of this development and to effectively contribute at improving coop-eration between Europe and India in this domain. The activity concerned Network

S.C. Lin and E. Yen (eds.), *Data Driven e-Science: Use Cases and Successful Applications of Distributed Computing Infrastructures (ISGC 2010)*, DOI 10.1007/978-1-4419-8014-4_4,
© Springer Science+Business Media, LLC 2011

and middleware aspects. Concerning the network component, the launch of the multigigabit low latency National Knowledge Network plan (www.tein3.net) represented the most prominent landmarks India attained in the field of e-Infrastructures during the period. NKN and TEIN3 set the premises for important developments and significant strengthening of the cooperation be-tween Europe and India in the domain of international connectivity. This was highlighted in the context of dedicated meetings held in January 2009, with par-ticipation of repre-sentatives from EU-IndiaGrid project, DANTE, the European Commission and the Indian Government. The peering to GEANT of the 1 Gbps CERN-TIFR link for LHC, completed also at the end of January 2009, represents not only an important result for the LHC community and Euro-India scientific col-laboration, but a step-ping stone for further cooperation in the domain of interna-tional connectivity as illustrated in the section dedicated to the Indian Network in-frastructure. http://www.knowledgecommission.gov.in/downloads/news/news333.pdf) and the involvement of India in the TEIN3 project (Concerning the middleware aspects, a solid cooperation was established with GARUDA, the Indian NGI, as well as with the regional WLCG (Worldwide LHC Computing Grid). As for the network do-main, the strong involvement and the primary position of Indian partners in these activities gave the project the opportu-nity to be involved in this process, and to contribute at improving Euro-India col-laboration. The landmarks in this field were:

– The establishment of the Indian Grid Certification Authority, recog-nised by APGRIDPMA, by CDAC.
– The GARUDA transition for Proof-of-Concept to Foundation Phase, in April 2008.
– The support and operation of a grid infrastructure, which provided ex-cellent service to applications. A measure of success is given by the evolution of its usage in the second reporting period, as reported in Fig-ure 3 below.

A particular effort was dedicated to the support of several user communities in-cluding Biology, High Energy Physics, Material Science, and Earth & Atmos-pheric Sciences.

For each user community specific applications were deployed on the grid in-fra-structure and each application was supported by a collaboration of European and Indian partners. A comprehensive overview of all applications main results was presented at the 3rd IEEE Conference on e-Science and Grid Computing with a keynote speech [1] and specific contributions for all applications [2]

In the wide area of Computational Biology two different applications have been successfully ported and routinely used on the EU-IndiaGrid infrastructure. The first package, the Multiscale Object-Oriented Simulation Environment (MOOSE) was ported by National Centre for Biological Science team in Banga-lore, collabo-rating with a team at the University of Cambridge. The second pack-age (BEMUSE) was developed as the result of the grid-enabling efforts of the specific algorithm Biased Exchange Metadinamics. This work has been performed jointly by ICTP EU-IndiaGrid team and CNR/INFM Democritos researchers interested in exploiting the EU-Grid infrastructure [3]. The maturity level reached in the se-lected applications was confirmed at 3rd IEEE Conference on e-Science and Grid Computing, in particular the poster "Approaching protein folding on the EU-IndiaGrid infrastructure" was awarded as "e-Science 2007 Best Poster".

The activities related to the High Energy Physics applications were fully integrated in the framework of the Worldwide LHC Computing Grid Collaboration with particular concern with the ALICE and CMS experiments active in India. Results from these specific activities were reported at several relevant conferences and Workshops [4]

Material Science applications, supported by ICTP and University of Pune, leaded to a set of relevant scientific results (see e.g. [5, 6]). In Material Science applica-tions the project teams exploited also interoperability at application level making applications capable of working on different grid infrastructure in a transparent way to the user [7].

Earth and Atmospheric Sciences applications were followed by C-DAC and ICTP teams These teams ported on the grid infrastructure applications dedicated to two main areas a) Seismic Data Processing related to exploration geophysics; b) At-mospheric sciences. In both cases the results were presented at relevant conferences and published on scientific journals. The major development under EU-IndiaGrid project was a coupled atmosphere-ocean regional modelling system applied to the simulation of Indian Summer Monsoon season [8].

The grid infrastructure made available by the project to the users was based on re-sources distributed across Europe and India. Over 180.000 jobs were executed corresponding to about 25 cpu time years and 45 Wall Time years. The accounting was performed using DGAS and the EGEE portal for EGEE sites like Cambridge. Figure 1 reports the job distribution (referred to DGAS accounting) among sites while figure 2 shows the usage according to the different applications and figure 3 indicates the evolution of the usage of the infrastructure during the project lifetime.

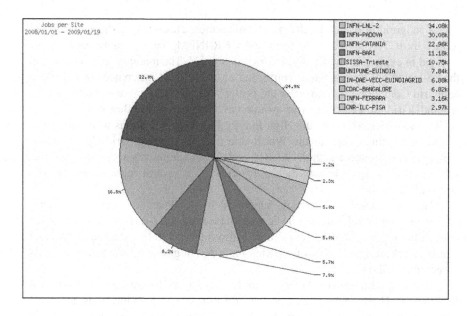

Fig. 1: Job per site distribution as accounted by DGAS, it does not include Cambridge and Pune University sites

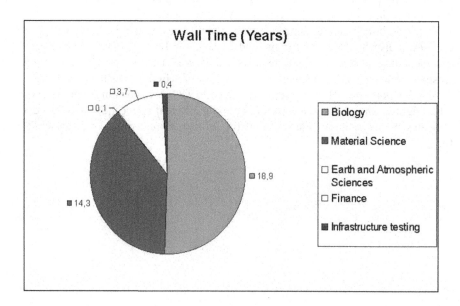

Fig. 2: Wall time per application field distribution as accounted by DGAS, it does not include HEP applications

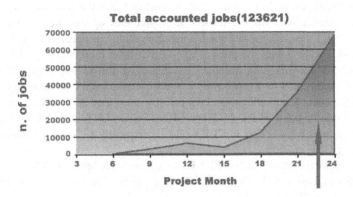

Fig. 3: The picture illustrates the growth in usage of the EU-IndiaGrid infrastructure by applications during the lifetime of the project in terms of jobs executed. By using the current infrastructure, applications can achieve in three months computational results that would have required 20 years of work on a single computer.

The increase of usage of the EU-IndiaGrid testbed, reported in figure 3 above, combined with scientific results obtained and presented at relevant international conferences or published on journals represent a clear measure of success of the user communities activity. The project Workshops and Conferences dedicated to the different applications were an important vehicle for the dissemination of results and for fostering the adoption of grid technology toward the scientific community and not only. In addition, supporting and addressing the problem of the interoperability at the application level further contributed to promote the use of advanced grid technology, and the cooperation between different projects and Institutes. Applications and user communities behind can thus be regarded as a key to sustainability, and they can help motivating the investment in e-Infrastructures.

3   THE PRESENT STATUS OF E-INFRASTRUCTURES IN INDIA

3.1   Network Infrastructure

In the last few years, the developments in the connectivity area in India were enormous, both at National and International level. EU-IndiaGrid Indian partners, in particular the Babha Atomic Research Centre (BARC), the Indian Education and Research Network (ERNET) and the Tata Institute of Fundamental Research (TIFR), had a leading role in this process, so EU-IndiaGrid found itself fully involved in this evolution and had the opportunity to act as a link between European and Indian e-Infrastructures. In October 2006, as part of EU-India co-operation in ICT and in coincidence with the EU-IndiaGrid project start-up, for the first time the GÉANT-ERNET link was established, interconnecting European and Indian research networks at 45 Mbps. At present the TEIN3 link interconnects the PanEuropean GEANT network with India at 2.5 Gbps. The TEIN3 link set-up was announced on January 2010 on the occasion of the EU-IndiaGrid2 Launch event.

The most prominent landmarks in the connectivity area since 2006 have been:

- The establishment of the 45 Mbps ERNET - GÉANT link and routing of re-gional WLCG data to CERN and subsequently EU-IndiaGrid traffic to EGEE in 2006;
- The upgrade of the GÉANT-ERNET link from 45 Mbps to 100 Mbps in 2008 and then to 175 Mbps in 2009 and upgrade of domestic bandwidth for regional WLCG network;
- The establishment of a dedicated 1 Gbps TIFR-CERN link for LHC re-search in 2008 and peering with GÉANT in 2009;
- The establishment of the National Knowledge Network (NKN) in April 2009;
- The connectivity of TEIN3: 2.5 Gbps Geant link to India in February 2010.
- The approval from Government of India of the full National Knowledge Net-work Plan in March 2010 with a budget of about 1 Billion euro.

EU-IndiaGrid Indian partners had a remarkable role in all these stepping stones in Indian network evolution while the EU-IndiaGrid project was always at the core of the development of improved collaboration services between European and Indian e-Infrastructures.

As remarked by Dr R. Chidambaram, Principal Scientific Adviser to the Gov-ern-ment of India, NKN and the participation of India to the TEIN3 project are crucial developments for Indian research: "The successful working of the initial phase of the multi-gigabit NKN, Indian Certification Authority, and participation in TEIN phase 3 are some of the important building blocks for supporting virtual research communities in India and their collaboration work with other countries." In the two sections below we provide a brief description of both initiatives.

3.1.1 National Connectivity: The Indian National Knowledge Network

The office of Principal Scientific Adviser to the Government of India and National Knowledge Commission (www.knowledgecommission.gov.in/) recommended the creation of the National Knowledge Network (NKN) as absolutely necessary for India's development. The objective of the National Knowledge Network is to bring together all the stakeholders in Science, Technology, Higher Education, Research & Development, and Governance with speeds of the order of 10s of gigabits per second coupled with extremely low latencies. NKN will interconnect all institutions engaged in research, higher education and scientific development in the country, over a period of time. It would enable use of specialized applications, which allow sharing of high-performance computing facilities, e-libraries, virtual classrooms, and very large databases.

In the initial phase of NKN, with 15 Core locations and about 57 institutes cover-ing leading national R&D labs and educational institutes have been connected at varying bandwidths of 100 to 1000 Mbps. In the final phase of NKN, around 5000 leading national academic and research institutes are going to be connected. On March 2010 the Government of India approved the full National Knowledge Net-work Plan in March 2010 with a budget of about 1 Billion euro. NKN with its multi-gigabit, low-latency, OFC-based backbone is acting as national transport for all existing networks. The Indian grid initiative GARUDA is riding on NKN as on today. The regional WLCG in India is going to be migrated to NKN. NKN will provide transport to ERNET replacing its existing backbone. The main design consideration for NKN is to create an infrastructure that can scale and adapt to fu-ture requirements. NKN will enable scientists, researchers and students from di-verse spheres across the country to work together for advancing human develop-ment in critical and emerging areas. NKN will catalyse knowledge sharing and knowledge transfer between stakeholders seamlessly – that too across the nation and globally. Education, Grid Computing, Agriculture and e-Governance are the main applications identified for implementation and delivery on NKN.

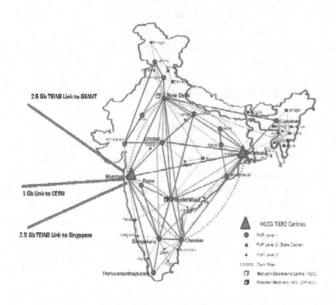

Fig. 4: India-1: NKN Connectivity

Concerning Sustainability it must be stressed that NKN has been proposed as na-tional programme. The network will be sustained through continuous government funding. The present Government approval established the funding for a period of 10 years.

In the design philosophy of NKN, high speed connectivity to global research net-works has been envisaged. To provide high-speed connectivity to users of NKN, it has been decided that TEIN3 connectivity will land in NKN POP in Mumbai. It had also been decided that exiting ERNET-GEANT connectivity and TIFR-CERN connectivity would be consolidated into a single link under TEIN3 link (see be-low).

3.1.2 International Connectivity: Trans Eurasia Information Network 3 (TEIN3) (http://www.tein3.net)

The Trans-Eurasia Information Network (TEIN) initiative was launched at the Asia Europe Meeting (ASEM) Summit in Seoul in 2000 to improve Euro-Asian research networking. India joined with its phase 3 (TEIN3) in 2009.

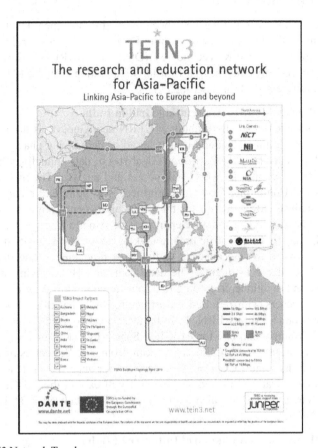

Fig. 5: TEIN3 Network Topology

As part of TEIN3 project, a TEIN3 Point Of Presence has been co-located at ERNET POP at Mumbai and it is acting as hub for connecting research networks in South Asia, except Pakistan. From Mumbai, two high speed links of 2.5 Gbps each has been commissioned to Europe and Singapore and are now operational providing direct connectivity to GEANT and TEIN3 POP at Singapore. India is now acting as hub for connectivity between Europe and Asia-Pacific countries. The European Commission is partly funding the connectivity under TEIN3. As part of this project, ERNET has been taking part in the meeting of TEIN3. At present TEIN3 POP is located in C-DAC campus in Mumbai. However in the long run, the TEIN3 POP in Mumbai will be relocated to NKN POP in Mumbai.

3.2   Grid Infrastructure

In India, two main Grid Initiatives have been taken at Government level: Regional WLCG set up by the Department of Atomic Energy (DAE) in coordination with the Department of Science & Technology (DST) and GARUDA National Grid Initiative. Both of them established a fruitful collaboration with the EU-IndiaGrid project and its successor EU-IndiaGrid2.

3.2.1   The Worldwide LHC Computing Grid in India

The Large Hadron Collider (LHC) built at CERN near Geneva, is the largest scientific instrument on the planet and it just started its data-taking phase. In full operation it will produce roughly 15 million Gigabytes of data annually, which thousands of scientists around the world will access and analyse. The mission of the Worldwide LHC Computing Grid (LCG) project is to build and maintain a data storage and analysis infrastructure for the entire high-energy physics community that will use the LHC. The Indian Department of Atomic Energy (DAE) is actively participating to the scientific program taking active part in CMS and ALICE experiments, devoted to find answers to the most fundamental questions at the foundations of matter constituents. The data from the LHC experiments will be distributed around the globe, according to a four-tiered model. Within this model, to support researchers with required infrastructure, India has also setup regional Tier-2 centres connected to CERN. In India there are two Tier2 centres: one for CMS in TIFR Mumbai and one for ALICE at Saha-VECC Kolkata. These centres provide access to CMS & ALICE users working from Tier III centres of Universities and national labs and LCG Data Grid services for analysis. TIFR is presently connected to CERN at 1 Gb/s and very soon it will exploit the 2.5 Gb/s TEIN3 link. Now TIFR & VECC are also being connected through NKN at 1 Gb/s for migration to NKN.

3.2.2   GARUDA: the National Grid Initiative of India

GARUDA India National Grid Initiatives (http://www.garudaindia.in/) is a collaboration of scientific and technological researchers on a nationwide grid comprising of computational nodes, mass storage and scientific instruments. It aims to provide the technological advances required to enable data and compute intensive science for the 21st century.

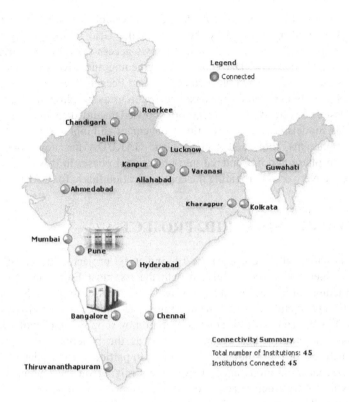

Fig. 6: Map of GARUDA Sites

C-DAC, one of EU-IndiaGrid's main partners, ensures progressive evolution and durable integration as manager of the Indian National Grid Initiative and from the start of its activity the EU-IndiaGrid project established an excellent collaboration with GARUDA.

GARUDA has transitioned form the Proof of Concept phase to the Foundation Phase in April 2008 and currently is in the third phase namely Grid Technology Services for Operational Garuda. This phase is approved for three years ending in July 2012.

Some of the envisaged deliverables of this phase include:
- Delivering Service based Grid with tools to support ease of use.
- On-demand provisioning of resources
- Ensure QOS and end-to-end reliability for applications
- Open and standards based implementation
- Supports Inter-operability across grids
- Deploy select identified application as service for end user consumption

The GARUDA project coordinator, CDAC established for the first time, in No-vember 2008, recognized by the Asia-Pacific Grid Policy Management Authority (http://ca.garudaindia.in), which allows access to worldwide grids for Indian Re-searchers. GARUDA aims at strengthening and advancing scientific and techno-logical excellence in the area of Grid and Peer-to-Peer technologies. It will also create the foundation for the next generation grids by addressing long term research issues in the strategic areas of: knowledge and data management, programming models, architectures, grid management and monitoring, problem solving environments, tools and grid services. GARUDA has now completed the foundation phase and has entered into operational phase. In this phase, National Knowledge Network is providing the communication fabric for GARUDA.

4   THE EU-INDIAGRID2 PROJECT

EU-IndiaGrid2 will leverage on the EU-IndiaGrid project achievements and the strong cooperation links established with the foremost European and Indian e-Infrastructure initiatives paving the way for successful sustainable cooperation across European and Indian e-Infrastructures. EU-IndiaGrid2 aims to procure sustainable EU-Indian e-Infrastructure cooperation by supporting a set of relevant applications, promoting their results, as well as the benefits and impacts of e-Infrastructures for Euro-Indian collaboration. In particular EU-IndiaGrid2 will address relevant Institutions and policy makers relying on the leading role of its partners in e-Infrastructure activities both in Europe and India. The main Objectives of the EU-Indiagrid2 project are summarised below:

1. Consolidate & enhance cooperation between European and Indian e- Infrastructures for the benefit of EU-Indian collaboration in e-Science
2. Support specific user communities in the exploitation of grid infra-structure in areas strategic for EU-Indian collaboration
3. ensure a sustainable approach to e-Infrastructures across Europe and India through dissemination actions, meetings & workshops
4. foster and enhance cooperation with other European Initiatives in the Asian region and worldwide

The project support activities are organised within four work packages besides the Project Management (WP1):

- Liaison with other Projects & Organisations (WP2) will pursue cooperation ac-tivities with the most relevant e-Infrastructure initiatives and Institutions both in Europe and India, capitalising on the leading role of its partners in the most relevant European & Indian e-Infrastructures projects and on the close links al-ready established with projects and relevant actors by the EU-IndiaGrid pro-ject;
- Operational infrastructure and interoperability support (WP3), will deliver sup-port to the Interconnection and Interoperation of e-

Infrastructures across Europe (EGEE -EGI) and India (WLCG, GARUDA and National Knowledge Network (NKN));
- User communities support (WP4), will sustain a set of applications within user communities strategic for EU-Indian cooperation fostering the benefits of tech-nology achievements on scientific collaborations; close cooperation with WP2, WP3, WP5 will contribute to identifying and performing the necessary actions to favour optimal resources ex-ploited by such user communities.
- Communication and Awareness raising (WP5) will reinforce the global rele-vance and impact of the results obtained by the project and will contribute to increasing awareness and use of joint e-Infrastructures, identifying engaging and supporting a Euro-Indian e-infrastructure community.

4.1 User communities

EU-IndiaGrid2 targets a number of user communities in the project:
- Climate change: Climate change is a worldwide concern and climate change studies are among the priorities in European and Indian research programs. In particular climate change is one of the flagship activities within the NKN program. EU-IndiaGrid2 aims to support climate change modelling studies on European and Indian e-Infrastructures thanks to the involvement of premier research groups with leading in-ternational repu-tations and a solid collaboration basis enhanced and strengthened in the course of EU-IndiaGrid.
- High Energy Physics: the Large Hadron Collider (LHC) program repre-sents one of the unique science and research facilities to share between India and Europe in the field of Scientific Research in general and in the ICT domain in particular. The Indian partners in the project represent both the ALICE and the CMS communities actively engaged in the LHC program. The role of the EU-IndiaGrid project in this specific ac-tivity has been widely recognised within the European Commission and the Indian Government and EU-IndiaGrid2 will continue its action in sustaining this community.
- Biology and Material Science: these broad areas require computational tools and techniques spawning different disciplines: they will challenge the project in setting up and providing cross disciplinary research ser-vices. The successful work of its predecessor EU-IndiaGrid, performed in these areas, allowed the establishment and the reinforcement of rele-vant EU-Indian collaborations supported by premier Institutions within the Consortium.

The project, approved within the call FP7-INFRASTRUCTURES-2009-1, started on January 2010 with duration of 24 months. The Project Launch and Kick-off Event happened in conjunction with the EU-India Workshop on Research Infra-structures where the interesting perspectives for the project activity were enhanced. In addition the recent announcement of the approval by Government of India of the multi-Gb high speed National Knowledge Network and the availability of a 2.5 Gb link from Europe to India and from India to Singapore in the context of the TEIN3 project set the conditions for extremely interesting opportunities for cooperation between Europe, India and the Asia-Pacific area in the e-infrastructures domain.

REFERENCES

[1]   S.P. Dhekne, 3rd IEEE International Conference on e-Science and Grid Computing, Bangalore, India (2007), Keynote tion, http://www.escience2007.org/keynotes.htm
[2]   3rd IEEE International Conference on e-Science and Grid Computing, Bangalore, India (2007) http://www.escience2007.org
[3]   R. di Meo, F. Pietrucci, A. Laio and S. Cozzini ICTP Lecture Notes Se-ries, Volume 24 LNS0924008 (2009)
[4]   A. Masoni, Advanced Computing and Analysis Techniques in Physics Research, Jaipur, India (2010), to be published on in "Proceedings of Science" (http://pos.sissa.it)
[5]   R. di Meo, A. Dal Corso, P. Giannozzi and S. Cozzini ICTP Lecture Notes Series, Volume 24 LNS0924010 (2009)
[6]   B.Pujari et al. Phys. Rev. B 78, 125414 (2008)
[7]   S. Cozzini, ICTP Lecture Notes Series, Volume 24 LNS0924002 (2009)
[8]   J. Venkata Ratnam, F. Giorgi, A. Kaginalkar and S. Cozzini, Journal Climate Dynamics 10.1007/s00382-008-0433-3

Pathway to Support the Sustainable National Health Information System

Naiyana Sahavechaphan, Jedsada Phengsuwan, Suriya U-ruekolan, Kamron Aroonrua, Jukrapong Ponhan, Nattapon Harnsamut and Sornthep Vannarat

National Electronics and Computer Technology Center, Thailand

Abstract   Heath information across geographically distributed healthcare centers has been recognized as an essential resource that drives an efficient national health-care plan. There is thus a need for the National Health Information System (NHIS) that provides the transparent and secure access to health information from different healthcare centers both on demand and in a time efficient manner. As healthiness is the ultimate goal of people and nation, we believe that the NHIS should be sustainable by taking the healthcare center and information consumer perspectives into account. Several issues in particular must be resolved altogether: (i) the diversity of health information structures among healthcare centers; (ii) the availability of health information sharing from healthcare centers; (iii) the efficient information access to various healthcare centers; and (iv) the privacy and privilege of heath information. To achieve the sustainable NHIS, this paper details our work which is divided into 3 main phases. Essentially, the first phase focuses on the application of metadata standard to enable the interoperability and usability of health information across healthcare centers. The second phase moves forward to make information sharing possible and to provide an efficient information access to a large number of healthcare centers. Finally, in the third phase, the privacy and privilege of health information is promoted with respect to access rights of information consumers.

1   INTRODUCTION

A national healthcare plan typically aims at the health treatment and promotion, the disease outbreak protection and control, the medical manpower development, the medical reimbursement, and any medical-related researches. It should thus be accomplished as either a year-based or an emergent plan to serve heath-related issues in a long or short period of time, respectively. To drive an efficient plan, heath information across geographically distributed healthcare centers has been recognized as an essential resource. Accordingly, there is a need for way to acquire such updated information both on demand and in a time efficient manner.

S.C. Lin and E. Yen (eds.), *Data Driven e-Science: Use Cases and Successful Applications of Distributed Computing Infrastructures (ISGC 2010)*, DOI 10.1007/978-1-4419-8014-4_5,
© Springer Science+Business Media, LLC 2011

Several approaches [1, 2, 4] have been proposed in the literature. Their goal is to propose the infrastructures that enable information consumers to access information from multiple repositories owned by different information providers. An information access in particular is done in a transparent and secure manner. This not only makes information consumers to gain information elsewhere with ease, but also guarantees information providers that only authorized consumers are able to access their information. However, the heterogeneity of information across different repositories are neglected, making the acquired information itself not ready for instant use. In addition, the performance to access information from a large number of repositories is not focused. It would therefore be time-consuming to get all necessary information. Moreover, the data security is often done at the service level (not the data level), exposing private information to all authorized consumers regardless of their intrinsic data access rights.

To address the above drawbacks, in this work, we must take the healthcare center and information consumer perspectives into account. Several issues in particular must be resolved altogether: (i) the diversity of health information structures among healthcare centers; (ii) the availability of health information sharing from healthcare centers; (iii) the efficient information access to various healthcare centers; and (iv) the privacy and privilege of heath information. Based on these, we propose to develop a sustainable infrastructure, namely NHIS (National Health Information System). Essentially, NHIS enables consumers to have the on demand access to standard health information from different healthcare centers in a transparent and time-efficient manner. It also restricts consumers to gain the information access based on their access rights.

To achieve the sustainable NHIS, this paper details our work which is divided into 3 main phases. Essentially, the first phase focuses on the application of metadata standard to enable the interoperability and usability of health information across healthcare centers. The second phase moves forward to make information sharing possible and to provide an efficient information access to a large number of health-care centers. Finally, in the third phase, the privacy and privilege of health information is promoted with respect to access rights of information consumers.

This paper is organized as followed. Section 2 gives the background. Details of each phase is given in Section 3 -Section 5. Section 6 concludes the paper.

2   BACKGROUND

Currently, in Thailand, there are about 10,000 healthcare centers geographically distributed throughout a nation. They can be classified into 3 main categories, ranging from small to medium and large healthcare centers. At least 30 hospital information systems (HIS') have been chosen and deployed at these healthcare centers. Beside healthcare centers, there are 4 significant governmental agencies (Ministry of Public Health (MOPH) [15], National Health Security Office (NHSO) [17], Social Security Office (SSO) [16] and the Comptroller General's Department (CGD) [18]) that require health information across healthcare centers. In particular, NHSO is mainly responsible for developing the national healthcare plan and then proceeding any activities related to the plan. Here, the summarized health information would be applicable. The rest are insurance plan agencies. They have focused on the reimbursement to healthcare centers that provide services to people using their insurance plans. They thus require the information based on health treatment of each individual patient. In addition, there would be other organizations (e.g. universities, pharmaceutical companies and insurance companies) that request heath information for their research and development. The existence of NHIS would enable these agencies to have an efficient application of health information and finally bring benefits to people and nation.

To the rest of this paper, we term healthcare centers as information consumers while the rest agencies are termed as information providers.

3   THE INFORMATION TRANSFORMATION PHASE

Unavoidably, healthcare centers throughout a nation deploy different HIS' that mostly serve their needs. Each of which has its own information structure and intrinsic coding scheme. The heterogeneity of heath information both in term of structure and coding scheme would thus be considered as a significant obstacle to its further application. Ideally, to facilitate this, the national health metadata standard should be developed. Healthcare centers must then transform their underlying information into a standard format. Health information across healthcare centers can now be in a good shape to be employed and interoperated. However, the healthcare domain itself is diverse and complex. It must also be dynamic to a new coming health-related issue. This reflects the national health metadata standard in such a way that its design should serve the application of health information in various dimensions (e.g. chronic disease treatment and antenatal care) and be dynamic to satisfy any changes.

Beside the complex and dynamic health metadata standard, the burden for transforming information into a standard format is on both software vendors and IT persons of healthcare centers. Each of which typically accomplishes it by manually writing a set of proper SQL and programs, and even creating a set of code mapping tables in a HISdatabase to lower the complexity of SQL and programs.

This method has been proved to be time-consuming and error-prone. In particular, line-by-line of SQL and programs must be written, modified and investigated in order to serve a standard. This phase thus focuses on the development of a generic tool to transform in any HISdatabases into a standard format.

Basically, we propose to develop the two significant (open source) tools: Metadata Mapping Tool (MMT) and Metadata Conversion Tool (MCT). MMTand MCTsupport healthcare centers to efficiently transform their information stored in any relational databases into a standard format with a small effort. Essentially, MMT facilitates a user to visually create the mapping configuration that captures the transformation knowledge between a specified HISdatabase and a metadata standard. The transformation knowledge encapsulates a set of mapping between each individual standard element and its source either based on a local element or a computation of one or more local elements. For example, Figure 1 visually shows that the standard element DateTime is mapped with the local element visit-date via its computation to transform the Christian Era into Buddhist Era. MCT, on the other hand, analyzes an assigned mapping configuration, generates an appropriate SQL and transforms information into a standard format. Figure 2 illustrates the relationship of MMTand MCT.

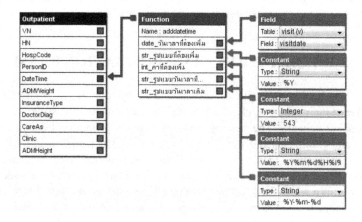

Fig. 1: The Transformation Knowledge of a Standard Element DateTime.

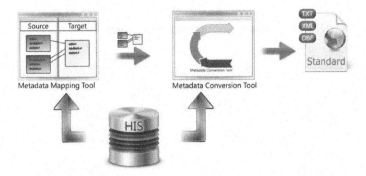

Fig. 2: The Relationship of MMT and MCT.

4   THE INFORMATION SHARING AND INTEROPERABILITY PHASE

Racall that the previous phase has coped with the heterogeneity of health information across various healthcare centers. Health information among healthcare centers is now in a standard format and hence ready to be employed and interoperated. However, the standard information has not yet been available to consumers, making them unable to access an information itself on demand to serve any ad-hoc events. This phase thus moves forward to make information sharing across healthcare centers possible and hence to promote the application of a standard information in an efficient manner.

It is likely that healthcare centers may deploy their HIS' based on different IT infrastructures. Each of which requires its own mechanism or technique to support an access of its underlying information. A steep learning curve is thus needed in order to acquire a standard information from such healthcare centers. Interestingly, Web Services Technology [5] has been developed to facilitate the interoperability of applications regardless of their underlying platforms and infrastructures. Based on this, we propose to develop an application as a service, namely Metadata Service (MS), for each individual healthcare center. MS accommodates not only the heterogeneity of IT infrastructure but also the availability of the information sharing and the information access on demand. Essentially, MSencapsulates the MCT's core engine and a proper mapping configuration with a standard protocol. As per an access request, MSautomatically analyzes its intrinsic mapping configuration, generates an appropriate query (SQL), accesses health information from a specified database and transforms it into a standard format. Figure 3 illustrates the deployment of MS' at healthcare centers regardless of their diversity in IT infrastructures and information.

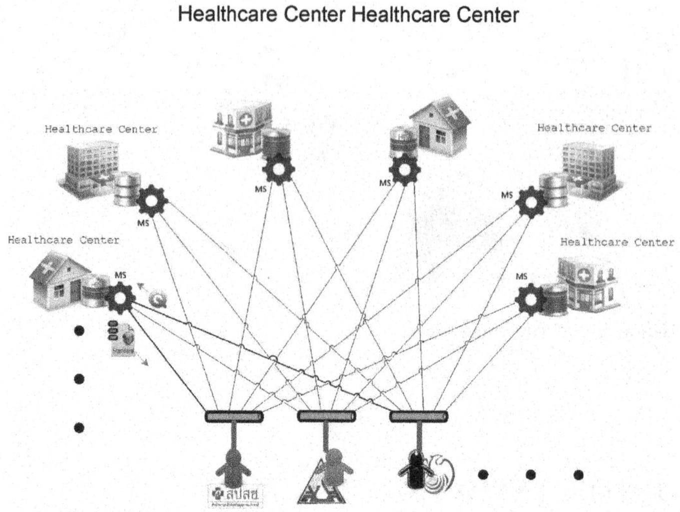

Healthcare Center Healthcare Center

Fig. 3: The Deployment of MS' at Healthcare Centers.

Here, a consumer can access information from different healthcare centers through their corresponding MS' standard protocol.

While an information access to each healthcare center is now simplified, it would still be nightmare for consumers to acquire information from a large number of healthcare centers. To address this, we propose to develop once again an application as a service, namely Metadata Broker (MB). Specifically, MB not only provides the linkage to a potential set of MS', but also accesses and integrates their information based upon a consumer's request. A number of MBalong with their communication are also deployed and developed using P2P technology [6] to facilitate an information access to a large number of healthcare centers as shown in Figure 4. An information access to various healthcare centers is thus allowed in a transparent and scalable manner. In addition, as per a request, MBis capable of decision-making on which MS' are applicable such that it would distribute them a request. Moreover, it is able to balance its load with other MB'. These two capability clearly makes the overall system performance more scalable.

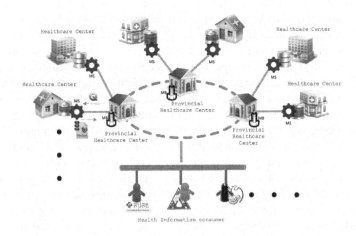

Fig. 4: The Deployment of MB' along with MS' at Healthcare Centers

5   THE INFORMATION SECURITY PHASE

Recall that the first phase has managed the heterogeneity of health information across various healthcare centers, while the second phase moves forward to make information sharing possible and to provide an efficient information access to a large number of healthcare centers. Standard health information from various healthcare centers can now be accessible by any consumers. Ideally, health information is private information and hence should be published to the proper consumers. As previously mentioned in Section 2, many consumers require health information to serve their needs in different dimensions. To lower any compromising risks, the access rights based on consumer roles should be taken into account. The access rights in particular can be defined based on the element and transaction levels. This phase thus promotes the privacy and privilege of health information with respect to access rights of information consumers.

Basically, in this phase, we propose to extend both MB and MS in such a way that they are able to authenticate the identity of an information consumer prior to his access allowance, authorize a consumer in a fine-grained manner to restrict an information access based on his access rights, delegate a consumer's identity and access rights from MB to its corresponding MS' as well as other MB' to serve the single sign on issue, and handle the privacy of information during its transportation among entities (MB', MS' and consumer).

To achieve the above extension, our work would (i) deploy the Public Key Infrastructure (PKI) [7] to support the issue of credentials (or identities) to consumers which is done based on X.509v3 end-entity certificate, and to facilitate the credential management. PKI is chosen due to its available security mechanisms such as confidentiality, integrity, authentication, and non repudiation; (ii) develop the Authorization System (AS) that uses X.509 Attribute Certificate (AC) to generate the policy attributes with respect to the access rights of consumers, and to support the authorization management. As access rights corresponds to the consumer roles, the Role Base Access Control (RBAC) [8] and the Privilege Management Infrastructure (PMI) [9] are chosen to form the basis of AS. In addition, the policy attribute issuer must be identified to make the ASitself reliable. Here, the Source of Author- ity (SOA) must thus be developed as part of AS and is responsible for providing the digital signature on each generated policy attribute. The architecture of AS is illustrated in Figure 5; and finally (iii) develop the WS-Security standards and Single sign-on (SSO) to guarantee privacy and integrity of the transported information as well as a single time authentication among multiple entities (MB, MS and consumers). In particular, the privacy and integrity of information is achieve by using XML-Encryption [10] and XML-Signature [11] respectively. The single sign on, on the other hand, is done via the application of Security Assertion Markup Language (SAML) [14].

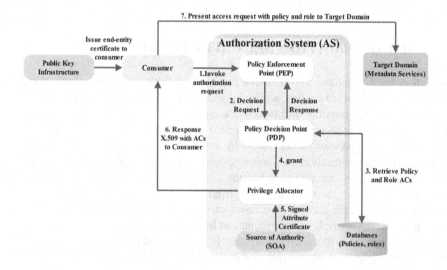

Fig. 5: The Architecture of AS.

6   CONCLUSION

This paper details our work which is divided into 3 main phases: the information transformation, information sharing and interoperability and information security phases as shown in Figure 6 - 8 respectively. We believe that this pathway enables the sustainable NHIS due to the intrinsic properties: transparency, data security, availability, extensibility and scalability. Currently, we are at the end of the first phase. The field evaluation of MMT and MCT will be conducted soon at about 20 healthcare centers that deploy at least 3 different HIS' and hence at least 3 different health information structures.

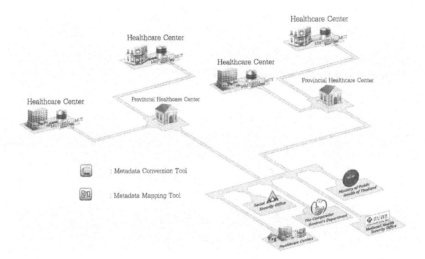

Fig. 6: The Information Transformation Phase.

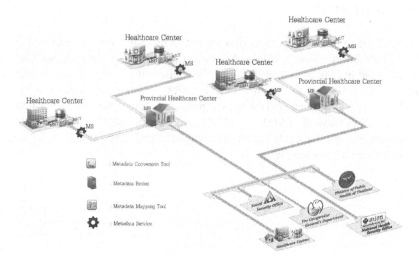

Fig. 7: The Information Sharing and Interoperability Phase.

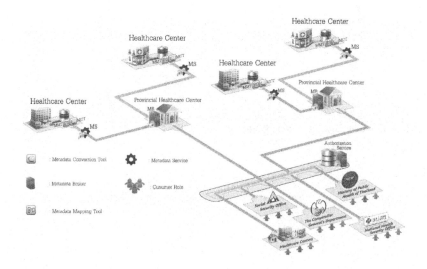

Fig. 8: The Information Security Phase.

REFERENCES

[1] S. Fiore, A. Negro, S. Vadacca, E. Verdesca, A. Leone and G.Aloisio. The GRelC Portal: A Ubiguitous and Seamless Way to Manage Grid Databases. In Proceedings of the 9th International Conference on Parallel and Distributed Computing, Applications and Technologies. (2008)

[2] Woehrer, A., Brezany, P., Janciak, I. Virtualization of Heterogeneous Data Sources for Grid Information Systems. (2004)

[3] Alpdemir, M. N., Mukherjee, A., Gounaris, A., Paton, W. N., Watson, P. Fernandes, A. A., and Smith, J. OGSA-DQP: A Service-Based Distributed Query Processor For The Grid. In the Proceedings of the Second e-Science All Hands Meeting. (2003)

[4] Pahlevi, M. and Kojima, I. OGSA-WebDB: An OGSA-Based System for Bringing Web Databases into the Grid. In Proceedings of the International Conference on Information Technology: Coding and Computing (ITCC) (2004)

[5] Web Services @ W3C. http://www.w3.org/2002/ws

[6] Stephanos Androutsellis-Theotokis, Diomidis Spinellis. A Survey of Peer-to-Peer Content Distribution Technologies. ACM Computing Surveys. v.66 n.4 (2004)

[7] Tom Austin. PKI: A Wiley Tech Brief. John Wiley & Sons Inc. New York (2000)

[8] D.F. Ferraiolo, J. A. Cugini and D. R. Kuhn. Role Based Access Control (RBAC): Features and Motivations. In the 11th Annual Computer Security Applications Proceedings (1995)

[9] D.W. Chadwick and A. Otenko. The PERMIS X.509 role based privilege management infrastructure. Future Generation Computer Systems. v.19 n.2 p.277-289 (February 2003)

[10] T. Imamura, B. Dillaway, E.Simon. XML Encryption Syntax and Processing. W3C. Available at http://www.w3.org/TR/xmlenc-core/

[11] M. Bartel, J. Boyer, B. Fox, B. LaMacchia and E. Simon. XML-Signature Syntax and Processing. W3C. Available at http://www.w3.org/TR/xmldsig-core/

[12] OASIS Web Services Security TC. WS-Security. OASIS, Available at http://www.oasis-open.org-committees/tc-home.php

[13] OASIS Security Services TC. Security Assertion Markup Language (SAML). OASIS. Available at http://www.oasis-open.org/committees/tc-home.php

[14] OASIS Security Services TC. Security Assertion Markup Language (SAML). OASIS. Available at http://www.oasis-open.org/committees/tc-home.php

[15] Ministry of Public Health. http://www.moph.go.th/

[16] Social Security Office. http://www.sso.go.th/

[17] National Health Security Office. http://www.nhso.go.th/

[18] The Comptroller General's Department. http:www.cgd.go.th/

Part IV
Grid Security and Networking

TERENA eScience PKI

Milan Sova

CESNET

Abstract   Several National Research and Education Networks associated in TERENA have joined their efforts to build a shared PKI able to serve potentially millions of users from their constituency. The TCS eScience Personal CA takes advantage of national identity federations to facilitate user identity vetting and enrollment procedures. The system uses identity management systems (IdMS) at participating institutions to perform the functions of registration authorities. The certificate enrollment application acts as a SAML Service Provider relying on information provided by IdMS performing as SAML Identity Providers (IdP). When applying for a personal certificate, users authenticate at their home IdP using credentials they normally use to access local services. The IdP controls the certificate issuance process by releasing SAML attributes specifying the user's eligibility for the service and the information to be included in the certificate such as the user's name and email address.

The TCS eScience Personal CA is part of the TERENA Certificate Service that uses a commercial PKI provider. Outsourcing the actual CA machinery to a specialized company results in professional-level services such as CRL and OCSP management.

The paper describes the legal, organizational and technical aspects of the TCS eScience PKI.

1   HISTORY OF TERENA CERTIFICATE SERVICES

1.1   Motivation

Academic institutions need to provide many services to their users. Some of them operate with sensitive data and require secure access to the server. The natural protocol of choice to build secure channels is TLS. Traditionally, many National Research an Educational Networks (NRENs) operated certification authorities (CAs) to issue public key certificates to servers within their constituency. However, these certification authorities were not implicitly trusted by the client software commonly used. The software confronted users with (usually rather incomprehensible) warnings and effectively defeated the purpose of server authentication.

S.C. Lin and E. Yen (eds.), *Data Driven e-Science: Use Cases and Successful Applications of Distributed Computing Infrastructures (ISGC 2010)*, DOI 10.1007/978-1-4419-8014-4_6, © Springer Science+Business Media, LLC 2011

Installing the certification authority root certificate into client software is cumbersome and demanding and was proved practically infeasible in the scale of European academic community. Some institutions decided to buy server certificates from commercial CAs recognized by clients by default. Nevertheless the certificates were expensive and the procedures to obtain a certificate were difficult.

1.2   Server Certificate Service

In 2004, Jan Meijer (SURFnet) first proposed to create a consortium of European NRENs for buying server certificates from a commercial provider as a service. The participating institutions should be able to get certificates for their server easily and at affordable cost. The idea has been adopted by 6 NRENs initially and TERENA (Trans-European Research and Education Networking Association) has been chosen as the legal representative of the consortium. In December 2004 the SCS (Server Certificate Service) has officially started.

After a couple of months spent on defining the service and market research, the Call for Proposals was issued in September 2005. The contract with Global-Sign NV/SA, the winner of the tender, was signed in January 2006. In the meantime, two other NRENs joined the project and the service became operational in March 2006 for 8 NRENs. In January 2007, the original one-year contract was prolonged by three more years.

1.3   TERENA Certificate Service

The service became very popular, there were 19 NRENs taking part in the project in 2009. After almost three years of using the service, the project members decided to test the conditions on a rapidly evolving market by preparing a new Call for Proposals issued in September 2008. As the result, a contract with Comodo CA Ltd. has been signed in April 2009. In addition to SSL server certificates, the new provider offered personal certificates and certificates for object signing. During the project negotiation, support for eScience (i. e. IGTF approved) certificates for both SSL servers and users was agreed upon. Based on the broader scope of provided services, the project name has been changed to TERENA Certificate Services (TCS).

The first phase of TCS was mainly oriented towards safeguarding the transition of the existing and popular server certificate service to the new provider. After having produced the Certification Practice Statement (CPS) for issuing server certificates and the web-enrollment application, first TCS server certificates have been issued in June 2009 giving the users six-months window for replacing their server certificates (the contract with the previous provider expiring in January 2010).

The objective of the second phase of the project was to prepare the new services, namely the personal certificates, the eScience personal and server certificates, and the object signing certificates. To enable both flavors of the personal certificates to scale at the European level, the project members decided to leverage the emerging infrastructure of Identity Federations within their community to provide the functions of registration Authorities to the TCS CAs. Being the larger expected service within many of the federations and bringing a rather new concept to both the PKI users and the CA operator, the definition of TCS Personal certificates service required significant effort both at the technical and organizational level. Finally the TERENA eScience Personal CA and the TERENA Personal CA have been opened to public in March 2010.

2   ORGANIZATIONAL STRUCTURE

The TCS organizational infrastructure is organized in three levels. At the top level, TERENA provides the umbrella representation of the project interacting with CA providers on the one hand and with participating NRENs on the other. The NRENs at the second level mediate access to the TCS for the institutions in their constituency. The institutions then represent the third organizational level of the structure. They use the service either directly (server and object signing certificates) or via their users (personal certificates).

Relations between individual parties are defined by a respective form of a legal contract. The overall conditions of the service are defined by the contract between TERENA and the supplier CA. As part of the process of joining the TCS, NRENs close a contract with TERENA. Similarly, individual institutions have to accept a Subscriber Agreement provided by their NREN. All these contracts refer the Certification Practice Statement of the respective service as the authoritative description of the service, the relevant responsibilities, and operational procedures. Thus, the liabilities are defined in a scalable and enforceable manner providing a trustworthy infrastructure.

2.1   TCS Products

Currently, the TCS offers five types of certificates each provided by its own Certificate Authority:

TERENA SSL CA

Provides certificates to SSL/TLS servers. The certificates may be valid for 1, 2, or 3 years. This is the continuance of the original SCS service.

TERENA eScience SSL CA

Issues SSL/TLS server certificates complying with IGTF requirements. These certificates may be used for servers and services within major grid infrastructures[1]. The certificates are valid for 13 month at most.

---

[1] At the time of this paper preparation, the accreditation of the TERENA eScience SSL CA was still pending. The process was expected to conclude in April 2010.

TERENA Personal CA

Issues general personal certificates usable for securing email using S/MIME and for end user authentication. Registration and verification of the users is provided by their home institutions using their local accounts and IDMS records. The certificates may be valid for 1, 2, or 3 years.

TERENA eScience Personal CA

Is a CA accredited by EUGridPMA for issuing personal certificates to grid users. The procedures and operational characteristics are almost identical to those of the TERENA Personal CA with some changes required by their orientation to eScience applications. The certificates are valid for 13 month maximally.

TERENA Code Signing CA

Issues certificates usable for signing code and other objects usually delivered from the network and intended to be run on the computer of a user. The issuance of object signing certificates is prescribed by industry standards and practices. This is the only TCS service requiring every request to be approved directly by Comodo.

All certification authorities are hosted and operated by Comodo in their secure environment. TCS participants access the CAs via Comodo HTTP API from secured enrollment web portals.

3 OPERATIONS

3.1 Server Certificates

A SSL/TLS server certificate in general binds one or more DNS hostnames to a public key. The registration authority responsible for approving a server certificate request has to verify that the requester is authorized to use the requested hostnames by the holder of the registration of the appropriate DNS zones. With the aim to achieve the maximum possible ease of use while providing all the required checks, the verification procedure has been implemented in two steps.

First, the institutions using the TCS SSL and the TCS eScience SSL services have to register with its NREN. For every institution, the NREN keeps a list of the DNS zones registered by the institution and a list of its authoritative representatives.

Server administrators apply for a certificate by uploading the relevant public key to an enrollment portal operated by the respective NREN. There they select the organization operating the server and amend the application with the DNS names of the server. The portal verifies that the requested DNS names correspond to the DNS zones pre-registered for the applying organization and submit the request for approval by an authoritative representative of the organization.

The representative then verifies that the requester is indeed the authorized administrator of the server and approves the application. After that, the application is automatically sent to the CA which issues the certificate usually within a couple of minutes. The portal then delivers the new certificate to the server administrator via email.

Revocation requests are generally handled by the authoritative representatives of the participating organizations as they have local means and procedures for identifying their server administrators. Whenever the organization is not able to process a revocation itself, the NREN TCS representatives can intervene.

These procedures are applied for both the TERENA eScience SSL CA and the TERENA SSL CA.

3.2 Personal Certificates

This section describes the properties of the TERENA eScience Personal CA service. However, it mostly applies for the TERENA Personal CA too, as it operates almost identically. The reader might find the minor differences by consulting the CPS for the services as published at the TCS repository[2].

As the expected size of the user base for the TCS personal certificates is in the order of millions, classical face-to-face registration procedures would not scale.

---

[2] https://www.terena.org/activities/tcs/repository/

On the other hand, academic institutions already have implemented processes and procedures for registering their students, personnel and other users. Those registrations and the corresponding user records could be easily reused for TCS. At the same time, the emergence of SAML standards and Identity Federations came up with the tools to unify access to individual user data independently on the technology used to implement the institutional Identity Management System (IdMS). Moreover, they provide a secure authentication framework reusable by external services.

The TCS enrollment process for personal certificates is based around the concept of a federated enrollment web portal. The portal, operated and/or managed by a participating NREN, serves as a self-service place for users to request and to manage their personal certificates.

The portal acts as a SAML Service Provider (SP) receiving relevant data form IdMS of participating organizations acting as SAML Identity Providers (IdP).

When an institution joins the project, its authoritative representatives[3] as well as its name and IdP metadata are registered with the portal. The representatives then can configure the mapping defining the particular attributes used by the IdP to deliver the required information.

3.2.1 Attributes

TCS Personal CAs use the following attributes when issuing certificates:

eduPersonEntitlement

This attribute plays critical role in the TCS system as it serves for authorization. By setting it to a particular value (prescribed by the portal), the issuing IdP represents that the user's identity has been vetted in compliance with the relevant CPS and that the institution entitles the user to obtain the requested certificate. The former enables the institution to use its IdP for any type of users and mark those who have been identified properly as eligible for the service. The latter enables the institution to apply local policy for issuing TCS personal certificates (e. g. exclude some category of users from the service, or ban some problematic users etc...)

3.2.2 Unique Identifier

An IdP must configure an attribute that will convey a unique and persistent identifier for the user within its scope. This identifier must never change for a given user and must not be reused or assigned to a different user. Some IdPs may use e. g. usernames, others, who reuse usernames, must find or create a different attribute for the purpose.

The identifier is used to prevent name conflicts; it is included in the certificate Subject name and thus should not reveal any personal information not intended to be published as a part of the certificate.

---

[3] The authoritative representatives of an institution for TCS personal certificates usually come from the user management group and are different from those responsible for server certificates (usually network or DNS managers)

commonName

The commonName attribute conveys a reasonable representation of the user's name and is without modification included into the CN attribute of the certificate Subject name (together with the unique identifier described above).

email

TCS personal certificates may contain up to ten email addresses of the certificate holder. The email addresses IdP sends to the portal must be verified by the IdP to make sure that they really belong to the user. The user may chose which of the addresses delivered by its IdP he or she wants to be included in the certificate during the application process. No direct editing of email addresses by the users is allowed.

3.2.3 Identity vetting

IGTF rules require an identity of every holder of a personal certificate to be verified by personally presenting his or her officially issued photo identity document to a registration authority officer. However, the majority of users of organizations participating in the TCS project have been already registered using the above mentioned procedure before being accepted to the institutional IdMS. Thus, the IdPs may reuse the existing registration as long as they are able to distinguish the registered users and as long as their accounts are continually used and have not been compromised.

3.2.4 Certificate Issuance

After setting up the enrollment portal for a particular organization, the actual process to obtain a certificate is very simple for the user.

The user accesses the portal where his or her identity as asserted by his or her home IdP is verified (the user might be required to authenticate with the IdP depending on the (non)existence of his single-sign-on session). The portal verifies that the user is eligible to apply for the certificate by checking the value of the eduPersonEntitlement attribute. Then the presence and content of the other required attributes is checked by the portal and the user is presented with the certificate application form. There he or she may select from the email addresses asserted by the IdP and the Subject of the certificate as constructed from the delivered attributes is presented. The user then lets the browser generate the private and public keys and send the generated public key to the portal. After a final consistency check, the portal submits the data to the CA. The certificate is usually issued within two minutes and can be installed into the browser. The portal notifies the user about every certificate issuance via email to enable the certificate download when the issuance step takes longer.

For use with grid middleware, the certificate must usually be exported from the browser to the storage used by the grid software. The appropriate tools are usually provided by the respective grid project.

3.2.5 Certificate Revocation

Revocation of compromised or no longer correct certificates is one of the essential services of any PKI. TCS implements several procedures to revoke a personal certificate. First, any user can revoke their own certificate using the enrollment portal. Access to the revocation service is controlled by the same federated identity used for the certificate request. Thus, any private key compromise can be immediately solved by the user himself.

In addition, TCS administrators of individual institutions may use the portal to revoke certificates issued to any of their users. This procedure may be used when the user is not available or when he or she is not trusted to proceed properly. TCS administrators also revoke all certificates of a user whose account with the IdP has been compromised or terminated or whose data has changed and are not correctly represented in the certificates any more.

Similarly, TCS NREN administrators may use the portal to revoke certificates issued to any user within their constituency. Moreover, they can even suspend a whole institution from using the portal if needed.

As a last resort, TERENA TCS administrators can revoke any TCS certificate using the supplier's web interface.

3.3 Certificate Profiles

TERENA eScience Personal certificates follow the rules for grid certificates as defined by Grid Certificate Profile [1]. All certificate subject names are prefixed with "/DC=org/DC=terena/DC=tcs" to guarantee their uniqueness. The rest of a subject name is constructed of the country code of the respective NREN (attribute C), the name of the institution (attribute O), optionally the name of an organizational unit (attribute OU), and the name of the certificate holder (attribute CN). The CN attribute contains the personal name of the certificate holder expressed in 7-bit ASCII and the unique identifier assigned to the person.

Certificate extensions are set to support TLS authentication and email protection, i. e. the Key Usage has the Digital Signature, Key Encipherment and Data Encipherment bits set; the Extended Key Usage contains object identifiers for TLS Client Authentication and Email Protection. User's email addresses are listed in the certificate Subject Alternative Name extension.

Subject names of TERENA eScience SSL certificates follow the convention described above for personal certificates. The CN attribute, however, contains a DNS name of the server. The Subject Alternative Name extension lists all DNS names of the server. Key Usage sets the Digital Signature, Key Encipherment and Data Encipherment bits, the Extended Key Usage contains object identifiers for TLS Server Authentication and TLC Client Authentication.

All TCS certificates list the CRL Distribution Point and the OCSP responder location of their issuing CAs.

For detailed description of TCS certificate profiles, see the relevant CPS [2, 3].

4   CONCLUSIONS

TCS operates two eScience CAs to support authentication in grid infrastructures. The services are profiled to fully comply with IGTF requirements. At the same time, great effort has been invested into making the services as user-friendly as possible.

Re-using the registration work already done by the institutions reduces significantly the cost of registration authority operations. Federated identity enables users to apply for a certificate any time and from any place. The time needed for getting a new certificate has been shortened from days to a couple of minutes when compared with the traditional model of a grid CA.

Thanks to the fact that the root certificate of the TCS supplier is by default accepted by major email client software, the TCS certificates can be directly used for securing email.

REFERENCES

[1] Groep D, Helm M, Jensen J et al (2008) Grid Certificate Profile. Global Grid Forum. http://www.ogf.org/documents/GFD.125.pdf

[2] TCS (2009) Certification Practice Statement - eScience Personal Certificates. TERENA. https://www.terena.org/activities/tcs/repository/cps-personal-escience.pdf

[3] TCS (2010) Certification Practice Statement - Server and Object Signing Certificates. TERENA. https://www.terena.org/activities/tcs/repository/cps-server.pdf.

Part V
Grid Operation and Management

SEE-GRID eInfrastructure for Regional eScience

Ognjen Prnjat[1], Antun Balaz[2], Dusan Vudragovic[2], Ioannis Liabotis[1],
Cevat Sener[3], Branko Marovic[4], Miklos Kozlovszky[5] and Gabriel Neagu[6]

1. GRNET, Greece
2. SCL, Institute of Physics Belgrade, Serbia
3. Middle East Technical University, Ankara, Turkey
4. University of Belgrade Computer Centre, Serbia
5. MTA SZTAKI, Budapest, Hungary
6. ICI, Bucharest, Romania

Abstract   In the past 6 years, a number of targeted initiatives, funded by the European Commission via its information society and RTD programmes and Greek infrastructure development actions, have articulated a successful regional development actions in South East Europe that can be used as a role model for other international developments. The SEEREN (South-East European Research and Education Networking initiative) project, through its two phases, established the SEE segment of the pan-European G ´EANT network and successfully connected the research and scientific communities in the region. Currently, the SEE-LIGHT project is working towards establishing a dark-fiber backbone that will interconnect most national Research and Education networks in the region. On the distributed computing and storage provisioning i.e. Grid plane, the SEE-GRID (South-East European GRID e-Infrastructure Development) project, similarly through its two phases, has established a strong human network in the area of scientific computing and has set up a powerful regional Grid infrastructure, and attracted a number of applications from different fields from countries throughout the South-East Europe. The current SEEGRID-SCI project, ending in April 2010, empowers the regional user communities from fields of meteorology, seismology and environmental protection in common use and sharing of the regional e-Infrastructure. Current technical initiatives in formulation are focusing on a set of coordinated actions in the area of HPC and application fields making use of HPC initiatives. Finally, the current SEERA-EI project brings together policy makers – programme managers from 10 countries in the region. The project aims to establish a communication platform between programme managers, pave the way towards common e-Infrastructure strategy and vision, and implement concrete actions for common funding of electronic infrastructures on the regional level. The regional vision on establishing an e-Infrastructure compatible with European developments, and empowering the scientists in the region in equal participation in the use of pan-European infrastructures, is materializing through the above initiatives. This model has a number of concrete operational and organizational guidelines which can be adapted to help e-Infrastructure developments in other world regions. In this

S.C. Lin and E. Yen (eds.), *Data Driven e-Science: Use Cases and Successful Applications of Distributed Computing Infrastructures (ISGC 2010)*, DOI 10.1007/978-1-4419-8014-4_7,
© Springer Science+Business Media, LLC 2011

paper we review the most important developments and contributions by the SEE-GRID-SCI project.

1   INTRODUCTION

Science is becoming largely digital -it needs to deal with ever increasing amounts of data and computational needs. Numerical simulations become more detailed, experimental science uses more sophisticated sensors to make precise measurements, and shift from the tradition of individuals-based science work towards more collaborative models now starts to dominate.

Computing resources and services able to support needs of such a new model of scientific work are available at different layers: local computing centers, national and regional computing centers, and European supercomputing centers. The gap between needs of various user communities and computing resources able to satisfy their requirements is addressed by introduction of Grid technology on the top of pan-European academic network.

Computing Grids are conceptually not unlike electrical grids. In an electrical grid, the wall outlets allow us to link to and use an infrastructure of resources, which generate, distribute, and bill for electrical power. When we connect to the electrical grid, we do not need to know details on the power plant currently generating the electricity we use. In the same way Grid technology uses middleware layer to coordinate and organize into one logical resource a set of available distributed computing and storage resources across a network, allowing users to access them in a unified fashion. The computing Grids, like electrical grids, aim to provide users with easy access to all the resources they need, whenever they need them, regardless of the underlying physical topology and management model of individual clusters.

Grids address two distinct but related goals: providing remote access to information technology (IT) assets, and aggregating processing and storage power. The most obvious resources included in Grids are processors (CPUs), but Grids also can encompass various sensors, data-storage systems, applications, and other types of resources. One of the first commonly known Grid initiatives was the SETI@HOME project, which solicited several millions of volunteers to download a screensaver, which was able to use idle processor time to analyze the astronomical data in the search for extraterrestrial life.

In the past 6 years the European Commission has funded through a number of targeted initiatives activating of new user communities and enabling collaborative research across a number of fields in order to close existing technological and scientific gaps, and thus bridging the digital divide, stimulating research and consequently alleviating the brain drain in the less-developed regions of Europe. This was especially successful in the South-East Europe (SEE), where a number of such initiatives show excellent results. In the Grid arena, the South-East European GRid eInfrastructure Development (SEE-GRID) project [1], through its two 2-

year phases, has established a strong human network in the area of scientific computing and has set up a powerful regional Grid infrastructure, attracting large number of applications from diverse fields from countries throughout the South-East Europe. The third phase of the SEE-GRID program (SEE-GRID-SCI) aims to have a catalytic and structuring effect on a number of SEE user groups, with a strong focus on the key seismological, meteorological, and environmental communities.

SEE-GRID-SCI (SEE-GRID eInfrastructure for regional eScience) involves three strategic international scientific communities (Virtual Organisations): seismology, meteorology, environmental protection. It aims to further stimulate the use and expansion of the existing regional eInfrastructure and its services, and capitalize on the existing human network to further strengthen scientific collaboration and cooperation among participating SEE communities in the area of eInfrastructures. The inclusion of the new scientific communities and the expansion of the infrastructure in terms of both size and geographical spread, together with a set of coordinated actions aimed at strengthening the National Grid Infrastructures (NGIs) in the region, ensures that at the end of the project each country in the region will be ready to join the long-term, sustainable European Initiatives as a full-fledged peer.

Overall, the project is composed of four Networking Activities (NA), one Service Activity (SA), and one Joint Research Activity (JRA). NA1 activity deals with the project administrative and technical management, while NA2 activity provides support to NGIs and coordinates international collaboration. It focuses on supporting non-EGEE countries of the Western Balkans, Moldova, Georgia and Armenia. Guidelines for NGI best-practices are developed and refined, and a set of coherent actions are carried out to ensure that NGIs reach the adequate maturity levels and organizational models for joining EGI. The other line of action is the dissemination of the NGI know-how to other peripheral regions, and establishing strong collaboration channels with other regional Grid initiatives as well as with pan-European initiatives. The collaboration goes beyond NGI issues and will also involve other project activities such as applications development and application-level services, operations, training and dissemination. NA3 activity deals with the dissemination and training, while NA4 activity provides round-the-clock support to user communities. Grid infrastructure operations and management of regional resources is done by the SA1 activity, which ensures that user community needs in terms of size and availability of computing, storage, networking and application-specific resources are catered for. In research activities, JRA1 deals with the development of application-level services and application-related operational extensions, customized to the needs of the specific user communities.

2   GRID INFRASTRUCTURE OPERATIONS

The regional Grid infrastructure [2] operated by SEE-GRID-SCI project is built on top of the pilot infrastructure established by the first SEE-GRID project (2004-2006), which was since then substantially extended and enlarged in terms of resources and number of Grid sites, and upgraded in terms of the deployed middleware and core services provided to existing and new user communities during the SEE-GRID-2 project (2006-2008).

The operations activity [3] adopted the pragmatic model of the 2-layered infrastructures in which mature sites move to EGEE production infrastructure while the start-up sites from new institutes and user communities incubate within the SEE-GRID infrastructure. In this way, both SEE-wide and national-level applications are able to benefit from the computing resources of both infrastructures, by mainly using the pilot infrastructure in the incubation phase and production infrastructure in the production phase. Moreover, this approach ensured that smaller sites, typical for the region, have a chance to be a part of the regional SEE-GRID infrastructure acting as an incubator for their maturing into EGEE production. As applications mature, new VOs spun off with the relevant core services supported by SEE-GRID-SCI. Discipline-specific services are deployed over the eInfrastructure and supported by SA1. Sophisticated operational tools some of them developed within JRA1 -are used to enhance infrastructure performance.

SEE-GRID-SCI project continues to operate and further extend, develop and improve this infrastructure, with the aim to cater for the need of all activated user communities in the region, with special emphasis on the three identified target areas: meteorology, seismology, and environmental sciences. Apart from computing and storage resources made available to these user communities, SA1 activity provides and maintains a set of existing and new operational and monitoring tools so as to ensure proper operation of the infrastructure, and a set of primary and secondary core services for all deployed VOs in order to ensure optimal geographical distribution according to the underlying network structure, load sharing, and quality of the service to end users.

Currently SEE-GRID-SCI infrastructure encompasses approximately 54 Grid sites, more than 6600 CPUs, and around 750 TBs of available data storage capacity, which is illustrated in Tab. 1 and in Fig. 1.

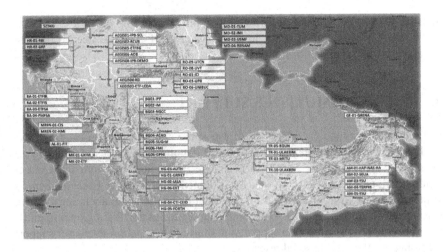

Fig. 1: Overview of the SEE-GRID-SCI infrastructure.

Table 1: SEE-GRID-SCI computing and storage resources.

Country	Total number of CPUs	Total storage [TB]
Greece	1200	66.8
Bulgaria	1210	42.3
Romania	120	4.0
Turkey	2380	528.0
Hungary	8	2.0
Albania	20	1.3
Bosnia-Herzegovina	80	1.1
FYR of Macedonia	80	4.1
Serbia	974	97.0
Montenegro	40	0.6
Moldova	24	6.5
Croatia	44	0.2
Armenia	424	0.2
Georgia	16	0.1
Total	6620	754.2

Overall number of CPUs has grown from 2400 at the beginning of the project in May 2008 to currently more than 6600, while the number of dedicated CPUs for SEE-GRID-SCI VOs is currently around 1500. Grid operations activity successfully maintains such a large, geographically disperse and ever growing infrastructure, harmonizing its operation with the pan-European EGEE infrastructure. In addition to this, one of the most important achievements of SA1 activity is transfer of knowledge and Grid know-how to all participating countries, and support to their NGI operation teams to reach the level of expertise needed for sustainable EGI-based operational model.

3   USER COMMUNITIES SUPPORT

SEE-GRID-SCI aims to accelerate e-Infrastructure uptake by new user groups extending over the region. Hence, the NA4 user communities support activities provide round-the-clock user support for a range of applications from three target fields: seismology, meteorology and environmental protection. Each of them is structured in the form of a virtual organization to facilitate collaborations among researchers from the field [4]. Dedicated support teams for the regional applications provide both gridification support and run-time production-level user support including training of interested researchers.

3.1   Meteorology VO

Weather forecasting is based on the use of numerical weather prediction (NWP) models that are able to perform the necessary calculations that describe/predict the major atmospheric processes. NWP applications require considerable processing power and data storage resources, and thus can benefit from the offerings of grid technologies.

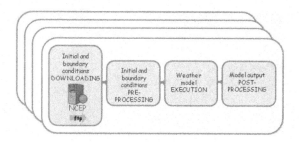

Fig. 2: REFS workflow.

In the frame of Meteorology VO two NWP applications are ported to the grid:
  - First, a regional scale multi-model, multi-analysis ensemble forecasting system (REFS) was built and ported on the grid infrastructure and it is currently in production phase. REFS is based on the use of four limited area models (namely BOLAM, MM5, ETA, and NMM) that are run using a multitude of initial and boundary conditions over the Mediterranean [5]. This activity involves the need of large infrastructure that is

not easily available at medium-scale research centers and institutions. Its workflow is summarized in Fig. 2.

- Moreover, the Weather Research and Forecasting Advanced Research WRF (WRF-ARW) prognostic model has been ported to the grid as the second application of this VO. The SEE region is a big challenge for the meteorologists because of the complexity of the reproduction/forecasting of the airflow over complex terrain. High resolution model grids are thus needed to study complex

- terrain airflow, and this is a quite demanding application in CPU, memory and data storage. To address these needs, WRF-ARW is used for weather research purposes as well as for operational weather forecasting.

3.2 Seismology VO

Scientists in the seismology field need computational resources for mathematical modeling of seismic phenomena, as well as storage resources for massive collections of seismic data from geographically distributed sensors. Seismology VO [6] aims to bring seismology data from the SEE region to the grid platform and also to gridify seismology applications that are of interest to not only the seismologists but also to the industry such as the insurance companies. To realize these goals, the Seismic Data Server Application Service (SDSAS) was developed to provide distributed storage and serving of seismic data from different partner countries, logical organization and indexing of distributed seismic data, and programming tools, developed for automatically downloading waveform data from the NERIES/ORFEUS datacenter in addition to the client interface for downloading earthquake event quakeml files from European-Mediterranean Seismological Centre.

The applications gridified within this VO include Seismic Risk Assessment, Numerical Modeling of Mantle Convection, Fault Plane Solution, Earthquake Location Finding, Massive Digital Seismological Signal Processing with Wavelet Analysis and Web Interface to SDSAS.

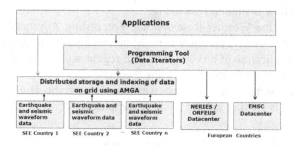

Fig. 3: Seismology VO platform.

3.3 Environmental VO

The applications from this VO, developed and deployed within the project, include Multi-Scale Atmospheric Composition Modeling [7], Monte Carlo Sensitivity Analysis for Environmental Systems [8], Refinement of surface and vegetation parameters in SEE region based on satellite images, Modeling System for Emergency Response to the Release of Harmful Substances in the Atmosphere, Groundwater Flow Simulation System, Changes of Environment with Remote Sensing, Modeling the assessment of climate change impact on air quality, based on an established methodology, Regional Ocean Modeling System. The use of Grid resources enabled the researchers to achieve results which they could not obtain using their local clusters or workstations. For example, the validation of the model for simulation of climate change impact on air quality for the period 1991-2000 takes tens of compute nodes with 8 CPU cores each for several days and produces terabytes of intermediate data (Fig. 4).

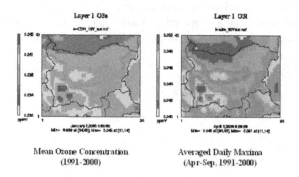

Fig. 4: Pollution levels for the period 1991-2000.

4   DEVELOPMENT OF APPLICATION-LEVEL SERVICES AND OPERATIONAL TOOLS

In course of the SEE-GRID-SCI project, a growing number of applications have been gridified within the regional user communities working in the three earth science disciplines. All three disciplines require inter-application teamwork in addressing common issues and emphasize the importance of data sharing and support for distributed collaboration.

The SEE-GRID-SCI JRA1 (Joint Research Activity) facilitates development and gridification of applications and usage of the underlying grid infrastructure by employing the expertise that goes beyond local communities. It aims to improve the usability of the infrastructure and Grid services for the end-users from target communities and manageability of the infrastructure by focusing in:

- Addressing some issues common to several user communities and their applications that are not addressed by the existing middleware and infrastructure, thus contributing to enhancement of services provided to end-users.
- Researching in the application-focused features of operational tools and development of new or extending of existing operational tools.

All SEE-GRID-SCI software developers were asked to provide their recommendations for development, deployment, internal and user documentation, maintenance, licensing, support practices and tools, and interaction of developed software with gLite grid environment. The resulting guidelines intend to address the quality of the software produced and facilitate support and extendibility of the tools and services.

Details of these services and operational tools are available at JRA1 commonalities wiki [9], which provides information on their purpose, status, architecture, requirements, deployment, code and documentation, usage, relation with other developments, dissemination, partnerships, practical and scientific impact, and expected long-term developments.

A number of application services was identified and developed, including: FMJ-API (SEE-GRID File Management Java API), DM-Web (Data Management Web Portal), SDSAS (SDS (Seismic Data Server Application Service, see Fig. 3), AWT (Advanced-Workflow Development Tool and Orchestration Service), ULMON (User Level Monitoring Tool), Work Binder, RAS (Rendering Application Service), ESIP Platform (Environment Oriented Satellite Data Processing Platform), CWRE (Common Workflow Repository Extension of P-GRADE Portal), Event Logger, and MEWS (Mathematical Expressions Web Service).

A set of applications services is already deployed and used by the grid applications demonstrating their usage and their benefits for the user communities of the project.

The JRA1 operational and monitoring tools developments include: JTS (Job Track Service), BBmSAM Extensions illustrated in Fig. 5, GSSVA (Grid Site Software Vulnerability Analyzer), NMTT (No Mercy Ticketing System), USGIME (User/Application Specific Grid Infrastructure Monitoring Extension), Logwatch-G, and Alert Messaging Service. GSSVA and Logwatch-G are related to site-level monitoring, while the others are related to grid-level monitoring and control. All 7 operational tools are in production usage.

Some of the developed applications services are already essential building blocks of specific applications, while other services and tools are used to facilitate user level monitoring and/or operational support for more effective and easy usage of the underlying grid resources.

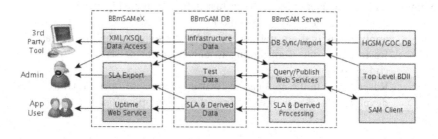

Fig. 5: BBmSAM overview.

A further effort was made to develop the application services using software engineering standards that would allow them to become more accessible and able to be adopted by any interested user community. Some application services are specifically promoted outside the scope of SEE-GRID-SCI. For example, Work Binder and ESIP Platform application services were submitted to EGEE for inclusion in its RESPECT program [10], while FM-J-API was a subject of a recent EUAsiaGrid lecture [11]. About 30 journal and conference papers were produced.

The expected overall impact of JRA1 activity will be to ease the involvement of new users, applications and resource providers, automating and simplifying common and burdensome tasks. In a wider context, it will make its results available to other regional and global initiatives, providing its most successful tools and components to other projects and contributing to optimal development and use of eInfrastructures and establishing a feature rich grid environment.

5   TRAINING AND DISSEMINATION

The SEE-GRID-SCI project established a central knowledge database on Grid-technology [12] including ready-made training materials, and a large set of grid technology educated trainers, who are able to train different Grid user groups (trainthe trainer concept). The SEE-GRID-SCI and its predecessor projects build up an effective training model with a training infrastructure and carry out lot of training events in order to raise the national-level and regional-level expertise and end-user adoption.

All SEE-GRID-SCI project partners are heavily involved in training activities, in total almost 40 trainers are qualified to deliver trainings in the SEE region (Fig. 6). Setting up a stable trainer community was an important milestone in the life of the project, enabling easy access to trainers and specialized knowledge.

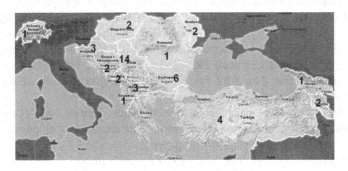

Fig. 6: Trainer community distribution within the SEE region.

Training infrastructure has been set up early in the project, and has proven to be a crucial tool for enabling flexible on-demand trainings. The training VO (SGDEMO VO) is supported on a set of smaller SEE-GRID sites. In addition to this, all core services are provided to this VO, so that during the training events the usage of Grid infrastructure can be fully demonstrated to users. The created training infrastructure offers a homogenous, reliable, grid-focused training environment, with standardized access control. To avoid delays and organizational overhead, special SEE-GRID Demo Certification Authority is used, which allows trainers to generate necessary number of temporary Grid certificates before any training event. These certificates are automatically added to the SGDEMO VO, so that users can access the Grid from the start of each training event. The training environment offers as additional service: annotated training material repository, a training agenda system, on-line surveys to evaluate the trainings and assure quality control. Older materials created from previous training events plays also an important knowledge resource, therefore it is accessible to everyone and can be reused for future trainings: these materials are freely available also by the wider public.

SEE-GRID-SCI project consortium performed focused dissemination events at regional and at national level during the project years, with the aim to bring together members of the targeted scientific communities and demonstrate to them examples of the Grid paradigm, strength scientific collaboration and cooperation among participating SEE communities in the area of eInfrastructures.

SEE-GRID-SCI is maintaining close ties with other key eInfrastructure projects, most notably the SEEREN initiative, the GEANT project, with EDGeS, EELA, BSI, GENESI-DR, BELIEF, as well as EGEE-III. The project participated both on numerous international conferences (EGEE Conference 2008 and 2009), User Forums (EGEE User Forum 2009 and 2010) and attracted a large audience, with a large number of dedicated project speeches during these conferences. The EELA2 project collaboration continues strongly on the basis of previous collaborations, mainly in the field of operations and SEE-GRID-SCI support for the Latin American National Grid Initiatives. The EGI DS project was provided with a number of concrete inputs from SEE-GRID-SCI, including operations, applications, and, most importantly, NGIs. GENESI-DR collaboration is reflected in exchange of scientific data and applications. BELIEF link is mainly exploited through disseminations and mutual PR support. The project established 5 Memoranda of Understanding during the first year of the project with the above mentioned key international projects.

The project has developed content-rich websites, generic and VO-specific posters, released 5 internal newsletters, carried out disseminations public media (TV, press releases, newspapers, e-newspapers). More than 80 scientific papers have been published as a result of the project's research work.

Main target of the developed training model is to provide discipline-specific trainings for the new SEE-GRID-SCI communities with a self-sustaining training environment. The project has created a trainer community, defined a "Grid evolution path". It categorized training community targets and materials, established a training material repository and supports trainers with information how to use or reuse these training materials.

6 CONCLUSIONS

The SEE-GRID series of projects have successfully led the Grid-related developments in the South-East Europe in the past 6 years. This included establishing, development, maintenance and operation of the largest computing resource in the region, training of users and site administrators and coordination of operations in all
countries of the region, reaching the level of sustainable NGI-based operations and
expertise needed in transition to the EGI operations model. In addition to the in-
frastructure-related achievements, the project has actively worked on the development of policy and international collaboration, and spearheaded the establishment
of NGIs in all partner countries. The dissemination events carried out by the project have substantially boosted public awareness of Grid technology and attracted
interest of policy makers to the development of distributed research infrastructures
in SEE countries, and their inclusion to the pan-European eScience infrastructures.

7 ACKNOWLEDGEMENTS

This work was supported by the European Commission under FP7 project SEE-
GRID-SCI (INFRA-2007-1.2.2 grant no. 211338), and by the Ministry of Science
and Technological Development of the Republic of Serbia (project no. OI141035).

REFERENCES

[1]   SEE-GRID-SCI Project, http://www.see-grid-sci.eu/
[2]   SEE-GRID-SCI Grid Infrastructure, http://goc.grid.sinica.edu.tw/gstat/seegrid/
[3]   SEE-GRID-SCI Grid Operations Wiki, http://wiki.egee-see.org/index.php/SEE-GRID Wiki
[4]   SEE-GRID-SCI VO Applications,
      http://wiki.egee-see.org/index.php/SEE-GRID Wiki#SEE-GRID-SCI VO Applications
[5]   K. Lagouvardos, E. Floros, V. Kotroni: A Grid-enabled Regional-scale Ensemble Forecast-
      ing System in the Mediterranean. Int. J. of Grid Computing, doi: 10.1007/s1072301091503
      (2010).
[6]   C. Ozturan, B. Bektas,, M. Yilmazer, C. S,ener, Challenges Faced in Building A Seismol-
      ogy VO for Southeastern Europe, e-Challenges Conference, Istanbul, Oct. 21-23 2009.
[7]   D. Syrakov, M. Prodanova, K. Ganev, N. Miloshev, E. Atanassov, T. Gurov, A. Karaiva-
      nova: Grid Computing for Multi-Scale Atmospheric Composition Modeling for the Balkan
      Region, Journal of International Scientific Publication: Ecology&Safety, Vol. 3, Part 1,
      2009, pp. 4-21.
[8]   E. Atanassov, A. Karaivanova, T. Gurov, S. Ivanovska, M. Durchova, Using Sobol Se-
      quence in Grid Environment, Proceeding of 32nd International Convention MIPRO/GVS
      2009, pp. 290-294.
[9]   SEE-GRID-SCI JRA1 commonalities wiki,
      http://wiki.egee-see.org/index.php/JRA1 Commonalities
[10] RESPECT program, http://technical.eu-egee.org/index.php?id=290
[11] EUAsiaGrid lecture, http://www.euasiagrid.org/wiki/index.php/Data Management Java
      API
[12] SEE-GRID-SCI Training Center, http://www.lpds.sztaki.hu/stc/

Peer-to-peer Cooperative Scheduling Architecture for National Grid Infrastructure

Ludek Matyska, Miroslav Ruda and Simon Toth

CESNET, Zikova 4, Czech Republic

Abstract   For some ten years, the Czech National Grid Infrastructure MetaCentrum uses a single central PBSPro installation to schedule jobs across the country. This centralized approach keeps a full track about all the clusters, providing support for jobs spanning several sites, implementation for the fair-share policy and better overall control of the grid environment. Despite a steady progress in the increased stability and resilience to intermittent very short network failures, growing number of sites and processors makes this architecture, with a single point of failure and scalability limits, obsolete.

As a result, a new scheduling architecture is proposed, which relies on higher autonomy of clusters. It is based on a peer to peer network of semi-independent schedulers for each site or even cluster. Each scheduler accepts jobs for the whole infrastructure, cooperating with other schedulers on implementation of global policies like central job accounting, fair-share, or submission of jobs across several sites. The scheduling system is integrated with the Magrathea system to support scheduling of virtual clusters, including the setup of their internal network, again eventually spanning several sites. On the other hand, each scheduler is local to one of several clusters and is able to directly control and submit jobs to them even if the connection of other scheduling peers is lost.

In parallel to the change of the overall architecture, the scheduling system itself is being replaced. Instead of PBSPro, chosen originally for its declared support of large scale distributed environment, the new scheduling architecture is based on the open-source Torque system. The implementation and support for the most desired properties in PBSPro and Torque are discussed and the necessary modifications to Torque to support the MetaCentrum scheduling architecture are presented, too.

1   INTRODUCTION

The Czech National grid Infrastructure—the MetaCentrum[1]—spans several sites across the country and provides some 1500 cores to its users. Its current scheduling system is fully centralized, running one PBSPro installation. This setup has

---

[1] https://meta.cesnet.cz

S.C. Lin and E. Yen (eds.), *Data Driven e-Science: Use Cases and Successful Applications of Distributed Computing Infrastructures (ISGC 2010)*, DOI 10.1007/978-1-4419-8014-4_8,
© Springer Science+Business Media, LLC 2011

clear advantages, as it allows to plan jobs between different physical clusters with the knowledge of the complete grid state, implement fair-share policies, schedule large jobs spanning several sites, support load balancing between clusters etc.

These advantages were until recently outweighing the disadvantages, but with steady growth of computational capacity, number of clusters and submitted jobs, this centralized architecture is slowly reaching its limits in the following aspects:

- Stability. While the stability of the central PBSPro installation improved significantly, the whole system needs far too many remote services to be accessible in a real time. Even the highly stable and internally redundant Czech academic network has short intermittent failures that have negligible impact on the standard stateless services but negatively influence the statefull scheduling. Increased number of sites and users increases probability of such network fluctuation to negatively impact the behavior of the whole system, with users seeing decrease in perceived stability.

- Scalability. The central setup is always a potential bottleneck and even with the current number of sites and clusters the central installation is not able to monitor all jobs and resources reliably. Similarly, the scheduler is reaching its limits, too. With large number of jobs submitted into queues at the same time unexpected hiccups and general slowdown of scheduling system are more and more frequent. The situation will become unbearable with the planned manyfold expansion of the national grid infrastructure and with increased small jobs ratio esp. for parametric studies.

- Single point of failure. The High Availability support for the central PBSPro installation still could not protect from the network fluctuations, where either users or some remote service (e.g. the cluster local queue) could not be reached. The worst effect is that users are not able to submit jobs even to their local cluster, as the accessibility of central and/or remote services is needed even if the job could be run locally. Short unavailability of a remote service causes cascade effects on the whole grid performance. The geographical span of the grid necessitates higher timeouts for the server services, slowing down the overall response even in case of redundancy, as the server must wait the longer timeout before using a different service.

- The PBSPro, being a commercial product, does not have too favorable pricing scheme work larger grid installations, as license fee is based on number of CPUs. Adding new resource provider with its cluster means to pay higher license fees, effectively de-motivating the grid expansion.

To deal with all the above mentioned problems, a new scheduling architecture, with higher autonomy of sites and cluster, is proposed. It is based on a peer to peer network of semi-independent schedulers for each site or larger cluster. Individual schedulers maintain their assigned clusters, while cooperating with their peers to support features that mimics the centralized planning. The semi-independence allow to accept jobs and submit them to the local cluster even if no external connectivity is available and other peers are not accessible, keeping jobs that could not be run on a local cluster in an appropriate queue, waiting for connectivity to re-establish. On the other hand, the system still supports central accounting of jobs, fair share of computational resources across all sites of the MetaCentrum, scheduling jobs over any resource on the grid as well as support for large jobs spanning several sites. Each scheduler represents an entry point to the grid, all these entry point are fully equivalent and accept jobs from all users for the whole grid (naturally, users usually tend to use the local entry point, but this is just a convenience, not a necessity). As MetaCentrum provides also virtualized resources (moving towards cloud provisioning [1]), the scheduling system is being integrated with the Magrathea system to support scheduling of virtual clusters. The actual implementation is based on the Torque scheduler, as it shares common roots with the currently used PBS-Pro while being an open source system posing no economic barriers to further grid expansion.

The proposed architecture is compatible with grid middleware stacks used in production in the global grid infrastructures. Namely, the support for gLite (used in EGEE), Globus (used in many community internal grids and also for demonstration and short time set-ups), and EMI (to be used in the EGI grid environments) is or will be included. However, instead of providing such interfaces for each cluster (and relaying on meta-schedulers internally), the proposed architecture supports direct inclusion of such gateways as a new component of the peer to peer infrastructure, providing access to the whole grid.

Compatibility with clusters managed by other batch systems will be also available. Torque-based systems, with external schedulers like Maui or Moab [2] could be supported via specialized routing queues supported by Torque. For other systems, possibility of deploying some form of gateway will be studied, either following standard Globus GRAM interface [3] implementation, or using our proposed gateway service. As an future extension, a study of a deeper integration with HTC (highthroughput) systems, like Condor or some pilot-job based systems, is also planned.

Details of the proposed architecture and its components are discussed in the following chapters, including analysis of Torque peer to peer capabilities, presentation of already implemented features, analysis of planned features and future challenges.

2   RELATED WORK

The usual scheduling setup includes a batch system managing one cluster or a set of clusters in one particular site. Some batch systems are freely available (Torque [4], SGE [5]), some of them are currently actively developed by user communities (Slurm [6], motivated with better support for clusters with large number of processors), some are commercial (PBSPro [7], LSF [8]). Scheduling is implemented either using internal schedulers or using external schedulers like the Maui one [9]. This scheduler is developed as an independent service, capable to manage jobs in various batch systems and often provides more sophisticated features than built-in schedulers.

Clusters can be integrated into a grid using some multi-cluster suites like Moab [2], or through a provisioning of grid interface (using Globus GRAM [3], gLite CE [10] or CREAM [11]) which is then used by multi-level schedulers. Support for specific batch systems is different in various grid interfaces, but Torque is clearly the most widely supported system.

Multi-level schedulers like Gridway [12] or gLite WMS [13] can schedule jobs across large number of clusters, using various low-level batch system and even through different grid interfaces in one instalation. However, multi-level scheduling brings also several problems, especially with incomplete knowledge of subordinated systems (jobs can be submitted directly to grid-interface or batch system, bypassing higher-level scheduler) and limited management or scheduling power (higher-level schedulers has limited power to influence ordering of jobs in batch system). Moreover, local scheduling policy or setup details are often hidden by grid interface and can be unpredictable for higher level scheduling system, which may lead to wrong estimates of waiting time for jobs and therefore incorrect scheduling decisions. This problem motivates research in the area of behavior predictions [14, 15].

Multi-level schedulers provide often only limited features for handling cluster outages or unpredicted overloads. Jobs already submitted to some local batch systems are "locked" in this system, waiting in the queue on dormant cluster even if other resources become available. This problem motivated some groups to develop pilot-job scheduling [16], by passing effectively the global scheduler decisions. Another area of problems covers multi-site jobs—support for jobs running across several clusters requires coordination of systems granting resources to the jobs in the same time. Co-scheduling of jobs was studied in several papers [17, 18, and 19], but is still problematic on production systems.

Condor [20], scheduling system developed originally for "hunting free cycles on workstations", evolved in time into system which implements most of our requirements. Using flocking technique, it supports cooperation of standalone clusters and moving of jobs between clusters. Condor systems can serve both as the standard local batch system, as well as higher-level system, capable to assign computational jobs into various batch systems, accessed through grid interfaces. Condor developers invented idea of glide-in, used for dynamic allocation of clusters nodes and reused in pilot systems. Due to its emphasis on high-throughput computing we decided not to use Condor system, but it served as an inspiration in some aspects of our design.

3 PROPOSED ARCHITECTURE

First, the current setup is described to serve as the basis for the new scheduling architecture.

3.1 The Current Setup

As mentioned in the Introduction, the current scheduling architecture uses a central PBS server to schedule all the jobs. The PBS system consists of the following three basic components. The Server, which keeps all the information and is responsible for the overall coordination and also serves as a mediator in almost all operations. Scheduler, responsible for decision making about which jobs will be run, when they will be run and where. The last component is a set of computational nodes (in the PBS-Pro/Torque terminology called MOMs).

The server can have an arbitrary number of queues with different properties, each job enters the system by being submitted to one of these queues. The job remains in the queue until it is executed on one of the nodes, or until it is transferred to another queue. In the current setup, one server and one scheduler is used, serving all the nodes (MOMs). When the scheduler is the only service talking to the server, it can work with the knowledge that the server's state is consistent with its assumptions.

3.2 Distributed Architecture

In the first step towards fully distributed scheduling architecture, we expand number of servers and schedulers, to assign a local server and a local scheduler to each cluster. It is not necessary to have a 1:1 correspondence between clusters and servers and schedulers, what is important to have a local server and scheduler available, with locality defined as within one site, usually within one computer room and in adjacent computer rooms. We also add a gateway, an equivalent of a user interface accepting. The setup for two sites is depicted in Fig. 1 and discussed bellow.

- Each server controls all the local queues for the managed cluster plus one routing queue for all the incoming jobs.
- The routing queue is filled by jobs user submits through a Gateway. While a native gateway is provided, gateways from other middleware stack systems could be connected, too (gLite CE or CREAM, Globus GRAM etc.). Gateway provides access also to all the job information system keeps track of.

Each scheduler has access to all the routing queues on all servers as well as to the local queues on its local server. Each scheduler queries the assigned queues, with a shorter period between requests for the local queues and a longer period for remote queues. Currently, each scheduler has knowledge about properties of all nodes, through direct contact with all servers.

- Each server sends a notification to each scheduler when a new job arrives to its routing queue, but notifies only its local scheduler if local job finishes (or if some change occurs on a local queue).
- Job accounting information is sent to a Logging and Bookkeeping (LB) server that keeps track of all the running jobs (we use a modified LB version integrated with the PBSPro [21]). There may be one or more instances of the LB server used, data from all LB servers will be finally stored in the associated Job Provenance server (a future work, not shown in the Fig. 1).

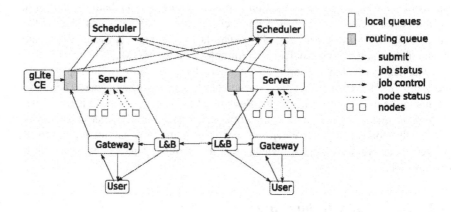

Fig. 1: The intermediate architecture

In this architecture, user interacts with a gateway and submits jobs into the routing queue. A new job stored in this queue triggers a server reaction, which notifies all schedulers. Upon awakening, each scheduler queries all the servers for new data and does the scheduling, using information about all jobs in all routing queues and its own local queues, matching it against properties of the local nodes directly served by the local queues on the local server. This way, if a job could be served by any one cluster, it will be eventually selected by the scheduler local for such a cluster. Scheduled jobs are moved to local queues (in a pull mode, the move is initiated by the local scheduler, not the eventually remote routing queue). The synchronization is done at the atomic job move command, i.e., the scheduler's request to move a job may fail due to the fact that the same job has already be taken by a different scheduler to its local queue. Such a failure of a job move request is simply accepted by the scheduler with no addition action taken. This way, no job is moved from its original routing queue until appropriate local queue is found for it. While the global state is not known to any scheduler (they do not have any information about node properties of remote clusters), the decision to move the job to a local queue is always taken by a scheduler local to such a queue, based on actual and accurate knowledge of its state.

All gateways and routing queues are equivalent, each user could submit his or her jobs through any gateway. For practical reasons, we expect users to use their "closest" gateway, with other gateways offering redundant service, used if the closest gateway is inoperational or inaccessible. As the gateway, server, and scheduler are all local to a cluster, the scheduling cycle works for local resources even is external connectivity is lost or if some other site is down. Users are therefore able to submit jobs (regardless whether for local or remote resources) and the local resources are not starving if they could be used for the locally submitted jobs.

The information stored in the LB servers could used to support the fair-share scheduling policy. The scheduler's local cache keeps information about all jobs in the whole grid, being updated regularly from the LB servers. There is no need to use always the freshest information, so the updates are done asynchronously to the scheduling cycle, having thus no slowdown effect. However, the current implementation of the fair-share policy uses the information available directly to all scheduler through their communication with all servers.

Gateways representing interfaces from other grid middleware systems submit jobs directly into the routing queue, by-passing the native gateway and its user interface. Apart from the input point, no changes in the overall system are necessary, as all internal actions are triggered by the job arrival to the routing queue. Also, if the external grid infrastructure uses LB or LB-compatible system for tracking jobs, the jobs could be tracked even inside the MetaCentrum grid.

3.3   Scalable Distributed Architecture

While the intermediate architecture has much improved stability and supports local submission of jobs, it still has scalability drawbacks. Therefore, a fully scalable peer to peer architecture is proposed, with the following features (see also
Fig. 2):

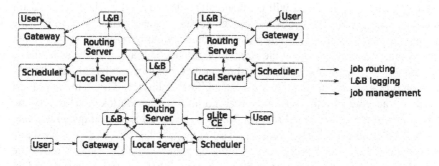

Fig. 2: The scalable architecture

● The routing queue is separated from the local server. It is managed by a special-
ized routing server that:
  – Notifies a local scheduler about any change in the routing queue.
  – Answers queries from the local scheduler about the state of the routing
    queue.
  – Sends asynchronously information about routing queue changes to all
    the other routing servers. Only meta-information is sent, the job body
    stays in the routing queue until it is moved to some local queue (either
    on the local server or on some remote non-routing server).
  – Updates routing queue with data received from remote routing servers
    (only meta-data about jobs in remote routing queues are provided).
  – Transfers (moves) jobs on a request to some non-routing server (either
    local or remote). The transfer is an atomic operation and if successful, it
    results in a complete job removal from the routing queue. Job is locked
    when the transfer is initiated, guaranteeing thus a job could be moved to
    one destination only (transfers are used as the synchronization events in
    case of race between schedulers).
  – Change state of a job when requested by the local scheduler.

● Each scheduler manages directly only two servers: the routing and local one.
All scheduling decisions are based on the information provided by these two
servers only, no remote query is ever initiated (naturally, for fair share some
global information is needed, too, but it is already provided asynchronously

from the LB server). The scheduler tags all jobs it could schedule on local resources. However, tagged jobs are not moved from the routing queue and could
be scheduled by remote scheduler, too. The job is eventually run on the resource that win the "move race"—this happens only when the resource is (almost) ready to accept the job. This way, jobs are scheduled as soon as an appropriate resource is available, while no scheduler does have a full information
about the grid. Tagging is always done in the local routing queue only, one job
could be tagged for different resources at the same time, but with the lazy job
transfer policy the number of job transfers is minimized. Local scheduler could
also untag a job (or even move it back from the local queue into the routing
one) if the local queue is closed or unavailable for any reason. Such job is eventually rescheduled on the local or remote resources.

- Each local server only communicates with its local scheduler and the local cluster nodes, removing itself as a bottleneck from the overall architecture.

Individual routing servers create thus a peer to peer network, that exchanges
control information—the metadata about submitted jobs stored in the routing
queues— and the actual content—job data. The control plane uses the push method for data exchange and is fully asynchronous (it is even possible to use an un-
reliable multicast to announce changes in the routing queue), while the data plane
uses pull methods, with the data always requested by the target local server (or its
scheduler). All scheduling decisions are made using only data available locally,
without any synchronous access to remote service. This guarantees full scalability,
as the local scheduling time does not depend on the number of sites or clusters. On
the other side, each scheduling decision of each schedulers always takes into account all the jobs in the system (or, more precisely, is based on the scheduler
knowledge of jobs). If the job could be scheduled, i.e. there are resources that fit
its requirements, it is eventually scheduled as the distribution scheme guarantees
that information about such a job arrives to a scheduler that manages appropriate
resources.

3.4   Advanced Features and Optimiz Ations

Both architectures are able to schedule all jobs that fit into an individual cluster.
However, jobs that do not fit into any one local queue specification could stay in
the system forever, waiting for a new resource that fits their requirements to appear. The detection of job requirements incompatible with any resources can done
at the source routing queue—the job can not be scheduled if it is not tagged by any
cooperating scheduler. However, as this may be result of temporary unavailability
of appropriate resource, we leave an implementation of the proper policy of the
job removal to a particular installation.

Both architectures support the fair-share, using the LB service as the source of
global information about users' consumption of resources. However, they are both
unable to directly cope with large jobs that need more than one cluster to run.

While this problem still requires a detailed analysis to be fully integrated, currently such jobs could be taken care of by a metascheduler that takes care only of such large jobs. This metascheduler should be connected to all the routing and local servers, having a global information about resources and jobs. With the job tagging, the metascheduler can implement priority override, making sure all the job parts are started synchronously on all target clusters. While not optimal, this approach demonstrates that even such a support is compatible with the proposed scheduling architecture.

The architecture also open ways for several optimizations, making sure it will work fast even on very large grid infrastructures. Routing servers could pack the information they are broadcasting, minimizing the load associated with sending and receiving routing queue updates. Also, they could immediately send information only about jobs that the local scheduler did not tag, while tagged info is sent with lower frequency (preferring thus local cluster for locally submitted jobs). Also, scheduler could keep some state about the last scheduling decision, not to repeat full scheduling cycle if nothing (important) changed since the last scheduling cycle.

4   IMPLEMENTATION

The current implementation of the distributed (but not fully scalable) scheduling architecture is based on the modified Torque servers and Torque schedulers. It also includes native gateway implementation and uses the gLite LB for job monitoring [21, 22].

The Torque scheduler directly support sequence scheduling of multiple servers, in a stateless scheduling cycle (all temporal information is always discarded at the end of a cycle). We extended the server with an implementation of new data structures that hold persistent information about available servers (there is currently no support for new server discovery, the topology is statically configured). Scheduler was also extended to support direct scheduling of virtual machines (we ported already implemented PBSPro extensions to support Magrathea system also into the Torque scheduler). We also added interruptibility to the scheduling cycle, allowing a scheduler to take immediately into account new incoming notifications about new jobs in some routing queue.

Torque servers were extended to support the globally visible routing queue. This information is used by the scheduler when it queries about the jobs in queues—only the local server sends also information about its local queues, all remote servers reply with routing queue information only.

The gateway implementation supports PBS API for job definitions and resource description. The gateway also recognizes Virtual Organization (VO) specific configuration, including specific profiles, default parameters, as well as tuned setting and views. Each gateway is also directly connected to the MetaCentrum monitoring system, serving as a monitoring sensor. It also provides interface between the user and the LB service, providing access to all the job information (regardless where the job was submitted and scheduled). The gateway is implemented as a command-line interface, again compatible with the standard PBS tools like qsub and qstat. A web interface is under development.

5   CONCLUSION

We proposed a fully scalable distributed scheduling architecture that has all the properties we identified as necessary for the large scale grid scheduling system. Local scheduling is extended through routing servers that communicate via a peer to peer protocol to exchange information about locally submitted jobs. All the scheduling decisions are taken using only information available on site, eventual race conditions are dealt with directly within the proposed architecture (with the job transfer from a routing to a selected local queue being the basic synchronization primitive).

As an intermediate step, we proposed and are currently also implementing a reduced distributed scheduling architecture that is more stable than the central manager and still supports the local job submission even in a disconnected state.

As a part of the migration of the current MetaCentrum PBSPro based central scheduling system we implemented necessary modifications and extensions of the Torque server and scheduler, to support the new features needed by the proposed architecture. Extensive simulations demonstrated the feasibility of our approach and the implementation, showing that the overhead of multiple servers and schedulers can be kept at a reasonable level [23].

6 ACKNOWLEDGEMENTS

This work was done with the support of Ministry of Education of the Czech Republic, research programs MSM0021622419 and MSM6383917201.

REFERENCES

[1] M. Ruda, J. Denemark, L. Matyska. Scheduling Virtual Grids: the Magrathea System, Second International Workshop on Virtualization Technology in Distributed Computing, USA, ACM digital library, 2007. p. 1-7. 2007, Reno, USA.

[2] Moab Workload Manager. http://www.clusterresources.com/products/moab-cluster-suite.php

[3] K. Czajkowski, I. Foster, N. Karonis, C. Kesselman, M. S. Smith, S. Tuecke. A resource management architecture for metacomputing systems. In Proceedings of the IPPS/SPDP Workshop on Job Scheduling Strategies for Parallel Processing. pp. 62–82, 1998.

[4] Torque Resource Manager. http://www.clusterresources.com/products/torque-resource-manager.php.

[5] Sun Grid Engine. http://gridengine.sunsource.net/.

[6] A. Yoo, M. Jette, M. Grondona. SLURM: Simple Linux Utility for Resource Management. In Job Scheduling Strategies for Parallel Processing, volume 2862 of Lecture Notes in Computer Science, pages 44-60, Springer-Verlag, 2003.

[7] The Portable Batch System. http://www.pbspro.com

[8] S. Zhou. LSF: Load sharing in large-scale heterogeneous distributed systems. In Proceedings of the Workshop on Cluster Computing.

[9] D. Jackson, Q. Snell, M. Clement. Core Algorithms of the Maui Scheduler. In Proceedings of 7th Workshop on Job Scheduling Strategies for Parallel Processing, 2001.

[10] LCG Computing Element. https://twiki.cern.ch/twiki/bin/view/EGEE/LcgCE.

[11] P. Andreetto et al., CREAM: A simple, Grid-accessible, Job Management System for local Computational Resources, Proc. XV International Conference on Computing in High Energy and Nuclear Physics (CHEP'06), Feb 13-17, 2006, Mumbay, India, Macmillan, p. 831-835.

[12] Eduardo Huedo, Ruben S. Montero ,Ignacio M. Llorente. The GridWay Framework for Adaptive Scheduling and Execution on Grids. Scalable Computing -Practice and Experience 6 (3): 1-8, 2005.

[13] P. Andreetto, S. Borgia, A. Dorigo, A. Gianelle, M. Mordacchini, M. Sgaravatto, L. Zangrando, S. Andreozzi, V. Ciaschini, CD Giusto, et al. Practical approaches to grid workload and resource management in the EGEE project. Proceedings of the International Conference on Computing in High Energy Physics (CHEP2004), Interlaken, Switzerland, 2004.

[14] D. Ch. Nurmi, J. Brevik, R. Wolski. QBETS: queue bounds estimation from time series. SIGMETRICS '07: Proceedings of the 2007 ACM SIGMETRICS international conference on Measurement and modeling of computer systems, 2007.

[15] W. Smith, V. Taylor, I Foster. Using Run-Time Predictions to Estimate Queue Wait Times and Improve Scheduler Performance. Proceedings of the IPPS/SPDP '99 Workshop on Job Scheduling Strategies for Parallel Processing, 1999.

[16] Vladimir V. Korkhova, Jakub T. Moscickib, Valeria V. Krzhizhanovskaya. Dynamic workload balancing of parallel applications with user-level scheduling on the Grid, Future Generation Computer Systems Volume 25, Issue 1, January 2009, Pages 28-34.

[17] I. Foster, C. Kesselman, C. Lee, R. Lindell, K. Nahrstedt, A. Roy. A Distributed Resource Management Architecture that Supports Advance Reservations and Co-Allocation. Intl Workshop on Quality of Service, 1999.

[18] K. Czajkowski, I. Foster, C. Kesselman. Resource Co-Allocation in Computational Grids.

Proceedings of the Eighth IEEE International Symposium on High Performance Distributed Computing (HPDC-8), pp. 219-228, 1999.

[19] H.H. Mohamed, D.H.J. Epema. KOALA: A Co-Allocating Grid Scheduler. Concurrency and Computation: Practice and Experience, Vol. 20, 1851-1876, 2008.

[20] M. Litzkow, M. Livny, M. Mutka. Condor—A Hunter of Idle Workstations. In Proceedings of the 8th International Conference of Distributed Computing Systems.

[21] M. Ruda, A. Krenek, M. Mulac, J. Pospisil, Z. Sustr A uniform job monitoring service in multiple job universes. In GMW '07: Proceedings of the 2007 workshop on Grid monitoring, ACM 2007. Pages 17–22.

[22] M. Ruda et al., Job Centric Monitoring on the Grid – 7 years of experience with L&B and JP services, Proc. CESNET Conference 2008.

[23] M. Ruda, S. Toth. Transition to Inter-Cluster Scheduling Architecture in MetaCentrum. Cesnet technical report 21/2009.

The EUAsiaGrid Roadmap
Paths to a Sustainable, Persistent e-Infrastructure in the Asia-Pacific Region

Alex Voss[1], Jan Kmunicek[2], Ludek Matyska[2], Marco Paganoni[3] and Simon C. Lin[4]

1. School of Computer Science, University of St Andrews, UK
2. CESNET, Zikova 4, Czech Republic
3. University of Milano-Bicoca and INFN, Italy
4. Institute of Physics, Academia Sinica, Taiwan

Abstract The EUAsiaGrid project has developed a Roadmap towards the establishment of a persistent and sustainable e-Infrastructure for research in the Asia-Pacific region. This paper describes its aims and context, the decisions make in its creation and outlines the proposal for an Asia-Pacific Grid Initiative that will allow partners from different countries in the region to coordinate their national initiatives and align themselves with the emerging infrastructure in the region as well as developments elsewhere in the world.

1   INTRODUCTION

The Asia-Pacific region has benefited from the development of a number of components of a full grid infrastructure driven by the participation of the region in the LHC experiments and the provision of support for this by Academia Sinica in Taiwan. The work conducted in the EC-funded EUAsiaGrid project[1] has provided support for the establishment of additional infrastructure components within the partner countries and for the development of user communities from a wide range of research disciplines. Thanks to EUAsiaGrid, researchers in these countries can now sign up to an existing infrastructure through certification authorities in their countries and join a generic virtual organisation, the EUAsia VO, that gives them access to the established EGEE resources in the region.

The current EGEE e-Infrastructure has been developed through a series of projects funded by the European Commission. The EGEE projects have contributed to the development of the basic technologies underpinning grid computing today and have established a worldwide operational e-Infrastructure supporting research applications spanning a wide range of disciplines from high-energy physics to the social sciences. In addition, the Commission funded a number of Coordination and

---

[1] http://www.euasiagrid.eu

S.C. Lin and E. Yen (eds.), *Data Driven e-Science: Use Cases and Successful Applications of Distributed Computing Infrastructures (ISGC 2010)*, DOI 10.1007/978-1-4419-8014-4_9,
© Springer Science+Business Media, LLC 2011

Support Actions that have helped to establish regional grid infrastructures in regions such as South-East Europe (SEE-Grid[2]), the Mediterranean (EUMedGrid[3]), Latin America (EELA[4]), China (EUChinaGrid[5]), India (EUIndiaGrid[6]) and, finally, the Asia-Pacific region through EUAsiaGrid.

Together, these projects have helped to expand the reach of the growing e-Infrastructure for research around the globe to facilitate research collaborations between different parts of the world. As the infrastructures mature and are being used by a growing number of researchers worldwide, the question of sustainability comes to the forefront. In order to make the existing infrastructure persistent and sustainable, the necessary technical, organisational and wider social arrangements need to be put in place to ensure that it can be taken for granted by researchers today and in the future.

In Europe, the EGI Design Study project has developed a blueprint (EGI-DS Consortium 2009) [1] for the establishment of a European Grid Initiative based on National Grid Initiatives within individual states that contribute to a common European infrastructure integrated with the other regions in the world and are coming together in the EGI Council to provide the necessary governance. To provide an operational basis for the EGI at the European level, a new organisation, EGI.eu, has been established under Dutch law. The arrangements put in place in Europe provide an example for other regions that wish to foster a persistent and sustainable e-Infrastructure but it is likely that rather than adopting this model one-to-one, other regions will need to come up with arrangements that reflect their cultural, socio-economic and political context.

It is in the light of this that EUAsiaGrid project has developed a roadmap (EUAsiaGrid Consortium 2010)[2] aiming to inspire the necessary political will and degree of collaboration amongst key stakeholders to drive forward the project of fostering a persistent, sustainable e-Infrastructure for research in the region. Aimed primarily at key decision makers at the national policy level and in senior management in institutions, the first part of the roadmap focuses on an assessment of the potential impact of such an infrastructure. It outlines the benefits that may be realised through increased scientific collaboration, resource sharing and the provision of an infrastructure that can be taken for granted by its users before highlighting the usage of the infrastructure in different research disciplines ranging from high-energy physics as an example of a discipline not only adopting but driving the development of grid technologies to the social sciences that are only beginning to develop models of e-Infrastructure usage that realise their full potential.

---

[2] http://www.see-grid.eu/

[3] http://www.eumedgrid.eu/

[4] http://www.eu-eela.eu/

[5] http://www.euchinagrid.eu/

[6] http://www.euindiagrid.eu/

The second part provides a blueprint for the technical and organisational structure. While the latter is largely inspired by examples like the European Grid Initiative and the Latin-American Grid Initiative (LGI), it also takes into account the specific characteristics of the Asia-Pacific region such as the immense heterogeneity and the at times difficult political context, both within countries and internationally, hindering the straightforward implementation of a hierarchical model such as those underpinning the EGI and LGI.

In the following sections, we first provide a description of the context and aims of the EUAsiaGrid Roadmap as well as an analysis of the strengths, weaknesses, opportunities and threats in relation to the currently existing e-Infrastructure in the Asia-Pacific region. Finally, we outline the structure of the proposed Asia-Pacifc Grid Initiative (APGI) and first steps towards its establishment.

2   AIMS AND CONTEXT

The aim of the Roadmap is to foster an e-Infrastructure for research that should be:

- **Persistent and pervasive:** the infrastructure is available at any point in time independent of specific uses. Researchers have access to it regardless of their location and affiliation as long as their use fits a defined set of criteria.
- **Embedded:** the infrastructure is provided for research use in a wide range of disciplines and research areas, it is not an end in itself. Consequently, ongoing community engagement activities will help to ensure that researchers from all disciplines will play a role in shaping its ongoing development.
- **Easy to use:** access to the infrastructure is easy enough for researchers without specific computing skills to start using it. The complexity of using advanced functionality should be proportional to their utility.
- **Managed**: the infrastructure is operated in a way that ensures a consistent and high quality user experience. The necessary coordination is ensured through internationally agreed governance mechanisms.
- **Supported:** education, training and user support are provided. Wherever possible, support will be provided at a local level in local languages and according to local needs. Their quality is en sured through international collaboration and a shared pool of resources such as training material underpins the provision of high-quality support.
- **Scalable:** the infrastructure is constructed in ways that ensure it can serve the needs of today and scale over time to support wider uptake by a larger number of researchers as well as supporting new research applications requiring larger capacities.
- **Homogenous in use:** the inevitable heterogeneity of resources and the technical and organisational arrangements around them are generally hidden from the users to provide ease of use.

- **Federated:** based on subsidiarity principle, what can (best) be done locally is done locally but in a way that local activities benefit from international collaboration and coordination.
- **Sustainable**: funding arrangements are put in place that ensure that the overall infrastructure is maintained even as individual resources become unavailable or as partners join or leave the collaboration.

These *core characteristics* guided the development of the EUAsiaGrid Roadmap and provide the fundamental yardstick by which the success of the Asia-Pacific Grid Initiative will measure the outcomes of its activities.

In order to understand the starting point for the roadmap, we conducted an in-depth analysis of the state of the existing e-Infrastructure in terms of both the technical resources and the social arrangements put in place to support its operation and usage. The overriding theme is that while the support provided by the EUAsiaGrid project has raised the baseline and given researchers access to significant resources, there is still much heterogeneity in the adoption of grid technologies in different countries in the region. While some have comprehensive national programmes, others are currently formulating their policies and programmes and some lack significant buy-in and are dependent on individual institutions taking the initiative. The existence of catch-all provision of key infrastructure services, support, certification services and a VO means that these issues do not pose insurmountable problems but the longer-term sustainability of the infrastructure will depend on wider and more homogeneous adoption.

Table 1 (next page) shows the strengths, weaknesses, opportunities and threats identified in a summary form.

Table 1: SWOT Analysis of e-Infrastructures

Strengths	The existence of a mature set of core services and operational arrangements across all areas with catch-all arrangements to compensate for heterogeneity at the national level. EUAsiaGrid has established a number of resource centres, ensured that CAs exist in all countries and established the EUAsia VO as a catch-all mechanism allowing researchers to access available resources.
Weaknesses	Lack of funding in many countries leading to a lack of e-Infrastructure re- sources as well as a lack of training and support capacity. Lack of national initiatives as well as international governance and national representation.
Opportunities	The establishment of EGI in Europe and LGI in Latin America are providing a strong template for the creation of a structure underpinning the Asia-Pacific Grid Initiative. In the context of the EGI-InSPIRE proposal, key resource providers in the Asia-Pacific region have formed a Joint Research Unit (JRU) that can form the basis for a growing Asia-Pacific Grid Initiative. The CHAIN proposal, if funded, provides an effective coordination mechanism linking the EGI with regional initiatives and realising economies of scale by combining previously separate efforts.
Threats	The lack of plans to establish national grid initiatives in most countries leads to the provision of resources and operational arrangements being dependent on local resources without any national coordination. Issues of sustainability are often caused by uncertainties about technical development, short-term, project-based funding arrangements and lack of funding and policy support for the formation of sustainable, persistent services.

One of the main issues that grid initiatives anywhere in the world face is the transition from project funding to more sustainable models that allow the provisioning of a dependable service. As already mentioned, the levels of funding available for e-Infrastructures in the Asia-Pacific region vary widely and the limited horizon for funding leads of problems such as staff fluctuation or conflicts between the requirements of service provision and research agendas. In addition, in many countries the resources provided are tied to specific subject areas, further compromising the aim of developing a generic, shared infrastructure.

Networking still plays an important role in the region as provision can differ between countries and between different institutions within a country. At the moment, the Asia-Pacific Advanced Network (APAN[7]) and the Trans-Eurasia Information Network (TEIN[8]) provide connectivity within the region and to Europe and the US. The provision of these inter-regional links is driven by the participation of countries in the LHC experiments at CERN. While overall connectivity to Europe and the US exceeds 50Gbits/s, connectivity within the region itself is less well developed. Changing this situation is one of the aims of the TEIN3 project, which will provide a larger number of countries with upgraded link capacities to the regional backbones. The provision of network capacity is gradually improving and international collaboration is also helping to address network disruptions such as in the case of taifun Morak, which took out important international links. In this instance, ASGCnet in Taiwan provided a backup route via its dedicated link to Europe.

At the middleware level, we can observe a degree of pragmatism in many countries with resource provides often supporting multiple middleware stacks to enable collaborations with partners in different parts of the world and with different technological commitments. Many countries have taken part both in EC-funded projects using the g-Lite middleware stack[9] and in the Pacific-Rim Applications and Grid Middleware Assembly (PRAGMA[10]), which focuses on interoperability with US grids using the Globus Toolkit[11]. In the longer term, it seems likely that the choice of middleware will not be one of selecting between different homogenous solutions rather be one of configuring a number of best-of-breed components together that inter-operate using commonly agreed standards. This is already visible in the approach being taken in Europe with regard to the Unified Middleware Distribution (UMD), which does not propose the development of a new, single middleware stack but rather aims to adopt components from g-Lite, ARC[12] and Unicore[13], three existing stacks developed within different contexts in Europe. Significant experience exists within the region with regard to interoperability, e.g., in Australia where the Australian Research Collaboration Service (ARCS[14]) has provided interoperability with different platforms of international importance through the use of national gateways. Rather than trying to control heterogeneity, ARCS has focused on bringing together different communities and institutions with different commitments. Ultimately, it will be important that while the need for interoperability is crucial for the provision of a shared

---

[7] http://www.apan.net

[8] http://www.tein3.net/

[9] http://glite.web.cern.ch

[10] http://www.pragma-grid.net/

[11] http://www.globus.org/

[12] http://www.nordugrid.org/arc/

[13] http://www.unicore.eu/

[14] http://www.arcs.org.au/

e-Infrastructure, this infrastructures ultimately exists to serve the needs of researchers and their projects, so a degree of flexibility will be required as no one solution will fit all needs. The more an e-Infrastructure will bend without breaking the more it will be fit to stand the test of time and deliver the expected support for driving forward science.

The provision of resources in the emerging Asia-Pacific e-Infrastructure has made significant progress through support by the EUAsiaGrid project. In contrast to initiatives such as PRAGMA, EUAsiaGrid has aimed from the start to foster the emergence of a persistent and sustainable e-Infrastructure that individual researchers can take for grants and simply use by signing up to a suitable virtual organization such as the EUAsia VO, which acts as a discipline-neutral catch-all VO for the region. A crucial achievement is that resources now exist in all the partner countries and the necessary human resources are being developed to sustain and expand these investments. Each country has a user interface (UI) machine through which researchers can access the resources provided by the EUAsiaGrid VO and other VOs. Local certification authorities with supporting registration authorities exist to provide end-user and server certificates to establish a trust infrastructure under the governance of the Asia-Pacific Grid Policy Management Authority (APGridPMA[15]). While the provision of an increased number of resources to meet future requirements is dependent on the provision of funds from national agencies, the support through EUAsiaGrid has helped to ensure that the baseline functionality and key services are readily available. Through the help of its training workpackage, the provision of training and support is being extended into the individual partner countries so they can become more independent from the catch-all provision of training and support. This is a key factor in ensuring scalability and sustainability.

3   TOWARDS AN ASIA-PACIFIC GRID INITIATIVE

In the short term, it is not possible to develop fully-fledged national grid infrastructures and an incorporated international organization such as EGI.eu in Europe. This is partly due to the lack of investment in e-Infrastructure in the region but also because problems exist with the lack of a political mandate at the national level for representation of countries through a single organisation. At the wider policy level, the lack of coordination within the region and the political problems that exist make it impossible to adopt the model provided by the EGI in a straightforward way.

Instead, the EUAsiaGrid Roadmap provides a proposal for the development of the Asia-Pacific Grid Initiative through a sequence of steps starting with the creation of the APGI Union, a lose federation of individual institutions and Joint Re-

---

[15] http://www.apgridpma.org/

search Units (JRUs) based on a set of *standard operating principles and proce-dures*.

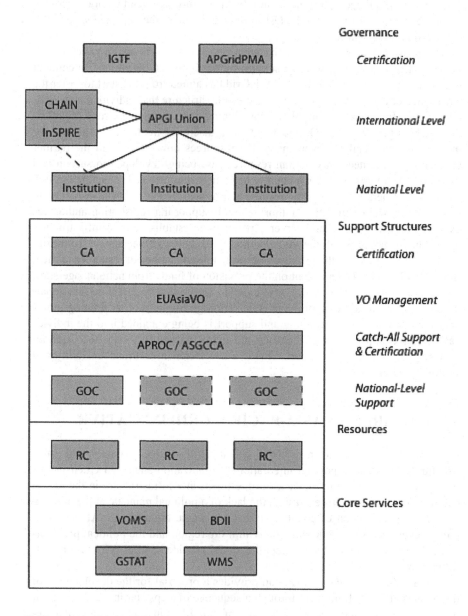

Fig. 1: Organisational and Technical Structure of the APGI Union

Figure 1 illustrates the structure of this proposed Union, which is based not on national representation but the participation of individual institutions as contributors to a shared infrastructure. The structure builds on the existing strengths identified in the SWOT analysis such as the availability of core services and the provision of key support services through the Asia-Pacific Regional Operations Centre (APROC[16]) and APGridPMA as well as the increased breadth of resources that are now available under the EUAsia VO. An important influence on the formation of the APGI Union will be the JRUs that are underpinning the participation of partners from the region in the EGi-InSPIRE and CHAIN proposals. These two projects will play an important role in the further development of a worldwide persistent and sustainable e-Infrastructure and the participation of key partners in the region, in particular, of Academia Sinica Grid Computing, will ensure that these efforts are well coordinated.

A crucial aspect of the usefulness of the structure of the APGI Union is that it does not fundamentally differ from the EGI model and that it will allow a gradual migration towards a model based on national representation. It is not currently possible to give a timeframe for this transition but experiences made in Europe show that the transition of a number of key players can lead to an 'avalanche effect' that will eventually lead to the universal adoption of the principles of national representation through NGIs and the establishment of a coordinating organisation similar to EGI.eu.

The standard operating principles and procedures for the APGI Union have been developed to allow the APGI Union to function as a regional grid initiative and to participate in international collaborations that will oversee the transition from the existing EGEE infrastructure to a persistent and sustainable infrastructure under the EGI and similar initiatives such as the LGI in Latin-America. Their formulation was based on experiences made in the context of PRAGMA and of APAN as well as a critical assessment of the current state of adoption and the formulation of governance structures in the region.

4   CONCLUSIONS

This paper has outlined the aims and context of the EUAsiaGrid Roadmap and the structure of the proposed Asia-Pacific Grid Initative, its initial form as the APGI Union based on contributions by individual institutions as well as the transition towards the full EGI/NGI model. We have described the reasons why we believe that an immediate and straightforward adoption of the model of national representation is unlikely to be successful and our motivation for proposing a model based on a gradual transition stating from an interim solution.

The funding of the EGI-InSPIRE and CHAIN projects by the commission will provide an important impetus for the establishment of the APGI Union and its

---

[16] http://aproc.twgrid.org/

gradual transformation into a regional grid initiative fully integrated with world-wide activities, supported by improved network and resource provision and legitimised through increasing evidence of impact on substantive scientific research. Ultimately, the success of this initiative will depend on the willingness of governments to provide the necessary policy frameworks and the funding necessary to develop and sustain national grid initiatives. We believe the EUAsiaGrid Roadmap has given policy makers the necessary evidence to inform and justify a decision to invest in the creation of the APGI and the infrastructure it support.

5   ACKNOWLEDGEMENTS

The work reported has been enabled by funding from the European Commission through the EUAsiaGrid project (FP7-INFRA-223791).

REFERENCES

[1]   EGI-DS Consortium (2009). EGI Blueprint. Available at:
      http://www.eu-egi.eu/blueprint.pdf
[2]   EUAsiaGrid Consortium (2010). EUAsiaGrid Roadmap: A vision for an Asia-Pacific
      e-Infrastructure for Research and Education. Deliverable D2.2, Policy Report / Technical
      Roadmap. Available at: http://www.euasiagrid.eu/roadmap

From EGEE Operations Portal towards EGI Operations Portal

Hélène Cordier, Cyril L'Orphelin, Sylvain Reynaud, Olivier Lequeux, Sinikka Loikkanen and Pierre Veyre

IN2P3/CNRS Computing Center, Lyon, France

Abstract Grid operators in EGEE have been using a dedicated dashboard as their central operational tool, stable and scalable for the last 5 years despite continuous upgrade from specifications by users, monitoring tools or data providers. In EGEE-III, recent regionalisation of operations led the Operations Portal developers to conceive a standalone instance of this tool. We will see how the dashboard reorganization paved the way for the re-engineering of the portal itself. The outcome is an easily deployable package customized with relevant information sources and specific decentralized operational requirements. This package is composed of a generic and scalable data access mechanism, Lavoisier; a renowned php framework for configuration flexibility, Symfony and a MySQL database. VO life cycle and operational information, EGEE broadcast and Downtime notifications are next for the major reorganization until all other key features of the Operations Portal are migrated to the framework. Features specifications will be sketched at the same time to adapt to EGI requirements and to upgrade. Future work on feature regionalisation, on new advanced features or strategy planning will be tracked in EGI- Inspire through the Operations Tools Advisory Group, OTAG, where all users, customers and third parties of the Operations Portal are represented from January 2010.

1 INTRODUCTION

The need of a management and operations tool for EGEE and WLCG (Worldwide LCG) lead in 2004 to the creation of the EGEE Operations Portal, later referred to as "the CIC Portal"[1]. Its main focus is providing an entry point for all EGEE actors for their operational needs.

The portal is an integration platform as shown in fig.1, allowing for strong interaction among existing tools with similar scope and filling gaps wherever functionality was lacking. It also implements numerous work flows derived from procedures for several of its features out of requirements expressed by end-users or administrators of Virtual Organizations (VO), Regional Operations Centres (ROC) or Resources Centres.

S.C. Lin and E. Yen (eds.), *Data Driven e-Science: Use Cases and Successful Applications of Distributed Computing Infrastructures (ISGC 2010)*, DOI 10.1007/978-1-4419-8014-4_10, © Springer Science+Business Media, LLC 2011

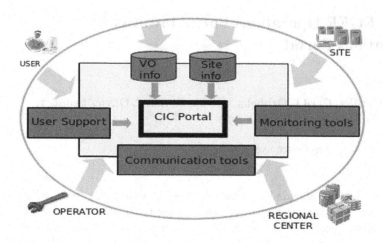

Fig.1: The integration platform concept

One of the most renowned representative features is the tool dedicated to daily operations of the grid resources and services through a set of synoptic views available to grid operators. After over 5 years of operations, this operations dashboard is now implementing a new decentralized operations model since June 2009, over a production infrastructure more than five times larger today than at the start of the project, i.e. over 250 sites and dozens of VOs.

2 EGEE OPERATIONS PORTAL: AN INTEGRATION PLATFORM

The Operations Portal is based on the "actor's view" principle where each EGEE actor has an access to information from an operational point of view according to his role in the project such as grid operator who daily monitors the status of resources and grid services, regular grid user and VO, site or ROC managers.

The information on display is retrieved from several distributed static and dynamic sources – databases, Grid Information System, Web Services, etc. – and gathered onto the portal. Linking this information enables us to display high level views where static and dynamic data yield representative views of the EGEE grid. This resulted in numerous tools that proved precious to sites like the User Tracking feature (to contact unknown users out of their DN in case of observed grid misuse) or the Alarm Notification feature (to subscribe to alerts upon monitoring failures).

Complementary to this informative goal, the portal also fosters communication between different actors, through channels like EGEE broadcast, and Downtime Notification Mechanisms and putting in place procedures to address their interaction needs.

Finally, it offers an implementation of official operations procedures – see §3.1, activity reporting for sites and ROCs or VO life cycle creation and update for VO Management. Last but not least, some integration of third party tools resulting from tight collaboration, like monitoring probes re-submission tool SAMAP (SAM Admin Page) or sites configuration tool (Yaim Configurator) proved useful to operators and sites.

3 A SPECIFIC USE-CASE: THE OPERATIONS DASHBOARD

3.1 The COD Story

When EGEE-I started, the infrastructure was smaller and managed centrally from the Operations Centre at CERN. While this worked quite well, troubleshooting of fifty sites was a difficult task, and the expertise of Grid Operations was concentrated in one place. In order to spread-out the expertise, several federations of countries shared shifts. Dubbed CIC-On-Duty (COD), this new system began in October 2004 [2], in which, the responsibility for managing the infrastructure was passing around the globe on a weekly basis. Indeed, this reduced the workload. However, requirements on tools synchronization and communication soared along with the complexity of the work. It then appeared necessary to have all the tools available through a single interface enabling a strongly interactive and integrated use of these tools. This resulted in the conception of a specific synoptic dashboard for operators and it became one of the main features of the Operations Portal dedicated to daily operations, the COD dashboard.

3.2   Operations Dashboard Concept

Accessing various tools from a single entry point is a key feature as the synoptic view and single operations platform proved invaluable gain for operators.

   Indeed, the interface with the EGEE central ticketing system (Global Grid User Support, GGUS [3]), and the interface with its monitoring framework (Service Availability Monitoring, SAM [4] since December 2004 and Nagios [5] since December 2009), provide to the operators at the decentralized or at the central level a single entry point for:

- Detecting problems through the Operations dashboard, by browsing notifications triggered by the monitoring tool and checking administrative status of the site;
- Creating a ticket in EGEE ticketing system, GGUS [3], for a given problem, linking this ticket to the corresponding monitoring failure, and notifying the relevant recipients extracted from the Grid Operations Centre database (GOC database [6]) through customized template e-mails;
- Browsing, modifying, and escalating tickets from the Operations dashboard directly according to procedures;
- Communicating between teams and reporting to the Operations Coordination Centre.
- The main result at the end of EGEE-II was that the combined set of operational procedures and tools and their constant evolution have been recognized key in stabilizing sites in production.

3.3 Overhaul of the Dashboard Feature during EGEE-III

Since the early days of EGEE-III, the operational model evolved and the daily operations are now under the regions responsibility, even if still under the guidance of the operational procedures. The project still operates some supervision on the unattended problems at sites, urgent security matters or project wide operational issues.

Status of the operations model in EGEE-III

The COD dashboard has evolved accordingly over the last two years into an Operations Dashboard, enabling the daily operations at the federation level through "regional views" hosted centrally; the central layer indeed being reduced a minima. This reflects the evolution in the operational model of EGEE-III [7]. Tools and procedures are now adequate for the switch of the production infrastructure of EGEE-III, to a sustainable production environment based on the operational entities at the national level -National Grid Initiatives or NGIs.

However, the constraint to provide an interoperable back-end that can be distributed to existing federations, and at the national level in the next future, lead us to restructure the EGEE Operations Portal [8] at the same time on a global scale. With this reorganization during last summer, the Operations portal development team is now able to provide a customized and reliable tool, dealing with operations overview at national, federal or central level without any service disruption as exposed in fig.2.

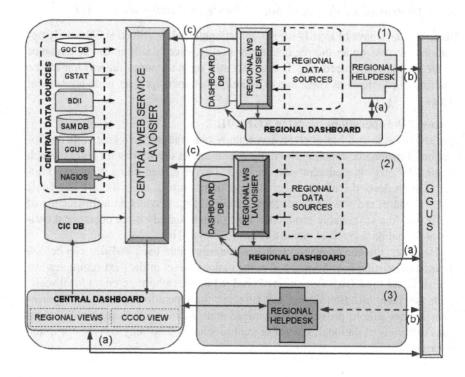

Fig.2. Operations dashboard concept

Legend of Fig.2:

(1) Full distributed model: regional help-desk, dashboard and database

(2) Partially distributed model : dashboard and database

(3) Help-desk distributed model

(a) update and creation of ticket

(b) synchronization between regional help-desk and GGUS

(c) synchronization between regional instance and central one

Scalability, Adaptability, Reliability

Together with the evolution of the operational model described above over the years, the portal also faced the evolution of all the third party tools it is coupled to, implying close interaction with their developers and administrators. The portal had been designed in such a way that neither the growth of the infrastructure to manage, nor the multiplication of the needs and procedures would overload or disrupt existing mechanisms. However, the range of tools proposed in the EGEE Operations Portal, becoming larger and larger, gradually induced an increased complexity in related development and maintenance.

To face this constant evolution and the EGI challenge on decentralisation and customisation as seen above, the global architecture of the portal evolved significantly and is summarized in §4.

General Work-flow - Lavoisier

We are highly dependent on the evolution of other tools: GOC DB, GGUS, SAM, Nagios (see fig. 2) and our technical solution was to implement a web service, in order to make the integration of these changes technically as transparent possible. Consequently, the main idea is to integrate each of the third party tools as a specific resource via Lavoisier.

"Lavoisier" [9, 10] has been indeed developed in order to reduce the complexity induced by the various technologies, protocols and data formats used by its data sources. It is an extensible service which provides a unified view of data collected out of multiple heterogeneous data sources. It enables to easily and efficiently execute cross data sources queries, independently of the technologies used. Data views are represented as XML documents [11] and the query language is XSL [12]. Lavoisier is distributed under the Apache 2.0 license like the Operations Portal.

The design of Lavoisier enables a clear separation in three roles: the client role, the service administrator role and the adapter developer role. The main client is the Operations Portal; it can retrieve the content of a data view in XML or JSON format through SOAP or REST requests. It can also submit XSL style sheets that will be processed by Lavoisier on the managed data views, and receive the result of this processing.

The service administrator is responsible for configuring each data view. He must configure the adapter, which will generate the XML data view from the legacy data source. He may also configure a data cache management policy, in order to optimize Lavoisier according to the characteristics and the usage profile of both the data source (e.g. amount of data transferred to build the view, update frequency, latency) and the generated data view (e.g. amount of data, time to live of the content, tolerable latency). Data cache management policy configuration includes:

- the cache type (in-memory DOM tree, on-disk XML file/files tree or no cache),
- view dependencies,

- a set of rules for triggering cache updates, depending on time-based events, notification events, data view read or write access, cache expiration, update of a cache dependency, etc.
- a set of fall-back rules for ignoring, raising errors or retrying cache updates in case of failure, depending on the type of the exception thrown,
- the cache time-to-live, to prevent from providing outdated information in case of successive cache update failures,
- a cache update time-out,
- the synchronization of the exposition of the new cache content for inter-dependant data views, in order to ensure data view consistency,
- the validation mode for generated views (conform to XML Schema [13], well-formed XML or no validation).

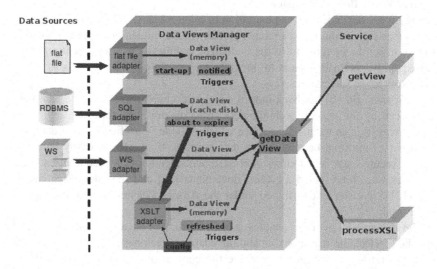

Fig. 3: Data Source Composition Service Lavoisier Configuration

Fig. 3 illustrates a very simple example of Lavoisier configuration with four data views. Data views obtained from flat file and RDBMS data sources are cached respectively in memory and on disk, while the data view obtained from the Web Service data source is regenerated each time it is accessed. The fourth data view is generated from the RDBMS data view, and refreshing of its in-memory cache is triggered when the cache of the RDBMS data view is refreshed. These two data views can be configured to expose their new cache simultaneously if consistency is required.

Lavoisier has proven effective in increasing maintainability of the Operations Portal, by making its code independent from the technologies used by the data sources and from the data cache management policy. Its design and interfaces made easier writing reusable code, and good performances are easily obtained by tuning the cache mechanisms in an absolutely transparent way for the portal code. Indeed, the different components work in a standardized way through the output of the Lavoisier Web Service. The translation of resource information into this standardized output is provided by different plug-ins.

Recently, a joint effort with EELA-II has been recently put into the configuration of Lavoisier, the structure of its caches and the rules of refreshing to have efficient, scalable and reliable data handling. Indeed, all information has been structured around the base component of the Operational Model: the site. We retrieve the global information about primary sources like GGUS, GOC DB, SAM and we organize it by sites. The main idea is to construct a summary of the different available information for a site: firstly, this organization permits to continue to work with the caches, even if a primary source is unavailable; then users access only information they need on the web page. Users' information is structured around a synoptic view of the site so they do not access the primary sources numerous times but a subset of them through the site view. Finally, we refresh the data sources only as needed and only when an action has been triggered. Last but not least, it is very easy to add a new data source in this model. In the configuration file of Lavoisier people can add the access to the relevant primary source and also the per site information split. This information is then readily available in the site synoptic view.

Web portal architecture
The advantages of adopting a framework are numerous. Namely, a framework streamlines application development by automating many of the patterns employed for a given purpose. It also adds structure to the code, prompting the developer to write better, more readable, and more maintainable code. Moreover, a framework makes programming easier, since it packages complex operations into simple statements. Additionally, several key features of a framework optimize the development of web applications, as these enable to:

- separate a web application's business rules, server logic, and presentation views,
- contain numerous tools and classes aimed at shortening the development time of a complex web application, and
- automate common tasks so that the developer can focus entirely on the specifics of its application.

On the other hand, adopting a framework induces a steep and long learning curve in itself. Also checking all the complex specifics - present and in the medium term - of operation portal was a pre-requisite before the start of the migration could take place. Proper feasibility and appropriate development of the operations dashboard started in August 2009 and was available for testing in December 2009

Indeed, the user interface is based on a View-Controller pattern and all the user requests are filtered out and checked by the main controller.

Whenever authorisation is needed, authentication is done using X509 certificate. Accepted requests are then forwarded to the sub-controller in charge of loading the requested page. In addition, the main controller uses abstraction layers to transparently connect to third-party applications like databases or web services. Connections are shared by all the sub-controllers thanks to inheritance mechanisms.

This approach improves organisation of source code, leading to a high rate of re usability. Moreover, all the operating system dependent implementations have been removed in order to ease configuration and deployment. It means also that the dashboard will be provided with a data schema and that with the help of the Symfony Framework you can generate on the fly the Database corresponding to the schema. This option is working with MySQL, Oracle, PostgresSQL and SQLLite.

The Symfony Framework is also giving additional features like a security layer assuming XSS and CSRF Protection, a set of different work environments different: test, prod and dev, and the use of plug-ins developed by the Symfony community. Finally, it has been thoroughly tested in various real-world projects, and is actually in use for high-demand e-business websites.

4   EGEE/EGI OPERATIONS PORTAL STATUS AT THE END OF EGEE-III

The portal architecture is still three-fold [8]: php web portal, database, and Data Processing System named Lavoisier [9, 10]; however, the php web interface is based now on a PHP Framework, Symfony [14] and the Data Processing system Lavoisier has recently been enhanced to increase the speed in the information handling. Taking advantage of the php framework features, the code factorization and reusability has increased. Also, the framework structure has eased the build-up of the local packages of the dashboard for which information sources and data base need customization.

The operations dashboard is the first feature of the portal to undergo such a overhaul to prepare for potential decentralisation and subsequent customization. On the 9th of December 2009, the reorganization of the operations dashboard has been completed and the Nagios based operations dashboard has been available for testing; it had been validated and released on March 1rst 2010.

Decentralization for the time being is achieved via "views hosted centrally" and the relevant operational entities – Regional Operation Centers in EGEE and National Grid Initiatives in EGI will be able to run their own instance of the tool upon request at the end of March 2010. In the mean time a dedicated beta-package is available and had been already tested by a couple of federations [15].

4.1   Installation Requirements for Decentralized Package

Any grid infrastructure will be able to install an Operations dashboard customized to its needs with a minimum set of requirements. A dedicated server will have to run PHP with a version over 5.2.4 with modules enabled such as SOAP and OCI, together with Java with a JDK version over 5.0 and a database of their choice MySQL, SQLLite, Oracle or PostgresSQL. The full package delivered will comprise the PHP code, the Database schema and the Lavoisier module, together with the relevant configuration files to proceed to necessary customization.

4.2   Conclusion and Description of Future Work in EGI -Inspire

Given our technical choices based on standards, we should be able to meet any scenario and associated requirements from any future operational entities like grid projects, federations or nations. Collaboration is already under way with EELA as a first example of adaptation to external DCI [16, 17, and 18].

In the mean time, current overhaul work comprises similar reorganization of the other features of the EGEE Operations Portal starting with EGEE broadcast and VO life cycle and VO operational metrics. We will then proceed with other key features.

In parallel, our goal is to provide a seamless access to the users regarding the sites' and the VOs' info, an easy access to administration interfaces for sites and VO managers, a standard access to information and standard formats for it, together with a scalable operations model for each scenario potentially required: national, federal or central.

Consequently, for user ergonomics and back-end simplicity the operations Portal development team is already working on common development plans with GOCDB developers [19]. Both developers' teams are part of the Operations Tools Advisory Group, OTAG, in order to cope with EGI/NGIs new features requirements and priorities. This newly formed advisory group will be transversal to all operational tools in EGI. Namely, potential decentralization of operational tools, migration and re-engineering of the existing features of the operations portal recognized as key for EGEE/EGI operations as well as strategic decisions are done in agreement with this joint Advisory Group: OTAG [20].

Finally, the structure of the back-end of the Operations Portal enables now any operational entity (NGIs or group of NGIs) to potentially customize their own configuration with the database of their choice, the relevant Lavoisier plug-ins and their specific set of php files. It is worth quoting that Lavoisier plug-ins developed externally -when developed in a generic way- might be reusable and made available to the community. Global trend clearly indicates customization as the motto for us to claim: we are aiming at delivering flexible services and customizable end-user interfaces.

5   ACKNOWLEDGEMENT

This work makes use of results produced with the EGEE (http://www.eu-egee.org) grid infrastructure, co-funded by the European Commission (INFSO-RI-222667)

REFERENCES

[1]   (2004) CIC Operations portal [online]: http://cic.Operations.org
[2]   H. Cordier, G. Mathieu, F. Scher, J. Novak, P. Nyczyk, M. Schulz, M.H. Tsai, Grid Operations: the evolution of operational model over the first year, Computing in High Energy and Nuclear Physics, India, 2006.
[3]   GGUS Web Portal [on line] http://www.ggus.org
[4]   SAM:http://goc.grid.sinica.edu.tw/gocwiki/Service_Availability_Monitoring_Environment
[5]   NAGIOS http://www.nagios.org/docs/
[6]   GOC portal: http://goc.grid-support.ac.uk
[7]   EGEE Operational procedures https://edms.cern.ch/document/840932
[8]   Aidel, O., Cavalli, A., Cordier, H., L'Orphelin, C., Mathieu, G., Pagano, A., Reynaud, S., CIC portal: a Collaborative and scalable integration platform for high availability grid operations: Grid Computing, 2007 8th IEEE/ACM Int. Conf; USA. 2007 Page(s):121 - 128
[9]   S. Reynaud, G. Mathieu, P. Girard, F. Hernandez and O. Aidel, Lavoisier: A Data Aggregation and Unification Service, Computing in High Energy and Nuclear Physics, India, 2006.
[10] Lavoisier documentation [online] : http://grid.in2p3.fr/lavoisier
[11] (1996-2003) Extensible Markup Langage (XML) [online] http://www.w3.org/XML
[12] (1999) XSL transformations [online] : http://www.w3.org/TR /xslt
[13] http://www.w3.org/XML/Schema
[14] Symfony http://www.symfony-project.org/doc/1_2/
[15] Operations Portal Forge: https://forge.in2p3.fr/documents/show/76
[16] EVENTUM http://eventum.eu-eela.eu
[17] EOC http://eoc.eu-eela.eu/doku.php?id=quick_guide
[18] C. L'Orphelin, H. Cordier, S. Reynaud, M. Lins, S. Loikkanen, O. Lequeux, P. Veyre "EELA Operations: A standalone regional dashboard implementation, Second EELA-II conference Choroni, Venezuela, 2009, p171-180
[19] Poster Session: EGEE Operations Portal: From an Integration Platform into a Generic Framework in EGI context, EGEE'09, Spain, 2009.
[20] OTAG meeting agenda: https://www.egi.eu/indico/categoryDisplay.py?categId=4

Kolkata Tier-2 Centre: Administration and Installation

Vikas Singhal and Subhasis Chattopadhyay

Variable Energy Cyclotron Centre, Department of Atomic Energy, Government of India, India

Abstract   Grid Computing has been considered as the solution for dealing with large amount of data produced in large experiments like ALICE, STAR etc. Grid comprises of many small sites geographically distributed across the globe. Therefore for this complex system, installation of a Grid site, day to day administration and management of the site and meeting the SLA (Service Level Agreements) and providing QA (Quality Assurance) services are challenging. This article describes Alice Grid as a whole, its architecture, tier based model, jobs of different tiers and procedure of job submission and storage with xrootd. One tier-2 grid computing centre has been installed at VECC-SINP campus in Kolkata, India for ALICE experiment under WLCG (Worldwide LHC Computing Grid). The article describes details of the installation of the Tier-2 site from scratch and bringing it upto the requirement of an experiment and describes, day to day administration and maintenance of the site.

   The installation procedure includes the discussion on infrastructure, cooling and power supply in addition to the procurement of computing hardware, building cluster, installing middleware as per the requirement of the WLCG and then maintaining software accordingly to the VO (Virtual Organization) requirement (for us ALICE experiment). The administration of the site requires continuous update of OS, middleware with respect to CE, SE, VOBOX and many other related to the security of the site. Apart from maintaining the Grid computing site, administrator has to provide computing infrastructure to the local users with sufficient storage and computing power in terms of a dedicated Tier-3 site. The challenges involved in all the steps related to the grid site will be discussed in this chapter with Kolkata tier-2 centre as a case study. It also explains Kolkata Tier2 connectivity with ALICE and explains Kolkata Tier-2 with its hardware, architecture and middle ware installation in whole for Cream-CE and Pure XrootD Storage.

1   GRID FOR ALICE EXPERIMENT:

ALICE experiment will collect data in lead-lead & proton-proton collisions from LHC and will produce simulation data. In one year of operation, ALICE will generate few Peta Byte (PB=1015 bytes) of raw and calibration data. ALICE has decided to use GRID environment for their computing need. It uses MONARC mod-

S.C. Lin and E. Yen (eds.), *Data Driven e-Science: Use Cases and Successful Applications*
of Distributed Computing Infrastructures (ISGC 2010), DOI 10.1007/978-1-4419-8014-4_11,
© Springer Science+Business Media, LLC 2011

el to deal with data processing involving installation of computing centres of various tiers depending on the load of computing.

GRID-based environment named AliEn2 (Alice Environment) has been implemented along with the WLCG, a framework providing Grid functionality. WLCG is built on top of the latest standards for information exchange & authentication (SOAP, SASL, and PKI) and common open source components (such as GLOBUS/GSI, OpenSSI, OpenLDAP, SOAPLite, MySQL, Perl5). AliEn2 provides a virtual file catalogue that allows transparent access to distributed data-sets and provides top to bottom implementation of ldap [1] (lightweight directory access protocol) which enables Grid to handle a large number of files (upto 2 PB data and 109 files/year, file size is 2GB each) which is distributed on more than 80 locations worldwide for the ALICE experiment.

2   INDIAN CONTRIBUTIONS TO ALICE

India is involved with CERN, since early 80s & started participation in detector building for deferent experiments. VECC [2] (Variable Energy Cyclotron Center) along with other collaborating institutes have developed one of the ALICE detectors named PMD (Photon Multiplicity Detector) and SINP [3] (Saha Institute of Nuclear Physics) has developed part of Muon Arms. (shown in Fig.1). Along with significant contribution for detector development, Indian institutions decided to participate in WLCG Grid as well. In this context one Tier-2 centre is setup at Kolkata since 2004.

Fig.1. ALICE Detector Model with PMD and Muon Arm detector.

3   GRID SITE FROM DIFFERENT PERSPECTIVES (CASE STUDY KOLKATA TIER-2)

In view of the VO (experiment), a Grid site is that some central services are running at a central place like CERN and then at site VOBOX service is running and behind this middleware services e.g. CE (computing element) and SE (storage element) are running. The CE and SE then contain of more and more computing nodes and storage disks or array of disks. This view is shown in fig.2. ALICE experiment supports CREAM-CE [4] as CE and Pure XrooD [5] as SE.

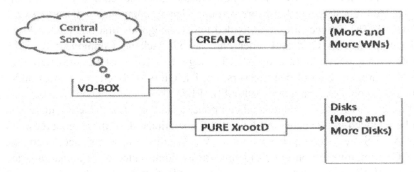

Fig. 2: Grid Site as per Experiment Requirement

In view of WLCG, a Grid site is that, some central services like WMS, My-Proxy, VOMS etc. are running at a central place and at Site lcg-CE, Site-BDII, Cream-CE, lcg-UI, SE services are running, and behind this more and more computing nodes and storage disks or array of disks are attached as shown in fig.3.

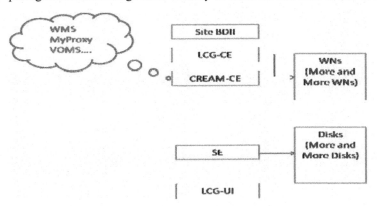

Fig. 3: Grid Site as per WLCG Requirement

Grid site at Kolkata is developed in many phases, as per the requirement of the hardware and budget approval, which results acquiring more and more resources of different architectures like 32bit, 64bit etc, and resources from different vendors like some international vendors HP, DELL, IBM etc or some from national (local) vendors. As network is basic infrastructure for any research or development, therefore in every country Government is concentrating on building good network infrastructure. In India from 2010 NKN (National Knowledge Network) is under development keeping this in mind. At Kolkata site, 2 networks are setup, one is Global Network by which site is connected with outside World and other is Local or internal network by which all the clusters and other component of the site is connected. On different hardware resources many components or services are configured. The services are here divided into 2 categories first one named Frontend Component of Grid and other one named Backend Component of Grid. VOBOX (2 voboxes in case of ALICE), lcg-CE, CREAM-CE, Site-BDII, SE, Xrootd redirector, Xrootd disk Servers, lcg-UI, Glite-MON etc are comes under Frontend component category and NFS, PBS, DNS, Installation, DHCP and Monitoring server falls into backend component category. Local Tier3 Cluster can also be included in this category. For 24 * 7 operations of all these resources, 3 * 40KVA UPS are installed in UPS room. We installed fire alarm, access control and CCTV monitoring on our Grid Site for avoiding entry of any unauthorized person. All Network, hardware, infrastructure and services together known as a Grid Site as shown in fig.4. Then somewhere some Central services like WMS, MyProxy etc are running which communicate with site services and confirm and publish a report that Grid Site is working fine.

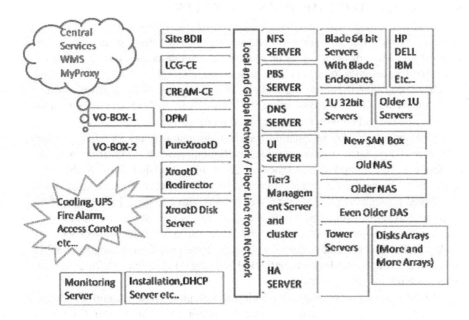

Fig. 4: Kolkata Site schematic

4 FRONTEND COMPONENTS OF SITE

All Grid middleware meta-packages can be installed through YUM (Yellowdog Updater, Modified) [6] and configured through YAIM (YAIM Ain't an Installation Manager) [7]. I used GLITE documentation and installation guide [8] for installing and configuring VO-BOX, Site-BDII, LCG-CE, LCG-UI etc. During Kolkata Site installation and configuration we experienced about RPM dependencies with JAVA, Security packages etc and learned how to resolve dependencies with help of rpm and yum commands. For all these issues, community mailing list helps a lot. For most of the installation and configuration related problem or any confusion one gets the solution from mailing list. As per ALICE experiment requirement we configured CREAM-CE as computing element and Pure-XrootD as storage element. Recently Cream-CE installation is also available as glite-CREAM meta package so we configured it through Glite user guide.

5   BACKEND COMPONENTS OF SITE

There are many different component and services which helps the Grid site to run successfully. Most of the services or component installation and configuration require good knowledge of Linux and networking concept. With help of Google search we configured router and switch. We configured NTP protocol on one server then sync all other server's time with this server. As NTP service is light so NTP service is clubbed with Pure Xrootd redirector server.

All other server's OS installation was done through network installation using PXE and TFTP. For respective services configuration we used Quattor tools. At our site we use common shared space for software and related files, for this on a server NFS (Network File System) runs and then on all other servers shared space is mounted through NFS. NFS server we clubbed with CE. On CE, PBS (portable batch scheduler) is running as batch scheduler. On the CE server we have 2 networks one global to connect internet and other one is local to connect with all worker nodes. Worker node cannot be accessed from outside therefore Firewall is configured through iptables and configured NATing on it so that worker node can access internet or outside world.

At Kolkata site one separate Tier-3 cluster with interactive and non interactive nodes are installed for local users and collaborators. On this cluster C3 RPMs (Cluster Command & Control (C3) [9] tool suite configured for easy use of all the nodes. All these, for monitoring every component of the SITE we configured one server which parses different log files and extract useful details. On this server MRTG is configured for Network Traffic Monitoring of router and also maps network profile of individual servers which is connected to a particular port on the switch.

6   SITE ADMINISTRATION & MAINTENANCE

At Kolkata site we perform preventive maintenance once in a year including cooling solution. During preventive maintenance we use to do the cleaning of whole hardware from inside and also recheck all the network connectivity for all servers and switches. By this activity we try to ensure that when system is running and contributing into production, there will not be any failure. Due to day by day increasing resources, cooling infrastructure is going to be upgraded. For better cooling, cooled air circulation should be proper. Cold air will be thrown from downward to upward and then hot air will be sucked by Precision AC units (so natural air circulation, cooled air is heavier then hot air, can be maintained.) as shown in fig. 5. For efficient cooling of hardware resources, we will prepare 2 zones, cold and hot. Cold zone will be formed by racks and then cold air will be thrown into this zone. All servers circulate air from front to back so hot air will be thrown in hot zone.

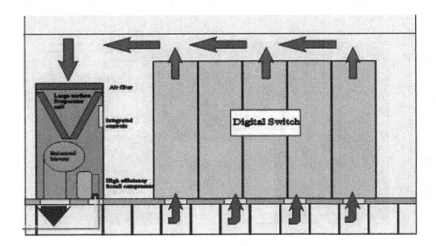

Fig. 5: Air circulation for proper cooling.

7   KOLKATA TIER2: STATUS AND FULL REPORT

At the beginning of 2004 we procured and configured one small 6 node cluster and participated in PDC04. After this 2006 we procured 13 Xeon 3.0 GHz dual CPU with 4GB RAM based cluster and configured as IN-DAE-VECC-01 site which is equivalent of 26KSI2k computing unit. We participated in PDC06, PDC07 and PDC08 with 34Mbps Network-Connectivity. On all hardware (for VOBOX, Computing Element, Storage Element, Worker Node etc) SLC OS installed and ALICE Environment (AliEn) is running on the VO-Box with AliEn-ClusterMonitor, AliEn-CE, AliEn-SE, AliEn-PackMan and MonaLisa-Monitoring agent. Time to time as per experiment and WLCG requirement we upgraded OS and all middleware services for all servers like from SLC3 to SLC4 and latest is SLC5.2 then reconfigured all compatible middleware packages like glite-VOBOX, lcg-CE, site-BDII, glite-MON etc.

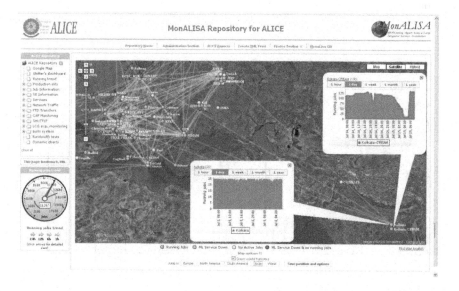

Fig. 6: Kolkata sites in MonaLisa repository for ALICE.

Wherever possible we try to maintain redundancy at all respect for making system reliable and achieving high availability. At Kolkata tier-2 we configured 2 name servers (naamak and suchak) for reverse and forward name resolution. Similarly all 13 worker nodes of IN-DAE-VECC-01 have 2 network cards and between these 2, bonding [10] is implemented. All nodes are connected to 2 different switches. (fig 7 shows the connectivity). All grid middleware services require host certificate therefore high availability (through redundancy) cannot be implemented for VOBOX, CE, SE etc. In year 2008 we procured 64 bit hardware which comprises 40 numbers of Dual core dual CPU 3.0 GHz blade server with 2GB

RAM/core and 2 hard disks on RAID 1 (Redundant Array of Independent disks) and 108TB of raw disk with 200 spindles of 500GB and 8 spindles of 1TB under 2 HP EVA6100 SAN boxes connected by two redundant SAN Switches with 4Gb host ports. After RAID5 and hot spare configuration of storage, we got 74TB of usable disk space which we connected through SAN with 2*HP 2U rack servers of 3.0GHz dual Xeon processor dual core CPUs with 8GB RAM, hardware shown in fig. 8.

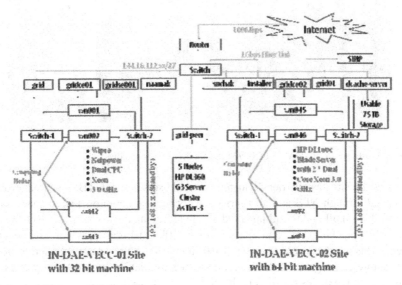

Fig. 7: Logical Diagram of Kolkata Tier2

After installation of x86_64 SLC4.6 OS, we configured lcg-CE as computing element with all 64bit blades as worker nodes which is Total 160 cores equivalent of 240KSI2k and configured D-CACHE[11] as storage element on a server as dcache head node and 2 disk servers (dcache-pool with 34TB usable space and dcacheclient with 40TB usable space.) These all are added as a new GOCDB site named IN-DAE-VECC-02 site. Then ALICE experiment suggested configuring CREAMCE as CE and Pure-Xrootd as SE. With the help of CREAM-CE developers we configured CRAM-CE on CE box (gridce02.tier2-kol.res.in) with 39 Worker nodes. ALICE submits jobs on CREAM-CE through different queue so it require a second VOBOX, we configured grid01.tier2-kol.res.in as second VOBOX [12]. Pure-XrootD configured as SE, on 3 Storage boxes, one as xrootd redirector and 2 as disk servers. After successful configurations and testing of all, second VOBOX, Cream-CE and Pure XrootD, are included into production and since March 2009 used under ALICE production. Ethernet bonding implemented in all 3 storage servers, for better performance of file transfer, and in IN-DAE-VECC-02 cluster. On both Xrootd Disk servers, internal and external both network is configured so that file transfer within Kolkata Site is done on gigabit network backbone and from outside it is by 100Mbps network line.

Fig. 8: Hardware for IN-DAE-VECC-02 Site (Blades servers and disks.).

Kolkata site has one tier-3 cluster for local users where 6 TB of shared space is mounted through NFS and all users have account on common shared space so all are visible on all nodes and installed all physics related softwares like ROOT, Geant, AliRoot, AliEn, etc and also included different libraries as per user requirement. This cluster contains 2 types of nodes, some nodes are interactive nodes where one can login and do there interactive simulation etc work and others are non-interactive nodes for running batch jobs.

8   CONCLUSION AND FUTURE ASPECTS:

Kolkata Tier2 contains 2 sites which are registered as production site in GOCDB (Grid Operation Center Data Base) named IN-DAE-VECC-01 & IN-DAE-VECC-02 and represented in MonaLisa Repository for ALICE as Kolkata and Kolkata-CREAM respectively shown in fig.6. Kolkata tier2 has its private dedicated network of 100Mbps and has 32 public IP addresses (144.16.112.x/27) which domain name is tier2-kol.res.in. Network connectivity is direct from Geant network to Mumbai and from Mumbai to Kolkata fibre pipe is laid. In India ALICE has 6 collaborators (Jammu university, Rajasthan University, Panjab University, AMU Aligarh, IOP Bhubaneswar and IIT Bombay) all are connected through 10Mbps private VPN network. Since 2009, both sites are participating under production. On IN-DAE-VECC-01 site, maximum 25 jobs can be run which equals to 25KSI2k and on IN-DAE-VECC-02 155 jobs can be run which equals to 250KSI2k as shown in fig.6. As per our pledged schedule we achieved 40% of our pledged resources of 600KSI2k with 240TB of usable space and 155 Mbps of network bandwidth. Kolkata Tier2 is under the umbrella of Asia Pacific and Software Functionality Tests are running daily thrice for ensuring Security & Site Functionalities. Kolkata Tier-2 is continuously participating in all Physics Data Challenges (like PDC04, PDC06, PDC07, PDC08 etc.) and also successfully completed CCRC08 (Common Computing Readiness Challenge before starting LHC). As per EGEE Availability and Reliability Report Kolkata tier2 sites have approximately 95% of Availability and reliability factor. As per present infrastructures Kolkata is contributing 1% of Total ALICE resources, shown in fig. 9. As per Kolkata Tier2 roadmap we will achieve pledged resource till end of year 2010 and will contribute approx 3% of total ALICE resources.

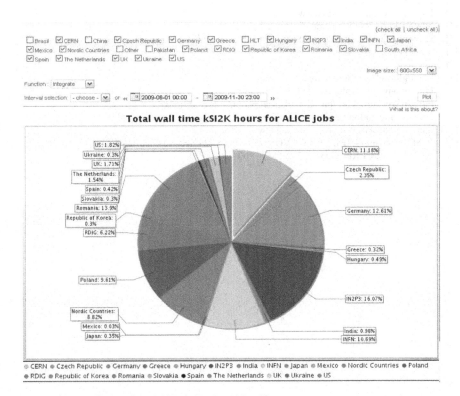

Fig. 9: Total Wall Time for ALICE during June-Nov 09.

9   ACKNOWLEDGEMENT

Kolkata Tier-2 comprises good amount of servers, storage and 100Mbps network bandwidth, the all procurement is supported from the grants of the Department of Atomic Energy and Department of Science and Technology, Government of India. I would like to thank the entire members of ALICE Grid, CERN and APROC Taiwan who helped in deployment of Grid middleware at Kolkata site.

REFERENCES

[1]   http://www.ldapman.org/articles/intro_to_ldap.html
[2]   http://www.vecc.gov.in/
[3]   http://www.saha.ac.in/cs/www/
[4]   http://grid.pd.infn.it/cream/
[5]   http://alien2.cern.ch/index.php?option=com_content&view=article&id=33&Itemi d=79
[6]   http://yum.baseurl.org/
[7]   http://yaim.info/
[8]   http://glite.web.cern.ch/glite/
[9]   http://www.csm.ornl.gov/torc/C3/
[10] http://www.kernel.org/pub/linux/kernel/people/marcelo/linux-2.4/Documentation/networking/bonding.txt
[11] http://trac.dcache.org/projects/dcache/wiki/manuals/YAIM
[12] P. M. Lorenzo, IT/GS, CERN, "VOBOXes and LCG Services" in Alice T1/T2 Tutorial for Site Admins, CERN, Geneva 26-27May 2009.

Performance Analysis of EGEE-like Grids in Asia and Latin America

Marco Fargetta[1], Leandro N. Ciuffo[2], Diego Scardaci[1] and Roberto Barbera[3]

1. INFN Catania, Italy
2. INFN Catania, Italy / RNP, Brazil
3. INFN Catania / Catania University, Italy

Abstract   A measure to estimate the value that Grids can provide to potential users can be obtained by assessing the resources availability, middleware overhead and infrastructure reliability incurred when running an application in a transcontinental e-Infrastructure like EGEE.

Celebrating the recent MoU between EELA-2 [1] and EUAsiaGrid [2] projects, both co-funded by EC under the Seventh Framework Programme, this paper aims at providing a comparative study between their respective Grid infrastructures.

Current monitoring tools provide information on the resources status. These figures are useful for Grid managers in order to check the availability of the services but not for end users because they do not provide any indication on the execution of users' applications, such as the average job delay.

In our approach, we randomly submitted 10 jobs per day during 1 week both project's infrastructures and measured its total execution time. No special requirements were set on the JDL files and we did not carry about the level of availability of the computing resources (CEs) neither about the number of jobs concurrently running at a giving moment. We let the core Workload Management System (WMS) of each project to automatically choose which CE to submit the jobs, considering both EUAsiaGrid and EELA-2 infrastructures as single entities.

The analysis of the results can be used to measure the quality of services provided by both projects to its respective user communities.

1 INTRODUCTION

Grid computing has established itself as a fundamental computational model for the support of e-Science activities in Europe and several other countries. This new paradigm has provided the computing power requested by modern experiments, which require data analysis and simulation of very complex systems, and at the same time, has fostered the co-operation among research centres spread around Europe.

S.C. Lin and E. Yen (eds.), *Data Driven e-Science: Use Cases and Successful Applications of Distributed Computing Infrastructures (ISGC 2010)*, DOI 10.1007/978-1-4419-8014-4_12, © Springer Science+Business Media, LLC 2011

In the last years, the European Commission has promoted Grid computing within new scientific communities in several regions of the world by providing grants to projects aiming at expanding the European Grid infrastructure to other continents (see Figure 1). As a result, many of these intercontinental projects have created good infrastructures with important research activities relying on them.

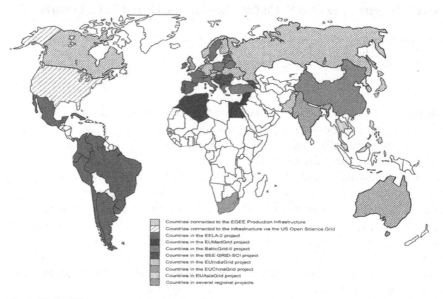

Fig. 1: World Grid coverage – adapted from [3].

Although these infrastructures are monitored by automatic tools and many people are involved in their management, the lower experience with this new computing model and the different maturity level of beneath technologies, such as the network infrastructure, the computing farms and so on, make the availability and the reliability of trans-continental Grid an issue for many applications.

Evaluating the quality of the infrastructure for their users is a troublesome activity. Current automatic tools are able to evaluate the status of each service available in the infrastructure but even if all of them are working properly the users can experience problems. In fact, the resources change continually and many error/problems raise only in specific resources, load condition or other not reproducible conditions. Consequently, scientists have frustration to use the Grid in order to run their activity and co-operate with other.

The work in this paper shows the result of 70 job submissions to both the Asiatic (EUAsiaGrid) and the Latin-American (EELA-2) Grid infrastructures in order to evaluate their quality from the user's perspective. Hence, our evaluation does not consider the activity of a single service/component but the Grid infrastructure as a whole. The common problems experienced were reported to the operators of both infrastructures providing an important feedback for the site administrators and VO managers.

The paper is structured as follows: next section gives an overview of the infrastructures analysed during this activity. Section 3 presents the approach used for the monitoring activity and describes the synthetic applications developed for the tests. Section 4 shows the results of the monitoring and the problems raised during the test. Finally, last section provides the conclusions and open several scenarios for the next monitoring activities.

2 THE INFRASTRUCTURES

Our analysis aims at evaluating the status of similar of EGEE-like Grid infrastructure outside Europe, in particular those provided by EELA-2 and EUAsiaGrid projects. The former is operating between Europe and Latin-America regions and the second is operating between Europe and South East Asia regions.

Both infrastructures are considered to be in production stage from more than one year, so their quality of service and their support level should be comparable.

EELA-2 and EUAsiaGrid projects adopt the gLite middleware [4, 5] - an European solution developed by the CERN jointly with the EGEE project [6]. A more detailed description of each infrastructure is in the following sections.

2.1 EELA-2

The EELA-2 project (E-science grid facility for Europe and Latin America) is EELA's second phase. It aims at building and operating a production Grid infrastructure, which provides computing and storage resources from selected partners across Europe and Latin America. Currently, the EELA-2 Consortium encompasses 78 member institutions from 16 countries (5 from Europe, 11 from Latin America).

The EELA-2 infrastructure operates middleware Core Services located in both Europe and Latin America1, and work with Grid sites that have demonstrated to have an adequate maturity level in par with what's expected from a production environment. It also maintains virtual organization services, with one main Virtual Organization (VO) - named prod.vo.eu-eela.eu – gathering the production-quality infrastructure services [7].

At the time of this writing, 18 Resources Centres (RCs) were connected to the EELA-2 infrastructure. It is spread over 11 countries and has more than 5000 job slots (CPUs). In the table 1 only the Latin-American partners are highlighted.

---

1 http://eoc.eu-eela.eu/doku.php?id=central_services

Table 1: Resources in the BDII for non EU partners of EELA-2

Organisation	Country	CPUs (job slots)	Storage (GB)
CEFET-RJ	Brazil	22	666
UFRJ-IF	Brazil	199	718
UFCG	Brazil	4	22
ULA-MERIDA	Venezuela	24	1039
UNIANDES	Colombia	108	379
UTFSM	Chile	52	1204
UNAM	Mexico	54	890
UNLP	Argentina	10	570

It's worth mentioning that the availability of job slots can vary several times a days, depending on the number of jobs running on the infrastructure. Also, site resources can be removed (or integrated) at any time due to hardware maintenance or network failures, for instance.

2.2 EUAsiaGrid

The EUAsiaGrid project started in March 2008 to enforce the scientific cooperation between Europe and South East Asia. The first and foremost goal of the project was to create a Grid infrastructure to support the activity of project partners.

Initially, the computational resources were provided by the European partners and the Academia Sinica (a project partner located in Taiwan), which was working with other project and had the expertise needed to manage the infrastructure. Other partners in the region have joined the infrastructure by integrating new Resource Centres during the first year of the project.

Table 2 shows the situation of non-European RCs retrieved from the BDII for the euasia VO, which is the VO for all resources, applications and users working in the project.

Table 2: Resources in the BDII for non EU partners of EUAsiaGrid

Organisation	Country	CPUs (job slots)	Storage (GB)
ITB	Indonesia	1	15
MIMOS	Malaysia	48	1246
UM	Malaysia	16	134
UPM	Malaysia	104	983
AM	Philippine	2	30
ASTI	Philippine	48	10
ASGC	Taiwan	3969	1474
HAII	Thailand	1	1028
NECTEC	Thailand	1	1474
IFI	Vietnam	4	733
IOIT	Vietnam	4	733

The central services, like VOMS and WMS, are managed by the Academia Sinica but many institutions provide a replica of them[2] so to increase the availability and reliability of the infrastructure.

The project will end in the middle of 2010 but the infrastructure should be operative after the end and actually a roadmap for its sustainability is investigated by the project partners.

3 ANALYSIS APPROACH

For the tests presented in this paper a synthetic application, written in C language, has been developed. In this application, each job can be parameterised with a variable that sets its local processing time. In our experiment, we set that value to 300 seconds.

Each job executes the following procedure:

1. Transfer a 1MB junk file using the InputSandbox;
2. Execute the synthetic application (sleep for 300 seconds);
3. Rename the junk input file and retrieve it back in the OutputSandbox.

Ten (10) normal Jobs were submitted per day during one (1) week. We did not take into consideration the level of availability of the computing resources (CEs) neither the number of jobs concurrently running at a giving moment. We have considered both EELA-2 and EUAsiaGrid infrastructures as a black box and observed the general properties of job submission.

No special requirements were set on the JDL file. We let the Workload Management System (WMS) to automatically choose which CE to submit the jobs. However, in order to focus our experiment on the computational value that Asiatic

---

2 The VOMS service is an exception because it has to be unique for the VO.

and Latin-American Resource Centres can add to each region's research, we set the JDL file to do not run on the European sites.

Additionally, only the core services located outside Europe were used. For the jobs submitted to EELA-2, we used the core services located in Brazil [8]. For the jobs submitted to EUAsiaGrid we used the core services located in Taiwan.

A second synthetic application to evaluate the ability of the infrastructure to manage parallel applications was developed. The basic schema of this application is quite similar to the one above. The main difference is that the job running the application asks 15 CPU Cores during the submission and the application is distributed on them for the execution. Nevertheless, all sites outside Europe, for both infrastructures, were not able to run this synthetic application correctly because the MPI libraries, needed to distribute the application among the cores, were not available or not configured correctly. Consequently, the tests for parallel applications are not reported in the following section but it is important to notice the lack of this important feature which can limit the use of more advanced applications.

4 RESULTS

Figures 2 and 3 show the makespan time (i.e., the total job delay) obtained by submitting 70 jobs to EELA-2 and EUAsiaGrid respectively. The jobs were sent between 8:00 AM and 6:00 PM in the Central European Time (CET). The times were obtained by querying the Logging & Bookkeeping service (LB) of each projects' core services. The difference between the red/dark part of the chart (total makespan time) and the light/yellow part is the delay incurred by the infrastructure's overhead.

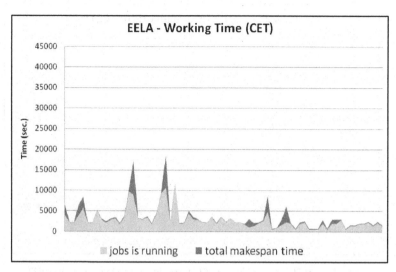

Fig. 2: Total job delay of 70 jobs submitted to EELA-2

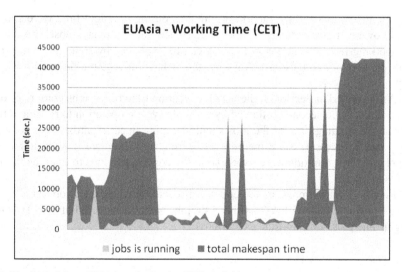

Fig. 3: Total job delay of 70 jobs submitted to EUAsiaGrid

One can note a huge delay in the jobs submitted to EUAsiaGrid. It could indicates some malfunction caused by communication problems between the CE and the LB. However, we also submitted others 70 jobs (10 submissions per day) during the night time (CET). Figure 4 presents the results.

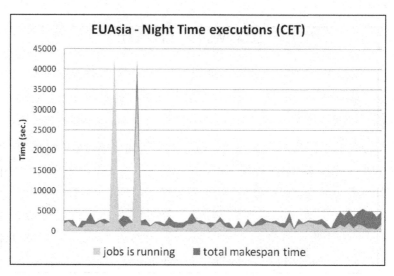

Fig. 4: Total job delay of 70 jobs submitted to EUAsiaGrid during the night time (CET)

The times obtained by submitting the jobs during the night time were similar to the overall times obtained in EELA-2. Hence, the big delays observed during the working-time executions in EUAsia can be explained by some network problem (e.g network congestion). Anyway, this behaviour requires further investigation.

As described in Section 3, the actual execution time of the jobs comprises of a sleep time of 300 seconds followed by a simple system operation to rename a file. Hence, the running time of the jobs should be quite linear regardless the computing power (processor, RAM memory, etc.) from the CE where it is executed. So, the charts show a middleware overhead in the communications to upgrade the job status in the LB.

Finally, Figure 5 presents the country distribution where each job ran. 70 jobs were considered in EELA-2 while 140 jobs were considered in EUAsiaGrid (night-time plus working-time executions).

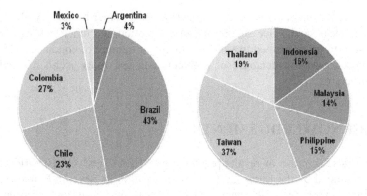

Fig. 5: Country distribution were each job ran

We observed a more uniform distribution among the Resource Centres integrated in EUAsiaGrid despite the fact that no jobs were sent to any site in Vietnam. Additionally, the only one CE in Indonesia received 15% of the jobs. This can retain several jobs waiting in the execution queue, which contributes to increase the total job delay.

On the EELA-2 side, the jobs distribution were rather proportional to the availability of CPUs on each country. However, no jobs were sent to Venezuela.

5 CONCLUSIONS

Grid infrastructures provide the computational power needed by most of the scientific experiments running in Europe and in other continents. However, build a good Grid infrastructure is a complex process requiring many years of experience but its quality is extremely important to increase the number of scientists using this new tool. Nevertheless, current automatic monitoring services do not provide useful information of the infrastructure quality, so it is difficult to improve the current situation, especially for newer infrastructure.

This paper has presented a set of tests performed in two new infrastructures developed with the collaboration of European institutes and located in different regions: EELA-2 and EUAsiaGrid. These tests consist of the periodical submission of synthetic applications and aims at evaluating the overhead to manage such application by the infrastructures.

Using this simple approach during a large time frame of several weeks was possible to identify many problems on the resources available and estimate the overall use of the resources and their reliability. As an example, the most important problem highlighted during the test was the impossibility to execute successfully a parallel application on both infrastructures. Additionally, apparently random problems and big delay to access some resources were observed.

Further test campaigns need to be performed in order to identify all the problems the users could face submitting an application and other synthetic applications need to be developed to simulate the major number of condition. This activity could generate a database of problems and test tools useful to verify new infrastructures.

6 ACKNOWLEDGEMENTS

This work makes use of results produced by EELA-2 and EUAsiaGrid projects, both co-funded by the European Commission within its Seventh Framework Programme. Authors thank the people involved with the set-up and management of both infrastructures during the tests for the provided support.

REFERENCE

[1]   EELA-2 project main page: http://www.eu-eela.eu/
[2]   EUAsiaGrid project main page: http://www.euasiagrid.org/
[3]   BIRD, I., JONES, R. & KEE, K.F. The Organization and Management of Grid Infrastructures, Computer, vol. 42, no. 1, pp. 36-46, Jan. 2009, doi:10.1109/MC.2009.28
[4]   gLite (2008). Documentation. Retrieved February 7, 2009, from:
       http://glite.web.cern.ch/glite/documentation/
[5]   LAURE, E., FISHER S.M., FROHNER, A., GRANDI, C. et al (2006) Programming the Grid with gLite. Computational Methods in Science and Technology. pp.33-45.
[6]   EGEE. (2008). Enabling Grids for E-sciencE. Retrieved February 8, 2009, from: http://www.eu-egee.org/
[7]   MARECHAL, B.M. et al. DNA1.2 – Acceptable Use Policy report. EELA-2 Consortium, 2008. Available at: http://documents.eu-eela.org/record/1016/files/
[8]   EELA-2 Central Services: http://eoc.eu-eela.eu/doku.php?id=central_services

GOCDB4, a New Architecture for the European Grid Infrastructure

Gilles Mathieu and John Casson

STFC, Rutherford Appleton Laboratory, UK

Abstract   The tool known as GOCDB, or Grid Operations Centre Data Base, consists of a central authoritative database which contains static Grid resource and topology related data. It stores information about regions, countries, sites, nodes, services and users, and links this information together in a logical way. Within the past years, GOCDB has imposed itself as a central authoritative repository for topology and site information within EGEE and WLCG. As for all other operational tools, the dramatic evolution of EGEE in order to prepare for a sustainable European Grid Infrastructure imposed many changes on GOCDB architecture. One of these changes is the requirement for a distributed architecture, where a central system can collect and display information maintained by regional instances of the system: in May 2010, GOCDB will become the official central topology repository for the European Grid Initiative (EGI), and will propose a regionalised model that will allow National Grids (NGI) to run their own instance of the system while keeping synchronised with the central EGI repository. These new requirements along with the limitations of GOCDB old model (known as GOCDB-3) led us to adopt an innovative database design based on a pseudo object database model (PROM). In this model, constraints and relations are built using meta-data. This allows for a large flexibility in the database schema, thus enabling different instances of the same tool to store different schemas while remaining interoperable. On top of this, a PHP-written input/output module gets and retrieves data in XML format, making the whole system as standard and configurable as possible. After reviewing GOCDB-3 architecture and explaining its limitations and the reasons for changing, the paper will describe GOCDB-4 inner architecture from general system overview down to technical details on database design, application level and standard interfaces. It will show how flexibility is achieved through the use of XML configuration files. Pros and cons of adopted model will also be assessed. The paper will finally review the overall distributed architecture and distribution scenarios, as well as interactions between GOCDB-4 and similar tools.

S.C. Lin and E. Yen (eds.), *Data Driven e-Science: Use Cases and Successful Applications*   163
of Distributed Computing Infrastructures (ISGC 2010), DOI 10.1007/978-1-4419-8014-4_13,
© Springer Science+Business Media, LLC 2011

1   CONTEXT

1.1   EGEE and WLCG

The general context of the work presented here lies within two worldwide grid computing projects: Enabling Grids for E-science (EGEE) [1] and the Worldwide LCG Computing Grid (WLCG) [2]. The EGEE Production Service infrastructure is a large multi-science Grid infrastructure, federating some 250 resource centres world-wide, providing some 40.000 CPUs and several Petabytes of storage.

WLCG is an application-level grid, running 140 sites in 33 countries, some of them a subset of EGEE together with other Grids like Open Science Grid, in order to do the computing for the four experiments running on the Large Hadron Collider at CERN.

1.2   GOCDB Purpose and Description

The tool known as GOCDB [3] (which stands for Grid Operations Centre Data Base) consists of a central authoritative database which contains static resource and topology related data about EGEE and WLCG. It stores information about regions, countries, sites, nodes, services and users, and links this information together in a logical way.

Information presented in GOCDB is static: data are maintained by the appropriate people with given roles. The reason for these data to be here is the need to have a reference, authoritative list: while dynamic data providers used by Grid middleware – such as BDII [4] or MDS [5] -present lists of resources that are available, GOCDB gives a list of resources that should be available. A short history of GOCDB is presented in [3].

1.3   Related Work

1.3.1   OIM

OSG Information Management System (OIM) [6] can be seen as the equivalent of GOCDB for the Open Science Grid [7] Project. It basically fulfils the same functions, storing and providing information about resources, users, services and downtimes. The main difference between OIM and GOCDB lies on the facility provided by OIM to store and map Virtual Organizations (VO). In EGEE this functionality is provided by the Operations Portal, a.k.a CIC portal [8].

1.3.2   HGSM

Hierarchical Grid Site Management (HGSM) [9] is a web-based management tool that stores static information about grid sites, used within the SEE-GRID project [10]. The set of information contained in HGSM is very similar to what GOCDB stores, and HGSM is often labeled as "a light version of GOCDB". Since some SEE-GRID sites are also EGEE sites, there is a clear overlap in terms of functionalities between the 2 tools, resulting in data duplication. Collaboration is under way for HGSM and GOCDB to be fully interfaced, as part of the work described later in this paper.

1.4. Why a New Architecture?

The third phase of EGEE, started in May 2008, has brought dramatic changes to the project's operational model compared to EGEE-I and EGEE-II [11]. These changes are proposed in order to achieve a successful transition from a central, project-based model to a sustainable infrastructure built on top of each EGEE region, possibly getting down to country level. This final requirement is a result from the European Grid Initiative (EGI) [12] design study where each participating country has the operational components responsibility of maintaining its own National Grid Infrastructure (NGI). These general evolution ideas have been discussed in EGEE-III OAT strategy document [13].

As a consequence of these evolution requirements, GOCDB had to evolve from the central database with a central interface described in [3] to a distributed model. The resulting architecture should allow for all the following points:

- Regional instances should be able to communicate efficiently with one another.
- In the event of a region not willing to host its data, GOCDB should provide a central "catch all" repository to host this information on their behalf.
- There should be a uniform way of accessing the data across all the regional instances, so that even if distributed, the model could also be seen as one.
- Regional instances should be customizable, i.e. adaptable to local needs.
- An adapter should be provided to allow interoperations with those regions that already have their information repository, without asking them to change their system.

2   GOCDB4 ARCHITECTURE AND DESCRIPTION

2.1   *Architecture of a GOCDB4 Module*

2.1.1   Overview

A GOCDB module comprises or the following components:

–   A database, where all data are stored. The system is currently designed to run on an Oracle Database.

–   An API which the database by providing access routines and low level business logic.

–   XML I/O modules which allow data to be sent and received in XML format

–   Web services and Programmatic Interfaces, which present data to third party tools and allow input from external systems

–   A GUI under the form of a web portal

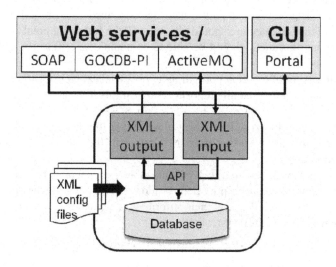

Fig. 1: Overview of a GOCDB module

Most components on top of the database can be configured using XML files, which allows for operating the module without need to change the code at any time. Fig.1 shows how these components interact with one another. They are described in details in the following sections.

2.1.2   Database model

2.1.2.1 Use of the PROM concept and tools

GOCDB4 database model has been designed and implemented following the pseudo-relational object model (PROM) described in [14]. The main idea behind this design is the concept of removing the physical aspects of any database into effectual 'meta-data'. By doing this it makes it possible to maintain links and table information outside of the actual data tables, allowing this data to be accessed in a uniform way, and changed with minimal, or no, changes to the actual design. This allows for faster deployment, standard data access routines, and the ability to grow the system without the need to redesign or re-implement the actual database.

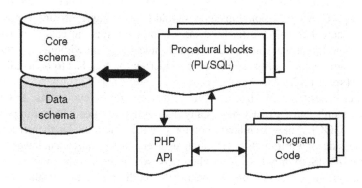

Fig. 2: General schema of a PROM database

The schema described on Fig.2 shows the main architecture of a PROM database as designed by its author. In our GOCDB architecture, the component here described as "program Code" is actually the XML I/O module.

The idea of using a PROM database for GOCDB came out of a design analysis based on the requirements described earlier in this paper. GOCDB previous version, known as GOCDB3, runs on top of a classic relational model as described in [3] and is hosted on an Oracle11g cluster. Distributing this model by splitting it into many instances is not a solution that would allow easy interoperations between these different instances.

The DB design will be required to be a central resource, with the ability to be installed in multiple locations, to cope with multiple grids. It is also understood that each Grid may need or want to vary the design to fit specific needs for that area. PROM seemed a suitable solution to answer these needs because of the inherent flexibility of the model.

2.1.2.2 GOCDB data schema

GOCDB4 data schema is object oriented and is described in [15]. The way PROM works makes it possible to store different objects in the same table provided they have a similar data structure. This is true for many GOCDB objects: Time zones, service types, site statuses are different objects in the PROM way but can all be described by two values: name and description. It is therefore possible to store them in a single database table that will precisely have these fields. This principle then shows a clear differentiation between the data schema, which is the description of all object types as well as possible links between them, and the database schema which shows which tables are used.

2.1.2.3 Benefits and limitations of the PROM approach

One of the benefits of using a PROM model is its easy deployment: installing and configuring a GOCDB regional instance should be as straight forward as possible. Integrating actual constraints to the dataset allows for such an easy deployment. Moreover, modifications can be made on the logical schema without affecting the overall design which is of great interest considering the tool has to be locally customizable (see 2.1.4.2).

Another benefit comes when thinking of possible future evolutions. At time of writing we don't know exactly how many distributed instance will run in parallel, so building GOCDB new architecture on top of a scalable model is then crucial.

On the side of limitations, performances seem to be somewhat lower than a standard RDBMS, mainly because of the many SQL joins that the model imposes. This is not an issue considering the relatively small size of the database we are dealing with, yet some specific queries have to be cached if we want to guarantee a fast access through the web portal or programmatic interface.

Another limitation to PROM is inherently linked to its flexibility: by not imposing constraints at database level it becomes easier to "break" the schema if PROM principles implemented at application level are not followed. To prevent that from happening data access should only be done through the PROM API and never inserted or modified manually in the database.

2.1.2.4 Adaptations and specific use

One of our key needs for GOCDB4 which is not provided by PROM is the notion of cardinality in object links. From a semantic point of view, some objects can only be linked to 1 object of a given type (e.g. a site to a time zone), while some can be linked to many (e.g. a site to a service endpoint). Even trickier, we needed to define a "level 2" cardinality, e.g. a site can be linked to many groups, but to only one group of each type (one country, one ROC, etc.). This has been achieved by introducing this cardinality in the gocdb_schema.xml description file (see 2.1.4.1). This cardinality parameter is then taken into account by the application whenever the need arises to create or modify links between objects.

While low level PROM API provides most of needed routines (see [14]), we found out that one was crucially missing, especially after introducing the notion of cardinality: the ability to simply remove a link between two PROM objects without necessarily deleting one of these objects. The method has consequently been implemented and added to the PROM API, and then interfaced with our code in a similar way to other routines.

2.1.3   Components Description

2.1.3.1 XML Input and Output
Interfacing between database, PROM API and higher level application is done through 2 modules called XML input and XML output. As the name suggest they provide or get data in XML format to/from the database.

XML output creates XML from a database query. A SQL query is read from a configuration file then executed against the database. Each row is then inserted into an XML template element. This template element is repeatedly filled with each row's results and added to the final XML file as described on Fig.3. Parameters can be used and passed to the application when calling the module to create the appropriate query plan.

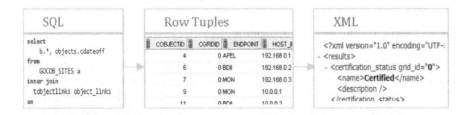

Fig. 3: From SQL to XML using the XML output module

XML input works in a similar way with flows in the other direction. It gets XML files, parses them according to predefined templates and calls appropriate PROM routines to insert, edit or delete objects and links in the PROM database.

2.1.3.2 Standard interfaces
GOCDB4 comes with a set of standard interfaces through which data can be gathered or input. The first of those interfaces is a REST [16] interface presenting XML formatted data over https. This interface, known as GOCDB Programmatic Interface or GOCDB-PI, is described in [17]. This interface uses XML templates and SQL queries defined within the XML output module. The GOCDB-PI is mainly used by third party tools that need to collect GOCDB information like site details, services or downtimes.

It is also planned to provide a SOAP [18] interface which will fulfill similar functions, and in addition will be used as the main interface to synchronize the central instance of GOCDB with its regionalized counterparts (see 2.2).

Finally, an Apache ActiveMQ [19] interface is planned in order to interface GOCDB with EGEE messaging system [20]. The main application use case would be to send through ActiveMQ downtime information to the EGEE message bus, thus allowing client application to build calendars or notification systems as appropriate.

2.1.3.3 Web portal

GOCDB4 web portal is a set of pages and scripts that display GOCDB information and allow for modification through a simple web GUI. The code is as application independent as possible, and most of GOCDB specific features are done at configuration level (see 2.1.4).

Initial requirements about the regionalisation of the tool imply that this portal should work on both read-only mode for the central instance and read-write mode for the regional instances (see 2.2). This is also achieved through parameterization in order to keep the code similar between two types of deployment.

GOCDB4 web portal provides a user management system based on X509 certificate DN authentication coupled with role management.

2.1.4 Configuration and Customization

2.1.4.1 Use of configuration files

Most of GOCDB configuration is made through a set of XML files in order to allow for easy changes without the need to touch the code. We've seen above that XML I/O modules were using XML templates to determine the format of the data to send – or to receive. On a more general tone, all GOCDB components work in a similar way in order to keep the code generic.

Initial deployment of a GOCDB module is also facilitated by a schema description file (gocdb_schema.xml) which describes in XML format the objects and classes hierarchy, the properties for each class (transformed into database fields) as well as the possible links between objects and their cardinality.

2.1.4.2 Data schema and components customization

PROM's flexibility allows for the data schema to be modified without necessarily breaking the initial version or over-complicating the design, which is a difficult challenge when using relational databases. Since object definition and relations are meta-data, new object types can be added and new link types created without the slightest modification made in the physical database. Customizing GOCDB4 schema in order to adapt to local needs doesn't imply to change the database schema, but only the logical schema.

Equally, it is possible to customize GOCDB interfaces by adding new XML output templates or modifying existing ones with little effort and no coding at all.

2.2 Interactions between Modules: The Ventral/Regional Architecture

As described in 1.4, GOCDB needs to run as a central system relaying information about EGI resources and topology while allowing the actual input system to be distributed and customized. This architecture is described in Fig.4 where three use cases are highlighted:

- Region 1: A region installs and runs its own GOCDB instance. It synchronizes with the central service by pushing its data through standard GOCDB4 interfaces.
- Region 2: A region uses the centrally provided input system
- Region 3: A region uses another tool to operate its topology information and synchronizes with the central GOCDB through an adapter.

The way the PROM model is designed allows for a differentiation of data stored in the same basic structure through the mean of a collection id or grid id: different objects can be stored in the same table and have different collection ids, thus referring to a different set of data. This is how data hosted in the central GOCDB system will be "logically split" into different regions. Regionalizing one of these subsets is then a simple question of separating from the main DB all data with the collection ID corresponding to this region.

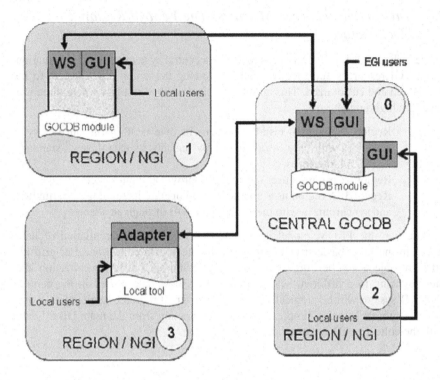

Fig. 4: Architecture of regional and central GOCDB

3 FUTURE WORK AND CONCLUSION

3.1 Future Developments

Current Version of GOCB4 is based on Oracle and low level PROM API is provided as an Oracle package of stored functions and procedures. Yet running an Oracle server is a non negligible limitation to GOCDB distribution, mainly because not all National Grids own an Oracle license. There are consequently plans to provide a MySQL version of the system, which will require the low level API to be rewritten.

Another axis for future development is related to the possible integration of GOCDB to other EGI operation tools. This includes the integration of GOCDB and CIC Operations portal [8] under a common interoperable toolkit for grid operations, starting with the integration of a common central human interface allowing users to access both central services through a single entry point, and then providing interoperable back ends for distribution to NGIs as a single package. Such development will require effort at data representation level as well as at interface and data transfer level.

Finally, some work can be done towards standardization of topology data representation. This is the continuation of a design study to better interface dynamic information systems such as the EGEE BDII with static repositories such as GOCDB. This work would require defining a standard schema for storing information (e.g. sites) as well as defining and implementing possible interfacing between static/dynamic models.

3.2 Early Analysis of the Benefits and Downsides of the Change

At the time of writing it is difficult to assess the global impact of the change from GOCDB3 to GOCDB4. The new system has to run in production for at least a few months before any useful metrics can be produced. Yet some benefits can already be noticed. Packaging of GOCDB4 module has eased standardization of the code and GOCDB release process. Additionally, the use of a PROM database has already helped coping quickly and easily with schema changes and new requests.

The only obvious downside to the system to be observed at the moment is the relative complexity of the system design: although PROM implements efficient concepts it is sometimes counter intuitive to people used to relational models. Yet experience has shown that once understood, the system is quickly adopted by whoever deploys it and initial reticence should not be considered a showstopper.

REFERENCES

[1]   Laure E, Jones R, "Enabling Grids for e-Science: The EGEE Project". EGEE-PUB-2009-
      001, http://cdsweb.cern.ch/record/1128647
[2]   The Worldwide LHC Computing Grid (WLCG), http://lcg.web.cern.ch/LCG
[3]   Mathieu G, Richards A, Gordon J, Del Cano Novales C, Colclough P, Viljoen
      M:"GOCDB, a Topology Repository for a Worldwide Grid Infrastructure", in Proceedings
      of Computing in High Energy and Nuclear Physics (CHEP09), Prague, Czech Republic,
      March 2009
[4]   Berkeley Database Information Index (BDII), 12
      https://twiki.cern.ch/twiki/bin/view/EGEE/BDII
[5]   Czajkowski K, Fitzgerald S, Foster I and Kesselman, C, "Grid information services for dis-
      tributed resource sharing" in Proceedings of the 10th IEEE Int. Symposium on High per-
      formance distributed computing (HPDC-10), San Francisco, CA, 7–9 August 2001
[6]   OSG Information management System (OIM), http://oim.grid.iu.edu
[7]   The Open Science Grid Consortium (OSG), http://www.opensciencegrid.org
[8]   Aidel O, Cavalli A, Cordier H, L'Orphelin C, Mathieu G, Pagano A, Reynaud S, "CIC por-
      tal: a Collaborative and Scalable Integration Platform for High Availability Grid Opera-
      tions", in Proceedings of The 8th IEEE/ACM International Conference on Grid Computing
      (Grid 2007), Austin TX, US, Sept. 2007
[9]   Hierarchical Grid Site Management (HGSM), http://hgsm.sourceforge.net
[10] South Eastern European Grid Infrastructure Development (SEE-GRID),http://www.see-
      grid.org
[11] Cordier H, Mathieu G, Schaer F, Novak J, Nyczyk P, Schulz M and Tsai MH, "Grid Op-
      erations: the evolution of operational model over the first year", In Proceedings of Comput-
      ing in High Energy and Nuclear Physics (CHEP06), Mumbai, India, 2006.
[12] The European Grid Initiative (EGI) design study, http://web.eu-egi.eu
[13] Casey J et al, "Operations Automation Strategy", https://edms.cern.ch/document/927171
[14] Colclough P and Mathieu G, "A pseudo object database model and its applications on a
      highly complex distributed architecture", In Proceedings of the IARA 1st international con-
      ference on advances in databases, knowledge and data applications (DBKDA 2009), Can-
      cun, Mexico, March 2009
[15] GOCDB4 data schema, http://goc.grid.sinica.edu.tw/gocwiki/GOCDB4_DB_Schema
[16] Representational State Transfer (REST) architecture, http://en.wikipedia.org/wiki/REST
[17] GOCDB-PI technical documentation,
      http://goc.grid.sinica.edu.tw/gocwiki/GOCDB_Technical_Documentation
[18] SOAP, http://en.wikipedia.org/wiki/SOAP
[19] Apache ActiveMQ, http://activemq.apache.org
[20] Casey J et al, "MSG - A messaging system for efficient and scalable grid monitoring",
      EGEE User Forum, March 09.

An APEL Tool Based CPU Usage Accounting Infrastructure for Large Scale Computing Grids

Ming Jiang, Cristina Del Cano Novales, Gilles Mathieu, John Casson, William Rogers and John Gordon

e-Science Centre, Science and Technology Facilities Council, UK

Abstract   The APEL (Accounting Processor for Event Logs) is the fundamental tool for the CPU usage accounting infrastructure deployed within the WLCG and EGEE Grids. In these Grids, jobs are submitted by users to computing resources via a Grid Resource Broker (e.g. gLite Workload Management System). As a log processing tool, APEL interprets logs of Grid gatekeeper (e.g. globus) and batch system logs (e.g. PBS, LSF, SGE and Condor) to produce CPU job accounting records identified with Grid identities. These records provide a complete description of usage of computing resources by user's jobs. APEL publishes accounting records into an accounting record repository at a Grid Operations Centre (GOC) for the access from a GUI web tool. The functions of log files parsing, records generation and publication are implemented by the APEL Parser, APEL Core, and APEL Publisher component respectively. Within the distributed accounting infrastructure, accounting records are transported from APEL Publishers at Grid sites to either a regionalised accounting system or the central one by choice via a common ActiveMQ message broker network. This provides an open transport layer for other accounting systems to publish relevant accounting data to a central accounting repository via a unified interface provided an APEL Publisher and also will give regional/National Grid Initiatives (NGIs) Grids the flexibility in their choice of accounting system. The robust and secure delivery of accounting record messages at an NGI level and between NGI accounting instances and the central one are achieved by using configurable APEL Publishers and an ActiveMQ message broker network.

1   INTRODUCTION

A computational Grid is a large scale virtual information processing infrastructure, which is spanning technologies, platforms, and organisations. In this infrastructure, various distributed information processing resources are "shared together and a common collaboration is established across multiple administrative organisations" [1].

In any computational Grid, a reliable and efficient accounting mechanism is the key to measure its resource usage and consumption accurately and provide ac-

S.C. Lin and E. Yen (eds.), *Data Driven e-Science: Use Cases and Successful Applications of Distributed Computing Infrastructures (ISGC 2010)*, DOI 10.1007/978-1-4419-8014-4_14,
© Springer Science+Business Media, LLC 2011

countable and valuable information for Grid resource providers and their users to optimise the provision and usage of these resources respectively [2].

In this paper, an open and flexible distributed CPU usage accounting infrastructure for the WLCG and EGEE Grids is introduced. The paper is organised as follows: In Section 2, the WLCG and EGEE Grids are introduced and the accounting mode of CPU usage by Virtual Organisation (VO) users of the Grids are explained briefly. In Section 3, APEL, a CPU usage accounting information collection, publication and storage tool is introduced and explained. In Section 4, the analysis design, implementation, and evaluation of CPU usage accounting infrastructure for the WLCG and EGEE Grids is reported. Finally, Section 5 presents future research topics and concludes the paper.

2 WLCG AND EGEE GRIDS

2.1 Grid Infrastructure

Historically the birth and development of Grid computing technology was largely driven by the High Energy Physics (HEP) community who demands huge amount of storage and computing resources for experimental data storage and analysis [3]. Most recently, the Worldwide LHC Computing Grid (WLCG) is built for the "entire" HEP community to use the Large Hadron Collider (LHC), the largest scientific instrument on the planet, at CERN to discover new fundamental particles and fields and analyse their properties [4]. It is estimated that around 15 Petabytes (15 million Gigabytes) of data will be produced by LHC experiments and its detectors. This data will be distributed around the globe, accessed and analysed by thousands of scientists worldwide.

Similar to the development history of Grid computing technology, the Enabling Grids for E-sciencE (EGEE) project started as a European infrastructure to open Grid facilities to multi-disciplinary applications [5]. The European part of the WLCG relies on the EGEE Grid as the underlying infrastructure provider [6]. The EGEE Production Service infrastructure federates 250 resource centres worldwide, providing some 40,000 CPUs and several Petabytes of storage.

2.2   The Role of Accounting in the Grids

In WLCG/EGEE Grids, jobs are submitted by users to computing resources via a Grid Resource Broker (e.g. gLite Workload Management System). The usage of these resources is measured by recording the CPU usage of each user's jobs to provide a complete description of usage of resources. Note that apart from the CPU usage accounting, there is also another purpose of accounting, such as the storage usage accounting and more general "Grid Services" accounting for the usage of core services, middleware and software licenses rather than CPU usage [7].

3   THE APEL ACCOUNTING TOOL

3.1   CPU Usage Accounting

The APEL (Accounting Processor for Event Logs) is a CPU usage accounting tool designed and deployed for the WLCG/EGEE Grids [8]. As a log processing application, it interprets logs of Grid gatekeeper (e.g. globus) and batch system logs (e.g. PBS, LSF, SGE and Condor) to produce CPU job accounting records identified with Grid identities. APEL publishes accounting records into a centralised repository at a Grid Operations Centre (GOC) for access from a GUI web tool. The functions of log files parsing, record generation and publication are implemented by the APEL Parser, APEL Core, and APEL Publisher component respectively.

Accounting Records Schema

APEL describes accounting data using two different schemas: an individual Grid job record, based on the Open Grid Forum Usage Record (OGF-UR) v.1 specification, and an aggregated record, based on a proposal for the OGF-UR v.2 specification. An individual Grid job accounting record describes the resources consumed by a single executing job. It contains information about the submitting user, the executing Site, the CPU usage amongst other job information (Table 1). An aggregated accounting record describes the resource usage by a collection of Grid jobs (Table 2 and 3).

APEL distinguishes between two different sets of accounting summaries. Anonymous data is public and describes resources consumed per site/VO/month (Table 2). User level data contains resource usage information for individual users (Table 3). Access to this data must be restricted as it contains personal information such as userDN and VOMS authorization information.

Table 1: Individual Job Records

Column name	Type
RecordIdentity	VARCHAR(255)
ExecutingSite	VARCHAR(50)
LocalJobID	VARCHAR(50)
LCGJobID	VARCHAR(50)
LocalUserID	VARCHAR(50)
LCGUserID	VARCHAR(255)
LCGUserVO	VARCHAR(50)
ElapsedTime	VARCHAR(30)
BaseCpuTime	VARCHAR(30)
ElapsedTimeSeconds	INTEGER
BaseCpuTimeSeconds	INTEGER
StartTime	VARCHAR(30)
StopTime	VARCHAR(30)
StartTimeUTC	VARCHAR(30)
StopTimeUTC	VARCHAR(30)
StartTimeEpoch	INTEGER
StopTimeEpoch	INTEGER
ExecutingCE	VARCHAR(50)
MemoryReal	INTEGER
MemoryVirtual	INTEGER
SpecInt2000	INTEGER
SpecFloat2000	INTEGER
EventDate	DATE
EventTime	TIME
MeasurementDate	DATE
MeasurementTime	TIME

Table 2: Anonymous Summary Record

Column name	Type
ExecutingSite	varchar(50)
LCGUserVO	varchar(255)
Njobs	int(11)
SumCPU	decimal(10,0)
NormSumCPU	decimal(10,0)
SumWCT	decimal(10,0)
NormSumWCT	decimal(10,0)
Month	int(11)
Year	int(11)
RecordStart	date
RecordEnd	date

Table 3: User-level Summary Record

Column name	Type
ExecutingSite	varchar(50)
LCGUserVO	varchar(255)
UserDN	varchar(255)
PrimaryGroup	varchar(255)
PrimaryRole	varchar(255)
Njobs	int(11)
SumCPU	decimal(10,0)
NormSumCPU	decimal(10,0)
SumWCT	decimal(10,0)
NormSumWCT	decimal(10,0)
Month	int(11)
Year	int(11)
RecordStart	date
RecordEnd	date

Encryption of UserDN

As part of the accounting data, APEL gathers and publishes the X.509 certificate DN of the submitting user. This information is considered to be personal data and therefore there is a requirement to protect it during transportation and when it is stored.

APEL encrypts user DN information based on a public/private key pair and a randomising function that reduces the likelihood of repeatable patterns arising in the encrypted string.

Before encryption of the DN string, two random numbers n1 and n2 are generated by the Bouncy Castle Crypto pseudo-random number generator and added to the input string according to the following format: *n1*DN_string*n2*.

The new string is then encrypted using a 1024-bit RSA key with PKCS1 v.1.5 padding. The size of the encryption key and the type of padding determines the length of the data that can be encrypted; in this case, the limit is 117 bytes. Doubling the size of the RSA key to 2048 bits would allow an input string of 245 bytes, but at the cost of greatly increasing the time needed to generate and operate the strings.

Although the 1024-bit key is enough to encrypt most of the user DNs in the EGEE project, in some occasions a longer DN is encountered and an algorithm is applied to shorten this input string before the encryption is applied. The random numbers are removed and common patterns in the DN (i.e. /OU=personal certificate/) can be reduced to simple strings (/ou=pc/).

To identify the encryption scheme used for decryption, the algorithm version header is added as a prefix to the encrypted cipher string. In the current version of APEL, the version header is *APEL V.0.2*.

Once the encrypted data has been published into the APEL server, it is stored in an offline database with restricted access. Only then the data can be decrypted using the header information together with the APEL private key. The random information is then removed using regular expression analysis.

CPU Time Normalization

As the CPU performance varies greatly between different resources, even within a single site, a reference is needed to provide a fair comparison of resource usage consumption.

APEL scales CPU time to a reference benchmark of 1K.SI2K hours. Each Grid site publishes a value for the CPU speed (described by the SpecInt2000 performance benchmark) for each site cluster as part of the site's GLUE schema. When generating accounting records, APEL interrogates the site Grid Index Information Service (GIIS) to obtain this data. Each individual record will then contain the CPU speed equivalent from the worker node where the job was executed. Once the record has been published into the APEL Accounting Server, the CPU time can then be normalized to the reference value (1K.SI2K Hours) by applying the following calculation:

Norm CPUTime = Glue Host Benchmark SI00/SI2 K * Base CPU Time, where SI2KRef is 1000. This procedure should be treated as an approximation as most sites are not homogeneous and describing a cluster by the performance of an average CPU is not entirely sufficient.

3.2   Scalable and Secure Transportation Mechanism

The APEL tool is at the time of writing in a transition phase. Current production system still uses of R-GMA (Relational Grid Monitoring Architecture) [9] as the transport mechanism for moving accounting records generated on each Grid client site to a centralised repository at a GOC. R-GMA Primary Producers for publishing records from each Grid site and a Secondary Producer for aggregating records into a centralised repository. A general topic publication and subscription messaging model enables distributed components in a system to publish and subscribe messages to/from a well defined topic that can be viewed as a virtual destination and source of messages. The definition of topics and low level reliable delivery of messages among components can be achieved by using a concrete message broker implementation to this model.

In the work reported here, such a model is investigated and implemented with a view to construct a distributed accounting infrastructure, which will includes a large number of NGIs and support flexible queries on accounting records generated by VOs across multiple NGIs.

3.3   Integration with External Accounting Systems

Some regions within EGEE, as well as some partner projects, have their own accounting infrastructure deployed. They are namely: INFN-Grid, which are using DGAS [10], NorduGrid with SGAS [11] and the OSG with GRATIA [12]. Getting accounting information from these regions is done by these systems publishing already processed data and summaries to the APEL front end.

4   AN OPEN AND FLEXIBLE ACCOUNTING INFRASTRUCTURE

4.1   New Requirements from EGI and NGI

The third phase of EGEE, started in May 2008, brings dramatic changes to the project's operational model compared to EGEE-I and EGEE-II. These changes are proposed in order to achieve a successful transition from a central, project-based model to a sustainable infrastructure built on top of each EGEE region, possibly breaking down to country level. This final requirement is a result of a European Grid Initiative (EGI) [13] design study where each participating country is given the responsibility of maintaining its own National Grid Infrastructure (NGI). Ideas for a general evolution in the years to come are discussed in the EGEE-III OAT strategy document [14].

This redefinition of the European Grid landscape induces many changes in all tools and services running on top of it, and APEL is no exception.

One of the first requirements of the system is to allow for each future NGI to have their own accounting repository should they wish to. This resulted in the design of a multi-level accounting system that will be described below. Along with changes in the architecture, distributing APEL massively across EGEE regions also implies a new design where automation, simplicity and scalability are key factors.

Knowing that some regions or partner projects use their own accounting system and will continue to do so, integration and interoperation is also a major requirement. Since there is a need for a central accounting repository for EGI, all participating NGIs should be able to report to it, whatever tool they use. This involves opening the system in such way that accounting data can transit from external tools to APEL in an easy way.

Another requirement lies in the generalized use of a shared communication mechanism between EGEE tools, which took the shape of a backbone message bus [15]. The replacement of the APEL transport layer has become one of its key evolutions, as explained in previous section.

Finally and in the long term, the general move towards standardization of accounting records format and the opening of data flows might result in a requirement for a standard infrastructure, which will also be described later in this paper.

4.2   Infrastructure Design

Based on the analysis in the previous section, the design of an open and flexible distributed accounting infrastructure aims to achieve these goals:

1. Multiple levels of publication should be supported (country -> region -> central),
2. Different regions should use a unified publication interface,
3. No significant operational changes to the existing Grid client side publication should arise,
4. A region should optionally be able to set up its local Accounting Server or use the Central Accounting Cache, and
5. The system should allow for potential interoperability and integration with other Grid middleware (e.g. Monitoring).

The infrastructure supports three major accounting publication modes: regionalized, non-regionalized and integration with the third-part accounting systems. However, due to the lack of available efficient distributed database query mechanism, a super central records cache of NGI or local Grid accounting instances will be set up to support accounting records queries across VOs.

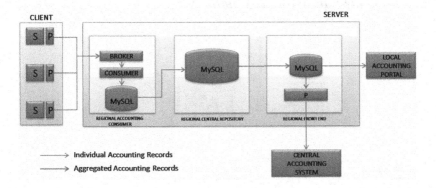

Fig. 1: A Regionalised Accounting System Connected to the Central Accounting System

Figure 1 illustrates the architecture of a single regionalised accounting system. The system may optionally connect to a central accounting system to publish an aggregated summary of accounting records. The central accounting system is illustrated in Figure 2, in which, Region A is "non-regionalised" direct publication of Grid sites; Region B is "regionalised" as in Figure 1; and Region C is a third party accounting system that is integrated into the infrastructure via a unified publication interface. An important design feature of the infrastructure is that the scalability of it can be increased by replicating the function components of a central accounting system into regional accounting systems that only republish aggregated accounting record summaries into the central accounting system.

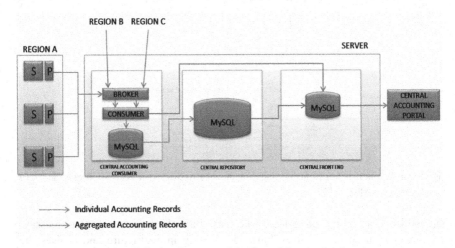

Fig.2: Three Accounting Publication Sources and the Central Accounting System

4.3   *Implementation and Evaluations*

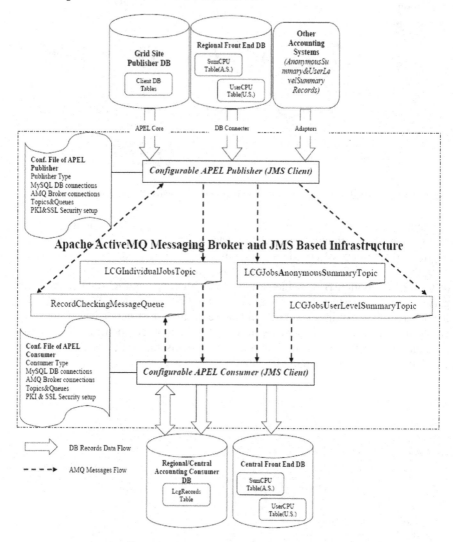

Fig. 3: An Accounting infrastructure based on Apache ActiveMQ Messaging Broker and Java Message Service APIs

The work reported here investigates the feasibility of adopting a general messaging model to implement a distributed accounting infrastructure and utilises the Apache ActiveMQ [16] message broker and Java Message Service (JMS) API based clients to implement the accounting records transport layer of APEL for robust delivery of accounting record messages. In this implementation, while the ActiveMQ message brokers will manage the delivery of accounting records message with secure mechanisms (SSL and PKI based authentication and DN based authorization), at a NGI level and between NGI accounting instances and the central records cache, the original user interfaces for existing APEL clients will remain consistent.

As illustrated in Figure 3, from top to bottom, there are three key groups of components in the implemented infrastructure:

1. Accounting record sources (see Section 4.2),
2. A configurable APEL accounting publisher and consumer (JMS Clients), and
3. Accounting record destinations (a regionalised accounting system or the central accounting system).

Although the ActiveMQ broker itself and its security configuration is not explicitly presented in the figure, various topics and queues of the accounting records messaging system are highlighted as they are defined and supported by a concrete message broker. The connection and configuration information of a concrete broker is set up in configuration files of APEL accounting publisher and consumer.

Another feature of this implementation is that the accounting messages are sent in a predefined plain text format (using key-value pairs). This allows interoperability with consumers other than the APEL client; provided the other client is authorized to use the broker network. This feature allows integration with other Grid middleware for wider applications.

Preliminary testing of the implementation with production CPU usage records demonstrates that the transport mechanism of the distributed accounting infrastructure is reliable and promising. More large scale testing is designed and prepared as the paper is being prepared.

5   CONCLUSION AND FUTURE WORK

In this paper, an APEL tool based CPU usage accounting infrastructure for the WLCG/EGEE Grids is presented. The infrastructure is designed and implemented to be open and flexible to regionalised accounting requirements in future NGI environments. Within the infrastructure, accounting records are transported from Grid sites APEL publishers to either a regionalised accounting system or the central one by choice via a common ActiveMQ broker network. The record messages can be generated according to a common format and delivered as plain text messages so that it may enable another Grid middleware (e.g. monitoring) to consume accounting information, provided it is authorised to connect to the common broker network.

In the short term, further investigations on the scalability (e.g. network of brokers) and fault tolerance features (e.g. failover pair, master/slave backup) of ActiveMQ will be conducted to construct a robust and durable accounting service.

Within the first months of EGI, there will be a strong validation test for all operational tools and systems within the current infrastructure. At that time, further work on interoperations with other Grid infrastructure will potentially join the efforts on distributing the system across NGIs.

In the longer term, progressing towards an open, standard and interoperable accounting system leads the way to the deployment of a Resource Usage Service (RUS) [17] as defined within the Open Grid Forum (OGF) [18]. Discussions and collaborations have been started in this area between APEL developers and the OGF RUS working group. It is expected that further inspirations and proposals may be produced in the future.

REFERENCES

[1]   I. Foster and C. Kesselman and S. Tuecke, The Anatomy of the Grid: Enabling Scalable Virtual Organizations, International Journal of Supercomputer Applications, 15(3), 2001.

[2]   Martin Waldburger, Matthias Göhner, Helmut Reiser, Gabi Dreo Rodosek and Burkhard Stiller: Evaluation of an Accounting Model for Dynamic Virtual Organizations. Journal of Grid Computing, Springer, Vol. Online First, No. DOI: 10.1007/s10723-008-9109-9, pages 1-19, Netherlands, September 2008.

[3]   The Large Hadron Collider (LHC), http://lhc.web.cern.ch

[4]   The Worldwide LHC Computing Grid (WLCG), http://lcg.web.cern.ch/LCG

[5]   Enabling Grids for E-SciencE (EGEE), http://www.eu-egee.org

[6]   Ian Bird, Bob Jones and Kerk F. Kee: The Organization and Management of Grid Infrastructures, pages 36-46, Computer, IEEE Computer Society, January 2009.

[7]   M. A. Pettipher, A. Khan, T.W. Robinson and X. Chan: Review of Accounting and Usage Monitoring, Final Report, e-Infrastructure Programme, 17 September 2007, JISC.

[8]   http://goc.grid.sinica.edu.tw/gocwiki/ApelHome

[9]   http://www.r-gma.org

[10]   http://www.to.infn.it/grid/accounting/main.html

[11]   http://www.sgas.se

[12]   The Gratia Accounting System, https://twiki.grid.iu.edu/bin/view/MonitoringIn formation/WebHome#Gratia_Accounting

[13]   European Grid Initiative, http://web.eu-egi.eu

[14]   J. Casey, et al, Operations Automation Strategy, https://edms.cern.ch/document/927171

[15]   J. Casey, et al, MSG - A messaging system for efficient and scalable grid monitoring, EGEE User Forum, March 09.

[16]   Apache ActiveMQ, http://activemq.apache.org

[17]   Resource Usage Service, http://www.ogf.org/gf/group_info/view.php?group=rus-wg

[18]   OGF, www.ogf.org

HLRmon, a Tool for Advanced Visualization of Resource Utilization

Enrico Fattibene[1], Tiziana Ferrari[1], Luciano Gaido[2], Giuseppe Misurelli[1] and Peter Solagna[3]

1. Istituto Nazionale di Fisica Nucleare CNAF, Bologna, Italy
2. Istituto Nazionale di Fisica Nucleare, Torino, Italy
3. Istituto Nazionale di Fisica Nucleare, Padova, Italy

Abstract   Monitoring resource exploitation in Grids is challenging due to the large scale and the distributed nature of the infrastructure. For this reason, the role played by the accounting service that collects information about resource usage, is crucial. Visualization tools are responsible for providing users – such as Grid managers, site administrators, VO managers and Grid end-users – with usage records aggregated into different views. In this paper we describe HLRmon, a web portal which provides a set of user-friendly views of accounting information gathered by the Distributed Grid Accounting Service (DGAS).

1   INTRODUCTION

Grid computing connects computers that are spread over a wide geographic area, allowing their computing power, data, instruments and storage space to be shared through harmonized interfaces regardless of their location and their specific implementation. It enables the resources of thousands of different computers hosted in university departments and data centers, national facilities, and even desktop PCs, to be combined to create a global computing facility.

In national Grids the accounting service is of paramount importance and is responsible of handling a huge amount of data, e.g. hundred thousands of records on a daily basis, as shown in Fig. 1.

Accounting information needs to be properly visualized in order to make this large amount of data useful to a human user. To satisfy this requirement, an accounting portal, called HLRmon, was designed and implemented to store and aggregate accounting data through a graphical user interface that intuitively guides the user to extract the exact subset of relevant information. HLRmon relies on the Distributed Grid Accounting Service (DGAS), a Grid middleware integrated and interoperating with the gLite Grid middleware distribution [1].

S.C. Lin and E. Yen (eds.), *Data Driven e-Science: Use Cases and Successful Applications of Distributed Computing Infrastructures (ISGC 2010)*, DOI 10.1007/978-1-4419-8014-4_15, © Springer Science+Business Media, LLC 2011

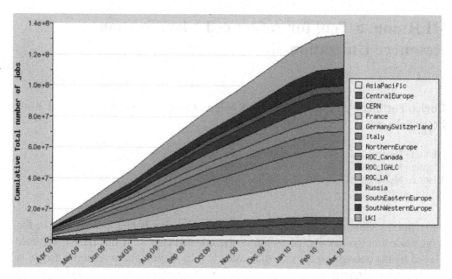

Fig. 1: Job workflow distribution per Region in the EGEE-III European Grid infrastructure (April 2009 – March 2010)[1].

This paper presents the architecture and implementation of HLRmon[2], as well as an extended version of the tool tailored for the Italian WLCG community to give Grid managers not only a report of computing usage, but also related information concerning the amount of installed storage capacity and its usage for a specified subset of Grid sites and VOs. While CPU usage records are collected by the DGAS system, storage accounting records are locally gathered by means of ad-hoc probes executed locally on the different storage elements deployed at sites. Ultimately both computing and storage records are stored in the HLRmon RDBMS for persistent storage and subsequent processing.

With respect to computing resources the HLRmon graphical user interface plots CPU and Wall clock time consumption normalized by the average compute power of logical CPUs from the local farm – expressed in terms of different compute benchmarks – provided by the gLite Information System. HLRmon graphs allow to visually compare the aggregated usage information against the overall available amount of installed capacity that was negotiated with the resource providers. This extended version of the HLRmon portal was originally implemented to report about the usage of the Italian WLCG Tier-1 and Tier-2 sites, but is easily applicable to other usage scenarios.

This paper is structured as follows. Section 2 provides information about the design of the HLRmon tool, while Section 3 provides an overview of the DGAS

---

[1] Source: EGEE accounting portal
    (http://www3.egee.cesga.es/gridsite/accounting/CESGA/egee_view.html)

[2] HLRmon Portal: https://dgas.cnaf.infn.it/hlrmon/welcome/welcome-lhc.html

accounting service used by HLRmon to gather usage records. Section 4 provides an insight into the process for accounting data acquisition, while Section 5 complements the HLRmon overview by illustrating the graphical user interface of the tool. The additional features added to HLRmon for WLCG accounting are detailed in Section 6, while in the following section HLRmon features are compared to other existing tools. Section 8 concludes the paper.

2 ARCHITECTURE

The HLRmon architecture, shown in Fig. 2, comprises different modules: a set of data collectors, persistent data storage, a data aggregation layer and a data presentation layer.

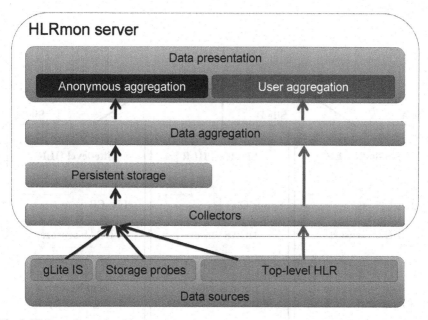

Fig. 2: HLRmon layered architecture.

At the bottom layer collectors retrieve anonymous aggregated accounting information from a usage records archive, named HLR (Home Location Register), to be stored in a local database. The aggregation layer is then responsible for data manipulation to produce charts and tables that are displayed by the graphical interface. Aggregated usage records for a specific user are retrieved from the HLR database at run-time and are just accessible by authorized users.

The HLRmon extension for WLCG resources includes a collector of storage accounting data retrieved by probes running on the SRM instances managed at a given site. Storage usage records are in XML format. An additional collector is responsible for retrieving GLUE attributes [2] about the weighted average computing power of a logical CPU from the gLite Information System.

3   ACCOUNTING INFRASTRUCTURE WITH DGAS

The Distributed Grid Accounting System (DGAS) [3][4][5] is a distributed tool for the implementation of national Grid accounting infrastructures; it is responsible for collecting, aggregating and storing the usage records, which are then displayed in the HLRmon web portal. DGAS is currently deployed in the Italian Grid Infrastructure, comprising 57 sites at the time of writing.

DGAS is designed to be geographically distributed and scalable. As illustrated in Fig. 3 the deployment model includes two main components: sensors and repositories.

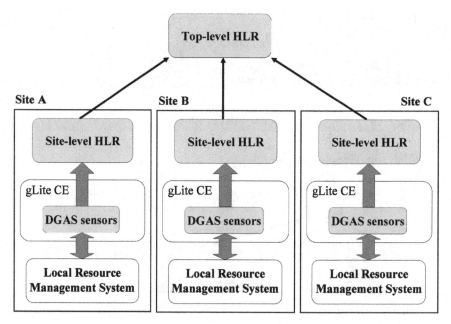

Fig. 3: Example of database hierarchy for the collection of usage records with DGAS in a national Grid infrastructure.

Sensors are installed on the Computing Element (CE) to collect accounting information and convert it into usage records. DGAS sensors are available for many different Local Resource Management Systems, such as Portable Batch System (PBS) and Load Sharing Facility (LSF).

DGAS collects accounting information for every job run by the batch system. On a daily timescale this produces a huge amount of usage records that need to be managed and manipulated efficiently. For example, the Italian production Grid runs about 100*103 jobs per day, totaling 60 million jobs during the past two years.

In order to scale with this huge amount of data, DGAS implements a hierarchy of data repositories, the HLRs, which are the building blocks that persistently storage usage records for future processing. At the bottom layer of the hierarchy site-level of VO-level HLRs (first-level HLRs) store usage records collected by sites. In parallel, at an upper layer of the hierarchy, second-level HLRs gather usage records from the first level HLRs. This approach can be recursively applied to implement an arbitrary number of layers according to the need. This results in a balanced and scalable architecture with multiple storage points. For example, the Italian accounting infrastructure implements a two layer database hierarchy, where the top-level HLRs are responsible of exchanging records with external Grid accounting domains, while usage records come either from multi-site HLRs aggregating information from several small sites, or per-site HLRs (deployed by the medium and large sites, such as the WLCG Tier-1 and Tier-2 sites).

4 HLRMON DATA ACQUISITION PROCESS

The main source of data for the HLRmon tool is a dedicated top-level HLR, which provides comprehensive information by aggregating records for all sites. Given the database size, HLRmon query latencies are crucial to expose a user-friendly web interface. Queries access a restricted set of the database. In addition, the database is mirrored from the top-level HLR in order to make data accessible even during maintenance periods and in case of outages of the top-level HLR.

The HLRmon data acquisition procedure gathers new accounting data from the top-level HLR on a daily base through the generic DGAS client, which performs SQL queries directly on the HLR job table named jobTransSummary. The usage records contained in this table follow the format recommendations of the OGF (Open Grid Forum) Usage Record Working Group [6]. Consequently, HLRmon aggregated information can be in principle retrieved by other accounting services following the OGF standard requirements. The data are aggregated directly as result of the SQL SELECT statement, using the GROUP BY clause. The fields in the GROUP BY clause, used as data aggregation keys for the charts displayed in the portal, are:

- Date, Site name, VO;
- CA - the Certification Authority that signed the user certificate;
- User FQAN - the second part of the user certificate subject, with VOMS groups and roles;
- Job type - "Grid" if submitted to the local resource manager through the Grid middleware or "local" if submitted directly.

The aggregated accounting metrics retrieved through the SELECT statement are:

- Job number - the number of job entries that match the group by values;
- CPU time and normalized CPU time - CPU time multiplied by the average computing power capacity of the logical CPU of the relevant site, expressed in terms of a benchmark of choice;
- Wall clock time and normalized Wall clock time.

Whilst HLR database contains more information about jobs, the aforementioned data are enough for most of the accounting data views required by the HLRmon users. In addition, aggregation considerably reduces the number of database entries involved. For example, the average amount of entries per day in the HLRmon database is about 500 for the whole Italian production Grid.

By default, the HLRmon data retrieval engine queries the HLR for the last 40 days: previous data are replaced by the result of the new query in order to add also jobs that, for some reasons, were recorded into the HLR many days after their end. The engine can retrieve accounting data from a configurable time interval. This can be handy to fix old entries, or to refresh the full HLRmon dataset if its database schema changed.

The HLRmon database is a "summarized" instance of the top-level HLR database, and in case of data corruption, for hardware failures or other reasons, it can be easily regenerated. For example, the HLRmon database can be populated with two years of accounting information of the Italian Grid in two or three hours.

5   GRAPHICAL USER INTERFACE

The HLRmon user interface is a PHP-based portal. The web pages are generated through the Smarty Template Engine to implement the separation between the business logic and the presentation logic to add flexibility to the management of both logics. By querying the local database, data are aggregated to produce a number of charts highly customizable by the users. Plots are generated through the JPGraph libraries and charts are presented in two sections of the portal: Report and Monthly. Moreover, the Ranking section shows a table of information on computing resource usage aggregated by Grid user, directly retrieved at run-time from the HLR database.

5.1   Report and Monthly Sections

Two portal views, named Report and Monthly, were designed to present different aggregation levels and to customize the required view. A valid personal X.509 certificate (released by a Grid accredited certification authority) is the only requirement to access those graphs, i.e. no registration is required by the portal.

The Report section includes the following metrics:
- – Number of jobs;
- – CPU time and normalized CPU time;
- – Wall clock time and normalized Wall clock time;
- – Job efficiency - ratio between CPU time and Wall clock time.

For each metric different types of aggregation can be selected: per day, per VO, per VOMS role and per Certification Authority, per site per day, per VO per day, per VOMS role per day and per Certification Authority per day, and finally per job type (local or Grid) per day. The user, by choosing a metric, loads a page showing the related chart set; in this way no more than 10 charts are loaded at a time.

The user can choose a subset of VOs, sites and a time period of interest to limit the dataset for the queries. Each chart can be magnified by simply clicking on it. In order to make charts more readable, only the first seven entries are plotted whereas the others are aggregated into a single plot and associated to the label "other".

The Report section includes also a tabular view of these aggregated data, offering the possibility to export the report in format suitable for spreadsheets. Finally, each session of a user (identified by the certificate installed in the respective browser) is saved by HLRmon in order to load the same set of options for subsequent view sessions.

The Monthly section was designed to show the month-by-month activity over the last year. The available plot types are: CPU time per day, CPU time and Wall clock time per VO.

5.2   Ranking Section

User-level accounting is necessary to track the behavior of individual users on the Grid. This feature is particularly relevant to VO managers, Grid managers and in case of security problems to identify unusual submission patterns.

The HLRmon database does not contain data grouped by user, as providing information at this fine granularity would dramatically increase the number of the needed entries in the database. In order to keep this feature usable, run-time queries need to be triggered on the HLR database. This is necessary as direct queries involving a broad time interval are usually affected by long delays and would turn the interface unusable.

For privacy reasons the access to the Ranking section is restricted to users registered on the portal with specific Grid roles. During the registration step, the user, identified by his/her personal X.509 certificate installed in the web browser, has to claim his/her Grid roles. After this step, the HLRmon administrator processes the registration request verifying the validity of the claimed roles. Different roles can coexist in order to visualize different subsets of information. In particular, several roles can be applicable at a time.

- ROC (Regional Operation Centre) manager: access open to any type of accounting information;
- VO manager: access restricted to the information of the users belonging to his/her VO;
- Site administrator: access open to any job submission activity relevant to the respective site;
- VO user: access restricted to the own accounting records.

6 VIEWS FOR WLCG

The HLRmon portal includes views customised to the needs of the Worldwide LHC Computing Grid (WLCG), such as the comparison between usage and amount of pledged resources (per site and per VO), and the availability of information about storage usage. The WLCG VOs are ALICE, ATLAS, CMS and LHCb. Sites listed in this section belong to the tiered architecture defined by WLCG computing architecture. Individual sites can support one or multiple VOs at a time. In all cases, it is important that the accounting infrastructure provides sufficient information to compare WLCG and non-WLCG usage of the pledged resources.

For what concerns the LHC experiments, each site hosts a certain amount of computing and storage resources, negotiated with the WLCG managers. The HLRmon views compare the LHC VOs accounting information against the total computing capacity and the total installed storage space available at each site.

6.1 Data Sources and Visualization

The data used to generate charts in the WLCG views come from different heterogeneous sources. In particular, computing resource usage, gathered by DGAS as explained earlier, is complemented by additional information retrieved from the gLite Information System (BDII) [7].

HLRmon plots the total number of job slots available at the site and the overall power capacity, which can be expressed in terms of different computing power benchmarks such as SpecInt2000 and HepSpec-06.

On the HLRmon instance dedicated to the Italian production Grid, the script queries the Italian top-level BDII once a day in order to retrieve, for each site, the value of the following attributes of the Glue Schema object named GlueSubClusterUniqueID [8]

- GlueSubClusterLogicalCPU: the number of job slots installed at the site;
- GlueHostBenchmarkSI00: the mean power capacity of the site expressed in SpecInt2000;

- GlueHostProcessorOtherDescription: the value of the attribute Benchmark, representing the mean power capacity expressed in HepSpec-06.

In addition, the HLRmon database also stores static information about the
amount of pledged resources for all the sites. These values are periodically updated.

Storage accounting data are collected through a simple script running once a
day on the SRM instances managed at a given site. The script includes:

1. a site-specific part that gathers the needed storage information from the
   SRM node, and is customized for various SRM implementations such as
   StoRM, DPM, dCache, and Castor. This script is typically tailored by site
   administrators according to the local configuration of the respective storage
   infrastructure.
2. a second general part that gathers disk utilization information, fills a XML
   document, and sends it to the HLRmon server.

Afterwards, once data have been gathered by HLRmon, automated routines
aggregate information for every single site, and insert it into the local database.
The HLRmon views for WLCG are organized in two main sections, named Computing and Storage. Each section presents chart sets with data aggregated over the
last month and the last year. For each site, links to site fabric monitoring tools
about computing, storage and network are provided. The Computing section contains six different chart sets, each showing aggregations for one of the following
metrics:

- CPU time expressed in time;
- Wall clock time expressed in time;
- CPU time normalized by the mean power capacity of the site, expressed
  both in kSpecInt2000 and HepSpec-06;
- Wall clock time normalized by the mean power capacity of the site;
- Number of submitted jobs;
- Job efficiency expressed as ratio between CPU time and Wall clock
  time.

For each set, charts can be grouped by Grid site or by LHC VO. The user can
compare the LHC VOs against non-LHC activity at sites, as well as Grid against
local submissions. When the user chooses one of the chart sets about CPU or Wall
clock time normalized, he/she can compare the VO usage against the WLCG
pledged resources and against the overall capacity of the site, computed as product
between the number of job slots and the mean power capacity of the site, as published by the gLite BDII.

In the Storage section the first plot of each box shows the total and free storage
space installed at the site per day, compared with the fraction used by each LHC
VO, while other charts indicate for each LHC VO the total storage space assigned
to the VO in the site, the total space used by the VO and the space used by each
Storage Area, if relevant in the storage under consideration.

7 RELATED WORK

The EGEE Accounting Portal [9] is the tool developed in the framework of the EC-funded EGEE-III project for the visualization of accounting information gathered by the individual regions that are part of the infrastructure and collected from a wide range of different accounting systems including: APEL, DGAS, Gratia, and SGAS .

APEL (Accounting Processor for Event Logs) [10] is a component of the EGEE CPU Accounting system, distributed as part of the gLite middleware. It parses batch system and Grid gatekeeper logs at Grid sites to generate usage records, published into a repository at EGEE GOC (Grid Operations Centre). The Gratia accounting system [11] aims to provide an accounting of OSG (Open Science Grid) jobs. It consists of probes operating on remote locations and uploading data to a network of reporting systems, such as the OSG Accounting Reports and the EGEE Accounting Portal. SGAS (SweGrid Accounting System) [12] is used by Grid infrastructures based on ARC middleware (e.g.. NorduGrid). What makes DGAS peculiar and unique in comparison with the aforementioned accounting systems, is the capability to partition the relevant Grid infrastructure into an arbitrary set of individual accounting domains, each associated to a dedicated accounting repository. This allows DGAS administrators to configure an arbitrary tree of distributed repositories storing usage records for different domains and publishing them externally to higher-level HLR databases, thus implementing an overall accounting infrastructure that is scalable, flexible and reliable at the same time.

The EGEE Accounting Portal presents Anonymous Statistical Accounting information organized in the Global view, including different sets of web views accessible by everyone, and User Related information in a restricted access section. This kind of organization is the same adopted by HLRmon. In the Global view the Web pages are designed to offer an amount of information for a large world-wide Grid, as the EGEE infrastructure is, giving the possibility to get statistics aggregated per EGEE ROC (Regional Operation Centre) and per country, while HLRmon relies on the assumption that sites belong to the same national or regional Grid. HLRmon allows the user to fully customize the information research, by selecting not only the relevant VOs but also the desired set of sites. In addition, HLRmon provides information about both local jobs (those jobs executed from batch submission framework rather than the gLite one), and Grid jobs. It aggregates data per VOMS role and per CA, and gathers information about storage resources.

8 CONCLUSIONS AND FUTURE WORK

This paper presents the architecture and the main features of HLRmon, a Grid accounting portal based on DGAS, the Distributed Grid Accounting System. The highly customizable views and the variety of aggregation levels that the tool offers are illustrated in detail. The flexibility of the database hierarchy - necessary for a persistent and reliable storage of usage records - and the maturity and stability of the DGAS source code, make HLRmon a web portal suitable and ready for deployment in national Grids. In addition to its standard views, the portal was enhanced to provide additional WLCG-specific features, which are easily customizable for an arbitrary set of sites and VOs. These views compare LHC and non-LHC job submission activities, analyse the job efficiency levels in the Grid, and compare the amount of power capacity utilised against the pledged resources. Within the WLCG section, HLRmon integrates information from the gLite Information System and storage accounting data retrieved at sites.

HLRmon will rely on the Grid configuration repository of EGEE (GOCDB) [13] in order to obtain Grid sites and downtime information, and to integrate these in the graphical interface. In particular, the GOCDB database provides also site certification status, showing if the site is active or not. This information would be useful to flag the currently inactive sites on the selection list on the web interface.

The HLRmon tool will shortly include a new graphical view providing data aggregated per scientific discipline; the mapping information between VOs and disciplines is currently retrieved from the EGEE CIC Operations Portal. The HLRmon team will study the possibility to receive accounting information through the ActiveMQ messaging system and a new consumer module will be implemented. Finally, the tool will be enhanced to adopt the usage record formats defined at the Open Grid Forum for increased interoperability.

9 ACKNOWLEDGEMENTS

HLRmon and DGAS are supported by the INFN Grid project. DGAS was also supported by the EU projects EGEE and EGEE-II, sponsored by the European Union under contract number INFSO 508833 and INFSO-RI-031688 respectively.

REFERENCES

[1] Laure E, Fisher SM, Frohner A, Grandi C, Kunszt P, Krenek A, Mulmo O, Pacini F, Prelz F, White J et al (2006) Programming the Grid with gLite. Computational methods in science and technology.

[2] Andreozzi, S.; Burke, S.; Donno, F. Et alt.; GLUE Schema Specification, version 1.3, Jan 2007.

[3]   Guarise A; Piro R, M, (2009) Distributed Grid Accounting System, Market Oriented Grid and Utility Computing., R. Buyya and K. Bubendorfer (eds), ISBN: 978-0470287682, Wiley Press, Hoboken, New Jersey, USA.

[4]   Piro R M; , Guarise A; Patania G; Werbrouck, A (2008). Using historical accounting information to predict resource usage of grid jobs., Future Generation Computing System , Volume 25, Issue 5, May 2009, pp. 499-510, doi:10.1016/j.future.2008.11.003.

[5]   Distributed Grid Accounting System: project home page (http://www.to.infn.it/dgas/index.html).

[6]   Usage Record – Format Recommendation (http://www.ogf.org/documents/GFD.98.pdf).

[7]   Ehm, F.; Field, L.; Schulz, M., W.; Scalability and Performance Analysis of the EGEE Information System; Int. Conference on Computing in High Energy and Nuclear Physics (CHEP'07), Journal of Physics: Conference Series 119 (2008) 062029, doi:10.1088/1742-6596/119/6/062029.

[8]   Burke S, Andreozzi S, Field L (2008) Experiences with the GLUE information schema in the LCG/EGEE production grid; Int. Conference on Computing in High Energy and Nuclear Physics (CHEP'07), Journal of Physics: Conference Series 119 (2008) 062029, doi:10.1088/1742-6596/119/6/062029.

[9]   EGEE Accounting Portal (http://www3.egee.cesga.es).

[10] Byrom R, Cordenonsi R, Cornwall L, Craig M, Abdeslem D, Ducan A, Fisher S, Gordon J, Hicks S, Kant D et al (2005) APEL: An implementation of Grid accounting using R-GMA. UK e-Science All Hands Conference.

[11] Gratia project wiki page (https://twiki.grid.iu.edu/bin/view/Accounting/WebHome).

[12] Gardfjall, P.; Elmroth, E.; Johnsson, L. et alt.; Scalable Grid-wide capacity allocation with the SweGrid Accounting System (SGAS); John Wiley and Sons Ltd.; Volume 20, Issue 18 (Dec 2008), pp. 2089-2122, ISSN:1532-062.

[13] GOCDB User documentation (http://goc.grid.sinica.edu.tw/gocwiki/GOCDB_User_Documentation)

Part VI
Grid Middleware and Interoperability

Interoperating AliEn and ARC for a Distributed Tier1 in the Nordic Countries

Philippe Gros[1]**, Anders Rhod Gregersen**[2]**, Jonas Lindemann**[3]**, Pablo Saiz**[4] **and Andrey Zarochentsev**[5]

1. Lund University, Div. of Experimental High Energy Physics, Sweden
2. NDGF -Nordic DataGrid Facility and Aalborg University, Denmark
3. LUNARC, Lund University, Sweden
4. CERN -European Organisation for Nuclear Research, Switzerland
5. St Petersburg State University, Russia

Abstract   To reach its large computing needs, the ALICE experiment at CERN has developed its own middleware called AliEn, centralised and relying on pilot jobs. One of its strength is the automatic installation of the required packages.
The Nordic countries have offered a distributed Tier-1 centre for the CERN experiments, where the job management should be done with the NorduGrid middleware ARC.

We have developed an interoperation module to allow to unify several computing sites using ARC, and make them look like a single site from the point of view of AliEn. A prototype has been completed and tested out of production. This talk will present implementation details of the system and its performance in tests.

1   INTRODUCTION

ALICE [1] is a heavy ion experiment at the Large Hadron Collider (LHC) at CERN. To access the large computing power and storage required for the processing of the data created, the ALICE collaboration has developed a set of grid tools called AliEn (ALIce ENvironment [2, 3]). AliEn allows to access the resources uniformly, and manage them centrally from CERN. The sites are managed using a front-end called a VO-box, which uses the local batch system to manage the resources, without any specific configuration on the nodes themselves.

The Nordic countries are individually small, but represent together an important contributor to the LHC. The decision was taken to pool their resources to create a distributed Tier-1 for the LHC computing grid. An entity called NDGF (Nordic Data Grid Facility [4]) was created to manage the Nordic resources and acts as a single entry point for CERN. The ARC middleware [5], developed by NorduGrid [6] in the Nordic countries was chosen for the management of the resources.

The goal of this work is to create an interface between AliEn and ARC to create such a distributed site. The data management is already unified using dCache

S.C. Lin and E. Yen (eds.), *Data Driven e-Science: Use Cases and Successful Applications of Distributed Computing Infrastructures (ISGC 2010)*, DOI 10.1007/978-1-4419-8014-4_16, © Springer Science+Business Media, LLC 2011

[7]. The interoperation solution presented here addresses only the job management.

In the first part, we will introduce the principle and the motivation for such an interface. Then a short description of the two middleware AliEn and ARC is given. In the fourth section, we show the mechanism in the realised interface. Finally, we describe the testing facilities and prototype performance, before concluding.

2   INTEROPERATION

In order to create a distributed Tier1, the AliEn and ARC software have to be interfaced. This interoperation should allow to create a machine which would appear as a front-end to the AliEn grid, but can manage jobs over a pool of computer clusters. This task has been initiated (see [7]), but no fully functional interface is used yet.

2.1   Motivation

The Grid has become a very important tool for science, but different strategies are chosen by different communities. We need then to interface the different solutions adopted to optimise the use of computing resources.

The AliEn paradigm is based on a single user (the ALICE collaboration), which receives jobs from the members of the collaboration, and submits them to the computing resources. The steering team at CERN has very much control over the whole system, but since the collaboration is not big enough, some tasks, such as the software installation, had to be automated.

ARC, on the other hand, provides a tool for many users, from different communities (different Virtual Organisations). It is very flexible, but requires involvement of the different scientific communities to provide access to useful resources.

Now when new big projects like International Linear Collider [8] or European Spallation Source, to be built in Lund [9], will start, they will also need grid solutions. If they want to access already existing resources, interoperability will be crucial. Besides, an interface between AliEn and ARC would bring several advantages for resource management.

- **Accounting**

The accounting of resource usage is simplified. For the central ALICE management, only one entry exists, so the information would come from a single contact. For the Nordic community, the ALICE site would use the resources in the same way as any other Virtual Organisation, and would be managed with the same tools.

- **Operation**

In term of operation of the system, the ALICE grid team only has one VO-box to maintain, instead of the current nine. This would make it much easier to provide the level of service required for a Tier-1 centre. All the sites already run ARC for other VOs like ATLAS. Besides, they benefit of the expertise of the many ARC developers in the Nordic region, while AliEn experts are mainly based at CERN.

- **Flexibility**

From a technical point of view, such a hierarchical system is more appealing. It should improve the scalability of the system. More clearly it greatly improves the flexibility, allowing to easily move and create new resources at a regional level, keeping only the total to the pledged value.

Of course, it also comes with some downsides. We increase the load on a single gateway machine. However, for the Nordic Tier-1, the combined size of all the federated sites should be comparable to a normal Tier-1 site, controlled by a single machine.

2.2 *Requirements*

The main requirement of such an interface is simplicity: For ALICE, the new VO-box should not create an exception, it has to be managed with the same configuration and management tools as any other VO-box. The code must be kept as much as possible to some simple modules, non invasive to the normal system.

For NDGF, the ARC "sub-sites" should not run any special services. The site managers should need as little knowledge of AliEn as possible. The VO-specific configuration should be done through an ARC RunTime Environment (see 3.2.2)

3   MIDDLEWARE

This project involves two pieces of middleware, with a hierarchical relation. AliEn is the master, and the very structure of the system has to be understood to create an interface. ARC is used as a client, and only the client's features are relevant, and not the actual structure of the grid.

3.1 *AliEn*

AliEn is the grid environment developed by the ALICE collaboration at CERN. It is using some centralised services at CERN. The computer clusters are managed by a set of service running on a front-end, called the VO-box.

AliEn is using a "pull" model. Pilot jobs, called Job Agents (JAs) which "pull" the actual jobs from the central database.

3.1.1   Job Management

The AliEn job management is done using a pull model and pilot jobs. The computer clusters are managed by a so-called VO-box, running several services to monitor and manage the pilot jobs. The three main services are the Computing Element (CE), the Cluster Monitor (CM) and the Package Manager (PackMan) (see figure 1).

The CE checks the available resources by querying the Local Resource Manager (LRMS) of the site. It also gets the list of packages available on the site from the PackMan. If there are jobs in the central queue matching these, it will send a corresponding number of Job Agents (JAs) to the node using the LRMS. If some extra packages are required, it will ask the PackMan to install them first.

The JAs (pilot jobs) check their environment on the node, and if there is a job matching in the central queue, it will pull it, download the corresponding data and start the job. When the job is finished, it uploads and registers the output. Then it can try to pull new jobs until it expires (usually after 48 hours).

The CM handles the communications between the different services. It acts as a proxy for the communication with the outside.

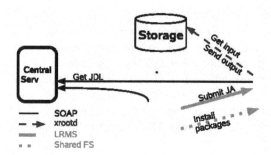

Fig. 1: AliEn job management process

3.1.2 Package Management

A strength of AliEn is that it automatically installs the software required by the jobs. The PackMan [10] originally relied on two assumptions: the cluster is homogeneous (all nodes have an identical platform) and the nodes share a file system with the VO-box where the PackMan is running. There is now a prototype [11] that allows the installation of the packages locally on the nodes, thus suppressing these two requirements.

The PackMan, when requested by the CE, downloads the package (tar ball) and installs (unpacks and runs as configuration script) on the shared file system. The configuration script usually just creates a file with the relevant environment variables, to be sourced when using the package.

3.2 ARC

ARC (Advanced Resource Connector [5]) has been developed originally by the Nordic community and has grown into one of the most widely deployed grid middleware. It is a highly distributed, multipurpose grid middleware.

3.2.1 Job Management

In ARC, the jobs are directly submitted from the client (user) to the batch system of a cluster, following a "push" model. It is then usually possible from the client to access the running directory of the job, to see any outputs created. In some site configurations, only the standard outputs are available before the job ends.

3.2.2 Package Management

In the ARC model, the packages are installed on the sites by the system administrators. Then, a RunTime Environment (RTE) script [12] is created to set the environment correctly for a job requiring the package. The RTE also advertises to the grid that the package is available on the site.

4 INTERFACE WITH ARC

We have developed an interface to allow a VO-box to submit and manage jobs using the ARC middleware. ARC can easily be used for the submission of Job Agents on a local cluster. However, to have a single VO-box submitting to remote sites via ARC, the package management has to be adapted.

4.1 Job Agent Submission

On an AliEn site, ARC can be used as a Local Resource Manager (LRMS) to manages the JAs. If the VO-box is set up for a single site (local area network and file system shared with the nodes), this works like any other AliEn site. The corresponding module is now included in AliEn and used in production on several site with high efficiency.

However, if we want the VO-box to submit the JAs to a remote site, communication with the JAs through firewalls has to be considered. Fortunately, all vital communication is done from the JA to the VO-box using SOAP. Therefore, only outbound HTTP connectivity is required, which is the most common situation.

For job monitoring, communication from the VO-box to the JA is done. With ARC, we can read the output produced by the jobs, so that the monitoring of the outputs can still be done. However, more advanced monitoring tools are still unavailable for remote JAs.

4.2   Package Management

In the case of a distributed AliEn site, the PackMan cannot rely on a shared file system to make the packages available to the nodes. The packages are therefore installed on a shared file system on each sub-site, using ARC jobs with special writing privileges.

The installation jobs use an AliEn command to install the package in the exact same way as the PackMan. That way, the package installation is as reliable as on any other AliEn site and the installation script does not require maintenance in itself.

Once the package is installed, an ARC RTE is created. The RTE contains all the relevant environment variables for the package, as created by the PackMan's post-installation script. It also instantly (within the one minute refreshing time of the database server of the ARC grid manager) advertises the existence of the software on the site. The PackMan on the VO-box can therefore check the available packages on its pool of sub-sites. The RTE can then be required when submitting JAs with package requirements.

If the installation script fails, no RTE is created, and a flag is put on the VO-box to retry later.

An AliEn PackMan prototype [11] using bittorrent [13] has been developed. Since it installs packages locally on the nodes, and gets the files from the central repositories and other node through peer-to-peer protocol, it works independently from the VO-box. It could therefore in principle replace efficiently this system for a distributed site.

4.3   Implementation

The AliEn native code is based on Perl. Besides a few minor modifications on the base code, the interface is contained into two Perl modules.

One handles the submission of the Job Agents using ARC. It is very similar to the other corresponding modules for other LRMS such as PBS or SGE.

The second handles the package installation. It is a completely new module, but the AliEn code already allowed the possibility to create and configure such a module.

The configuration of the VO-box in the central configuration database allows to use these modules instead of the default ones. It is also used to configure the system (by giving for instance the list of sub-sites).

5   TESTING

An interface prototype has been tested in Lund. To avoid interfering with ALICE production, a test bed was created. A more limited version of the interface (not supporting multiple sites) is currently used for production on several Nordic sites.

This test allowed to confirm the viability of the interface, and to address some potential issues.

5.1   A Simple Test-bed

To avoid interfering with the production grid at a critical time, a test bed had to be set up to test prototypes of the interface. A complete AliEn grid system was installed in Lund fig. 2), with a corresponding Virtual Organisation (VO). Its purpose was to validate the principle of the interface in a simple environment, not to test it in heavy load situation.

The test bed had three components:

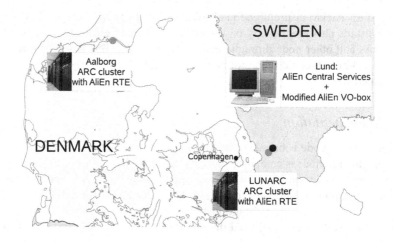

Fig. 2: Test bed for the interface prototype. Only the computer running AliEn services in Lund is dedicated to the test.

- **AliEn Central Services**

The basic AliEn Central Services (CS) were installed on a machine in Lund and were associated to a test VO. They were absolutely not modified from the ones used at CERN.

- **One AliEn VO-box**

A single VO-box was created, on the same machine as the CS. There the interface was included (2 specific modules, and some minor modifications on some services). The site was configured accordingly in the CS database.

- **Two ARC clusters running ARC**

Two ARC sites participated in the exercise: LUNARC and Aalborg. These sites are used for grid production. On each site, an AliEn RTE was created. Directories were created for the installation of the packages and their associated RTE. Two grid users were added: one for running JAs, with normal user rights; the other for package installation, having writing privilege on the previous directories. A simple plugin had to be added in LUNARC to bypass a configuration that prevented writing possibility for the RTE directory.

5.2   Results and Observations

Jobs requiring ROOT [14] packages were submitted to the AliEn CS. The VO-box installed the packages on the two sites. It then submitted JAs. The JAs ran the jobs successfully, producing outputs. For the test, the ARC job manager was set to distribute the jobs randomly between the sites. Better algorithm are of course available for a large scale submission. The test was very successful. However, it appeared that overloaded sites can have minor problems (time out) at the installation stage. This should be improved by setting high priority to the installation jobs. Checking for RTE before retrying the installation greatly reduces the impact of such situations.

Besides, the interface limited to a single sites (and not addressing the question of package management) has been used successfully on several Nordic sites (e.g. Aalborg). The efficiency and stability of the interface is comparable and maybe higher than with direct submission to the LRMS [15].

6   CONCLUSION

It is possible to create a distributed Tier-1 for AliEn. A prototype has been successfully tested in a reduced environment. A limited part of the interface is already used in production. A fully distributed site needs to be tested with high loads before it is used for ALICE production.

Since the ARC functionalities used in the interface are not very middleware-specific, it is probable that the same work could be applied to other flavors of middleware such as gLite or UNICORE.

REFERENCES

[1]   ALICE Technical Proposal for A Large Ion Collider Experiment at CERN LHC, CERN/LHCC/95-71, 15 December 1995

[2]   Saiz, P. et al.: AliEn–ALICE environment on the GRID. Nucl. Instr. and Methods A 502 (2003) 437-440

[3]   Bagnasco, S. et al.: AliEn: ALICE environment on the GRID. J. Phys.: Conf. Ser. 119 (2008)

[4]   Fischer, L., Grønager, M., Kleist, J., Smirnova, O.: A distributed Tier-1. J. Phys.: Conf. Ser. 119 (2008)

[5]   Ellert, M. et al. Advanced Resource Connector middleware for lightweight computational Grids, Future Generation Computer Systems, vol 23, 2007, p. 219-240

[6]   M.Ellert et al.: The NorduGrid project: Using Globus toolkit for building Grid infrastructure. Nucl. Instr. And Methods A 502 (2003) 407-410

[7]   C Anderlik et al: ALICE -ARC intergration. J. Phys.: Conf. Ser. 119 (2008)

[8]   J. Brau et al., "International Linear Collider reference design report. 1: Executive summary. 2: Physics at the ILC. 3: Accelerator. 4: Detectors,"

[9]   http://www.ess-scandinavia.eu

[10]   Buncic, P. and Peters, A. J. and Saiz, P., and Grosse-Oetringhaus, J.F.: The architecture of the AliEn system, CHEP 2004, Interlaken, Switzerland (2004)

[11]   Saiz, P. et al.: Modern methods of application code distributions on the Grid. CHEP09. http://indico.cern.ch/contributionDisplay.py?contribId=452&sessionId=62&confId=35523

[12]   ARC Runtime Environment Registry. http://gridrer.csc.fi/

[13]   http://www.bittorrent.com/

[14]   Brun, R. Rademakers, F. Nucl. Instr. and Meth. A 389 (1997) 81; http://root.cern.ch/.

[15]   http://pcalimonitor.cern.ch/map.jsp

Toward SVOPME, a Scalable Virtual Organization Privileges Management Environment

Nanbor Wang[1], Gabriele Garzoglio[2], Balamurali Ananthan[1], Steven Timm[2] and Tanya Levshina[2]

1. Tech-X Corporation, CO, USA
2. Fermi National Accelerator Laboratory, IL, USA

Abstract   Grids enable uniform access to resources by implementing standard interfaces to resource gateways. In the Open Science Grid (OSG), privileges are granted on the basis of the user's membership to a Virtual Organization (VO). However, individual Grid sites are solely responsible to determine and control access privileges to resources. While this guarantees that the sites retain full control on access rights, it often leads to heterogeneous VO privileges throughout the Grid and hardly fits with the Grid paradigm of uniform access to resources. To address these challenges, we developed the Scalable Virtual Organization Privileges Management Environment (SVOPME), which provides tools for VOs to define, publish, and verify desired privileges. Moreover, SVOPME provides tools for grid sites to analyze site access policies for various resources, verify compliance with preferred VO policies, and generate directives for site administrators on how the local access policies can be amended to achieve such compliance without taking control of local configurations away from site administrators. This paper describes how SVOPME implements privilege management tools for the OSG and our experiences in deploying and running the tools in a test bed. Finally, we outline our plan to continue to improve SVOPME and have it included as part of the standard Grid software distributions.

1   INTRODUCTION

The Grid computing environment has emerged as the leading technology for coordinated resource sharing among participating institutions and individuals. It enables execution of large-scale computation jobs by providing uniform access to distributed resources such as computational cycles and data storage, shared among participating institutes. The Virtual Organization (VO) is a key concept in grid computing. A VO manages members from different home institutes with common interests. Multiple VO's can coexist and share a common set of resources in a Grid. Meanwhile, the structure and membership of a VO are dynamic, as groups and individuals may join and leave VO's based on their interests and needs.

S.C. Lin and E. Yen (eds.), *Data Driven e-Science: Use Cases and Successful Applications*
of Distributed Computing Infrastructures (ISGC 2010), DOI 10.1007/978-1-4419-8014-4_17,
© Springer Science+Business Media, LLC 2011

Grid middleware aims to provide uniform access to all the resources made available at various distributed sites for members of a VO. The Grid Security Infrastructure (GSI) [1] provides the core security capabilities such as secure communication and mutual authentication between users and resources, using X.509 certificates. A VO is responsible for managing user memberships to groups and roles according to its organizational structure [2]. Individual sites enforce the resource usage privileges according to VO specifications through underlying OS' access control mechanisms.

1.1   Challenges in Reconciling VO and Site Policies

Within a Grid body such as the Open Science Grid (OSG) [3] or European Grid for E-sciencE (EGEE) [4], a VO establishes resource-usage agreements with Grid resource providers to grant access of site resources to group of users within a VO. Modern Grid middleware provides both the mechanisms and tools to enable the fine-grained, role-based access control. However, it comes up short in providing a streamlined and consistent distributed user privilege management across VO's and sites. Currently, this lack of automatic policy instantiation/reconciliation mechanism is handled manually via verbal discussions between VO administrators and site administrators. Such manual propagation of VO policies is a brittle and time-consuming process. As privilege policies change dynamically, which is becoming more common for large VO's, and new VO's are onboard, Grid utilization suffers as legitimate users may not be able to access resources which are otherwise perfectly usable.

1.2   The Need for Managing VO User Privileges

To realize the vision of providing uniform access to distributed resources in Grid Computing, there is an urgent need to bridge the gap between VO privilege policy specifications and local Grid site configurations. VO user roles and privilege policies must be able to propagate to Grid site automatically, yet allowing site administrators to retain full control over site policies. Furthermore, with the ever changing numbers of VO's, organizations, and privilege policies, there need to be tools to help VO and site administrators alike to verify that policies at VO's and sites are consistent with one another.

2   RELATED WORKS

SVOPME project is synergistic to many projects on authorization management. For example, the GPBox [5] project is a policy management framework for the Grid environment to globally modify the execution priorities of jobs submitted from VOs at sites. Compared to GPBox, SVOPME project does not attempt to configure site policies directly. Instead, SVOPME produces compliance reports about local configurations that hint on how the configurations could be modified for the site to provide better support for VO's. We believe that leaving local site administrators in full control of site configuration will give them peace of mind and reduce their resistance toward the eventual adoption of SVOPME.

Another synergistic effort to the SVOPME project is the EGEE Authorization Service [6]. Similar to SVOPME, the EGEE Authorization Service aims to provide consistent authorization decisions for distributed services over the Grid. It provides software components for defining privilege policies at services. These policies are then used to answer queries about whether a particular action is permissible by certain users. Although the EGEE Authorization Service also aims at providing a set of consistent authorization policies over the Grid, unlike SVOPME, the new Authorization Service does not focus on the VO policies. The two projects will be able to leverage the work done by each other.

Another effort closely related to SVOPME is the Authorization Interoperability project [7]. This project defines an attribute and obligation profile for authorization interoperability across Grids as described in Section 3. We will leverage the efforts from this project to integrate SVOPME into OSG and other Grid infrastructure.

3   VO POLICIES AND GRID SITES

Fig 1 illustrates the security model in OSG. Other modern Grid software stacks, such as EGEE, also adopt similar security models [8]. The figure depicts the procedures for performing authentication on the VO side and authorization on Grid sites. The Authorization Interoperability project standardizes the terms and formats used in the authorization process between security components, specifically Policy-Enforcement-Point (PEP), such as gLexec, and Policy-Decision-Point (PDP) [9], such as GUMS [10]. This profile is based on the eXtensible Access Control Markup Language (XACML) [11] and the Security Assertion Markup Language (SAML) [12]. However, as highlighted by Fig. 1, the existing Grid security model does not provide support for a policy-administration-point (PAP), i.e., how a VO can define its privilege policies. The SVOPME project, therefore, fills this gap and utilizes XACML as its VO privilege policy definition language for administering policies over the Grid.

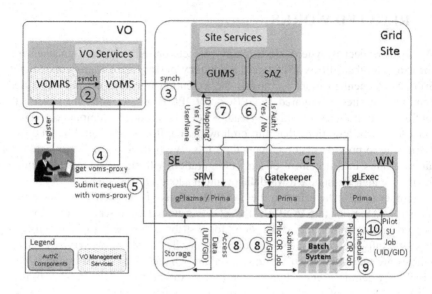

Fig. 1: The OSG Security Model.

4   THE SVOPME ARCHITECTURE

We develop the Scalable Virtual Organization Privilege Management Environment (SVOPME) to address the challenges in administering and maintaining user privileges over multiple VOs and grid sites. Built on top of the existing OSG privilege infrastructure, the SVOPME project is an extension to the OSG VO Services project [7]. The work fills a common gap that many Grid privilege management infrastructures share, as we pointed out in Section 1. **Fig. 2** illustrates the main data entities and operations performed in SVOPME that help VO administrators and grid site administrators maintain a consistent view of privileges across the Grid. Furthermore, SVOPME identifies inconsistencies in user privileges and help transform them into appropriate site configurations. These key data entities include:

- **VO Privilege Policies:** A VO administrator defines a set of VO's organizational privilege policies for users of different groups and roles.

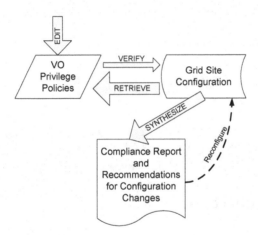

Fig. 2: SVOPME Helps Distribute and Realize VO Privilege Policies.

- **Site Configurations:** A collection of all relevant Grid site system and software configurations that enforce the local privilege policies. These configurations include the local user account settings, local user group setting, identity mapping (GUMS) configurations, batch system configuration, storage element configurations, etc. Like the VO Privilege Policies, SVOPME will also need to codify and transform these configurations into a document that can be reasoned on and compared against VO policies.
- **Compliance Report and Recommendations for Site Configurations:** SVOPME generates this document on each Grid site to provide
  - detailed evaluation of how many of the VO policies are supported and,

   – recommendations on how to modify the local configurations to fully
     support VO privilege policies for site administrators.

   Note that the site administrators maintain full control over their site configurations and need to reconfigure the site manually.

   Figure 3 illustrates the architecture of the SVOPME tools that we developed.
Four key components provide the core functionality of SVOPME. They include
support for VO administrators to define and generate VO privilege policies, and
for site administrators to automatically generate local site privilege policies based
on existing site configurations.

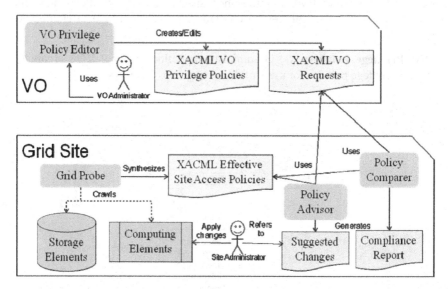

Fig. 3: Overall SVOPME Architecture.

To allow easy extension of the policies supported, we design the tools to use policy templates. The use of policy templates allows us to support new policy types by simply adding new templates into the tools chain without modifying the core implementations. SVOPME currently supports the following common VO privilege policies:

- Account mapping policies allow a VO to define how users of a particular group or role should be mapped to local accounts. This mechanism grants members of the same group the inherent OS-level protections at Grid sites. One policy is for all users of a VO group or role to be mapped to a single shared local "group account". Alternatively, a pool account policy maps users of a specific VO group or role into one of a pool of local accounts.
- Relative priority policies allow a VO to specify that jobs submitted by a particular VO group or role should be executed with higher priority than those submitted by another group or role. For example, a VO may want to grant the highest execution priority to jobs from members of the production team to ensure highest throughput in producing science.
- Pre-emption policies define if jobs submitted from a group or role should be allowed to run for consecutive hours without pre-emption to ensure quick turnaround time of these tasks.
- Permission policies define if users from a specific group or role are allowed to access certain storage areas. For example, a VO may want to grant only users playing the "software administrator" role the permission to install software into the $OSG_APP area for the VO.
- UNIX group sharing policies allow a VO to define finer grained permission management. For example, a VO may want to specify that local accounts of two groups share the same group ID on Grid sites to ensure that they can freely exchange data, if needed.
- Job suspension policies let a VO to specify if jobs submitted from a particular group or role are not to be suspended.
- Data privacy policies allow a VO to specify that files created by a group of users should be accessible only by that group by default.
- Disk quota policies allow a VO to specify the maximum disk usage by a group of users.
The remainder of this Section describes these tools in more details.

4.1   VO Components

Fig. 4 illustrates all the utilities SVOPME provides for VO administrators. In the core of VO supports is the XACML VO Policy Editor. As we mentioned earlier, the VO Policy Editor uses XACML as the internal representation of privilege policies. This provides a generic mechanism for describing, combining, and reasoning with policies. However, XACML as a language is too complex and verbose for VO administrators to express their policies. Furthermore, XACML is a generic language for defining privilege policies and defines a very limited set of standard attributes about resources, actions, etc. Each community, therefore, needs to define a vocabulary (i.e., XACML profile) to frame the concepts in its domain and VO administrators may not be expert in it.

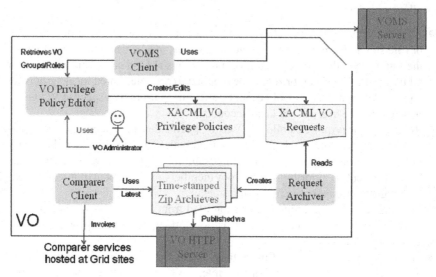

Fig. 4: VO Tool interactions.

In order to address these issues, we develop a "domain-specific" GUI-based VO policy editor. The editor enables its users to create individual privilege policies as separate XACML files. As opposed to a generic GUI-based editor for arbitrary XACML documents, our VO Policy Editor predefined a set of VO policy types and attributes that users can generate and edit.

VO administrators can then use the editor to create new VO privilege policies by selecting from a list of pre-defined policy types and filling in the key information for the type of policy being created. For example, when defining an account mapping policy, an administrator only needs to specify the kind of users (their group and role attributes) to which the policy will be applied and the kind of account to which these users should be mapped (group or pool account). Furthermore, VO Policy Editor is now capable of detecting and prevent user from redundant and contracting policies. A utility tool called "VOMS Client" [13] in Fig. 4 contacts the VO's VOMS server to retrieve the VO structural information and offers the information to the editor. This alleviates users from having to remember and type out all the group and role combinations.

For every VO policy defined by the VO Policy Editor, a matching XACML verification request is generated. These requests define the operations that must be permitted at a Grid site supporting the VO, and are used to test the compliance of

Grid sites. A "Request Archiver" enables a VO to package all these test queries into a time-stamped archive, which can then be published on the VO's web site. Timestamps allow other tools to retrieve only the latest set of test queries.

The "Comparer Client" provides VO administrators and users access to the policy comparer Web Services hosted on Grid sites. Users can use the comparer client contact to verify the degree of VO privilege support at individual sites using a set of test requests.

4.2 Site Components

This Section describes the 3 site-specific components in SVOPME, namely, Grid Probe, Policies Advisor, and Policies Comparer.

4.2.1 Grid Probe

Mechanisms for enforcing Grid site privilege policies currently are scattered at different locations on a Grid site. There is no one centralized entity to manage and configure existing Grid middleware infrastructure. For example, the VO group and role to local user ID mapping is managed by the Grid site's GUMS database. However, setting up local user ID and group ID, which are the basic subject entities for enforcing local policies, has to be done via OS tools. Batch system and storage elements, too, have their own configuration points to control privileges such as priority and permissions.

To try to compare and reason on VO policies directly with all these configuration points will result in ad hoc software tools that are very complicated and hard to maintain and expand. To address this issue, we developed the Grid Probe tool that scans and gathers configuration information from various tools and mechanisms. The Grid Probe then analyzes this information and generates the effective local privilege policies in XACML.

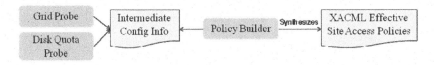

Fig. 5: SVOPME's site mechanisms for synthesizing effective site policies.

One contentious issue in deploying tools like SVOPME is the need to run the probing with special privileges. For example, to scan the disk quota configurations for all relevant local user accounts, the probe needs to have root privilege. As a result, local site administrators may become very suspicious about the adoption of SVOPME site tools. Moreover, different sites may have different configuration strategies. To address these concerns, SVOPME separates the actual probing components into multiple, small scripts/programs that are easy for administrators to examine. These probes can be scheduled to run periodically using accounts with minimal privileges required. The probes collect the site configurations into intermediate files which are used by the Policy Builder component to synthesize the actual equivalent site XACML policies. The approach of using customized probes also allows SVOPME to easily adapt to the differences in site configuration strategies.

Current Grid Probe implementations support the scanning of the following configuration points:

- GUMS configurations provide mappings from user identity and VO's group and role membership to a specific local GID and UID. GUMS mappings are used to generate account type and mapping policies. Many other policies also require information of local user identification.
- Unix group memberships of various users are needed to determine if they can share information.
- Unix directory permissions are needed to determine a series of privilege policies such as software installation and user data privacy.
- Condor configurations are used to determine site policies in job execution priority, pre-emption, and suspension/resumption privileges.
- Disk quota of all local users.

4.2.2 Analyzing Site Configurations

SVOPME uses the verification queries generated by the VO policy editor to verify if policies defined by a VO are supported on a site. Using the VO Request Retriever, the site checks periodically if a VO has published a new set of verification queries, and downloads them when necessary. As shown in **Fig. 6**, the requests for VOs are cached locally at Grid sites and are used to verify the site configurations as described in the remainder of this Section.

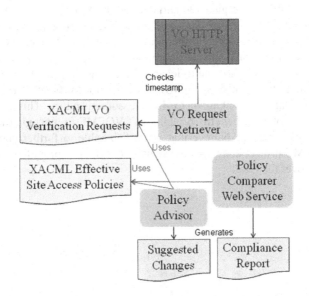

Fig. 6: VO requests are used to verify site configurations.

4.2.2.1 Policy Advisor

The Policy Advisor runs on Grid sites. It verifies if the VO privilege policies are supported at the site by issuing VO verification requests against the local privilege policies, generated by the Grid probe. If the site fails to comply with a specific policy, the Policy Advisor will analyze and recommend a way to modify the site configuration to correct the problem.

4.2.2.1 Policy Comparer

The Policy Comparer is a Web/Grid Service invoked by a VO administrator or any VO user to verify the degree of support of the site of their VO privilege policies. Site compliance test can be done by using the Policy Comparer Client VO tool with a set of test queries to check if the VO policies are supported at the site. By providing the Policy Comparer Web Service, we avoid publishing the site configurations information in the form of site equivalent policies while allowing the VO users to verify site compliance by producing a pass/fail response to each query.

5   EXPERIMENTAL DEPLOYMENTS

Since our last report in iSGC 2009, we continued to enhance and harden the SVOPME implementation. In particular, we defined and implemented how verification requests flow among many VO's and grid sites through standardized mechanisms. Furthermore, we deployed the SVOPME tools in a realistic, large-scale Grid environment using FermiGrid's integrated test bed (ITB). To evaluate the effectiveness of SVOPME, we gathered and defined the VO policies for the DZero and the Engage VO's of OSG as our target VOs. The experiment motivated several enhancements in Grid tools. Furthermore, we were able to identify some inconsistent and unconventional site configurations in our target site environment.

Some of the differences are due to legacy site configurations known to the administrators. More importantly, SVOPME was able to identify some inconsistencies in the ITB that were unknown to the site administrators. This experiment demonstrated the potential benefits brought by SVOPME to managing a Grid. If deployed in large scale, we believe that we will be able to further demonstrate how the SVOPME project addresses the scalability issues in providing consistent resource usage over the Grid.

6   PROJECT OUTLOOK AND CONCLUSIONS

To address the scalability issues in providing consistent access to Grid resources, we develop a set of tools and services to realize a Scalable Virtual Organization Privilege Management Environment. We have demonstrated the feasibility and the effectiveness of this project in a test bed environment to allow VOs and sites to communicate the VO privilege policy needs and to verify the degree of site support automatically. Fully deployed, the SVOPME project can greatly reduce the costs in running and maintaining VO's and sites alike. Similarly, SVOPME allows sites to advertise and prove their degree of support for a VO. For a site to support a new VO and its privilege policies, there are now semi-automatic mechanisms to amend site configurations. Equally important is that Grid sites do not relinquish the privilege enforcement to the VOs. Rather, SVOPME informs the site administrators with a formal VO policy assessment.

We are currently soliciting VO's and sites interested in testing out SVOPME in a production environment. We will continue to enhance and harden SVOPME tools based on the feedbacks and experiences from these early adopters. For example, we may implement the following policies previously discussed for future extension based on the needs:

- Policies on job resubmission semantics instruct the underlying batch system to execute jobs from a specific group or role at most once. This is particularly important in some high energy physics data processing, where the workflow must guarantee that output data is not duplicated.
- Network policies allow a VO to request outbound network connections for jobs submitted by a group of users.
- File retention policies defines for how long files owned by users of a specific group or role should be kept in the storage.

We intend to have SVOPME incorporated in the Virtual Data Toolkit (VDT), the de facto standard Grid middleware distribution.

7   ACKNOWLEDGMENTS

The SVOPME project is partially funded by the Office of Advanced Scientific Computing Research, Office of Science, United States Dept. of Energy under contracts DE-FG02-07ER84733 and DE-AC02-06CH11357, the Fermi National Accelerator Laboratory, and the Tech-X Corporation. Fermilab is operated by Fermi Research Alliance, LLC under Contract DE-AC02-07CH11359 with the U.S. Department of Energy.

REFERENCES

[1] Foster I and Kasselman C 1997 Globus: A Metacomputing Infrastructure Toolkit International Journal of Supercomputer Applications, 11(2) 115-128

[2] Ceccanti A, Ciaschini V, Dimou M, Garzoglio G, Levshina T, Traylen S, Venturi V 2009 VOMS/VOMRS Utilization patterns and convergence plan Proceedings of Computing in High Energy Physics and Nuclear Physics 2009, Prague, Czech Republic

[3] Pordes R et al. 2007 The Open Science Grid Journal of Physics: Conference Series 78 15

[4] Laure E et al. 2004 Middleware for the next generation Grid infrastructure Proceedings of Computing in High Energy Physics and Nuclear Physics 2004, Interlaken, Switzerland 826

[5] Cesini D, Ciaschini V, Dongiovanni D, Ferraro A, Forti A, Ghiselli A, Italiano A, Salomoni D 2008 Enabling a priority-based fair share in the EGEE infrastructure Journal of Physics: Conference Series 119 062023 DOI:10.1088/1742-6596/119/6/062023

[6] The EGEE Authorization Service:
     http://twiki.cern.ch/twiki/bin/view/EGEE/AuthorizationFramework
     Accessed on May 13, 2009

[7] Garzoglio G et al. 2009 Definition and Implementation of a SAML-XACML Profile for Authorization Interoperability across Grid Middleware in OSG and EGEE Journal of Grid Computing DOI: 10.1007/s10723-009-9117-4

[8] Garzoglio G et al. 2009 An XACML profile and implementation for Authorization Interoperability between OSG and EGEE Proceedings of Computing in High Energy Physics and Nuclear Physics 2009, Prague, Czech Republic

[9] Garzoglio G et al. 2008 An XACML Attribute and Obligation Profile for Authorization Interoperability in Grids Fremilab White Paper CD-doc-2952-v2

[10] Lorch M, Kafura D, Fisk I, Keahey K, Carcassi G, Freeman T, Peremutov T, Rana A S 2005 Authorization and account management in the Open Science Grid The 6th IEEE/ACM International Workshop on Grid Computing, 2005

[11] Moses T et al. 2005 Extensible access control markup language (xacml) version 2.0 Oasis Standard

[12] Cantor S, Kemp J, Philpott R, Maler R 2005 Assertions and Protocols for the OASIS Security Assertion Markup Language (SAML) V2. 0 OASIS SSTC

[13] Alfieri R et al. 2004 VOMS, an authorization system for virtual organizations Proceedings of European across Grids conference No1, Santiago De Compostela, Spain 2970 33-40

The D4Science Approach toward Grid Resource Sharing: The Species Occurrence Maps Generation Case

Leonardo Candela and Pasquale Pagano

Istituto di Scienza e Tecnologie dell'Informazione "Alessandro Faedo" - Italian National Research Council (CNR), Italy

Abstract   Nowadays science is highly multidisciplinary and requires innovative research environments. Such research environments, also known as *Virtual Research Environments*, should be powerful and flexible enough to help researchers in all disciplines to manage the complex range of tasks involved in carrying out *eScience* activities. Such research environments should support computationally-intensive, data-intensive and collaboration-intensive tasks on both small and large scale. The community to be served by a specific research environment is expected to be potentially distributed across multiple organizational domains and institutions. This paper discusses the approach put in place in the context of the D4Science EU project to enable on-demand production of Virtual Research Environments by relying on an innovative, grid-based Infrastructure. In particular, the foundational principles, the enabling technology and the concrete experience resulting from developing (*i*) a production Infrastructure and (*ii*) a Virtual Research Environment for generating predictive species distribution maps are described.

1   INTRODUCTION

Today research activities require collaborations among parties that are widely dispersed and autonomous. Collaborations are often cross-discipline and require innovative research environments that make available data, processing and interaction intensive workflows to produce new knowledge able to stimulate further research.

To support such a demanding scenario a very promising approach is based on *e-Infrastructures*. By definition, an e-Infrastructure is a framework enabling secure, cost-effective and on-demand *resource sharing* [1] across organisation boundaries. A resource is here intended as a generic entity, physical (*e.g.* storage and computing resources) or digital (*e.g.* software, processes, data), that can be shared and interact with other resources to synergistically provide some functions serving its clients, either human or inanimate. Thus, an e-Infrastructure poses as a "*mediator*" in a market of resources having the role to accommodate the needs of resource providers and consumers. The infrastructure layer supports (*i*) resource

S.C. Lin and E. Yen (eds.), *Data Driven e-Science: Use Cases and Successful Applications of Distributed Computing Infrastructures (ISGC 2010)*, DOI 10.1007/978-1-4419-8014-4_18,
© Springer Science+Business Media, LLC 2011

providers, in "selling" their resources through it; (*ii*) resource consumers, in "buying" and orchestrating such resources to build their applications. Further, it provides organizations with logistic and technical aids for application building, maintenance, and monitoring. A well-known instance of such an e-Infrastructure is represented by the Grid [2], where a service-based paradigm is adopted to share and reuse low-level physical resources. Application-specific e-Infrastructures are in their turn inspired by the generic e-Infrastructure framework and bring this vision into specific application domains by enriching the infrastructural *resource model* with specific *service* resources, *i.e.* software units that deliver functionality or content by exploiting available physical resources.

This potentially not-limited market of resources allows a new development paradigm based on the notion of *Virtual Research Environment* (VRE) [3, 4], i.e. integrated environment providing seamless access to the needed resources as well as facilities for communication, collaboration and any kind of interaction among scientists and researchers. This is built by aggregating the needed constituents after hiring them through the e-Infrastructure. In this development paradigm, the resulting research environments are considered as organised "*views*" built atop the pool of available assets, ranging from computers and servers to collections and services.

In the context of the D4Science [5] EU project this vision has been realised. An e-Infrastructure managing in a seamless way computing and storage facilities as well as services, softwares and data resources has been built and operated. Through this e-Infrastructure a set of Virtual Research Environments have been defined and operated to serve scientific scenarios ranging from ocean chlorophyll monitoring and vegetative land cover activities to species distribution maps generation, country profiles production and fishery statistical data management.

The remainder of this paper is organised as follows. Section 2 describes the design principles governing the definition and implementation of the D4Science innovative infrastructure supporting the development of Virtual Research Environments. Section 3 discusses the enabling technology that has been developed to realize such a kind of infrastructure. Section 4 describes the infrastructure that has been developed and operated in the context of the D4Science project to implement the envisaged service. Section 5 reports on the Virtual Research Environment that has been realized to provide biodiversity scientists with an innovative cooperation environment supporting a seamless access to the rich array of data sources and facilities needed to produce enhanced reports on species distributions. Finally, Section 6 concludes the paper and discusses the future activities leading to enhanced versions of the D4Science infrastructure and its Virtual Research Environments.

2 D4SCIENCE: BUILDING AN E-INFRASTRUCTURE FOR VIRTUAL RESEARCH ENVIRONMENTS

D4Science[1] [5] is a project co-funded by European Commissions Seventh Framework Programme for Research and Technological Development involving 11 participating organizations. It continues the path that GÉANT[2], EGEE[3] and DILIGENT [6] projects have initiated towards establishing networked, grid-based, and data-centric e-Infrastructures that accelerate multidisciplinary research by overcoming barriers related to heterogeneity, sustainability and scalability.

D4Science as a system falls in the category of *Service Oriented Infrastructures, i.e.* those infrastructures resulting from the application of the Service Orientation principles. This manifests in facilities for the reusability and dynamic allocation of the resources forming the infrastructure itself. In addition, D4Science supports a very flexible and agile application development model based on the notion of *Platform as a Service (PaaS)* [7] in which components may be bound instantly, just at the time they are needed, and then the binding may be discarded. Such development model materialises in the support for Virtual Research Environments representing a distinguishing feature of D4Science. According to it, user communities are enabled to define their own research environment by simply selecting the constituents (the services, the data collections, the machines) among the pool of resources made available through the D4Science e-Infrastructure. The cost of operating each defined VRE is completely outsourced to the infrastructure that by applying economies of scale to the operation of the applications (*sharing and re-use*) can offer better, cheaper and more reliable applications than single communities themselves can do.

From a service point of view, the D4Science project has been conceived to deploy and operate a production quality e-Infrastructure guaranteeing a 24/7 service. The primary consumers of such a service have been two large scale, multidisciplinary, scientific communities including environmentalists, earth scientists, foresters, fisheries and livestock specialists, nutritionists, social scientists, statisticians, agronomists, economists. These communities are the *Environmental Monitoring* (EM) community lead by the European Space Agency[4] (ESA) and the *Fisheries and Aquaculture Resources Management* (FARM) community lead by the Food and Agriculture Organization of the United Nations[5] (FAO).

---

[1] DIstributed colLaboratories Infrastructure on Grid ENabled Technology 4 Science (D4Science) www.d4science.eu

[2] GÉANT www.geant.net

[3] Enabling Grids for E-sciencE www.eu-egee.org

[4] European Space Agency www.esa.int

[5] Food and Agriculture Organization of the United Nations www.fao.org

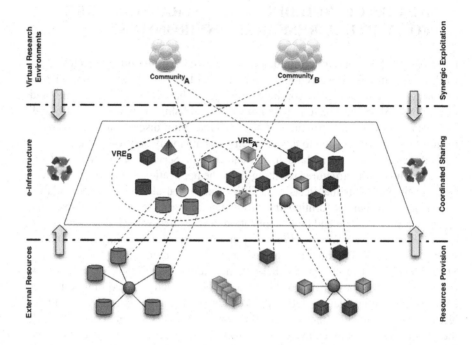

Fig. 1: Building Virtual Research Environments through an e-Infrastructure

From an organisational point of view, the D4Science infrastructure operates as a "broker" in a market of resources accommodating the needs of resource providers and consumers (Fig. 1). It distinguishes among: (*i*) external resources, managed by third-party resource providers which maintain and make the resources available to the e-Infrastructure under certain policies, and (*ii*) VREs, implemented as applications enabled by the e-Infrastructure, specifically designed to meet the needs of the scenarios addressed.

To implement the e-Infrastructure described above an innovative and features rich software platform, *i.e. gCube*, has been developed.

3   THE ENABLING TECHNOLOGY: GCUBE

gCube[6] [8] is a distributed system for the operation of large-scale scientific infrastructures. It has been designed from the ground up to support the full lifecycle of
modern scientific enquiry, with particular emphasis on application-level requirements of information and knowledge management. To this end, it interfaces pan-
European Grid middleware for shared access to high-end computational and storage resources [9], but complements it with a rich array of services that collate, describe, annotate, merge, transform, index, search, and present information for a variety of multidisciplinary and international communities. Services, data and
metadata collections, and machines are infrastructural resources that communities
select, share, and consume in the scope of collaborative *Virtual Research Environments*. gCube is built by combining in a Service Oriented Architecture a number of subsystems according to the Reference Architecture [10] depicted in Figure
2.

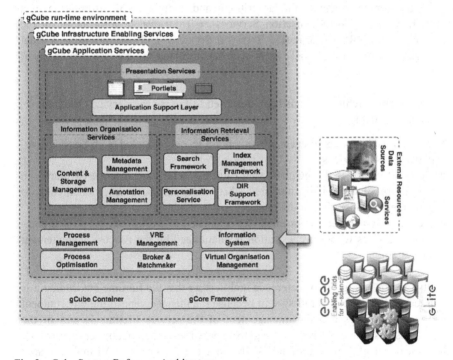

Fig. 2: gCube System Reference Architecture

---

6 www.gcube-system.org

Such subsystems are organised in a three-tier architecture consisting of:

- the gCube run-time environment, named gCube Hosting Node (gHN), is the set of subsystems equipping each gCube empowered machine and forming the platform for the hosting and operation of the rest of system constituents. Namely, it consists of (*a*) the gCube Container (to run gCube Services), (*b*) the gCore Framework, named gCF (to leverage the services from the unnecessary complexities introduced by a distributed infrastructure), (*c*) a number of local services, namely Deployer, gHNManager, Delegation, and ResultSet and (*d*) a number of libraries and stubs needed to manage the communication with all other gCube services;
- the gCube Infrastructure Enabling Services is the set of subsystems constituting the backbone of the gCube system and responsible to implement (*i*) the operation of an e-Infrastructure supporting resources sharing and (*ii*) the definition and operation of Virtual Research Environments;
- the gCube Application Services is the set of subsystems implementing facilities for (*i*) storage, organisation, description and annotation of information in a VRE (Information Organisation Services), (*ii*) retrieval of information in the context of a VRE (Information Retrieval Services) and (*iii*) providing Virtual Organisations [1] and VRE users with an interface for accessing such an e-Infrastructure.

The overall architecture has been designed following the Service Oriented Architecture principles:

- the main constituents of each subsystem are loosely-coupled Web Services (actually WSRF services);
- the constituents of the gCube-based e-Infrastructure are discovered thanks to the Information System subsystem that, as usual, becomes fundamental to guarantee the operation of the rest;
- such loosely-coupled Services can be organised in workflows as to form compound services whose orchestration is guaranteed by the Process Management subsystem.

It is worth noting in this reference architecture that the runtime environment is an integral part of the overall system because the management of the environment hosting the services and the management of the service lifetime is part of the gCube business logic. Thanks to the gHN capabilities, other gCube services can be dynamically deployed on remotely gHNs to serve the needs of Virtual Research Environments.

In the remainder of this section the constituents of the Reference Architecture are introduced starting from the lower layer.

The *gCore Framework (gCF)* [11] is a Java framework for the development of high-quality gCube services and service clients. It provides an application framework that allows gCube services to abstract over functionality lower in the web services stack (WSRF, WS Notification, WS Addressing, etc.) and to build on top advanced features for the management of state, scope, events, security, configuration, fault, service lifetime, and publication and discovery.

The *gCube Infrastructure Enabling Services* is the family of subsystems implementing the foundational services that guarantee the operation of the e-Infrastructure. Such functions are organised in four main areas: (*i*) organisation and execution of Virtual Research Environments (VRE Management) by guaranteeing an optimal consumption of the available resources (Broker and Matchmaker); (*ii*) registration of the infrastructure constituents (Information Service); (*iii*) authentication and authorization policy enforcement enabling the highly controlled sharing of infrastructure constituents (Virtual Organisation Management); and (*iv*) definition and orchestration of complex workflows (Process Management) by guaranteeing an optimal consumption of the available resources (Process Optimisation).

The *gCube Application Services* is the family of subsystems delivering three outstanding functions of any Virtual Research Environment: (*i*) storage, description and annotation of information in a VRE (gCube Information Organisation Services), (*ii*) retrieval of information in the context of a VRE (gCube Information Retrieval Services) and (*iii*) providing VRE users with an interface for accessing such an information and the rest of functions equipping a VRE (gCube Presentation Services).

The *gCube Information Organisation Services* is the family of subsystems implementing the foundational services guaranteeing the management (storage, organisation, description and annotation) of information by implementing the notion of Information Objects, *i.e.* logical unit of information potentially consisting of and linked to other Information Objects as to form compound objects. Such functions are organised in three main areas: (*i*) the storage and organisation of Information Objects and their constituents (Content and Storage Management) including the management of statistical data and metadata objects like time series (Time Series Management); (*ii*) the management of the metadata objects equipping each Information Object (Metadata Management); and (*iii*) the management of the annotations objects potentially enriching each Information Objects (Annotation Management).

The *gCube Information Retrieval Services* is the family of components offering Information Retrieval (IR) facilities to the gCube infrastructure, i.e. allowing searching over data and information by a wide range of techniques. The IR family of services can be decomposed in three major categories, which are presented below and are entitled as frameworks due to the fact that they are not standalone services. Instead, they are rather large collaborating systems based on protocols, specifications and software, which add remarkable extensibility to the gCube system they empower [12, 13].

The *gCube Presentation Services* form the logical top layer of a gCube-powered infrastructure. Their objective is twofold: (*a*) to provide the means to build user interfaces for interacting with and exploiting the gCube system and infrastructure and (*b*) to provide a full range of user interfaces for achieving interaction with the system, out-of-the-box. The gCube presentation layer is based on the Application Support Layer (ASL), which is a framework that abstracts the complexity of the underlying infrastructure so that the front-end developer focuses on the objectives of presentation rather than on the details of the protocols and rules for interacting with the underlying (WSRF) services. The ASL exposes to the developer well known tools as session and credential management and is accessible through various interfaces (currently HTTP and JAVA-native). On top of the ASL the developer can develop the user interface components needed for a particular application, depending on the execution environment that will host them (*e.g.* php web server, desktop application, application server). The execution environment is normally provided by existing systems and can be powered by bare Operating Systems / Virtual Machines (*e.g.* desktop applications), plain html pages, dynamic web-sites (php, asp, jsp etc), portals, application servers, etc. gCube presentation layer offers an initial set of components currently running under the JRS168 specification, hosted by GridSphere and LifeRay portlet container. It is based on Java and servlets technologies for offering its services. These components, which are called "portlets", cover end-user and administrative functionalities.

By relying on this rich software framework the D4Science team has deployed and operated the D4Science gCube-based e-Infrastructure.

4   THE D4SCIENCE GCUBE-BASED E-INFRASTRUCTURE

The basic constituents of every gCube-based e-Infrastructure are gCube nodes, i.e. the servers equipped with the gCube run-time environment (cf. Sec. 3) making them ready to host gCube services. 60 gCube nodes have been deployed in 5 sites – CNR -Pisa (IT), NKUA -Athens (GR), ESA -Rome (IT), UNIBASEL -Basel (CH), FAO -Rome (IT) – providing a total of 53 physical machines, offering 408 GB RAM, 38 TB disk space, and 166 processor cores.

In addition to that, the D4Science e-Infrastructure (thanks to the gCube capability to interact with gLite-based nodes, *i.e.* the enabling technology of the EGEE project) is interoperable with the EGEE infrastructure. In the context of the EGEE infrastructure a D4Science VO has been created and through it the D4Science infrastructure has access to more than 3,000 worker nodes and more than 240 TB of storage space.

A gateway to the D4Science e-Infrastructure manifest in its portal[7].

This e-Infrastructure supported the operation of two virtual organizations corresponding to the two communities served by the project (cf. Sec. 2). The EM lead to the creation of approximately: 27 content collections containing more than 20,000 compound Information Objects; 59 metadata collections with multiple metadata schema including Dublin Core, ISO19115 and proprietary formats containing more than 40,500 metadata records; and more than 250 WS-Resources representing full text, forward and geo indices supporting the search over these data. The FARM lead to the creation of approximately: 15 content collections containing more than 8,800 compound Information Objects; 38 metadata collections with multiple metadata schemas including Dublin Core and a proprietary format containing more than 13,800 metadata records, and more than 130 WS-Resources representing full text and forward indices supporting the search over these data.

This e-Infrastructure supported the development and operation of these VREs:

- *Fishery Country Profiles Production System* (*FCPPS*) supports scientists in the generation of fisheries and aquaculture reports. The production of country profiles requires complex aggregation and editing of continuously evolving multilingual data from a large number of heterogeneous data sources. Availability of the FCPPS VRE permits to the scientists producing them to update and webpublish these important reports as frequently as the community requires, while also having access to additional resources when needed.
- *Integrated Capture Information System* (*ICIS*) supports scientists in integrating regional and global capture and distribution information of aquatic species, from a number of Regional Fishery Management Organisations (RFMOs) and international organisations (FAO, WorldFish Center) into a common system. The VRE provides not only access to the necessary data but also a number of

---

[7] portal.d4science.research-infrastructures.eu

services for, providing a harmonised view of catch statistics and allowing the community to overlay according to pre-defined reallocation rules.

- *Global Ocean Chlorophyll Monitoring* (*GCM*) offers to scientists an environment that integrates satellite data of microscopic marine plants and sea surface temperature. This environment supports research on biodiversity, by facilitating process like the measuring the distribution, monitoring and modelling of phytoplankton (microscopic marine plants), the provision of forecasts of sea state and currents, the monitoring of algal blooms and marine pollution and the measuring of changes in the ocean productivity.
- *Global Land Vegetation Monitoring* (*GVM*) provides a virtual environment that integrates satellite images of vegetative land cover. It facilitates specific research on how climate changes and land cover influence environmental resources. By having access to the data and tools of this VRE scientists can determine important measures like the total green leaf area for a given ground area, how much water will be stored and released by an ecosystem, how much leaf litter it will generate, and how much photosynthesis is going on.

In addition to them, a Virtual Research Environment dedicated to support the Fisheries scientists to produce species distribution maps has been developed: the AquaMaps Virtual Research Environment.

5   THE AQUAMAPS VIRTUAL RESEARCH
ENVIRONMENT

AquaMaps is an approach to generate model-based, large-scale predictions of currently known natural occurrence of marine species. Models are constructed from estimates of the environmental tolerance of a given species with respect to depth, salinity, temperature, primary productivity, and its association with sea ice or coastal areas. The resulting maps show the color-coded relative likelihood of a species to occur in a global grid of half-degree latitude / longitude cell dimensions, which corresponds to a side length of about 50 km near the equator. Predictions are generated by matching habitat usage of species, termed environmental envelopes, against local environmental conditions to determine the relative suitability of specific geographic areas for a given species. Knowledge of species distributions within FAO areas or bounding boxes is also used to exclude potentially suitable habitat in which the species is not known to occur.

The modeling approach used by AquaMaps was originally developed by Kristin Kaschner and colleagues to predict global distributions of marine mammals [14]. The approach was based on incorporating expert knowledge into an environmental envelope or ecological niche model. The use of expert knowledge compensated for the effects of species misidentifications, effort biases, and the non-representative coverage of large-scale species distributions. Such data gaps and problems are widespread in publicly available occurrence data sets that are compiled from different sources.

The approach developed for marine mammals was subsequently modified in collaboration with FishBase staff to make it more suitable for a greater range of marine organisms and to make use of data and information available in FishBase and OBIS/GBIF [15] online databases.

This approach is currently implemented by the AquaMap Service [16] which permits the community to establish/predict species geographic distribution based on species ecological envelopes according to a transparent algorithm that can be handled by species experts. However, such a service and the overall approach underlying AquaMaps is a computationally-intensive and cooperation-intensive task that greatly benefits from a Virtual Research Environment.

The AquaMaps VRE has been developed to provide a research environment for scientist to find, share, generate, modify and validate predictions of marine species distribution computed using species distribution models. Such predictions are generated based on the investigation of statistical relationships between the documented presence (and absence in some cases) of a species at a given location and the associated environmental conditions. These relationships are then extrapolated and/or interpolated to other un-sampled areas to provide an indication of the relative probability of a species to occur such areas.

This Virtual Research Environment is equipped with: (a) a dedicated suite supporting a detailed selection and customisation of the data and algorithms to be used to produce certain maps and relying on the distributed computing facilities for the computationally intensive data crunching activities; (*b*) a flexible report management suite supporting the definition and production of complex reports of various genre, i.e. documents composed by multiple parts of different media; (*c*) a workspace suite providing the researchers with a working environment implementing modern file manager facilities on a rich array of compound information objects and promoting their effective sharing with co-workers; (*d*) a powerful information discovery suite allowing a seamless access to the heterogeneous data sources these researchers need.

This environment has been designed and developed very quickly by relying on the gCube VRE deployment facilities [17]. Some screenshots of the resulting environment are in Figure 3.

Fig. 3: AquaMaps VRE Screenshots: AquaMaps Generation Service

Through this environment scientists have successfully produced in a few months of activity more than 10,000 AquaMaps objects each consisting of 15 images (a 2D map of the whole Earth plus 2 3D views for the Poles, 6 3D views for the Continents, and 6 3D views for the Oceans) with the relative metadata.

6 CONCLUSION AND FUTURE WORK

eScience scenarios demand for innovative research environments supporting computationally-intensive, data-intensive and collaboration-intensive tasks on both small and large scale. This paper described an approach for supporting such a kind of activities based on an e-Infrastructure enabling the definition and operation of *Virtual Research Environments*. It has been discussed the implementation of such an approach realised in the context of the D4Science EU project. Moreover, it has been presented how this approach has been exploited to serve concrete and challenging scenarios in the Environmental Monitoring and Fisheries and Aquaculture Resources Management.

Since October 2010 the second phase of the D4Science project started in the context of the D4Science-II project. The objective of this second phase is to reinforce the D4Science e-Infrastructure by making it interoperable with diverse other data e-Infrastructures that are running autonomously thus creating the core of an e-Infrastructure Ecosystem. The resulting e-Infrastructures Ecosystem will serve a significantly expanded set of communities dealing with multidisciplinary, scientific and societal challenges including the mining of bibliometric data with the aim to compute hybrid metrics, the production of enhanced publications, the production of enhanced species occurrence maps, the reallocation of catches statistics, the building of improved country profiles.

7 ACKNOWLEDGEMENTS

The work reported has been partially supported by the D4Science project, within FP7 of the European Commission, INFRA-2007-1.2.2, Contract No. 212488 and by D4Science-II project, within FP7 of the European Commission, INFRA-2008-1.2.2, Contract No. 239019. The authors would like to thank Pedro Andrade, Nicolas Bailly, Kristin Kaschner, Andrea Manzi and Fabio Sinibaldi for their fundamental role in implementing the AquaMaps VRE.

REFERENCES

[1] I. Foster, C. Kesselman, and S. Tuecke. The Anatomy of the Grid: Enabling Scalable Virtual Organization. The International Journal of High Performance Computing Applications, 15(3):200–222, 2001.

[2] I. Foster, C. Kesselman, J. Nick, and S. Tuecke. The Physiology of the Grid: An Open Grid Services Architecture for Distributed Systems Integration. Open Grid Service Infrastructure WG, Global Grid Forum, June 2002.

[3] M. Fraser. Virtual Research Environments: Overview and Activity. Ariadne, 44, 2005.

[4] L. Candela, D. Castelli, and P. Pagano. On-demand Virtual Research Environments and the Changing Roles of Librarians. Library Hi Tech, 27(2):239–251, 2009.

[5] L. Candela, D. Castelli, and P. Pagano. D4Science: an e-Infrastructure for Supporting Virtual Research Environments. In M. Agosti, F. Esposito, and C. Thanos, editors, Post-

proceedings of the 5th Italian Research Conference on Digital Libraries - IRCDL 2009, pages 166–169. DELOS: an Association for Digital Libraries, 2009.

[6] L. Candela, F. Akal, H. Avancini, D. Castelli, L. Fusco, V. Guidetti, C. Langguth, A. Manzi, P. Pagano, H. Schuldt, M. Simi, M. Springmann, and L. Voicu. DILIGENT: integrating Digital Library and Grid Technologies for a new Earth Observation Research Infrastructure. International Journal on Digital Libraries, 7(1-2):59–80, October 2007.

[7] I. Foster, Y. Zhao, I. Raicu, and S. Lu. Cloud Computing and Grid Computing 360-Degree Compared. In Grid Computing Environments Workshop, 2008. GCE '08, 2008.

[8] L. Candela, D. Castelli, and P. Pagano. gCube: A Service-Oriented Application Framework on the Grid. ERCIM News, (72):48–49, January 2008.

[9] O. Appleton, B. Jones, D. Kranzmuller, and E. Laure. The EGEE-II project: Evolution towards a permanent european grid initiative. In L. Grandinetti, editor, High Performance Computing (HPC) and Grids in Action, volume 16 of Advances in Parallel Computing, pages 424–435. IOS Press, Amsterdam, Mar. 2008.

[10] S. Boutsis, L. Candela, P. Di Marcello, P. Fabriani, L. Frosini, G. Kakaletris, P. Koltsida, L. Lelii, D. Milano, P. Pagano, P. Polydoras, P. Ranaldi, P. Roccetti, F. Simeoni, M. Simi, V. Tsagkalidou, R. Tsantouli, and A. Turli. D4Science System High-level Design. Deliverable DJRA1.1c, D4Science, November 2009.

[11] P. Pagano, F. Simeoni, M. Simi, and L. Candela. Taming development complexity in service-oriented e-infrastructures: the gcore application framework and distribution for gcube. Zero-In e-Infrastructure News Magazine, 1(1):19 – 21, 2009.

[12] F. Simeoni, L. Candela, G. Kakaletris, M. Sibeko, P. Pagano, G. Papanikos, P. Polydoras, Y. E. Ioannidis, D. Aarvaag, and F. Crestani. A Grid-Based Infrastructure for Distributed Retrieval. In L. Kovács, N. Fuhr, and C. Meghini, editors, Research and Advanced Technology for Digital Libraries, 11th European Conference, ECDL 2007, Budapest, Hungary, September 16-21, 2007, Proceedings, volume 4675 of Lecture Notes in Computer Science, pages 161– 173. Springer-Verlag, 2007.

[13] E. Floros, G. Kakaletris, P. Polydoras, and Y. Ioannidis. Grid Computing: Achievements and Prospects, chapter Query Processing Over The Grid: the Role Of Workflow Management, pages 1–12. Springer, 2008.

[14] K. Kaschner, R. Watson, A. W. Trites, and D. Pauly. Mapping world-wide distributions of marine mammal species using a relative environmental suitability (RES) model. Marine Ecology Progress Series, 316:285–310, July 2006.

[15] M. Costello, K. Stocks, Y. Zhang, J. Grassle, and D. Fautin. About the Ocean Biogeographic Information System. http://www.iobis.org/, March 2007.

[16] K. Kaschner, J. S. Ready, E. Agbayani, J. Rius, K. Kesner-Reyes, P. D. Eastwood, A. B. South, S. O. Kullander, T. Rees, C. H. Close, R. Watson, D. Pauly, and R. Froese. AquaMaps: Predicted range maps for aquatic species. http://www.aquamaps.org/, 2008.

[17] M. Assante, L. Candela, D. Castelli, L. Frosini, L. Lelii, P. Manghi, A. Manzi, P. Pagano, and M. Simi. An Extensible Virtual Digital Libraries Generator. In B. Christensen-Dalsgaard, D. Castelli, B. A. Jurik, and J. Lippincott, editors, 12th European Conference on Research and Advanced Technology for Digital Libraries, ECDL 2008, Aarhus, Denmark, September 14-19, volume 5173 of Lecture Notes in Computer Science, pages 122–134. Springer, 2008.

An Efficient Grid Data Access with StoRM

Riccardo Zappi, Elisabetta Ronchieri, Alberto Forti and Antonia Ghiselli

INFN-CNAF, Bologna, Italy

Abstract   In production data Grids, high performance disk storage solutions using parallel file systems are becoming increasingly important to provide reliability and high speed I/O operations needed by High Energy Physics analysis farms. Today, Storage Area Network solutions are commonly deployed at Large Hadron Collider data centres, and parallel file systems such as GPFS and Lustre provide reliable, high speed native POSIX I/O operations in parallel fashion. In this paper, we describe StoRM, a Grid middleware component, implementing the standard Storage Resource Manager v2.2 interface. Its architecture fully exploits the potentiality offered by the underlying cluster file system. Indeed, it enables and encourages the use of the native POSIX file protocol (i.e. "file://") allowing managed Storage Element to improve job efficiency in data accessing. The job running on the worker node can perform a direct access to the Storage Element managed by StoRM as if it were a local disk, instead of transferring data from Storage Elements to the local disk.

1   INTRODUCTION

The term Grid computing refers to the computational and networking infrastructure, designed to provide pervasive and reliable access to data and computational resources over wide-area network across organizational domains. A Grid connects a collection of hundreds of geographically distributed computers and storage resources located in different parts of the world to facilitate sharing of data and resources [1], [2], [3], and to allow users to transparently use them without knowing where their data resides and where it is processed and analysed. The term storage resource refers to any combination of the storage system with the controlling software (e.g., file system). There are several types of storage resources like CASTOR[1], DPM[2] and dCache [4] (see Fig. 1), for example related to disk and tape, providing each different levels of quality of service and access technologies.

---

[1] CASTOR: CERN Advanced STORage manager, http://castor.web.cern.ch/castor

[2] DPM: LCG Disk Pool Manager, https://twiki.cern.ch/twiki/bin/view/LCG/ DpmAdminGuide

S.C. Lin and E. Yen (eds.), *Data Driven e-Science: Use Cases and Successful Applications of Distributed Computing Infrastructures (ISGC 2010)*, DOI 10.1007/978-1-4419-8014-4_19,
© Springer Science+Business Media, LLC 2011

Fig. 1: Example of storage resources.

An increasing number of High Energy Physics (HEP) applications require the searching over billions of data and accessing data from various distributed storage systems. These data-intensive applications involve large amounts of data, which are vital to large HEP collaborations dispersed over wide-area networks. The HEP usage of Grid is intended to allow them to manage data at very large scales of both size and distribution, and to access secure resources shared across organizational boundaries. Ensuring efficient access to such huge and widely distributed data is a serious challenge to speed up common analysis jobs on scientific data and to enable some previously impractical analysis jobs. For example, in the field of HEP the analysis of a set of collision events may require to read only the wanted events. The major barrier to supporting fast data access in a Grid is the high latencies of wide-area networks and the Internet, which impact the scalability and fault tolerance of the total Grid system. Therefore, high-performance Storage Area Network (SAN) solutions with parallel and cluster file systems, like IBM General Parallel File System (GPFS) [5] and LUSTRE offered by SUN[3], are used in HEP analysis farms to provide reliability and high speed I/O operations, to provide high availability and fault tolerance, to handle the explosive growth of data, and to satisfy the most demanding applications. These solutions are deployed at the Large Hadron Collider (LHC) at the European Centre for Nuclear Research (CERN) that generates data of the Petabyte order for the major HEP experiments such as Alice, ATLAS, CMS and LHCb. This LHC data is distributed and persistently stored at several dozens of sites around the world building the LHC data Grid on the base of the Worldwide LHC Computing Grid (WLCG)[4].

Nowadays network-oriented computing environments require high-performance and network-aware file systems enabling to satisfy both the data storage requirements of individual systems and the data sharing requirements of work groups and clusters of cooperative systems. The access to data is becoming the main bottleneck in such data intensive applications because the data cannot be replicated in all sites. Developing a data service that guarantees service performance, scalable throughput, high availability, and reliability is both a critical imperative and a huge challenge for large organizational domains. Storage Resource Manager (SRM) [6] is middleware software module whose purpose is to manage what resides on the storage resource, interacting with mass storage systems to perform

[3] Lustre, High Performance and Scalability, http://wiki.lustre.org/index.php/ Main_Page

[4] The Worldwide LHC Computing Grid (WLCG), http://lcg.web.cern.ch/LCG/

file archiving and file staging and invoking middleware components like GridFTP [7] to perform file transfer operations. It is able to manage multiple storage resources at a site, giving the site the possibility to move files around between two different storage devices for example without changing the file name. SRM is adopted in the context of LHC. In this paper, we present StoRM, an implementation of SRM interface version 2.2, as a suitable solution to face access data problems, joined to the WLCG world and designed to allow direct access to the storage resource using the native file protocol [8] as well as other standard Grid protocols like GridFTP and Remote File I/O (RFIO) [9]. StoRM takes advantage from high performing cluster file system, like GPFS and Lustre, and supports also any standard POSIX file systems with ACL enabled.

This paper is organized as follows. Section 2 introduces the problem statement. Section 3 describes StoRM as suitable solution at the problem. Section 4 explains how StoRM is able to access data using file protocol. Finally, Section 5 concludes the paper.

2   PROBLEM STATEMENT

In the context of WLCG, a Storage Element (SE) is an abstraction of the storage Grid infrastructure, being the smallest units in the chain of data access and data processing. SEs must be able to communicate each other in order to transfer data between sites running different storage systems, and to provide local data through standard methods to allow Grid jobs to access data files in a site by hiding storage characteristics and allowing interoperability. Each site may provide large amounts of storage technologies from custodial long-term tape storage to shorter-term disk based storage that have to be transparent to the users, therefore an abstract layer on top of the particular storage implementation used at each site has to be provided.

The SRM working group[5] within the Open Grid Forum (OGF) defined a standard asynchronous control interface, called SRM, to Grid storage systems and supervises this protocol. The SRM services in the WLCG context are interoperable thanks to an international effort made by the developers of different SRM implementations to eliminate functional differences and to feedback from the HEP community [10], [11].

SRM defines a set of commands to be implemented by the local storage system to enable remote access, to prepare data for remote transfer, and to negotiate appropriate transfer mechanisms. It is essential in a Grid environment, because it provides smooth synchronization between shared resources by pinning files, releasing files, and allocating space dynamically. The SRM service provides a way of managing local storage by means of the control protocol SRM, providing and receiving data by basic wide area transport protocols, like GridFTP [12] and

---

[5] SRM collaboration working group, https://sdm.lbl.gov/srm-wg/

http(s) [13], and making storage available to local native I/O access protocols (like dCap [14], and RFIO [15]). SRMs usually rely on GridFTP for wide area data transfer. GridFTP is a modified version of the standard FTP protocol [16]. This protocol builds on standard FTP to incorporate X.509 based security [17] allowing interaction with Grid Security Infrastructure (GSI) [12], and to include further extensions [18]. In the current Grid infrastructure, the high-level storage control protocol (i.e., SRM) mostly chooses GridFTP for wide area transfers. Alternative protocols could be selected if supported by client and server.

The rfio and dCap server-dependent protocols were designed in the HEP community to provide access to hierarchical mass storage devices such as Castor [9] and dCache [19]. The RFIO protocol was designed for the transfer of files in a trusted environment with a minimum of overhead. It does not use a secure authentication and therefore lays open the overhead of authentication when comparing with other protocols like GridFTP. RFIO provides a full POSIX-inspired access mechanism to the remote files via adapted open, read, write and close commands using a file number as handler. RFIO has a problem with many concurrent request. The dCap protocol supports regular file access functionality. dCap offers the POSIX open, read, write, speek, stat, close calls. It supports pluggable security mechanisms where the GSSAPI [20] and ssl security protocols are implemented.

In Grid, a file is referred by different names: Logical File Name (LFN), Storage URL (SURL) and Transport URL (TURL). The LFN is a user friendly high level name created by a user to some item of data (e.g., lfn : dteam/20030203/ run2/track1); there can be several LFNs (aliases) for one file.

The SURLs contain information related to the location of the physical replica and its access, whilst the LFNs identify a file without considering its location. The mapping between LFNs and SURLs are kept in a file catalogue service, whilst the files themselves are stored in SEs. The only file catalogue officially supported in WLCG is the Logical File Catalogue (LFC).

Two site scenarios are described in Fig. 2: site A provides jobs indirect access to data via RFIO, whilst site B allows jobs to direct access data via file protocol thanks to the usage of a cluster GPFS file system. For these site scenarios a set of use cases were identified: 1. an application may need to store data in SE from a WN; and 2. an application may need to copy data locally into a WN and use them. Each of these use cases is easily transformed in a list of operations:

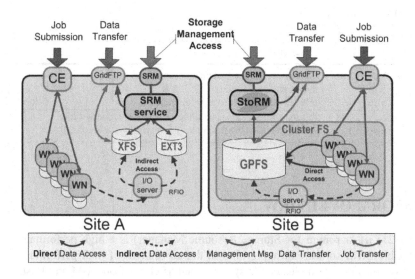

Fig. 2: Two site scenarios: site A represents a classic site, whilst site B is a StoRM site.

1. to store data in the SE from a WN, an application needs to create a new LFN entry in LFC obtaining a SURL, to run srmPrepareToPut (see Table 1) with the resulted SURL, to transfer the file for storing it in the SE, and to run srmPutDone (see Table 1) with the resulted SURL;

2. to retrieve data stored into the SE onto the WN, an application needs to query the file catalog to retrieve the SURL from the LFN, to run srmPrepareToGet (see Table 1) with the resulted SURL, to transfer the file for read it from the SE, and to run srmReleaseFile (see Table 1) with the resulted SURL.

Applications need to access a big set of data: therefore copy data into the WN could not be the best solution, whilst remote access might be more convenient in some cases. Furthermore, applications might require standard POSIX I/O and might want to take advantage of the local optimized storage infrastructure (e.g., parallel file systems, and storage area network).

Table 1: Description of operations

Operation	Description
srmPrepareToPut	creates a reference that clients can use to create new files in a storage space.
srmPutDone	tells the SRM that the write operation is done.
srmPrepareToGet	returns a reference to an online copy of the requested file.
srmReleaseFile	marks as releasable the copies generated by srmPrepareToGet

3   STORM OVERVIEW

StoRM [21] it] (acronym for Storage Resource Manager) is a high performance and flexible SRM solution bringing in Grid the advantages of high performance storage systems based on cluster file system, such as GPFS from IBM and Lustre from SUN. The latest stable version of StoRM (v1.5.x) enables also the management of hierarchical storage resource through a generic interface; indeed, in this configuration, it is currently used at the Italian Tier-1, at the CNAF, in Bologna, where it manages a hierarchical system based on GPFS and TSM.

It is designed to allow local access to the shared storage resources using the native protocol, that is the "file://" protocol, supporting as well as other data access libraries like RFIO [9]. StoRM decouples the file system from the SRM service, in the sense that the data access functionality can be provided by any POSIX file system with Access Control List (ACL) support [22], like XFS and ext3, while StoRM specifically provides just the SRM functionality. StoRM uses the mechanism of ACL provided by the underlying file system to implement the security model allowing the use of native access to the file system by authorized users and applications. This allows applications to perform a standard POSIX operation without interacting with any external service that emulates data access (e.g. RFIO) with the result of improving considerably the benefits in terms of I/O throughput, mostly in presence of high performance parallel and cluster file systems.

3.1   StoRM Architecture

The StoRM architecture is shown in Fig. 3. StoRM has a multilayer architecture composed by two main stateless components, called Front-End (FE) and Back-End (BE) and one database. The FE exposes the SRM web service interface, manages user authentication, stores SRM requests data into a database and retrieve the status of ongoing requests, and interacts with the Back-End. The Back-End is the core of StoRM service since it executes all synchronous and asynchronous SRM functionalities. It processes the SRM requests managing files and space, it enforces authorization permissions and it can interact with other Grid services, such as external authorization service and mapping service. Moreover, the Back End is able to use advanced functionalities provided by some file systems, like GPFS [5] and XFS, to accomplish space reservation requests. The BE uses a plug-in mechanism to easily extend new support for different file systems. The database is used to store only SRM requests data and space metadata; it does not hold any crucial information but only transient data. An accidental loss of the full database simply leads to failing ongoing SRM requests; space metadata will be recreated at next restart.

The StoRM service is capable to satisfy the high availability and scalability requirements coming both the small and growing centre and Tier1-scaled centre of HEP community. Most of the StoRM components support replication enabling the capability to deploy multiple instances in different hosts, to avoid bottleneck and enhance load balancing. Multiple Front-End instances can be deployed on separate machines and configured to work on the same database and the same Back-End service. For the load balancing a simple dynamic DNS configuration can be used.

StoRM has a light and flexible mechanism providing the mapping between the SURL and the physical location of the file. The standard approach used by other SRM implementation is to query, for each SRM request, a persistence service to resolve the SURL in TURL. StoRM leverage the underlying file system structure, and the mapping are done without interacting with any database service but evaluating a set of rules with a simple and effective algorithm [23].

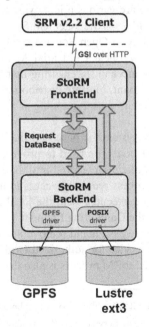

Fig. 3: StoRM Architecture.

4   ACCESSING DATA WITH STORM

As mentioned in the previous section, one of the StoRM peculiarities is its ability to create and manage TURLs through a system of rules rather than through the usage of a database. This flexible mechanism allows StoRM to manage new protocols very easily. Currently, StoRM is able to properly manage the mapping between SURL and TURL with protocols such as xroot, gsiftp, root, rfio and the native POSIX file protocol. However, StoRM is intended also to manage http and https protocols in the near future.

In order to fully exploit the presence of cluster file system, or to simply allow legacy applications to use Grid files without any modification, it is needed to use the data access protocol exposed by the file system natively. The job running on the WN should be able to perform direct access to files using the native file protocol, as if the files were in a local disk, instead of transferring data from the Grid SE. The management of the file protocol through StoRM is possible by assigning access privileges on files for those local users resulting from the mapping operation of the Grid users authorized to access.

Typically, Grid users have a certificate X.509 with VOMS extensions in which the roles and membership in groups are expressed. These information are used to map Grid credentials to local user and group identifier (i.e., uid and gid). This mapping is based upon the role and VO group membership and it is implemented in a service or library. There are various middleware that implement the mapping service: for example, the Grid User Management System (GUMS)[6] service developed at BNL, and used mainly in Open Science Grid (OSG). In gLite Grid middleware it is used the library Local Credential Mapping Service (LCMAPS)[7], which uses the pool account mechanism ensuring that different individuals on the Grid remain distinct Unix account. In gLite distribution there is a plan to adopt the system Argus[8], which may return a user mapping as an obligation result of the authorization phase.

Access control in UNIX systems is based on the credentials with which it is running a process. The credentials are used to prove eligibility to access the file and the associated security policies are stored into the Access Control List (ACL). In the scenario of use, the process requiring access to the file is the job submitted by a Grid user, which will be executed with the local credentials returned by the mapping service queried by the Computing Element.

StoRM operates on ACL to assign and remove access privileges to local users resulting from the mapping service for authorized Grid users. StoRM is granted to modify the ACL because the StoRM process is also the owner of files it manages.

---

[6] Grid User Management System (GUMS), https://www.racf.bnl.gov/Facility/ GUMS/1.3/

[7] LCMAPS, Local Credential Mapping Service https://www.nikhef.nl/pub/ projects/grid/gridwiki/index.php/LCMAPS

[8] Argus, EGEE Authorization Service, https://twiki.cern.ch/twiki/bin/view/ egee/authorizationframework

The named ACL entries (ACE) are added both to files and to directories. For example, when a user requests the reading of a file (i.e., srmPrepareToGet), the following entries are added:

group:<gid>:r--# on file

group:<gid>:--x # on each path element

where <gid> is the mapping result of the user requesting the srmPrepareToGet operation. In the case of a writing request, the following entries will be added to the file:

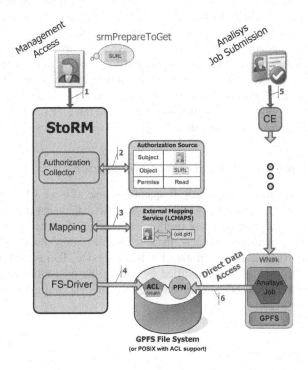

Fig. 4: A simple sequence diagram for data access with file protocol.

group:<gid>:-w-# on file
group:<gid>:--x # on each path element

In this way the job running with the local account (with Group ID <gid>) resulting from the pool account mechanism will have enough privileges to perform the wished operations on the target file. The added ACE entries could be removed when the access operation lifetime expires, or at the end of the request denoted by srmReleaseFile in case of a reading request, and by srmPutDone in case of a writing request.

4.1 A Sequence of Actions for Data Access with File Protocol

In Fig. 4 it is illustrated a simple sequence of actions describing how StoRM allows the use of file protocol to read a file. A Grid user with a valid Grid credentials wants to read a file pointed by SURL, so he/she performs a srmPrepareToGet call to StoRM holding the wished file (see point 1 in Fig. 4). When StoRM receives the call, first of all it verifies if the Grid user identified by the Distinguish Name (DN) and the VOMS attributes (FQANs) is authorized to perform srmPrepareToGet on that SURL (point 2). If the user is authorized, then StoRM retrieves the local mapping for the requestor (point 3); it is important observe that the same mapping service will be used by the Computing Element service in order to share the same user mapping results. After that StoRM sets up an ACL entry to the physical file and in every directory traversed corresponding to the wanted SURL (point 4). These entries could be removed when the pin expires or when the file will be released by the user. When the user obtains the TURL from StoRM, he is able to submit the job (point 5) with the certainty that the TURL will be accessible from any worker node using the native file protocol (point 6).

4.2 Local and Grid Data Access Cohabitation

Recently it is becoming increasingly frequent the case of users who do not want, or cannot for some reason, access to files using Grid data management tools such as SRM services. In practice, these users wish to access files using its own local account within its own farm. Clearly, these users must know the absolute path of the file, the TURL, without prompting the SRM service. To respond to this scenario of use, StoRM has been modified by adding the possibility to add, in the execution of srmPrepareToGet, a list of ACE definable via configuration.

5   CONCLUSIONS

Nowadays, a plethora of different storage resources are commonly adopted in Grid data center, such as CASTOR, DPM and dCache; some of which are developed to respond to the requirements coming from HEP community. These mentioned solutions, although solid and well supported, currently do not support the usage of the native file protocol and the file access is only possible using proprietary protocols, like dCap and RFIO protocols. Recently storage systems based on SAN and cluster file systems are becoming increasingly widespread and, correspondingly there is a growing need to exploit the access performance from a node of the farm offered by these storage resource types.

In this paper, we outlined the design of StoRM showing how it meets the HEP requirements in terms of performance maintaining the adhesion to the standard SRM. StoRM differs from other SE solutions in many aspects, but the main distinguish feature is surely the one that allows the usage of the file protocol with enormous advantage in terms of data access throughput, legacy application reuse and a clear justification of the adoption of SAN and cluster file system.

The scalability of StoRM is granted by the modular architecture, whilst the mechanism of driver allows to hide the specificity of different file systems making StoRM able to manage any POSIX file system supporting ACL. Indeed the support of the file protocol is guaranteed through a particular set up of ACL as described in a simple sequence of actions.

The flexibility of StoRM allows to satisfy the requirement of the users who do not want, or may not for some reason, use the Grid middleware to perform data access to local files from nodes belonging to their farm. Storage resources managed by StoRM are accessible to local users without requiring the use of any Grid middleware and, at the same time, they are available as SE in Grid.

REFERENCES

[1]   Allcock, W., Bester, J., Bresnahan, J., Chervenak, A., Foster, I., Kesselman, C., Meder, S., Nefedova, V., Quesnel, D., Tuecke, S.: Secure, Efficient Data Transport and Replica Management for High-Performance Data-Intensive Computing. In: IEEE Mass Storage Conference (2001)

[2]   Foster, I.: The Grid: A New Infrastructure for 21st Century Science. Physics Today. 54:2 (2002)

[3]   Stevens, R., Woodward, P., De Fanti, T., Catlett, C.: From the I-WAY to the National Technology Grid. Communications of the ACM. 40:11, 50–61 (1997)

[4]   De Riese, M., Fuhrmann, P., Mkrtchyan, T., Ernst, M., Kulyavtsev, A., Podstavkov, V., Radicke, M., Sharma, M., Litvintsev, M., Perelmutov, T.: dCache, the Book. Nov. (2006) http://www.dcache.org/manuals/Book/

[5]   Schmuck, F. and Haskin, R.: GPFS: A Shared-Disk File System for Large Computing Clusters. USENIX FAST 2002 Conference on File and Storage Technologies. (200) http://www.usenix.org/events/fast02/full_papers/schmuck/ schmuck.pdf

[6]   Shoshani, A., Sim, A., Gu, J.: Storage Resource Managers: Essential Components for the Grid. chapter in book: Grid Resource Management: State of the Art and Future Trends. Ed-

ited by Jarek Nabrzyski, Jennifer M. Schopf, Jan weglarz, Kluwer Academic Publishers (2003)

[7]   Allcock, W.: GridFTP: Protocol extensions to FTP for the Grid. Global Grid Forum GFD-R P.020 (2003) http://www.ggf.org/documents/GWD-R/GFD-R.020.pdf

[8]   Borland, M.: A self-describing file protocol for simulation integration and shared postprocessors. In: Particle Accelerator Conference. (Dallas,TX) 4, 2184–2186 (1995)

[9]   Barring, O., Baud, J., Durand, J.: CASTOR Project Status. In: Computing in High Energy Physics. Padua, Italy (2000)

[10]   Donno, F., Abadie, L., Badino, P., Baud, J.-P., Corso, E., De Witt, S., Fuhrman, P., Gu, J., Koblitz, B., Lemaitre, S., Litmaath, M., Litvintsev, D., Lo Presti, G., Magnoni, L., McCance, G., Mkrtchan, T., Mollan, R., Natarajan, V., Perelmutov, T., Petravick, D., Shoshani, A., Sim, A., Smith, D., Tedesco, P., and Zappi, R.: Storage Resource Manager Version 2.2: design, implementation, and testing experience. J. Physics: Conference Series. 119 (2008)

[11]   Sim, A., Shoshani, A., Donno, F., and Jensen, J.: Storage Resource Manager Interface Specifiation v2.2 Implementation Experience Report. Global Grid Forum GFD-E.154 (2009) http://www.ogf.org/documents/GFD.154.pdf

[12]   Foster, I., and Kesselman, C. and Tuecke, S.: A Security Architecture for Computation Grid. In: ACM Conference on Computer and Communications Security. (San Francisco, CA, USA) 83–92 (1998)

[13]   Fielding, R., Gettys, J., Mogul, J., Frystyk, H., Masinter, L., Leach, P., Berners-Lee, T.: Hypertext Transfer Protocol – HTTP/1.1. June (1999) http://www.w3.org/Protocols/HTTP/1.1/rfc2616.pdf

[14]   Ernst, M., Fuhrmann, P., Mkrtchyan, T., Bakken, J., Fisk, I., Perelmutov, T., and Petravick, D.: Managed Data Storage and Data Access Services for Data Grids. In: Computing in High Energy Physics and Nuclear Physics 2004. Interlaken, Switzerland, 27 Sep -1 Oct (2004)

[15]   Heiss, A. and Schwickerath, U.: RFIO/IB Project. http://hikwww2.fzk.de/hik/orga/ges/infiniband/rfioib.html

[16]   Postel, J., and Reynolds, J.: RFC959, File Transfer Protocol. The Internet Society. (1995) http://www.faqs.org/ftp/rfc/pdf/rfc959.txt.pdf

[17]   Horowitz, M., and Lunt, S.: RFC2228, FTP Security Extensions. The Internet Society. (1997) http://www.faqs.org/ftp/rfc/pdf/rfc2228.txt.pdf

[18]   Hethmon, P., and Elz, R.: Feature negotiation mechanism for the File Transfer Protocol. (1998)

[19]   Ernst, M., Fuhrmann, P., Gasthuber, M., Mkrtchyan, T., and Waldman, C.: dCache, a Distributed Storage Data Caching System. In: Computing in High Energy Physics. Beijing, China (2001)

[20]   Linn, J.: Generic Security Service Application Program Interface, Version 2, Update 1. Network Working Group. (2000) http://www.ietf.org/rfc/rfc2743.txt

[21]   Ghiselli A., Magnoni L., and Zappi R.: StoRM: a Flexible Solution for Storage Resource Manager in Grid. In: Nuclear Science Symposium Conference Record, 2008 (NSS '08) IEEE. Dresden, Germany (2008)

[22]   Grnbacher, A.: POSIX Access Control Lists on Linux. In: USENIX 2003 Annual Technical Conference, FREENIX Track. 259–272 (2003) http://www.usenix.org/event/usenix03/tech/freenix03/full_ papers/gruenbacher/gruenbacher.pdf

[23]   E.Corso, A.Forti, A.Ghiselli, L.Magnoni, R.Zappi: An effective XML based name mapping mechanism within StoRM. In: International Conference on Computing in High Energy and Nuclear Physics (CHEP'07) IOP Publishing, Journal of Physics: Conference Series 119 (2008)

Design and Implementation of a Multi-Grid Resource Broker for Grid Computing

Chao-Tung Yang and Wen-Jen Hu

Department of Computer Science, Tunghai University, Taiwan (ROC)

Abstract   Grid computing integrates geographical computing resources across multiple virtual organizations to achieve high performance computing. A single grid often could not provide huge resources, because virtual organizations have no adequate of computing resources restriction on the scale of organizations. In this paper, we present a multi-grid, new grid architecture for integrating multiple computational grids from different virtual organizations. A resource broker is built on multiple grid environments; it integrates a number of single grids from different virtual organizations without the limitation of organizations. The multiple grid resource could be utilized efficiently and precisely.

Keywords   Grid computing, Multi-Grid, Resource Broker

1   INTRODUCTION

Grid technology plays a major role in tackling large-scale problems by integrating distributed resources to provide users with a supercomputer liked capacity for data sharing and computation [1, 2, 3, and 4]. Participating sites may be physically distributed, heterogeneous, and governed by different administrative domains. Many grid related studies and projects has been proposed for solving large scale scientific problems such as earthquake simulation, atmosphere and ocean simulation, high energy and nuclear physics, astronomy, bioinformatics [5], and medical image processing [6]. There are more and more proposed grid projects such as Globus [4, 7], Condor, LEGION, Grid PP, EGEE, P-Grid, DutchGrid, ESnet, and Grid Bus.

We use the Ganglia and NWS tools to monitor resource status and network-related information [8, 9, and 10], respectively. Understanding influence of each parameter is not only crucial for an application to achieve good performance, but would also help to develop effective schedule heuristics and design high quality Grids. In Taiwan, some research institutes has devoted to build grid platforms for academic research use such as Tiger Grid [11] and Medical Grid [6] that integrate available computing resources in some universities and high schools. They respective use their grid resource, but some of virtual organizations have no the adequate of computing resources restriction on the scale of organizations [15]. For this rea-

S.C. Lin and E. Yen (eds.), *Data Driven e-Science: Use Cases and Successful Applications*
of Distributed Computing Infrastructures (ISGC 2010), DOI 10.1007/978-1-4419-8014-4_20,
© Springer Science+Business Media, LLC 2011

son, we construct a multi-grid resource broker [13] integrate those single grid environment as a multiple grid environment so that resources can be used more effectively.

In this paper, we propose a multi-grid resource broker architecture to solve the resource sharing problems in grids [14, 15, and 16]. When a new grid joins in the multi-grid environment by the proposed system, the user can use entire multi-grid resources, and get more computing resource. This approach could help these virtual organizations to possess more computing resources without any extra overhead. We chose the Globus Toolkit as the middleware of grids. Although Globus provides a monitor tool, which is called MDS, is not capable of providing the rich set of all the requisite information. Thus we used another monitor tool "Ganglia" [17, 18, 19, and 20] on the multi-grid system. The Ganglia is a scalable open source distributed system for monitoring status of nodes in wide-area systems based on clusters.

2 MULTI-GRID RESOURCE ARCHITECTURE

The system architecture of the resource broker is shown in Fig. 1. Users could easily make use of our resource broker through a common Grid portal [21, 22, 23, and 24]. The primary task of Resource Broker is comparing requests of users and resource information provided by Information Service. After choosing the appropriate job assignment scheme, Grid resources are assigned and the Scheduler is responsible to submit the job. The results are collected and returned to Resource Broker. Then, Resource Broker records results of execution in the database of Information Center through the Agent of Information Service. Users can query the results from Grid portal.

Our resource broker architecture includes four layers: web portal, resource brokering subsystem, multi-grid manager center, and multi-grid resource. The multi-grid resource consists of many single grid environments. When a new single grid joins our multi-grid environment, the grid administrator should register at the web portal and provide the personal file and the related information of the grid, such as the CA package, the grid-mapfile of Globus, and the machine lists. The multi-grid system deploys the environment according to the registered information, and then assigns a resource broker account to a single grid user. This account could access the resource which was supported by the resource broker on the multi-grid environment, Fig. 1 shows the concept. The multi-grid manager center has cross grid authentication service and cross grid information service, that is the important part on entire multi-grid environment, which controls the access of grid and the information gather, the details described in following section.

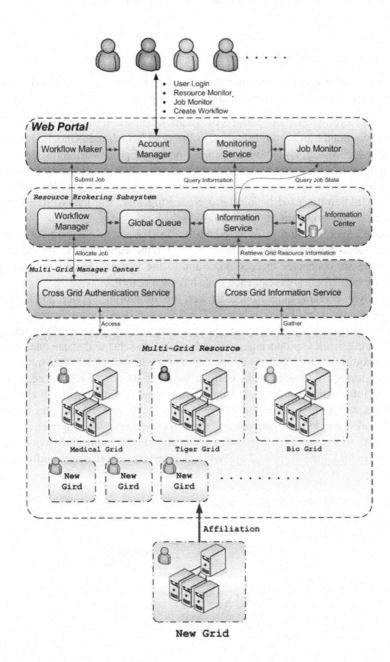

Fig. 1: Resource Broker system architecture

3   SYSTEM DESIGN AND IMPLEMENTATION

3.1   Software Stack Diagram

The system software stack includes three layers which were constructed using a bottom-up methodology. The layers are described below:

- Bottom Layer: principally consists of Nodes, as shown in Fig. 2. The layer contains two main blocks, the Information Provider, which uses Ganglia to gather machine information on Nodes, such as number of processors/cores, processor loading, total/free memory, and disk usage, and NWS, which gathers essential network information such as bandwidth and latency. The second block contains Grid Middleware, used to join Grid Nodes together, and the MPICH-G2 required for running parallel applications on the Grid.
- Middle Layer: contains grids as shown in Fig. 3. Each grid consists of several nodes located in the same place or connected to the same switch/hub. All nodes in a site are connected to each other and to the Internet. Moreover, grids are usually built as clusters with each node having a real IP.
- Top Layer: contains the Resource Broker, the Monitoring Service, and the multi-grid manager, as shown in Fig. 3. The Resource Broker coordinates Grid resources, dispatches jobs to resources, and monitors job statuses. One contribution of this work is proposing a resource allocation scheme that can handle user jobs requiring more Grid resources than one dedicated cluster can supply. To make strategic decisions in dispatching jobs, the Re-source Broker needs currently information on the Grid from the Monitoring Service, which also provides a web front-end for users to observe job progress. Monitoring Service, which also provides a web front-end for users to observe job progress. The task of multi-grid manager is integrating the grids into the multi-grid environment, which includes the cross grid authentication service and cross grid information service.

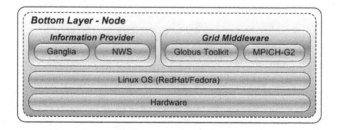

Fig. 2: The software stack of all nodes

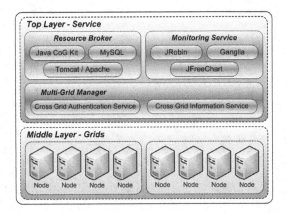

Fig. 3: The software stack of all sites and the service

3.2   Cross Grid Authentication Service

The Globus Toolkit authentication is issued by the certificate of GSI. Each user and service is certificated to identify and authenticate the trust between users or services. If two parties have the certificate and both of them trust the CAs, then these two parties could trust each other. This is known as the mutual authentication. A subject name, which identifies the person or object that the certificate represents. The cross grid authentication service manages the several certificates and the subject of grid, and we know these messages from the registered information via web portal. All of nodes on multi-grid environment should setup the cross grid service tool, which written in the shell script program, show in Fig. 4. The cross grid service tool contains some procedures to regular automatic update with multi-grid manager center, such as the IP and domain of host list, the certificates, and the subject. Any single grid user on our multi-grid environment makes use of the multi-grid resource through the tool to update with multi-grid manager center. The primary task of cross grid information is gathering the IDL file, which contains the several attributes of hosts on grid, the detail describe in next section.

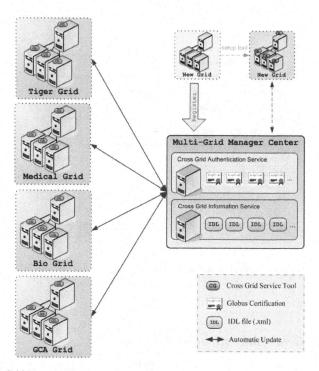

Fig. 4: Multi-Grid Manager Center

3.3 Cross Grid Information Service

The monitor tool is one of the most important components in a grid environment [17, 18, and 25]. A good monitor tool could help grid administrator to manage and monitor the machines. On the other hand, the middleware could gather the resource information to find the suitable resource via the monitor tool. There are common monitor tools, such as MDS, Ganglia, Cacti, and Condor. On a multi-grid environment, grids use different monitor tools with different information formats. Therefore, we define a new information format to integrate different formats. The proposed format is called IDL (Information Describing Language), as shown in Fig. 5. It is responsible to exchange and translate resource information among grids, and to perform the post-transfer filtering to ensure that only necessary information is passed to clients, end users, and software components.

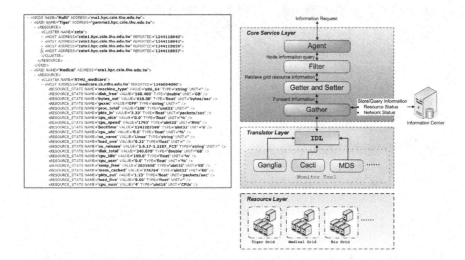

Fig. 5: Information Describing Language.

Fig. 6: Cross Grid Information Service architecture

The CGIS consists of three layers: the Core Service Layer, the Translator Layer, and the Resource Layer, as shown in Fig. 6. The Core Service Layer contains the Agent, Filter, Getter and Setter, and Gather. These components are installed in every grid environment for information gathering and maintenance. The Translator Layer supports a variety of format conversion monitor tools, such as Ganglia, Cacti, and MDS. The information in different monitor tools would be transformed into the IDL format. The Resource Layer describes resource information from different grid environments. In this study, it includes Tiger Grid, Medical Grid, and Bio Grid [15].

3.4 Web Portal

We provides a registration page for a new single grid to join our multi-grid environment, the register service will automatic send mail to the multi-grid administrator, administrator adjustment and configure the setting of multi-grid environment as receive the registration page. Simultaneously, the register service informs the new single grid to download the cross grid service tool from multi-grid server for finishing the step of registration, as shown in Figure 7.

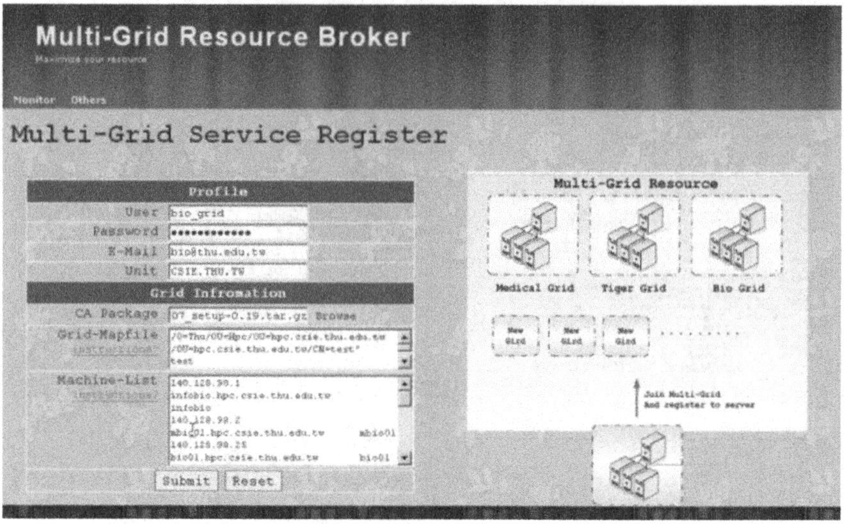

Fig. 7: Registration page of Multi-Grid Resource Broker

We use IDL XML format to exchange of the information between multi-grid resources. The collected information not only is utilized while submitting job, but also be referenced while monitoring the status of grids. The Monitor Service could monitor the resources supported by the multi-grid resource broker. We provide the interface to observe the status of Hosts Info, Daemons, and Ganglia. Hosts Info show the status include the number of CPU, CPU speed, the average of load in one minute, the average of load in five minute, the size of free memory and the size of free swap , as shown in Figure 8. Daemon Status is another service that monitors the services' status of machines by the NMAP, which parses the list of host by IDL file and scans the fix ports through the list, and then gets the status whether the service to be on or not, as shown in Figure 9. In this study, we rewrite the Ganglia codes and modify its setting to support the multiple grids. Our Ganglia page presents the multi-level architecture: Tiger Grid, Medical Grid, Bio Grid, and GCA Grid in the web portal, as shown in Figure 10.

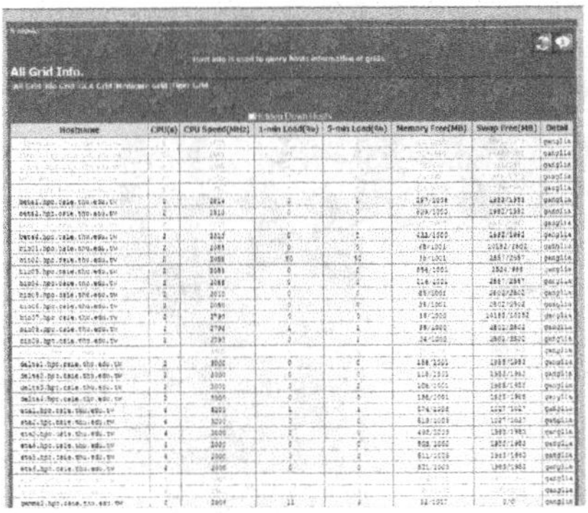

Fig. 8: Hosts Info 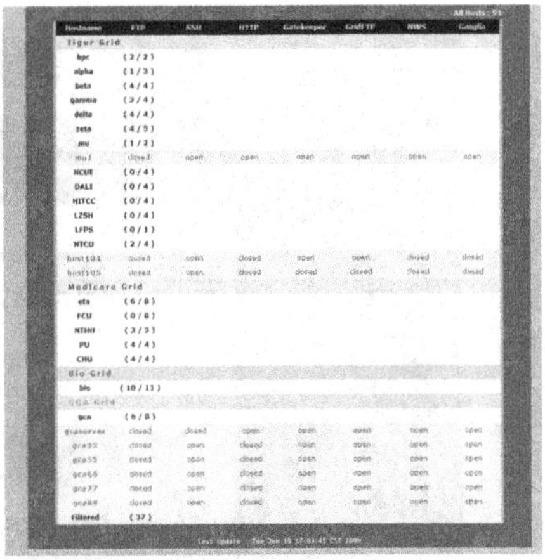   Fig. 9: Daemon Status

The Tiger Grid contains the network measure service; we use the NWS to achieve the point to point network bandwidth measure. However, the NWS tool lacks the database to conserve the statistics, so we stored the statistics into round-robin database every five minutes, and then draw the graph through JRobin, as shown in Figure 10. JRobin is a 100% pure Java implementation of RRDTool's functionality. The function pages have a web page of help manual in our web portal, which describes the capability of page and the function of hyperlinks. With the friendly manipulated interface, details are abstracted from the users who no longer have need of expertise in multi-grid environment, as shown in Figure 11.

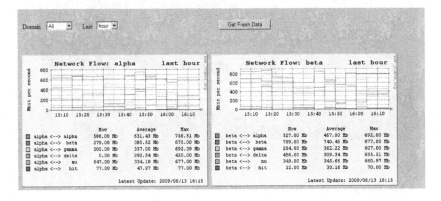

Fig. 10: NWS Information

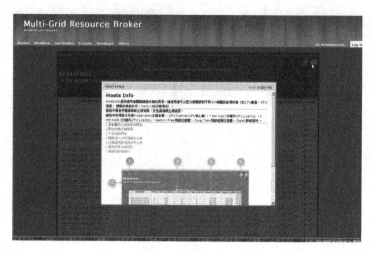

Fig. 11: Help Page

The user could execute a parallel program via the resource broker and describe the requirements for the execution of the hosts when submitting the job, as shown in Figure 11, and retrieve the result form the Job Monitor Service, which shows the many detail messages in execute time, such as scheduling log, machine list, result message, running log, debug message, and turnaround time.

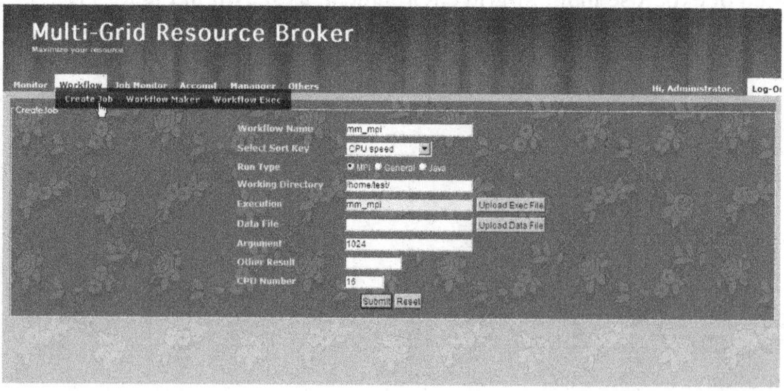

Fig. 12: Job Monitor

4   CONCLUSIONS AND FUTURE WORK

In this paper, we construct a resource broker for multi-grid computational environment which integrates the four single grids into our environment, and provides the cross grid service. The resource broker facilitates users to submit job via web portal. The user executes the workflow to achieve more high-performance computing by web portal without comprehend complicated instructions, and that can monitor status of multi-grid or grid itself. With the multi-grid platform, as more and more virtual organizations join into the multi-grid environment, a huge computing resource would be progressively grown up.

In the future, we focus on efficiently integrating the different grid middleware, such as Globus and GLite. Although most organizations utilize the Globus as the grid middleware in Taiwan, the GLite still has plenty of users in global. We will continually invite other universities or research centers to join our architecture, and allocate the account to use resource broker.

REFERENCE

[1]   Foster and N. Karonis, "A Grid-Enabled MPI: Message Passing in Heterogeneous Distributed Computing Systems," Proceedings of 1998 Supercomputing Conference, 1998, pp. 46- 46.

[2]   J. Tang, and M. Zhang, "An Agent-based Peer-to-Peer Grid Computing Architecture," Semantics, Knowledge and Grid, 2005, SKG '05, First International Conference on, 2005, pp.57-57.

[3]   F. Ian and K. Carl, "Globus: A Metacomputing Infrastructure Toolkit," International Journal of Supercomputer Applications, 1997, vol. 11, pp. 115-128.

[4]   F. Ian and K. Carl, The Grid: Blueprint for a New Computing Infrastructure, Morgan Kaufmann, 1st edition, 1999.

[5]   Bio Grid, http://140.128.98.25/ganglia/

[6]   Medical Grid, http://eta1.hpc.csie.thu.edu.tw/ganglia/

[7]   V. Laszewski, I. Foster, J. Gawor, and P. Lane, "A Java commodity grid kit," Concurrency and Computation: Practice and Experience, 2001, vol. 13, pp. 645-662.

[8]   C.T. Yang, P.C. Shih, and S.Y. Chen, "A Domain-Based Model for Efficient Measurement of Network Information on Grid Computing Environments," IEICE - Trans. Inf. Syst. 2006, vol. E89-D, pp. 738-742.

[9]   R. Wolski, N. Spring, and J. Hayes, "The Network Weather Service: A Distributed Resource Performance Forecasting Service for Metacomputing," Future Generation Computing Systems, 1999, vol. 15, pp. 757-768.

[10]   D.H. Kim, K.W. Kang, "Design and Implementation of Integrated Information System for Monitoring Resources in Grid Computing," Computer Supported Cooperative Work in Design, 2006, pp. 1-6.

[11]   Tiger Grid, http://gamma2.hpc.csie.thu.edu.tw/ganglia/

[12]   W. Zhang, B. Fang, H. He, H. Zhang, M. Hu, "Multisite resource selection and scheduling algorithm on computational grid", Proceedings of Parallel and Distributed Processing Symposium, 2004, pp. 105-115.

[13]   Multi Grid, http://gamma2.hpc.csie.thu.edu.tw/

[14] C.T. Yang, P.C. Shih, and K.C. Li, "A high-performance computational resource broker for grid computing environments," Advanced Information Networking and Applications, 2005. AINA 2005. 19th International Conference on, 2005, vol.2, pp. 333-336.

[15] C.T. Yang, K.C. Li, W.C. Chiang, and P.C. Shih, "Design and Implementation of TIGER Grid: an Integrated Metropolitan-Scale Grid Environment," Proceedings of the 6th IEEE International Conference on PDCAT'05, 2005, pp. 518-520.

[16] C.T. Yang, C.F. Lin, and S.Y. Chen, "A Workflow-based Computational Resource Broker with Information Monitoring in Grids," Proceedings of Fifth International Conference on Grid and Cooperative Computing (GCC'06), 2006, pp. 199-206.

[17] F.D. Sacerdoti, M.J. Katz, M.L. Massie, and D. E. A. C. D. E. Culler, "Wide area cluster monitoring with Ganglia," Cluster Computing, 2003. Proceedings of 2003 IEEE International Conference on, 2003, pp. 289-298.

[18] C.T. Yang, T.T. Chen and S.Y. Chen, "Implementation of Monitoring and Information Service Using Ganglia and NWS for Grid Resource Brokers," Proceedings of 2007 IEEE Asia-Pacific Services Computing Conference, 2007, pp. 356-363.

[19] F.D. Sacerdoti, M.J. Katz, M.L. Massie, D.E. Culler, "Wide Area Cluster Monitoring with Ganglia," Proceedings of IEEE Cluster 2003 Conference, 2003, pp. 289-298.

[20] Ganglia, http://ganglia.sourceforge.net/

[21] G. Aloisio and M. Cafaro, "Web-based access to the Grid using the Grid Resource Broker portal," Concurrency Computation: Practice and Experience, 2002, vol. 14, pp. 1145-1160.

[22] K. Krauter, R. Buyya, and M. Maheswaran, "A taxonomy and survey of grid resource management systems for distributed computing," Software Practice and Experience, 2002, vol. 32, pp. 135-164.

[23] C.T. Yang, C.L. Lai, P.C. Shih, and K.C. Li, "A Resource Broker for Computing Nodes Selection in Grid Environments," Proceedings of Grid and Cooperative Computing - GCC 2004: 3rd International Conference. 2004, vol. 3251, pp. 931-934.

[24] C.T. Yang, S.Y. Chen, and T.T. Chen, "A Grid Resource Broker with Network Bandwidth-Aware Job Scheduling for Computational Grids," Proceedings of Grid and Pervasive Computing - Second International Conference. 2007, vol. 4459, pp. 1-12.

[25] L. Baduel and S. Matsuoka, "Peer-to-Peer Infrastructure for Autonomous Grid Monitoring," Proceedings of Parallel and Distributed Processing Symposium, 2007, vol.35, pp.1-8.

Part VII
Digital Library and Content Management

The Quality in Quantity
- Enhancing Text-based Research -

Patrick Harms[1], Kathleen Smith[2], Andreas Aschenbrenner[3],
Wolfgang Pempe[4], Mark Hedges[5], Angus Roberts[6], Bernie Ács[7] and
Tobias Blanke[8]

1. State and University Library Goettingen, Germany
2. University of Illinois at Urbana-Champaign, USA
3. State and University Library Goettingen, Germany
4. State and University Library Goettingen, Germany
5. Centre for e-Research, Kings College London, UK
6. University of Sheffield, UK
7. National Center for Supercomputing Applications, UIUC, USA
8. Centre for e-Research, Kings College London, UK

Abstract   Computers are becoming more and more a tool for researchers in the humanities. There are already several projects which aim to implement environments and infrastructures to support research. However, they either address qualitative or quantitative research methods, and there has been less work considering support for both methodologies in one environment. This paper analyzes the difference between qualitative and quantitative research in the humanities, outlines some examples and respective projects, and states why the support for both methodologies needs to be combined and how it might be used to form an integrated research infrastructure for the humanities.

1   INTRODUCTION

A vision of how reference networks of books, annotations, and other sources are creating an additional layer of knowledge beyond the mere words was illustrated when Gregory Crane asked "What Do You Do with a Million Books?" [1]. This vision is driven by experiences in the arts and humanities for dealing with unstructured, context-dependent and often distorted information, yet it is also informed by statistics and other scientific methods. [2]

Exploring the opportunities in text-based research has brought about many projects that can be classified as either focused on qualitative or quantitative mechanisms. Examples for qualitative orientation include virtual research environments that provide a consistent and useful set of interfaces to enable or allow for the collation, annotation, and sharing of work in a community of peers. The quantitative orientation focuses on providing frameworks for computational analysis,

S.C. Lin and E. Yen (eds.), *Data Driven e-Science: Use Cases and Successful Applications*
of Distributed Computing Infrastructures (ISGC 2010), DOI 10.1007/978-1-4419-8014-4_21,
© Springer Science+Business Media, LLC 2011

automated content manipulation, and the production of various visual representations or summaries of textual content for researchers.

Qualitative and quantitative approaches can be complimentary when the two are joined to provide the researcher with tools and services in an integrated research environment that provides an extensible functional infrastructure to support individual and communitybased research efforts. Existing tools and services can be brought together in one integrated research infrastructure through which

1. distributed textual resources can be shared in secure environments;
2. methods can be shared, co-developed, and discussed; and
3. researchers can
   – manage, analyze and visualize large bodies of text and subsequently drill down into specific works, sections, sentences or smaller pieces;
   – edit a specific text by contextualizing it in networks of related works and supplementary resources.

The opportunities in integrating existing methods go beyond research in the arts and humanities and also include existing approaches for text mining in biotechnology, machine-assisted annotation and contextualization of documents in knowledge management systems, and so on. The integration of quantitative and qualitative approaches will enhance the research opportunities for researchers in the digital humanities and stimulate new research by connecting the academic communities.

The following sections will show how qualitative and quantitative research methodologies are distinguished, how they can be combined as well as how infrastructure projects might address this methodological interaction.

2 QUALITATIVE AND QUANTITATIVE RESEARCH IN THE EHUMANITIES

When using the terms qualitative and quantitative, it is necessary to clarify how they are understood within the context of this article.

2.1 Quantitative Research

Quantitative research in the eHumanities is expected to deal with the processing of large amounts of data, perhaps retrieved from many data sources. However, one file, i.e. one data source, of several megabytes in size could store a complete novel, which could already be considered a large amount of data for textual research. As a consequence quantitative research must be defined without considering the amount of data but by considering the way the data is used.

Quantitative research can be characterized by a sequence of functional steps:

1. preparing the data (cataloging, automated annotation, and so on)
2. collecting information by
   - applying natural language processing techniques (tokenization, part of speech tagging, etc)
   - extracting entities or patterns from the data and annotated data (data mining, pattern matching, and so on)
   - generating statistical analyses based on the data and annotated data (statistical evaluation)
3. aggregating this information into a format to be evaluated by the researcher (different methods of visualization)

Considering these steps, the following definition for quantitative research in the eHumanities could be used:

Quantitative research in the eHumanities focuses on answering research questions by interpreting aggregated information based on the data.

2.2 Qualitative Research

Correspondingly, the definition of qualitative research is also based not on file sizes or data source counts, but on the way the data is used. Qualitative analysis of data in the eHumanities implies a more intensive interaction with the data. This interaction with the subject "content" can be seen as "adding value" or "enhancing the quality" through study, observation, and documenting findings.

Some examples of qualitative research work are:

1. observing the data (e.g. by reading a text, watching a movie or listening to a soundfile)

2. understanding the data (e.g. translating it, recognizing the semantics of values, and so on)
3. analyzing the information contained in the data
4. annotating the data with the results of the analysis

There are more ways of working with the data in qualitative research. However, these examples are already sufficient to demonstrate the differences between qualitative and quantitative research. While quantitative research considers aggregated information, which is based on data, qualitative research is defined as follows in our article:

Qualitative research in the eHumanities focuses on answering research questions by directly interacting, interpreting, and enhancing the data itself.

3   SCHOLARLY PROCESSES AND THE RESEARCH LIFECYCLE

There are many different theories about the ways in which qualitative and quantitative research methods are or are not linked in research processes. Examples include the phase model, the convergence model and the complementarity model, which are all summarized in [3]. All of these models describe how qualitative and quantitative research methods can be combined and how their different outcomes can be considered in analyzing research best practices. However, all of these models treat the two research methods as distinctly separate.

The distinction between qualitative and quantitative methods is not always as straightforward as specified in these research models. Instead, the degree to which quantitative and qualitative methods are applied depends on the specific research question and the precise research context.

Figure 1 illustrates a general view on research work in form of a research lifecycle as it could be adapted to many different disciplines, contexts, and methodologies (inspired by [4], section 6[1]). Two aspects in this graph are of particular importance for this paper:

1. Research is not a linear, deterministic process. The process may iterate over some steps, lead to a dead end and backtrack, or skip some of the steps.
2. In addition to being non-linear, research is often a succession of activities that directly interpret and explore specialized questions, and of aggregating interpretations that aim to understand the questions in their context and their implications.

---

[1] http://www.archimuse.com/papers/ukoln98paper/section6.html

It is this non-linear nature, and the succession of direct and aggregate methods, that is supported by the combination of qualitative and quantitative approaches. To underline this point, the following discussion of the individual steps in a research cycle shows how each step is inherently influenced by either qualitative (direct) or quantitative (aggregate) evaluation or interpretation. Researchers intuitively explore the domain and evaluate the right choice of tools and methodologies as they carry out their research.

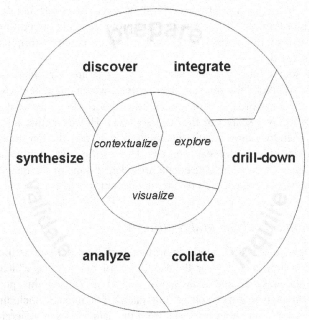

Fig. 1: Research Lifecycle: Within the research process, the three stages shown in this figure are complimentary rather than rigidly progressive.

3.1   Prepare: Discover and Integrate

A research question is usually defined broadly during the initial research phase to allow for a more focused conceptualization at a later stage. One initial step for preparing research could be the discovery of data providers (such as libraries, digital repositories, journal databases, and so on), in which relevant data sources could be located. The discovery of data providers would be considered a quantitative task since it does not directly consider the contents of the data provided by that resource, but rather the information about the specific provider (i.e., a comparative evaluation rather than intrinsic). Once a data provider is selected, the researcher could retrieve information about the data sources that data provider makes available. At this stage, the evaluation would be qualitative because the specific data sources are evaluated based on their relevance.

3.2   Inquire: Drill-Down and Collate

After relevant data providers have been selected, our hypothetical researcher could perform a search for relevant data sources (articles, monographs, and so on) available from the data provider. This search might reveal other relevant data providers or else it might turn out that a specific data provider is not suited to the research topic. At this stage, more concrete research questions could be formulated and hypotheses generated.

The data source inquiry would also be dual in nature. First there is a quantitative selection of potentially relevant data sources, which could be performed based on a search for keywords, author names, item descriptions (metadata) and so on (i.e., by a drill-down search of the data sources). However, this initial selection could be verified by a more qualitative method (such as collation) to assess the intrinsic relevance of a specific data sources. This verification might lead to discarding the reference or even the entire data provider, if none of the quantitatively selected data sources of a specific provider is relevant.

3.3   Validate: Analysis and Synthesis

The central part of research work could therefore be described as the process of answering research questions or the validation of hypotheses, which arose in a preceding data provider and data source selection. During this phase, the researcher might analyze a data source in a quantitative manner, including the combination of information either retrieved from the data source or generated based on the data source. A subsequent synthesis of the results into a research outcome would again be qualitative since it considers in-depth the data generated based on the preceding analysis.

3.4   Research Characteristics

The different research procedures applied during the phases of preparation, inquiry and validation share some characteristics, which depend on the way a researcher works. Such characteristics are for example exploration, visualization and contextualization.

During the data provider and data source selection the specific details of a research question or hypothesis might not always be clear. Therefore the work of a researcher is not always driven by a concrete but more intuitive goal. As a result this part of the research work could be seen as an exploration of the research topic.

When finishing the data source selection as well as in the initial research validation researchers could restructure the information relevant for the research topic and also visualize it in formats, which help them to formulate concrete research questions and hypotheses and also to have initial ideas for answering or validating them. Therefore this part of the research work would concentrate on the visualization of the research topic.

The validation of the research questions and hypotheses as well as the linking of the appropriate results with other work in the same or in related topics would be the contextualization of the research topic and its outcome. Since it could be the basis for future research work the contextualization extends also to the discovery of data providers.

4 RESEARCH INFRASTRUCTURE PROJECTS FOR HUMANITIES

The previous section argued that when conceptualizing the research process, qualitative and quantitative methods should be combined. This combination is performed intuitively by matching the requirements of research in a specific context or phase. But how is the work of researchers supported by existing tools, environments and infrastructures? How do these tools foresee the support of qualitative and quantitative work?

There are several projects currently addressing the implementation of research infrastructures in the eHumanities in the North American and European contexts. In the following paragraphs some of those projects are described briefly, to allow for a short analysis of their orientation regarding qualitative and quantitative research.

4.1 TextGrid

TextGrid [5] is a community grid project for the Arts and Humanities in Germany. It is working to develop a virtual research environment (VRE) including tools for the editing, annotating, analysis and publishing of texts and other resources. TextGrid is extensible and allows for sharing tools, workflows, primary sources and supplementary material within the user community.

TextGrid supports the observation of data in different formats (text, images, and so on), the annotation of the data, and data analysis with the help of integrated tools such as dictionaries. Since all these features address direct data analysis, TextGrid can be primarily categorized as an environment for qualitative research. However, an integrated workflow tool for combining streaming services allows for quantitative text analysis as well.

4.2 SEASR

SEASR [6] addresses the needs of the humanities by providing a data flow environment for analytical processing. SEASR focuses on the application of processing algorithms that include natural language processing, data mining, entity extraction and visualization to a sample of texts or other data.

The SEASR infrastructure supports the creation of data flows to convert, or extract content from input data. The researchers analyze the results of such data processing, which gives SEASR a quantitative character. However, SEASR tools can also support the viewing of documents (in whole or as extractions) which suggests some qualitative research applications as well.

4.3 TEXTvre

The TEXTvre [7] project intends to create a virtual research environment for the humanities based on TextGrid. Its major aim is to extend TextGrid with further functionalities to allow for improved data editing, analysis and linking. Linking in particular will be achieved by the application of technologies for a better search and retrieval on humanities texts.

Since TEXTvre is based on TextGrid its basic orientation is qualitative as well. However, for some extensions, e.g. similarity detection for texts, TEXTvre will apply algorithms that create data extracts for special text analysis. It has therefore quantitative aspects as well.

4.4 GATE

GATE [8] is a natural language processing framework. It provides tools and components for developing text mining, information extraction, and other language engineering applications. GATE is designed to handle small sets of texts as well as large corpora.

GATE concentrates on the application of processing algorithms on data. The results can be analyzed by a researcher. However, most of these results will be aggregated information derived from the data processing. The orientation of GATE is therefore quantitative.

4.5 Qualitative and Quantitative Project Orientation

To provide a more generalized view on the qualitative and quantitative aspects of these projects, Figure 2 shows the intensity of the respective orientations in form of a diagram and allows for a better understanding of the projects' focus. In an ideal world there would be a balanced qualitative and quantitative environment, as indicated with the star. However, current tools align more in one orientation.

In section 3, qualitative and quantitative methods can be seen as closely linked during the research process. However, a brief overview of some projects intended

to support research work in the eHumanities shows that this methodological interaction is not yet fully supported. There is a need for improvement and extension,
which will be the focus of the next sections.

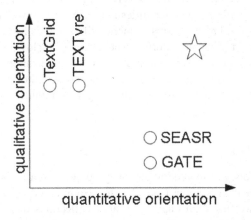

Fig. 2: Qualitative and Quantitative Orientation of some eHumanities Infrastructure Projects

5   COLLABORATIVE STRUCTURES: PRACTICAL
       APPLICATIONS

Researchers can be supported in their explorations of research domains by changing perspectives (e.g., through statistical analyzes and visualizations), and by contextualizing research results with related resources and other results. Both exploration and contextualization can be supported by offering researchers the appropriate
tools at the right point in the research process - without performing any radical
changes in scholarly practice, and without the need for inventing novel technologies. This section highlights some existing success stories and the lessons learned
from them, and focuses on the following questions: What are the guiding principles in designing research environments in which qualitative and quantitative
methods are joined in a complimentary fashion? Where are we headed?

5.1   Be Proactive

Researchers are used to their traditional scientific processes and systems, and the
suggestions in this paper are not an attempt to "reform" them. Aiming to change a
culture from the outset is unlikely to earn the sympathy of the researchers. Therefore, the suggestion of a systematic combination of qualitative and quantitative
approaches aims to empower researchers by offering additional vantage points and
context in the otherwise unaltered research process.

In its Firefox/Zotero Plugin, SEASR integrates in the native system environment of researchers and offers visualizations of text analyses where the researchers are performing their scientific tasks. Similarly, the Microsoft Research Desktop [9] aims to embed these types of tools right into the research environment.

By proactively offering functionalities and gateways between different (qualitative and quantitative) methods, researchers will have the chance to explore them with minimum effort. They may not even be aware of it. However, there is a great variety of potential quantitative analyzes (e.g. contextualization, visualization; cf. [10]). For the most impact, the research environment and the choice of tools to be offered may need to be tailored to a specific target community and research workflow.

5.2 Switch Modes

Where diverse tools and methodologies may support each other, the researchers will appreciate their integration. Consider, for example, one of the greatest stumbling blocks in creating high quality research collections of scientific texts: the creation of metadata that describes individual objects and collections, and which therefore allows their retrieval, analysis, and reuse. The burden of creating metadata is often perceived as excessively high by researchers, even though a large percentage of the metadata could be captured automatically (see [11]). Rather than manually typing metadata, the metadata could be extracted from existing files or generated from the context upon creation. With regard to quantitative analyzes, there are algorithms to automatically extract keywords, to create summaries, to identify authors [12], create links to related resources, and so on. Thus the combination of semi-automatic and quantitative methods may finally reduce the burden of metadata creation to a minimum.

Vice versa, manual cleaning can support the creation of large scale analyses. TextGrid for example allows the definition of virtual corpora. Such definitions might include works with different data and metadata structures which need unification or adaptation to match certain standards. Such homogenization could be the basis for further automated or manual analysis.

Therefore switching between different modes (manual -> semi-automatic -> analysis) in a way that allows ongoing refinement (e.g., beginning with a visualization of research references, bibliometrics, and then successively improving the graph) may offer opportunities to the researcher without being obtrusive.

5.3 Share

Scholars not only work with textual data, they modify existing data and produce new data. To this purpose they might access distributed resources as data (as well as tools/services and methods) and interlink them as needed. On the other hand, they also might want to share their own resources in a secure environment, enabling collaboration with colleagues – also from other academic disciplines. Virtual

Research Environments (VRE) like TextGrid and TEXTvre provide the technical framework to support both scenarios.

When equipped with a suitable working environment, scholars would be able to prepare the basis for their analysis by collecting, annotating, structuring, enriching and linking digital content. The underling infrastructure should implement a robust and flexible interoperability layer to enable the creation of virtual collections, connecting heterogeneous resources.

Using a virtual collection as corpus for analysis, the infrastructure must support the execution of data-intensive flows and computing-intensive operations as linguistic analysis (e.g. tree-tagging) or text mining. The resulting data sets could be further analyzed, annotated and eventually edited as basis for a publication, for further processing or as the basis for interdisciplinary scholarly/scientific work.

6   CONCLUSION

In its article "The End of Theory,"[2] *Wired* magazine presented several examples in which statistical analysis and visualization open up a totally new vantage point to access and understand a set of data (e.g., crop prediction and modeling epidemics)[3][13]. Based on these examples, Wired argued that the traditional approach to science — hypothesize, model, test — is becoming obsolete.

Current virtual research environments often model traditional methodologies in the digital domain and in doing so they fail to take full advantage of the opportunities offered by digital technologies in supporting the non-linear nature of research processes. Qualitative and quantitative are often perceived as disparate paths in doing research, while in fact they are complimentary and may support each other. The combination of qualitative and quantitative methods could smooth out the transitions between the investigation of specialized questions and the contextualization of results. We therefore posit that a paradigm shift in research does not require the development of entirely new technologies and methodologies. Rather, it is precisely the seamless combination of existing tools and approaches that could drastically alter the face of text-based scholarship.

REFERENCES

[1]   Crane, G (2006) What Do You Do with a Million Books? D-Lib Magazine 12.3. http://www.dlib.org/dlib/march06/crane/03crane.html. Accessed February 2010

[2]   Commision on Cyberinfrastructure of the ACLS (2006) Our Cultural Commonwealth, The report of the American Council of Learned Societies Commission on Cyberinfrastructure

---

[2] http://www.wired.com/science/discoveries/magazine/16-07/pb_theory published in the issue "The End of Science" http://www.wired.com/wired/issue/16-07

[3] http://www.wired.com/science/discoveries/magazine/16-07/pb_intro

for the Humanities and Social Sciences. American Council of Learned Societies. http://www.acls.org/cyberinfrastructure/. Accessed February 2010

[3]   Prein G, Kelle U, Kluge S (1993) Strategien zur Integration quantitativer und qualitativer Auswertungsverfahren, Arbeitspapier 19. Universität Bremen Sonderforschungsbereich 186, Bremen

[4]   Bearman D, Trant J (1998) Unifying Our Cultural Memory: Could Electronic Environments Bridge the Historical Accidents that Fragment Cultural Collections? Archives & Museum Informatics. http://www.archimuse.com/papers/ukoln98paper/. Accessed February 2010

[5]   http://www.textgrid.de. Accessed February 2010

[6]   http://www.seasr.org. Accessed February 2010

[7]   http://textvre.cerch.kcl.ac.uk. Accessed February 2010

[8]   http://gate.ac.uk. Accessed February 2010

[9]   http://research.microsoft.com/en-us/projects/researchdesktop/. Accessed February 2010

[10]   Wattenberg, M (2008) Selected Research. http://www.bewitched.com/research.html. Accessed February 2010

[11]   ERPANET (2003) ERPANET Training Seminar, Marburg – Final Report. Metadata in Digital Preservation. ERPANET.
        http://www.erpanet.org/events/2003/marburg/finalMarburg%20report.pdf. Accessed February 2010

[12]   Argamon, S (2008) Interpreting Burrows's Delta: Geometric and Probabilistic Foundations. Scientific Commons. http://en.scientificcommons.org/49978669. Accessed February 2010

[13]   Anderson C (2008) The End of Theory: The Data Deluge Makes the Scientific Method Obsolete. Wired Magazine 16.07. http://www.wired.com/science/discoveries/magazine/16-07/pb_theory. Accessed February 2010

Grid Application Meta-Repository System: Repository Interconnectivity and Cross-domain Application Usage in Distributed Computing Environments

Alexandru Tudose[1], Gabor Terstyansky[1], Peter Kacsuk[2] and Stephen Winter[1]

1. Centre for Parallel Computing, University of Westminster, London, UK
2. SZTAKI, Budapest, Hungary

Abstract   Grid Application Repositories vary greatly in terms of access interface, security system, implementation technology, communication protocols and repository model. This diversity has become a significant limitation in terms of interoperability and inter-repository access. This paper presents the Grid Application Meta-Repository System (GAMRS) as a solution that offers better options for the management of Grid applications. GAMRS proposes a generic repository architecture, which allows any Grid Application Repository (GAR) to be connected to the system independent of their underlying technology. It also presents applications in a uniform manner and makes applications from all connected repositories visible to web search engines, OGSI/WSRF Grid Services and other OAI (Open Archive Initiative)-compliant repositories. GAMRS can also function as a repository in its own right and can store applications under a new repository model. With the help of this model, applications can be presented as embedded in virtual machines (VM) and therefore they can be run in their native environments and can easily be deployed on virtualized infrastructures allowing interoperability with new generation technologies such as cloud computing, application-on-demand, automatic service/application deployments and automatic VM generation.

1   INTRODUCTION

The number of Grid applications has been growing steadily in recent years. Applications are now stored in repositories which offer better options for their management by storing objects in a structured manner, following a model defined by the repository administrator. The repository provides functions for classification, storage, management and retrieval of the components stored there. [1] However, there are many repository frameworks on the market and they vary in terms of access interface, security system, implementation technology, communication protocols and transfer protocols. Moreover, administrators are free to choose among those technologies and also have free choice in defining a specific repository model. This growing diversity has turned into a significant limitation in terms of interoperability and inter-repository access.

S.C. Lin and E. Yen (eds.), *Data Driven e-Science: Use Cases and Successful Applications of Distributed Computing Infrastructures (ISGC 2010)*, DOI 10.1007/978-1-4419-8014-4_22,
© Springer Science+Business Media, LLC 2011

This paper presents a solution to this issue by creating a generic repository architecture which allows GARs to connect to the system independent of their underlying technology.

For a better understanding of this solution we have set the following GAR requirements:

- *(R1) APPLICATION PUBLISHING*: Any GAR needs an intuitive, friendly user interface such as graphical clients or web-based solutions, which would make application publishing easy for both Grid administrators and users.
- *(R2) APPLICATION DISCOVERY*: GARs should permit the discovery of applications stored by them following several principles:
  - *(R2.1) Expose their application to the Web*: GARs should be built using technologies that interact with popular web search engines and web metadata harvesters. It is desired for GARs to expose interfaces such as HTTP/REST [2, 3] and OAI-PMH [4], which would make the application discovery process easier to both human users and services.
  - *(R2.2) Be interoperable with any OGSI/WSRF Grid Service*: GARs should expose an OGSI/WSRF Grid Service interface [5], which would make them able to interact seamlessly with any other OGSI/WSRF Grid Service in a standard, serviceable manner.
  - *(R2.3) Linked with other GARs*: While GARs are currently not connected in any manner, a service able to connect different GARs and to find whether a desired Grid application is stored in any of the connected Grid repositories would prove very valuable to both human users and services.

- *(R3) OBJECT EXCHANGEABILITY and REUSEABILITY*: GARs should permit the exchange and reusage of Grid application objects and application-related objects with other repositories. It would allow administrators to easily find and relocate objects in fresh repositories in an automatic manner and would also permit services to simultaneously extract metadata and objects from GARs.
- *(R4) VERSATILITY*: GARs should extend the scope of the distributed environments where the applications stored by them can be used to include computing concepts similar to Grid such as *application-on-demand, cluster-on-demand* and *cloud computing*.

2   RELATED WORK

This section presents an overview of the related work that has already been undertaken in the areas of Grid Application Repositories and GAR models.

2.1   Grid Application Repository-GAR

One of the oldest examples of application repository that can be found on Grid is the Berkeley Database Information Index -BDII [6]. BDII stores information about resources commissioned to Grid by each site, as well as about the Grid applications installed on them. However, BDII is not able to store any application-related object and lacks an intuitive user interface for publishing applications. BDII does not interact with neither popular web search engines nor OGSI/WSRF Grid Services. Furthermore, BDII has no connection to any other GAR -neither in gLite/lcg-based Grids infrastructures nor on any other Grids -and is not able to exchange and reuse objects with any other GAR.

The CHARON iSoftrepo (Interactive Software Repository) [7] is a step forward in that respect, as it comes with a collection of static web pages where administrators can manually enter the information about the applications stored in the repository. This makes the application visible to web search engines but with the obvious drawback that any change in the application description or any new application added to the iSoftrepo requires manual intervention from administrators.

An excellent example in highlighting the importance of application exposure to web is the *myExperiment* [8] repository which employs a HTTP/REST interface. The ability to find information about Grid applications straight through popular search engines, combined with myExperiment's intuitive and user-friendly interface made this system very popular -as shown by the increasing number of myExperiment users (e.g. 1000 registered users in July 2008, 2478 registered users in July 2009) and the growing number of applications (e.g. 321 registered applications in July 2008 -635 registered applications in July 2009) stored in the repository.

Grid Execution Management for Legacy Code Architecture (GEMLCA) [9, 10], NGS Application Repository [11, 12] and myExperiment expose user-friendly graphical interfaces, which makes them easily accessible both by Grid-knowledgeable users and by non-Grid users. Notably, GEMLCA highlights the importance of interoperability with OGSI/WSRF Grid Services. GEMLCA is built as an OGSI/WSRF Grid Service and is therefore fully interoperable with other Grid Services. In terms of making GARs more versatile, GEMLCA, NGS Application Repository and my-Experiment store not only application descriptions but also other application-related objects. However, the attributes used for their reference (such as Files or Packs) make the application objects indistinguishable for automatic retrieval. Without a structured naming scheme to be followed by publishers, even human users can have difficulties distinguishing between user documentation, source code or binary. This approach limits the discovery of specific application-related objects and impedes automatic retrieval of these objects.

With regard to the ability of exchanging repository objects, only myExperiment is built on on a repository solution which comes with an OAI (Open Archive Initiative) provider able to support OAI-PMH and OAI-ORE [13] protocols. These protocols permit metadata indexing and searching on the objects stored in the repository, as well as the exchange of objects between repositories.

Currently, GARs are not connected in any manner and this is a straightforward consequence of the different repository frameworks used as GARs. Moreover, there is no service, which users or other services can inquire and find if a desired Grid application is stored in any of the Grid repositories.

In conclusion, existing GAR solutions could only partly meet the requirements outlined in Section 1 (R1 -R4).

2.2   Grid Application Repository Model

Repository models are a formal way to structure information and to describe relations between various objects stored in a repository. When applied to GARs, the models refer to the metadata associated with the following objects/actors: applications and application-related objects, users, security policies and accounting policies (and the relations between them).

As part of this research we investigated five of the repository models currently used in GARs (myExperiment, NGS Application Repository, GEMLCA, WS-PGRADE/gUSE [14] and CHARON iSoftrepo). In most cases, the technology used for repository implementations is generic and imposes little or no restrictions on what administrators define in their models. The models vary significantly from one repository to another, even though they may refer to similar objects. Beside the metadata associated with users, security and accounting policies, there is very little information that can be found about the actual application. For example, these repositories have in common the following information: application name, application version, the creator of the application description document, a free-text description of the application, creation date, last modification date and particular fields used internally by the system such as universal identifier, modification history or usage statistics.

Moreover, GAR models refer strictly to application description documents as objects stored in the repository. myExperiment, NGS Application Repository and GEMLCA do allow additional objects to be stored beside application descriptions, but make no formal distinction between the types of objects can be added on. This is because such repositories are usually tightly-coupled with one particular Grid and the applications run on platforms well known by repository administrators. Therefore, applications exist only in their binary form and are either already deployed on the execution sites or they can be staged there from storage facilities other than the repository itself. This means that scenarios involving prerequisite application-related actions such as getting the source code, compiling the code, solving licensing issues, solving software dependencies and deployment are done by Grid site administrators independent of what is actually stored in the repository.

3   GRID APPLICATION META-REPOSITORY SYSTEM (GAMRS)

Following the Grid Application Repository requirements identified in Section 1 this research proposes a new GAR called Grid Application Meta-Repository System. GAMRS represents a collection of services which work together in a system meant to provide the following functionality:

- *PUBLISHING*: GAMRS provides an intuitive Web user interface, where users can easily publish applications and application-related objects into the repository. Furthermore, GAMRS provides an OGSI Grid Service interface that can be used by Grid Services to interact with the system and a HTTP/REST interface that can be used by non-Grid Services to publish directly applications into GAMRS.
- *DISCOVERY*: GAMRS connects different GARs and allows users and services to discover the Grid applications stored in them. It provides web visibility for all applications in the repositories connected to GAMRS, even if the majority of GARs do not provide it natively. Furthermore, Grid applications stored or referenced by GAMRS can be discovered by any Grid service compliant with the OGSI standards stack and the HTTP/REST interface mentioned above allows search engines to discover applications. Moreover, GAMRS employs an OAI provider, which other services can use for application metadata discovery (through the OAI-PMH protocol).
- *EXCHANGEABILITY and REUSEABILITY*: The OAI provider also allows the exchange and reuse of application-related objects between repositories by using the OAI-ORE protocol. Object metadata and the actual object can be imported as well as exported automatically using XML documents written in FOXML (i.e. a language capable to embed datastreams into object descriptions) [15].
  VERSATILITY: GAMRS allows applications to be deployed embedded in virtual machines; therefore, the application runs in its native environment and can be used in *application-on-demand, cluster-on-demand and cloud* architectures. GAMRS can also embed commercial applications that require licence acceptance and paid services. It offers a framework for deploying and running of commercial applications provided a taxation model is put in place. Through its architecture and model capabilities GAMRS allows Grid administrators to find and use all the required objects for Grid application deployment in one place - its repository.

3.1 Architecture

Figure 1 depicts the GAMRS architecture: its three core services (Publisher, Meta-Repository and Matchmaking) were designed and implemented separately so that they can also be used independently and can easily be extended with new methods in the future. If new repository standards for publishing emerge in the future, they can always be added to the Publisher service. If new GARs were added to Grid, the Meta-Repository (MR-Service) would already have a connection interface and new adapters would be written and integrated to it. The Matchmaking[1] module nfinds similar applications in repositories connected to GAMRS. It is also implemented separately as a service in order to allow new matchmaking methods to be added to it. The three core services are backed up by the GAMRS Backend[2] module, which is responsible with the actual storage of repository objects.

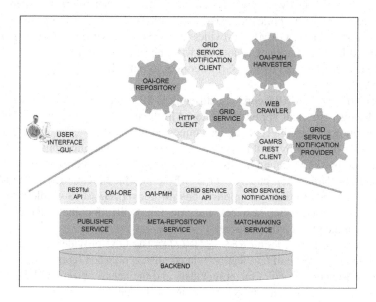

Fig. 1: Grid Application Meta-Repository System architecture

---

[1] The Matchmaking module will not be discussed in detail in this paper.

[2] The Backend module will not be discussed in detail in this paper.

3.1.1 GAMRS Publisher Service

This service is responsible for the publishing of Grid application information for various clients. This service contains the actual repository technology as the main part of the module. It exposes all the necessary interfaces through which the objects stored in the repository can be accessed or published: HTTP/REST, OAI protocols (i.e. PMH and ORE) and an OGSI/WSRF Grid Service interface. Examples of such services that can access the GAMRS are: HTTP clients, other OAI-ORE compliant repositories, any OGSI/WSRF Grid service, web crawlers, OAI-PMH harvesters and WS-Notification subscribers. Human users can use the graphical interface (GUI) to search, publish and retrieve Grid application information and application-related objects from the repository.

3.1.2 GAMRS Meta-Repository Service (MR-Service)

The MR-Service is responsible for connecting together any type of GAR, independent of the underlying technology these are built on, as it leverages through their different methods of access and authentication, communication protocols and transport protocols. In this way the service grants access to any application stored in connected Grid repositories, notwithstanding the differences of the methods mentioned above.

The MR-Service is implemented as an OGSI/WSRF Grid Service and exposes an OGSI-compliant API. Moreover, it exposes methods of accessing and retrieving applications from connected repositories through its API. Therefore, even though the majority of current Grid repositories cannot be queried directly by OGSI/WSRF Grid Services, if they are connected to the MR-Service the applications stored in them become visible through the OGSI/WSRF interface. This module is also connected to the Publisher service, which makes all the applications stored in those GARs connected to the MR-Service visible on the web.

The MR-Service allows any type of repository to be connected to it through the use of Adapters. From the MR-Service point of view an adapter provides a uniform connection to other repositories. The MR-Service defines high-level interfaces and commands for interaction with the connected repositories (such as *connect, authenticate, get application x, get all applications, get application metadata, get all metadata for application x, get metadata x for application y*, etc.). However, an adapter has to translate the high-level commands into those protocols understood by connected repositories. In order to accomplish that the adapter implements the following four modules (Figure 2):

- The *Communication protocol module* is responsible for accessing the connected repository. This requires knowledge of the repository API.
- The *Authentication and authorization module* helps the MR-Service to mediate the authentication process on connected repositories. Usually, the authentication process differs from one GAR to another (e.g. GSI, username/password, free access). This module is required to implement the authentication process appropriate to each of the repository connected to the MR-Service.

- The *Transport protocol module* helps the service retrieve the application metadata and the application-related objects stored on the connected repository. Every repository can implement a different transport protocol (e.g. HTTP, SOAP, GridFTP). Subsequently, the adapter must implement the transport protocol appropriate to the repository technology which connects to MR-Service.
- The *Meta-Repository interface* is the module responsible for the management of commands received from MR-Service as well as for formatting the responses according to those interface specifications accepted by the MR-Service.

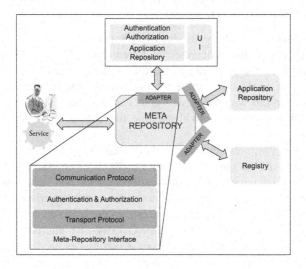

Fig. 2: Meta-Repository Adapter architecture

3.2   Repository Model

Traditional GAR models revolve around two objects: *the user* who described the application and *the application* itself. More advanced GAR solutions do allow application-related objects to be stored. However they store them without any categorization or name-pattern tagging, which makes them indistinguishable for searches or meaningful automatic retrieval.

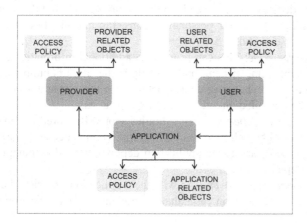

Fig. 3: GAMRS repository model

The GAR interconnectivity requirement (R2.3) requires another object to be placed in the repository model, *the provider*. Figure 3 shows the core three objects of the model: the provider, the application and the user, along with the first level in the hierarchy of objects related to each of them.

The *Access Policy* object is a high level representation of a collection of policies, which deal with security, visibility and permission attributes for each of the object they relate to. The *Provider Related Objects* refers to the provider-related objects that may be needed to be stored in GARs to give a comprehensive description of a provider and to ensure proper access and connectivity to it (e.g. PKI public certificate, WS client, etc.). The *User Related Objects* refers to the user-related objects that can be stored in GARs and can be used for identification, application running or data staging (e.g. X509 proxies, PKI public keys, username/password sets, etc.).

The *Application Related Objects* described by the GAMRS repository model are:

● *Application description documents*: These should be stored in GARs as they provide the link to those submission systems, which allow users to run the application on Grid. Moreover, administrators can use preconfigured description files with resource attributes and other Grid specific attributes already filled in (such as the minimum CPU frequency, the minimum amount of memory or the minimum number of file descriptors required for the application to run).

- *Application binaries*: The application binaries are referenced in the application description document but in most cases they are already deployed on a Grid site, and cannot be retrieved, only accessed. Once the application binary is stored in the repository, services which deal with automatic deployment or automatic virtual machine generation can make use of the binary. Furthermore, if the application deployed on a Grid site becomes unavailable but the user insists to use that particular site for personal reasons, the executable could still be staged and run on-demand.
- *Application source code*: This can provide an additional information source to application matchmaking systems and can help in the case of automatic deployment of applications on heterogeneous machine architectures and operating systems as it can be compiled directly on the target systems.
- *Application libraries (dependencies)*: Libraries should be stored on application repositories as they can help in cases when compilation is needed. They can also help in the case of automatic application deployment and automatic virtual machine generation.
- *Application dependency software*: As with the Application libraries, the dependency software is necessary in cases that require automatic application deployment.
- *Application documentation*: This is a useful set of objects for users and administrators who want to know more about the application than the short summary available in the application description document under the attribute Description.
- *Application test files*: These application-related objects can help in matchmaking. Matchmaking systems can run a candidate-match application with the set of test input files. If the output files prove to be the same as the test output files there is a high possibility that the applications are the same.
- *Virtual Machine-embedded application*: In order to make the application easily deployable in virtualized environments, one solution is to embed it from the beginning in a virtual machine. That allows the application to run in its native environment, thus overcoming potential architecture-related issues or operating system-related issues. The repository model proposed in this paper allows such application-objects to be stored in the GAR.
- *Hash sums*: Hash sums were added to the model to help check the integrity of records after the completion of a data transfer. However, hash functions are also used by matchmaking systems in their algorithms to speed up the matching process.
- *Application licenses*: Since this repository model can also be used to accommodate commercial applications, the application license acceptance is a necessary prerequisite to any automatic deployment process or job submission involving commercial software.

4 CROSS-DOMAIN APPLICATION USAGE IN DISTRIBUTED COMPUTING ENVIRONMENTS

One of the application-related objects modelled by the new formalism is the virtualmachine-embedded (VM-embedded) application. By storing this type of objects in the repository, applications are ready to be used not only in Grid but also in distributed computing paradigms similar to Grid. Figure 4 shows how VM-embedded Grid appplications can be run on virtualized infrastructures and cloud infrastructures.

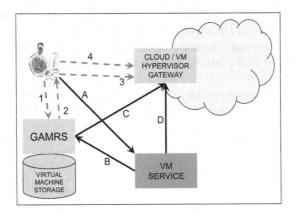

Fig. 4: Using GAMRS in virtualized architectures

The user can search the GAMRS for a certain application (*action 1*) which s/he wants to deploy and run on a virtualized infrastructure. If the collection of application-related objects contains the VM-embedded object, the user can then download it on his/her computer (*action 2*). Next, the user can connect to a cloud gateway or virtualization hypervisor access interface and upload the virtual machine on the virtualized infrastructure (*action 3*). The machine will remain saved in the pool of virtual machines and the user can instantiate it (even multiple copies, creating a cluster) any time s/he wants and use it to solve his/her problems (*action 4*).

The transfer of the virtual machine from the repository to the user's computer and from the user's computer to the virtualized infrastructure represents a drawback. Virtual machines are usually large in size (i.e. several gygabytes) and they can be costly in terms of networks usage and disk usage, hampering the normal utilization of the user's computer.

This paper presents a solution which overcomes this drawback. It involves the creation of a new service (*VM Service*) which is able to communicate both to GAMRS and to virtual infrastructure hypervisors. The *VM-embedded* application object stored in GAMRS contains in its associated metadata the path to its storage location, the protocol needed for access and staging the object, and the VM technology used in formatting the virtual machine (although, nowadays, most virtual machines are described in the standard Open Virtualization Format -a format known by most virtualization hypervisors currently in production).

The cloud/virtualized hypervisors are stored as *provider* objects in the GAMRS. They too have metadata associated with them, such as location, methods of access, protocols and security information. The user submits to the VM-Service the information (*action A*) about the VM-embedded application and about the hypervisor on which s/he would like to deploy the VM. The VM-Service finds the virtual machine archive on GAMRS (*action B*) and initiates a direct transfer of that archive between the GAMRS storage and the virtualized hypervisor storage (*action C*). Upon successfull completion, the VM-Service connects to the hypervisor access interface (*action D*) and unpacks the virtual machine files. Next, it registers the virtual machine as a template in the pool of virtual machines and, if so specified by user, can also clone an instance for the user, power the instance on and, preferably, can start a VNC (Virtual Network Computing) server on the virtual machine to enable remote desktop connections to it. The user can then access the application through the cloud interface or directly through a VNC viewer.

5 CONCLUSIONS

GAMRS architecture shows that Grid technology can be combined with web technologies to provide a wide range of interfaces to make applications easily accessible both to human users and services. We have already implemented a pilot GAMRS solution and connected three GARs (GEMLCA, myExperiment and NGS Application Repository) to the system making their applications visible and usable through the GAMRS interfaces.

The new repository model is richer than old GAR repository models and expands the area of usage of Grid applications to other distributed architectures such as cloud architectures and application-on-demand architectures. Moreover, GAMRS can store Grid application-related objects such as: binaries, source code, dependencies, documentation and test files. These objects can be used by Grid administrators for application deployment processes.

In addition to that, the VM-embedded approach allows applications to be run in their native environment making the porting of application on different machine architectures or different operating systems unnecessary. We have implemented a pilot VM-Service and used a VMWare virtualized infrastructure to deploy applications that are stored as VM-embedded objects in the GAMRS, thus demonstrating the application's usability not only in Grid but also in cloud computing or other virtualized technologies.

In conclusion, GAMRS sets the milestone for a new generation of GRID Application Repositories able to support different distributed computing architectures, while being easily accessible both to human users and services.

REFERENCES

[1] Stephens T (2005) Knowledge: The essence of Meta Data: The Repository vs. The Registry. http://www.dmreview.com/article sub.cfm?articleId=1025672. Cited 4 Nov 2009
[2] Fielding R T, Taylor R N (2005) Principled Design of the Modern Web Architecture. In: ACM Transactions on Internet Technology (TOIT), Association for Computing Machinery 2, New York, pg 115-150, ISSN 1533-5399
[3] Fielding R T (2000) Architectural Styles and the Design of Network-based Software Architectures. In: Doctoral dissertation, University of California, Irvine
[4] Lagoze C, et al. (2008) Open Archives Initiative Protocol for Metadata Harvesting http://www.openarchives.org/OAI/openarchivesprotocol.html. Cited 4 Nov 2009
[5] OGSI -Web Resource Framework Specifications version 1.2 http://docs.oasis-open.org/wsrf/wsrf-ws resource-1.2-spec-os.pdf. Cited 4 Nov 2009
[6] Field L, Schulz M W (2004) Grid Deployment Experiences: The path to a production quality LDAP based grid information system. In: Proceedings of the International Conference on Computing in High Energy and Nuclear Physics (CHEP 2004)
[7] CHARON/iSoftrepo http://meta.cesnet.cz/charonwiki/isoftrepo/site.php?site=voce. Cited 4 Nov 2009
[8] myExperiment Repository http://wiki.myexperiment.org. Cited 4 Nov 2009

[9]   Delaitre T, Goyeneche A, Kacsuk P, Kiss T, Terstyanszky G Z, Winter S C (2004)
       GEMLCA: grid execution management for legacy code architecture design. In: Proceed-
       ings for 30th Euromicro Conference, pp. 477-483, ISBN: 0-7695-2199-1
[10]   Delaitre T, Goyeneche A, Kacsuk P, Kiss T, Terstyanszky G Z, Winter S C (2005)
       GEMLCA: Running Legacy Code Applications as Grid Services. In: Journal of Grid Com-
       puting, Volume 3, no.1-2, pg. 75-90, ISSN 1570-7873
[11]   NGS Application Repository Portal https://portal.ngs.ac.uk/JobProfiles.jsf. Cited 4 Nov
       2009
[12]   Meredith D, et al. (2007) A JSDL Application Repository and Artefact Sharing Portal for
       Heterogeneous Grids and the NGS. In: Proceedings of the UK e-Science All Hands Meet-
       ing (AHM 2007)
[13]   Open Archive Initiative -Object Reuse and Exchange, OAI-ORE specifications and user
       guide, version 1.0 http://www.openarchives.org/ore/1.0/toc. Cited 4 Nov 2009
[14]   WS-PGRADE/gUSE Project http://www.guse.hu/?m=architecture&s=0. Cited 4 Nov 2009
[15]   FOXML   Introduction   to   Fedora   Object   XML,   http://www.fedora-
       commons.org/documentation/3.0b1/userdocs/digitalobjects/introFOXML.html.
       Cited 4 Nov 2009

Part VIII
Grid Computing and Cloud Computing

Integration of Cloud and Grid Middleware at D-Grid Resource Center Ruhr

Stefan Freitag

Dortmund University of Technology, USA

Abstract   Starting in 2007 commercial providers introduced Cloud Computing as new technology. Like Grid Computing, this technology enables users to utilize remote resources and services, not only but also for submitting jobs or storing data. In direct comparison to current Grid middlewares, Cloud middlewares already incorporate virtualization of network, storage, and compute resources in their software stack. For evaluation of Cloud Computing and the integration into the D-Grid software stack, the D-Grid Resource Center Ruhr, a D-Grid and LCG site with about 2,000 CPU cores and 100 TByte storage, has been transformed into an OpenNebula Cloud. On the one hand this paper will present experiences made and on the other hand identify missing elements for the integration with D-Grid.

Keywords   Grid Computing, Cloud Computing, D-Grid

1   INTRODUCTION

In 2008 the D-Grid Resource Center Ruhr (DGRZR) was established at Dortmund University of Technology. DGRZR provides 2,000 CPU cores and 100 TByte storage to D-Grid users. To access this resources D-Grid users have to use one of the supported Grid Middlewares gLite[1], Globus Toolkit[2], and UNICORE[3].

The ongoing hype about Cloud Computing makes it necessary to consider the benefits of this technology for D-Grid and therefore identify required steps for the integration into the D-Grid software stack and the D-Grid reference installation[4]. To this end, with OpenNebula a Compute Cloud middleware was installed and evaluated at DGRZR.

A survey on existing work is given in Section 2. It is followed by a brief introduction of Cloud Computing. Here the focus is put on Compute Clouds providing SaaS, PaaS and IaaS. Section 4 describes the integration of Open-Nebula at D-Grid Resource Center Ruhr (DGRZR). Issues to tackle down for a complete inte-

---

[1] http://glite.web.cern.ch/glite/

[2] http://www.globus.org/toolkit/

[3] http://www.unicore.eu/

[4] http://dgiref.d-grid.de/wiki/Introduction

S.C. Lin and E. Yen (eds.), *Data Driven e-Science: Use Cases and Successful Applications of Distributed Computing Infrastructures (ISGC 2010)*, DOI 10.1007/978-1-4419-8014-4_23, © Springer Science+Business Media, LLC 2011

gration of a Cloud Middleware into the D-Grid software stack are presented in Section 5.

2   EXISTING WORK

At present a focus is set on the installation, configuration and execution of Grid middleware services as part of a Compute Cloud [1]. In this context three variants have been identified: i) the dynamic deployment of virtualized Grid workernodes in a private Cloud; ii) if physical resources of one provider do not suffice, he leases capacities from other cloud providers and integrates them into his private Cloud. As in variant i) workernodes are deployed, but this time on leased physical resources; iii) not only single services or workernodes but a complete Grid site is deployed on demand in a Cloud.

In [2] Buyya et al. set their focus on the orchestration of Cloud services. Information from different Cloud providers (e. g. costs per CPUh or availability) are aggregated and made available. A Cloud resource broker can use this information to improve the quality of its matchmaking process, i. e. achieve a better match between the customer requirements and the available resources.

A third approach noticed in Cloud Computing is the development of lib-cloud[5]. Similar to the design of libvirt[6] libcloud provides users with an API that encapsulates APIs to various compute cloud providers (e. g. Amazon EC2[7]).

3   CLOUD COMPUTING

Three years ago Cloud Computing emerged as new enabling technology in the IT sector. The hype about this topic is still ongoing and confirmed by an increasing number of queries to Internet search engines. Figure 1 juxtaposes search trac at Google caused by queries for Grid and Cloud Computing. Noticeable is the gradually, but steadily decreasing interest in Grid Computing and that the emergence of Cloud Computing did not boost the loss of interest in Grid computing.

---

[5] http://incubator.apache.org/libcloud/

[6] http://libvirt.org/

[7] http://aws.amazon.com/ec2/

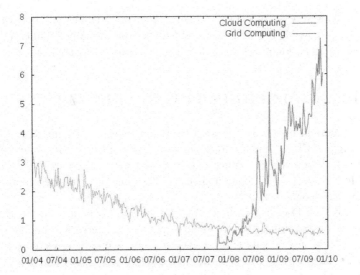

Fig. 1: Google Trends results for Grid and Cloud Computing (09.12.2009).

Until now and similar to Grid Computing, Cloud Computing lacks of a commonly accepted definition. Vaquero et al. compared in [3] various Cloud definitions to identify a least common denominator. This comparison provided no clear result, but three characteristics were mentioned in many definitions: i) scalability, ii) virtualization, and iii) a pay-per-use model.

In contrast to the similarity of a missing definition, the concepts of Cloud and Grid Computing differ in their origin. The development and dissemination of Cloud computing was and still is enforced by enterprises. This enterprises were interested in means to open their not fully utilized resources for third party usage. Business models (e. g. pay-per-use, flat rate) transform the increased utilization to an increased income. In contrast to this, Grid Computing originated in the idea of resource sharing in scientific collaborations and is non-profit oriented.

Depending on the provided service three cloud categories exist:

- Infrastructure-as-a-Service (IaaS) Customers use interfaces like EC2 or OCCI [4] to request infrastructure. Depending of the infrastructure type, virtual appliances can be deployed (i. e. Compute Cloud) or data stored (i. e. Storage Cloud). To keep pace with changing customer demands Cloud providers make use of virtualization technology [5] to dynamically reconfigure their free capacities.
- Platform-as-a-Service (PaaS) With PaaS customers gain access to software platforms (e. g. Google Apps Engine[8]). On top of those platforms customers develop their own services and have access to tools (e. g. accounting, billing, quotas) supplied by the PaaS provider.

---

[8] http://code.google.com/intl/de/appengine/

- Software-as-a-Service (SaaS) Providers setup software in a cloud infrastructure and make it available for SaaS customers via network, usually the Internet. One example for this is GoogleDocs [9] offering a word processing application.

4 GRID AND CLOUD COMPUTING AT DGRZR

Some of the current endeavors focus on the deployment of Grid middleware services in Compute Clouds and on the creation of Grids of Clouds. In context of the youngish D-Grid project[10] the integration of Cloud and Grid computing concepts into a uniform model for compute and storage resource provisioning seems a desirable long term goal.

Since 2008 the D-Grid Resource Center Ruhr (DGRZR) acts in the D-Grid project as resource provider. Currently it supports three compute middle-wares (gLite, UNICORE and Globus Toolkit) and two storage middlewares (dCache and OGSA-DAI). Additionally to this Grid middlewares with Open-Nebula[11] a Compute Cloud middleware was installed and promoted DGRZR to a new type of resources in D-Grid.

A prerequisite for this extension was the installation of all services in virtual machines. This is not only restricted to the aforementioned Grid middlewares, but also includes additional services (e. g. user management). At present Xen 3.2.3 is used as platform virtualization software.

Figure 2 shows the various layers of DGRZR. Entry points to DGRZR are the Grid middleware frontends (e. g. gLite CE, Globus WS GRAM, dCache SE) and the new Compute Cloud middleware frontend. In contrast to the Grid middleware frontends this one is located directly on top of the virtualization layer.

At present OpenNebula 1.4 is installed as Cloud middleware. It provides a Compute Cloud interface (EC2 and OCCI). Eucalyptus[12](Eucalyptus), an Open-Nebula competitor, provides additionally to EC2 support a simple Storage cloud interface, but at DGRZR there was no need for this kind of interface.

---

[9] http://docs.google.com

[10] http://www.d-grid.de

[11] http://www.opennebula.org

[12] http://eucalyptus.com/

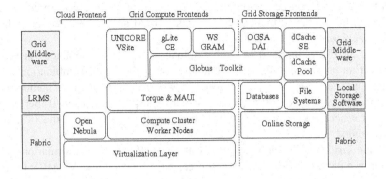

Fig. 2: Middleware layers at D-Grid Resource Center Ruhr

Users register their virtual appliances with OpenNebula via EC2 or OCCI and start them afterward. The OpenNebula daemon oned monitors the execution of the virtual appliances and therefore checks the status of the appliances and the execution hosts periodically. Figure 3 shows a typical output of the command *onevm list*. This command gives an overview on the deployed virtual appliances. Aside of the appliance status and the reserved RAM, the name of the execution host is displayed. Noteworthy is that a virtual appliance that is not registered with Open Nebula and running on an execution host will not be monitored by oned.

```
ID   USER    NAME    STAT CPU MEM  HOSTNAME    TIME
16 oneadmin centos.5  runn  0  262144  udo-bl1107  10 19:47:33
17 oneadmin ubuntu9   runn  0  262144  udo-bl1106  10 19:42:26
18 oneadmin debian.5  runn  0  262144  udo-bl2313  10 14:17:47
```

Fig. 3: Output of *onevm list*

5   OPEN ISSUES

A wide experience in the operation and the full integration of DGRZR in D-Grid allowed to identify open issues concerning i) the (inter-)operation of Grid and Cloud middleware interfaces on a D-Grid resource, and ii) the interoperation of a Cloud middleware (i. e. OpenNebula) with D-Grid central services. Each of the following sections describes one of the identified issues in detail.

5.1   User Management and Authentication

OpenNebula stores user information in the user pool table of the central SQLite3 database one.db. These users are classified in two categories: i) the super user oneadmin and ii) all others. Latter ones are created by oneadmin and are only allowed to manage resources belonging to/ registered by themselves. In contrast to this, oneadmin is able to manage all objects (virtual appliances, networks, hosts and users) existing in OpenNebula.

Before an EC2 command (e. g. for uploading a virtual appliance via econe-upload) of an user is executed his authentication with a valid combination of access key and secret key is required. access key corresponds to a user name known to OpenNebula, secret key is a secret password chosen by the user. If there exists no entry for access key in the SQLite3 database, the execution of the EC2 command is denied.

For the Grid middlewares supported at DGRZR the user information is not stored in a database located at the resource, but in the remote VOMRS (Virtual Organization Membership Registration Service). This service is used by every virtual organization [6] supported at DGRZR. Virtual organization members are mapped via Grid middleware mechanisms to local user accounts. In Globus Toolkit 4.0 a grid-mapfile (see Listing 1) contains the mapping from the Grid user X.509 certificate[13] to one or more local accounts.

Listing 1 grid-mapfile example

```
1   "/C=DE/O=GermanGrid/OU=TU-Dortmund/CN=XXXXXX XXXXXX"
    dt0061
2   "/C=DE/O=GermanGrid/OU=TU-Dortmund/CN=YYYYYY YYYYYY"
    kg0081
3   "/C=DE/O=GermanGrid/OU=TU-Dortmund/CN=ZZZZZZ ZZZZZZ"
    hp0007
```

To enable a virtual organization to use OpenNebula for each member a corresponding OpenNebula user has to be created. For the automation of this task, a mechanism is required that queries the information from the VOMRS server and creates the users in the user pool table. The name space for the OpenNebula users can follow the schema proposed in D-Grid: two characters of choice, two characters identifying the virtual organization and a four digit number. Nevertheless at present groups, roles and attributes as they exists in virtual organizations can not be transferred to OpenNebula.

Additionally to the aforementioned mechanism, the OpenNebula authentication procedure needs an extension to become compatible with D-Grid. The users in D-Grid are used to authenticate themselves with their X.509 user certificate and not with a username/ password combination. A possible solution to this issue exists with the creation of a transparent service on the host running OpenNebula. This service interacts on the one hand with users and requires from them an X.509 based authentication. On the other hand the service has access to all username/ password values and interacts with OpenNebula on behalf of the authenticated user.

---

[13] The distinguished name (DN) of the X.509 certificate is used.

5.2   Information System

Each of the Grid middlewares supported in D-Grid runs a separate information system. The gLite middleware uses a combination of site and top level BDII, the Globus Toolkit uses the Monitoring and Discovery System (MDS), and CIS (Common Information Service) is used in UNICORE6.

The D-MON[14] project aims at the development and implementation of an information system capable of collecting, aggregating and publishing information from the three aforementioned information systems. For information retrieval D-MON uses an adapter for each of the supported Grid middlewares. Figure 4 shows the simplified architecture of the D-MON software.

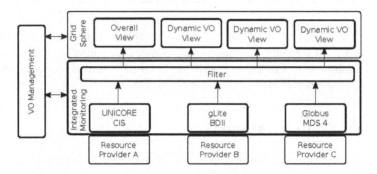

Fig. 4: Simplified D-MON Architecture

To integrate information provided by a Cloud Middleware in D-MON a new adapter must be developed. Before this, relevant facts to publish for a Cloud have to be identified. This facts may include the used virtualization software (e. g. Xen, VMware), available virtual appliances/ templates and limits concerning the maximum amount of CPU cores and RAM per virtual appliance.

5.3   Accounting

Until now all submitted jobs to DGRZR pass one of the installed Grid middlewares on the way to the LRMS (see Figure 2). The introduction of a Cloud middleware implies a change in this procedure: jobs (i. e. virtual appliances) submitted via the Compute Cloud interface do not start at LRMS, but at fabric level.

In D-Grid accounting of compute resources is done with DGAS (Distributed Grid Accounting System). To generate job-specific accounting data a local service parses the LRMS accounting logs and publishes them in the OGF-UR (Open Grid Forum – Usage Record) format.

---

[14] http://www.d-grid.de/index.php?id=401

At present OpenNebula lacks an accounting service, but with the information provided in the SQLite3 *database one.db* such a service can be developed. Joining the information from several tables of this database (e. g. history table, see Table 1) should suffice to generate the required usage record.

Table 1: Excerpt of the history table in one.db

vid	host_name	stime	etime	pstime	petime
13	udo-bl2313	1258384216	1258384219	1258384216	1258384219
12	udo-bl1107	1258384210	1258384247	1258384210	1258384244

The *vm attributes* table (see Table 2) is another table to inspect for the creation of usage records. It contains information about resources required by a virtual appliance. To subsume, it is proposed to make use of the UR format for the accounting of used resources provided by Compute cloud middlewares.

Table 2: Excerpt of the vm attribute table in one.db

id	name	type	value
12	CPU	0	0.5
12	MEMORY	0	256
12	NAME	0	centos.5-3.x86
12	VMID	0	12

5.4   Integration of the Grid Batchsystem and OpenNebula at DGRZR

At DGRZR the batch system consists of a combination of Torque[15] and MAUI[16]. Latter one is used as scheduler. Every job submitted via the Grid middleware to the batchsystem is forwarded by the scheduler to a workernode for execution.

OpenNebula uses an internal scheduler for assigning a virtual appliances to a physical server. At present this scheduler supports the rank scheduling policy and can be replaced by more sophisticated ones. If the support for advance reservation is required Haizea[17] can be used as replacement.

As OpenNebula and the batchsystem act at DGRZR on the very same physical resources a cooperation or at least a coordination is needed. An example for such a cooperation is the dynamic deployment of job-specific workernode virtual appliances [7]. Presuming a limited number of different job types in the batchsystem, each job type corresponds to a virtual appliance and a batchsystem queue. The virtual appliances fits to the software requirements of the job type and the queue parameter maxrunning specifies the upper bound for the simultaneously active virtual appliances for a job type.

Periodically a daemon parses the batchsystem status (i. e. via qstat -x). If a queue A lacks of jobs but has assigned resources and in another queue B jobs are idling because of missing resources, the daemon initiates the reconfiguration of the free resources by issuing commands to OpenNebula. Workernodes compatible with queue B are instantiated and after the boot process is finished, they register themselves with the batchsystem server.

6   CONCLUSION

Cloud Computing emerged in the last years as new enabling technology in enterprise IT. Therefore it can not be neglected that Cloud Computing had an still has a higher impact than Grid computing on markets. Nevertheless, Grid Computing and Cloud Computing are complementary concepts and an integration of both into a uniform model for dynamic provisioning of storage, compute and network resources is highly desirable.

To this end the integration of OpenNebula as a representative for Compute Cloud middlewares into the D-Grid software stack at D-Grid Resource Center Ruhr was evaluated. The evaluation showed open issues in the areas of accounting, authentication, information system, and user management that need to be overcome.

---

[15] http://www.clusterresources.com/products/torque-resource-manager.php

[16] http://www.clusterresources.com/pages/products/maui-cluster-scheduler.php

[17] http://haizea.cs.uchicago.edu/

REFERENCES

[1] Llo09. Dynamic Provisioning of Virtual Clusters for Grid Computing, M. Rodr´ı guez, D. Tapiador, J. Font´an, E. Huedo, R. S. Montero, and I. M. Llorente, Proceedings Euro-Par 2008 Workshops -Parallel Processing: VHPC 2008, UNICORE 2008, HPPC 2008, SGS 2008, PROPER 2008, ROIA 2008, and DPA 2008, Las Palmas de Gran Canaria, Spain, August 25-26, 2008, Revised Selected Papers, Pages 23–32, 2009.

[2] Buy09. Cloudbus Toolkit for Market-Oriented Cloud Computing, R. Buyya, S. Pandey, and C. Vecchiola, Lecture Notes in Computer Science, Vol. 5931, Pages 24–44, 2009.

[3] Vaq09. A break in the clouds: towards a cloud definition, L. M. Vaquero, L. Rodero-Merino, J. Caceres und M. Lindner, ACM SIGCOMM Computer Communication Review, Volume 39, No. 1, Pages 50–55, 2009.

[4] OCC09. Open Cloud Computing Interface Specification Version 5, A. Edmondsm,S. Johnston, G. Mazzaferro, T. Metsch and A. Merzky, Open Grid Forum, September 2009.

[5] Fre09. Virtualisierungstechnologien in Grid Rechenzentren, S. Freitag, 2. DFN-Forum Kommunikationstechnologien, GI Proceedings, Volume 149, Pages 137–146, 2009.

[6] Fos01. The Anatomy of the Grid: Enabling Scalable Virtual Organizations, I. Foster, C. Kesselman, and S. Tuecke, International Journal of Supercomputer Applications, Volume 15, 2001.

[7] Kon09. Dynamisches Management virtueller Maschinen auf den High-Performance Computing Ressourcen der Technischen Universitt Dortmund, B. N. Konrad, Diploma thesis, 2009.

Distributed Parametric Optimization with the Geneva Library

Rudiger Berlich[1], Sven Gabriel[2], Ariel Garcia[1] and Marcel Kunze[1]

1. Karlsruhe Institute of Technology, Steinbuch Centre for Computing, Germany
2. Gemfony scientific

Abstract   Geneva is an Open Source library implemented in C++, targetted at large-scale parametric optimization problems. One of its strengths is the ability to run on resources ranging from multi-core machines over clusters to Grids and Clouds. This paper describes Geneva's architecture and performance, as well as intended deployment scenarios.

1   INTRODUCTION

The tell-tale acronym "Geneva" stands for "Grid-enabled evolutionary algorithms".

Geneva targets large scale parametric optimization problems. Here "large scale" refers to problem domains that cannot be solved by a single processor alone, e.g. due to the sheer need for computing power, or due to the memory requirements, which do not allow execution on a single system. Consequently, optimization programs will likely be long-running, putting additional emphasis on the need for stability and dependability of the architecture.

As the name suggests, the library started life in particle physics, where it was used to perform tasks as diverse as training of neural networks or the optimization of particle physics analysis'. In this computationally very demanding example an improvement of 45% of the chosen figure of merit could be observed [1]. Geneva has since been reimplemented and Open Sourced, and is available from the software portal Launchpad [2]. Supported devices range from single-and multi-core machines over clusters to Grids and Clouds. Geneva's architecture makes only very few assumptions about the underlying optimization problem.

While Geneva initially focussed on using Evolutionary Algorithms ("EA") [4] for tackling optimization problems whose parameters can be expressed with fioating point numbers, different parameter types (such as boolean, integer or even arbitrary object types) are possible. Parameter types may be mixed freely in order to express a given optimization problem. EA, inspired by natural selection processes, work with populations of candidate solutions and perform a cycle of duplication/recombination of the best known solutions ("parents"), followed by mutation

S.C. Lin and E. Yen (eds.), *Data Driven e-Science: Use Cases and Successful Applications of Distributed Computing Infrastructures (ISGC 2010)*, DOI 10.1007/978-1-4419-8014-4_24, © Springer Science+Business Media, LLC 2011

and selection (i.e. evaluation and sorting) of the resulting individua. Evolutionary Strategies ("ES") [5], one well-known EA-variant, use fioating point variables as parameters, whereas Genetic Algorithms ("GA") use bit-vectors. Evolutionary strategies perform particularly well in the presence of local optima.

Apart from EA, the architecture also allows for the implementation of further optimization procedures, such as Swarm algorithms [6] and gradient descents, both of which will be available in the near future. Geneva attempts to become a general-purpose collection of distributed optimization algorithms.

Parallelization of these optimization procedures is done easiest on the level of the evaluation of candidate solutions, as these will not depend on each other. Parallelization will consequently yield the best results for optimization problems involving long-lasting evaluation cycles.

2　DESIGN PRINCIPLES AND IMPLEMENTATION

The (re-)design of the Geneva library followed a number of distinct principles:

- Efficiency: Geneva is implemented in C++ because it gives users the option to write very efficient code and, moreover, with the emergence of the Boost library collection [7] many high-quality, peer-reviewed library components have become available that facilitate C++ programming for networked applications.
- Portability: dependencies on external libraries have been limited to Boost, which is itself very portable[1]. The library has been tested with different versions of the GNU Compiler Collection on different Linux platforms, and has been successfully compiled with the Intel C++ Compiler on Linux.
- Stability over efficiency: Since the Geneva library targets very large scale optimization problems where the evaluation of the candidate solutions will consume most of the program's running time, the focus is on stability.
- Specification of parameters: Geneva's data structures do not make assumptions about the underlying optimization problem. Particularly, Geneva allows for both discrete (integer, boolean) and (quasi-)continuous (floating point) parameters to be used in the specification of a parameter set.
- Transparency: It is up to the user to specify how a given parameter set should be evaluated. However, he should not have to be aware of whether his code runs in a parallel environment or not. Some restrictions nevertheless apply:
  - User-code should not rely on global variables, or else there might be problems with multi-threaded execution (execution in a networked environment will be unproblematic, though).
  - External data needed for the evaluation needs to be available at the site where the evaluation function is executed, either by making it available through the network, on shared storage in a local cluster, or using the appropriate data management tools in Grid-and Cloud-environments.
  - Serialization using the Boost-Serialization library cannot be done transparently, if the user's objets rely on own, local data structures for their evaluation. In this situation, the user needs to specify which data needs to be serialized. Doing so, however, is usually very easy.

- Connectivity: As Geneva intends to be usable in Grid-and Cloud environments, only very few assumptions have been made about the network environment: the compute nodes should just have outbound network connectivity. Geneva's network-mode is thus strictly implemented as "client-server", leaving little room for techniques such as de-central, server-less sorting. All communication is initiated by the compute nodes, asking for work and returning results to the server. This way only the server needs a public IP.

---

[1] Note that, at the time of writing, Geneva is nevertheless almost solely being developed on the Linux platform.

- Fault tolerance: Applications running in a networked environment need to cope with missing responses from clients. Geneva's EA populations can repair themselves in case of missing results, and can cope with varying numbers of individuals (i.e. candidate solutions). Other optimization algorithms have stronger restrictions.

2.1 Architecture

Geneva consists of a set of largely independent modules:

- In EA-mode, optimization problems are specified by assigning adaptors (responsible for the adaption[2] of parameters) and evaluation modules to parameter collections. Both the type of the parameters in a collection and the mutations applied to them can be chosen freely by the user. A number of common choices are implemented in the library and will be extended as it evolves further. Different parameter types, such as double precision-, integer-and boolean-values, can form a joint parameter collection. They can be accessed with an interface that closely resembles the C++ standard template library STL[3]. In case of networked execution, parameter sets are serialized and shipped to the clients, where the evaluation function is executed. Network clients access parameter collections through a base class, making use of C++-style polymorphism, and thus do not need to possess special knowledge about them.
- Population objects take care of the optimization cycle of duplication, mutation and selection. Multi-threaded execution is implemented on the level of these population objects, using the Boost.Thread library. For networked execution, populations ship the individuals to be evaluated to a broker, which takes care of (de)serialization and communication with clients. The broker uses the Boost.Asio library [10] for network communication and is discussed in more detail in section 2.2.
- Populations possess an interface that allows them to be subjected to an optimization cycle themselves. Thus, from Geneva's perspective, there is no difference between "simple" parameter collections and populations as they both have the same API.
- A random number "factory" constantly fills a buffer with packages of random numbers that are consumed locally by proxy objects. They create random numbers with a particular distribution from this raw material. One important example are random numbers with a Gaussian distribution, which are needed in evolutionary strategies. In networked mode, clients have their own random factory. Each of these factories receives a starting seed from the server. The use of a "factory" generator allows to produce random numbers at times when the sys-

---

[2] or mutation in the case of evolutionary algorithms

[3] Indeed, the corresponding classes wrap STL containers

tem would otherwise be idle, as it is waiting for a response from the remote partner.

2.2 The Broker

Distributed execution is performed by starting one or more client application remotely. These request work items (i.e. serialized individuals) from a server, deserialize them, process them, serialize the results and send them back to the server. Geneva does not require a fixed number of clients, and can cope with their responses not coming back. Populations will repair themselves in those cases. **Geneva's parallelisation framework is able to deal with an unknown number of producers and consumers,** responding to requests for work items and shipping processed items back to the originator.

This is taken care of by a broker. Populations put work items (i.e. individuals to be processed) into –and receive processed items from– their own private threadsafe queues, "raw" and "processed" respectively. The broker takes work items from the raw queues in a round-robin fashion whenever a client makes a request. Processed items get into the corresponding processed queue. Populations then poll their "processed" queue and re-integrate available items into their data structures.

In a networked environment, processed items might easily arrive too late or not at all, if the client dies for instance. Geneva measures the time t0 until the first work item *of the current generation returns*. Later processed items are accepted in the originating generation if they arrive within a configurable multiple of t_0. When that timeout is reached, the current population is completed with copies of other individuals, and the next generation is started. Late arrivals will be re-integrated into the then-current generation, still allowing them to compete.

2.3 Further Development

The Geneva library currently largely avoids the creation of child individuals from more than one parent in Evolutionary Algorithms, e.g. by performing cross-over operations. Modifications involving multiple individuals are difficult to handle in parallel. However, the architecture allows the implementation of new recombination methods in the future. Multi-criterion optimization is currently not implemented. However, it is believed that implementation can be performed on the level of populations without changing the rest of the architecture (such as the parallelization framework). Over time, other optimization algorithms will be implemented. Swarm algorithms are being worked on, and gradient descents are foreseen.

2.4   Availability / Licensing

The software is freely available under an Open Source (Affero GPL v3) license in the Launchpad Open Source portal [2]. The chosen license puts very few restrictions in the way particularly of scientific usage of the code.

2.4.1   Sample Use-cases

Fig. 1: Modeling the Mona Lisa using 300 semi-transparent overlapping triangles. On the left, arbitrarily choosen intermediate steps in the optimization run. On the right, the middle image shows the result after 20% of the generations compared to the initial (left) and final (right) states of the optimization.

For most real-life optimization problems, it is not possible to decide whether the current best parameter set represents the globally best solution or just "a" good solution, such as a local optimum. Hence it is difficult to know how well an optimization algorithm has performed, and whether there is any further potential for improvement.

An exception to this rule is given here as a usage example of the Geneva library. In this optimization problem, 300 semi-transparent triangles had to be assembled in such a way that they most closely resembled the Mona Lisa. As each triangle is described by 6 coordinates, 3 colors, and its opaqueness, Geneva had to find suitable values for 3000 variables (normalized to [0:1]). The chosen figure of merit was simply the squared sum of each pixel's difference in color between target and candidate images. Thus, no special knowledge or face or image recognition was involved at all. As the triangles were allowed to overlap and were sorted according to their opaqueness, this leads to additional difficulties for the optimization algorithm: slight modifications of the opaqueness can result in large changes of the overall figure of merit, and a highly "jagged" quality surface. A visual inspection of the best solution found at the end of the optimization allowed to make a statement about the level of success. Figure 1 (left side) shows several states of this optimization in succession, with the target image at the lower right corner[4].

The compute time needed for the evaluation of each candidate solution scales quadratically with the diameter of the target image. Hence, by varying the size of the latter, it is also possible to simulate different levels of complexity of the evaluation function, when performing scalability tests. This optimization was per-

---

[4] Visit http://www.gemfony.com for a color and higher resolution version of the picture

formed in parallel in a Linux-cluster, showing good stability and scalability. A noteworthy feature of this particular optimization problem is that over 95% of the improvement of the chosen figure of merit were achieved in the first 20% of the optimization cycles. Figure 1 (right side) shows the best solution at the start of the optimization cycle, after 20% of the cycles and at the end of the procedure. The improvement between the last two pictures is visibly minor. The authors have seen similar results for other optimization problems. **This makes it likely that, with the Geneva library, optimization even of very large problem domains in distributed environments is a "low-hanging fruit".**

Another optimization problem tackled with Geneva relates to the optimization of the geometry of the Dodeka-L-Alanin protein by minimizing the molecule's potential energy, and the distributed training of feed-forward neural networks. This example is demanding as evaluation was done by an external application, with which Geneva needed to communicate.

The training of Neural networks presented a good test case as the ability of a neural network to recognize data patterns is a good measurement for the success of the optimization.

The authors invite readers from both science and industry to propose other possible real-life deployments of the Geneva library.

3 PERFORMANCE AND SCALABILITY

3.1 Test Setup

A number of scalability tests were performed on a dual-socket Intel Nehalem (8 core) system (16 logical cores, taking into account hyperthreading), a cluster of identical AMD Opteron systems (all running Scientific Linux 5), and on the GridKa cluster[5]. The Nehalem and Opteron nodes used for this test were "ideal" in the sense that they were under the full control of the testers. No other applications were running on the same nodes, and the test-applications were started by hand, not by using a batch submission system.

GridKa compute nodes (albeit not cores) and the network on the GridKa cluster were shared with other applications, and the local PBS batch submission system was used to submit Geneva's components. Therefore this gives an idea on how Geneva behaves in a production compute environment.

The tests were based on a population of 16 child individuals, each with 1000 double precision parameters (resulting in close to 100 KByte of serialized data per individual, including data needed for Geneva's internal management and the serialization framework). The choice of a population with 16 child individuals was

---

[5] A Tier-1 centre in the LHC Computing Grid, running in production mode

inspired by the wish to fully utilize the 16 logical cores of a dual-Nehalem system, when doing comparisons between networked-and multi-threaded modes of Genva.

To the Geneva server, client applications are a black box. All it knows about them is the data transferred to and from the clients, and the time it took for answers to evaluation requests to arrive. Except for (de-)serialization of objects, which can be CPU-intensive, and some sorting and management work, no part of the evaluation process happens on the server. Therefore one can measure the overhead introduced through the parallelisation procedure by replacing client-side calculations with sleep-cycles of defined length.

Communication between client and server will then be virtually independent of the CPU-load on the client nodes. It even becomes possible to run 16 networked clients on a local host with a sufficient number of cores, using local networking inside of the machine's RAM, and to compare those timings with the ones found in a "physical" networked environment.

Such measurements in ideal environments of course cannot reflect any performance impact that concurrently running applications on the same host might have on the optimization in real life, but will give quite accurate figures for the maximum achievable speedup as a function of the amount of time needed to evaluate a given parameter set (or, more generally, running times of clients). Furthermore, in production enviroments such as the GridKa cluster, the effect of a shared network can be studied.

In the tests, the average length of each generation was measured.

- for serial execution on a single core
- for multi-threaded execution on 16 logical cores, using 16 threads
- using local networking with all 16 client applications plus the server running on the Nehalem system
- using 16 clients running on an Opteron cluster under full control of the test-team, with the server again running on a Nehalem machine
- using 16 clients running on the GridKa cluster
- using an oversupply of 20 clients running again on GridKa

The timings for serial execution were then divided by the timings for networked and multi-threaded execution, resulting in a measurement of the speedup in different constellations.

Sleep-/Evaluation-times varied from 10 milliseconds to 120 seconds. Time-measurements were restarted for each new time-setting, while the client and server kept running. On GridKa, clients were started short time before the server, thus limiting the effects of the batch submission system. Clients were started on the processing nodes quickly as, at the time of the measurement, the GridKa Cluster was unusually empty, with only some 3000 of its 8500 Cores busy with other user-applications. Hence the overhead involved in the usage of the batch submission system was small. Nevertheless the measurement for the first time-setting will likely have been impacted. Also note that, in a production environment, there can be no control over concurrent network transfers (possibly from the same host, and in GridKA often quite demanding) by other applications.

3.2 Measurement Results

The results of the measurements are shown in figure 2. It is noticeable that there is only a negligible overhead for multi-threaded execution. The speedup deviates from the maximum factor 16 only for very short evaluation periods.

The curves for local and "ideal" Opteron-cluster-based networking are so similar that they appear as one in the picture. This indicates that the network is less of a bottleneck for Geneva than one might think. Instead, the bulk of the parallelization overhead seems to stem from the (de-)serialization and the communication between population and broker[6]. This is fortunate as, from the perspective of Geneva, the network's architecture and settings cannot be changed. Bottlenecks that are inherent to Geneva's architecture or the libraries being used, however, can be more easily dealt with. Thus further improvements of the core library seem possible. The similarity between both curves also supports the assertion that the different architectures (Nehalem vs. Opteron) used for the "ideal" networking measurement had no measurable effect (as it should be, as the clients mostly perform sleep cycles). Likewise, that similarity also confirms the reasoning that the server running on the same node as the clients for the local measurement should only have a minimal effect.

---

[6] Note that communication between client and server happened in text mode. Switching Geneva to binary-transfers can both reduce the serialization overhead and the size of the exchanged messages.

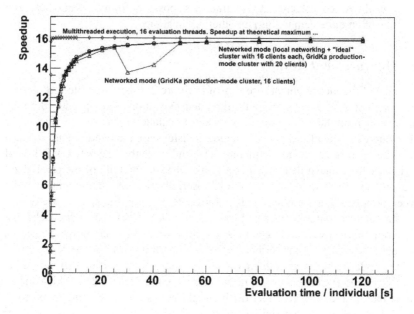

Fig. 2: Speedup for a problem involving 16 or 20 concurrent evaluations in different modes.

Note that in realistic scenarios clients will not return results at the same time, e.g. due to different speeds of worker nodes or due to other applications running on the same node or communicating over the same network. This has the positive effect of reducing the server's load (or else handling 1000 clients, as was done during stress testing of the Geneva library, would likely have been impossible), but has the negative effect that sometimes more clients might be needed than there are candidate solutions to be evaluated, so that there is always a free worker node willing to process a new work item. A slight oversupply of clients should thus be planned for.

This is shown in the two remaining curves. 16 clients running on the GridKa cluster, together with some 3000 other applications, led to a noticable impact on the scalability for some measurements. Note again that the exact reasons for such a deviation cannot easily be determined in a networked environment, as there is no control over other user's applications and it would require detailed network monitoring data for each node. Reasons will however likely involve large network transfers or possibly other "demanding" applications running on the same node. Also, the effects will not be reproducable. A measurement with 20 clients (an oversupply of 25%) did not show any significant deviation from the local networking or "ideal" cluster case, as in this situation clients were always readily available to accept workloads even if part of the "usual" 16 nodes were still occupied.

As shown in figure 2, despite the parallelization overhead in the case of networked execution, significant speedup levels could already be achieved for comparatively short-running evaluation functions (in the range of a few seconds). This seems to make many large-scale deployment scenarios feasible.

4   CONCLUSION

Geneva has matured enough to be usable for various computational optimization problems as Particle Physics, Life Sciences (geometry optimization of proteins), engineering or as shown here simply finding the optimal parameterset to resemble an arbitrary picture from a given number of triangles. In particular Geneva provides a framework to make use of distributed compute environments, ranging from local clusters to Grids and Clouds. The development of Geneva is focused on the computational boundery conditions imposed by these technologies, such as the network (private/public IPs, latencies), dynamic number of heterogeneous compute nodes of different architectures, no dependance on a particular Grid-Middleware.

5   ACKNOWLEDGEMENTS

The authors would like to thank the Steinbuch Centre for Computing (SCC) at Karlsruhe Institute of Technology, as well as the Helmholtz Association, for their help with this study and the implementation of the library. The measurements presented in this paper were performed at the GridKa compute centre in SCC. The SCC staff was helpful in all situations. Likewise, the EGEE team has given a scientific home for this work.

REFERENCES

[1]   Dr. Rudiger Berlich; PhD Thesis; Ruhr-Universit at Bochum; February 2003; Application of Evolutionary Strategies to Automated Parametric Optimization Studies in Physics Research

[2]   Source code of the Geneva library: http://www.launchpad.net/geneva

[3]   Web page of Gemfony scientific: http://www.gemfony.com

[4]   Evolution¨are Algorithmen : genetische Algorithmen, Strategien und Optimierungsverfahren (German) / Ingrid Gerdes; Frank Klawonn; Rudolf Kruse; Wiesbaden : Vieweg, 2004; ISBN 3-528-05570-7

[5]   Evolutionsstrategie '94 (German); Ingo Rechenberg; Stuttgart : Frommann-Holzboog, 1994; ISBN 3-7728-1642-8

[6]   Swarm intelligence : introduction and applications / Christian Blum (ed.); Berlin ; Heidelberg : Springer, 2008; ISBN 978-3-540-74088-9

[7]   The Boost library collection: http://www.boost.org

[8]   The Boost shared ptr class template: http://www.boost.org/doc/libs/1 42 0/libs/smart ptr/shared ptr.htm

[9]   Bjarne Stroustrup; Die C++ Programmiersprache; pp. 390ff; Addison Wesley, 2006; ISBN 3-8273-1660-X

[10] The Boost ASIO library: http://www.boost.org/doc/libs/1 42 0/doc/html/boost asio.html

[11] The Karlsruhe Institute of Technology: http://www.kit.edu

[12] JMol, an open-source Java viewer for chemical structures in 3D: http://jmol.sourceforge.net/

Determining Overhead, Variance & Isolation Metrics in Virtualization for IaaS Cloud

Bukhary Ikhwan Ismail, Devendran Jagadisan and Mohammad Fairus Khalid

MIMOS Berhad, Malaysia

Abstract   Infrastructure as a Service cloud provides an open avenue for consumer to easily own computing and storage infrastructure. User can invent new services and have it deploy in a fraction of a time. As services being consumed, user expect consistent performance of their virtual machines. To host an IaaS, virtualization performance and behaviour need to be understood first. In this paper we present virtualization benchmarking methods, results and analysis in various resource utilization scenarios. The scenarios are Performance Overhead; the cost of virtualization compared to physical, Performance Variance; the VM instance performance when more VM is instantiate and Performance Fairness or Isolation; the study of fairness on each of the guest instances under stress environment. These studies provides us the fundamental understanding of virtualization technology.

1 INTRODUCTION

"Infrastructure as a service" (IaaS) is a commodity base resource based on pool of physical servers. The underlying infrastructures consist of hardware i.e. servers, storage & network switches of heterogeneous nature. On top of these, software stacks such as hypervisors, operating system and hardware drivers play important role in the assembling of IaaS. Any changes on the technology stack will affect the performance of the Virtual Machines or guest instances. In order to control and manage the service effectively, we need to understand the performance or problem of each technology stack.

In this paper, we present benchmarking methods, tools and results based on our first initial infrastructure setup. KVM will be use as our deployment hypervisor. Benchmarking includes in the areas of performance overhead, variance, isolation or fairness and overhead of guest OS. To direct our findings, we create test case based on the needs of IaaS designer and application developers who interest in the performance. By understanding virtualization behaviour, it can guide us on design decision for cloud deployment infrastructure.

Section 2 describes brief review of virtualization technology. Section 3 explains our test strategies, metrics, methodologies and rationale behind each met-

S.C. Lin and E. Yen (eds.), *Data Driven e-Science: Use Cases and Successful Applications of Distributed Computing Infrastructures (ISGC 2010)*, DOI 10.1007/978-1-4419-8014-4_25,
© Springer Science+Business Media, LLC 2011

rics. Sec-tion 4 discusses on tools and setup. Section 5 and 6 shows results & discussion. Lastly, we present our summary.

2 VIRTUALIZATION

Virtualization is the main ingredient blocks for cloud computing. Virtualization is a process of hiding the underlying physical hardware and makes it transparently usable and shareable by multiple VM.

2.1 KVM

One of the most important innovations on Linux is the transformation into a Hypervisor. KVM, Lguest, UML, IBM Zvm, are some of the examples of Linux based hypervisor. They provide isolated virtual hardware platform for execution that in turn provide the illusion of the full access to the guest OS. Updates or optimization on Linux components will benefit both the host and the guest OS. 2

KVM, turn Linux OS into hypervisor by loading KVM modules into the kernel. Every KVM process is treated as normal Linux process. Linux consist of Kernel & User Mode. KVM add third mode called Guest Mode. In Guest Mode, reside guest own Kernel & User mode.

KVM consist of 1) device driver for managing the virtual hardware and 2) user space component for emulating PC hardware. Linux kernel handles this very efficiently. Compared to non-kernel based hypervisor, other hypervisor put great effort on their scheduler and memory management system. [1]

2.2 Memory

Memory is virtualizes through KVM. It provides virtualization of memory through /dev/kvm device. This involves sharing the physical RAM with dynamically allocating it to VM. VM memory is very similar to the virtual memory used in modern OS. Applications see it as a contiguous address space that is tied to the underlying RAM in the host. The OS keeps the mappings of virtual page numbers to physical page numbers stored in page tables [2, 3]

Each guest operating system has its own address space that is mapped when the guest is instantiate. A set of shadow page table are maintained, to support the translation from VM physical address to host physical address. [4]

2.3   I/O Operation

I/O operation for VM operating system is provided by QEMU[5]. QEMU is a platform virtualization solution that allows virtualization of an entire PC environment (including disks, graphic adapters, and network devices). Any I/O requests a VM OS makes are intercepted and routed to the user mode and emulated by the QEMU process.

3   BENCHMARKING

3.1   Testing Methodologies

Experiments are designed to evaluate, Virtualization Overhead, Variance and Isolation of resource elements. from these 3 metrics, we will measure the CPU, memory, storage and application behaviour (database and Java). Results obtain from this studies, will act as initial result for further studies. Next, we justify the chosen metrics.

- Overhead - is the performance differences of the guest VM versus the actual bare metal host. From this metric, it will give us the insight of all resource elements and support the explanation of variance, isolation and fairness properties.
- Variance - In virtualization environment, resources are shared among guest OS. By incrementally increase the amount of guest OS within single host, we can discover the performance effects
- Isolation or fairness is the act of securing and providing the resources to VM in isolated container where other VM may co-exist in the same host. Ideally, all the host resources must be shared equally. It is the desirable metrics in this environment in order to guarantee SLA. For example, if one VM starts misbehaving, i.e. consuming up all its own memory, other VMs are not affected and should continue to run normally. Here we test by simultaneous running resource intensive application to see the effects of non-isolation behaviour for VM guest server.

Another area of isolation studies is security. For example, for any reason, an at-tacker attacks a VM or part of it and the VM is well isolated, it will not jeopardise other VM. [6]. For this point, we will not test it. Isolation metric is among discussed topics in virtualization studies. [7, 8, 9]

- Application Specific Behaviour - VM guest overhead, variance and isolation shows the perspective of micro-level resource utilization and behaviour. Server applications consume all resources and produce macro level results. Here we test SQLLite and Java to benchmark our guest OS.

3.2 Setup

Below are the testbed configuration and VM setting.

Table 3: Host System Specification

Processor	4 Cores Intel Xeon CPU E5405 @ 1.99GHz
Mainboard	DellPrecision WorkStation T5400
Chipset	Intel 5400 Chipset Hub
Memory	2 x 4096 MB 667MHz
Disk	750GBHitachi HDS72107
Graphics	nVidia Quadro FX 1700,
OS	CentOS 5.3 64bit
Kernel	Kernel:2.6.18-128.4.1.el5 (x86_64)
File System	EXT3

Table 2: Guest VM Specification

Processor	QEMU Virtual CPU 0.9.1 @ 7.97GHz (Total Cores: 1)
Mainboard	Unknown
Chipset	Unknown
Memory	512MB
Disk	12GB GEMU Hard disk
Graphics	Nil
OS	Fedora release 10 (Cambridge) (Eucalyptus Image)
Kernel	Kernel: 2.6.28-11-generic (x86_64)
File System	ext3

3.3   Testbed Setup

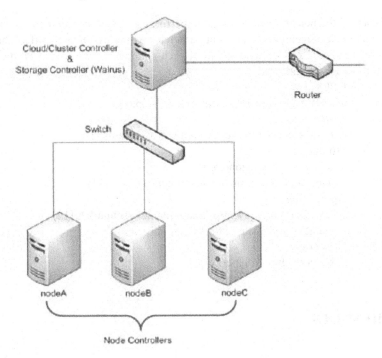

Fig. 1: Testbed Setup

Test environment use CentOS 5.3 as the based operating system due to stability and reliability of the OS. The following libraries are used. [10]

- KVM 85
- KMOD-KVM -2.6.3.0.1
- Libvirt-0.6.5
- QEMU-KVM 10.6.0

KVM 85 and KMOD-KVM-2.6.3.0.1 installed using yum repositories while lib-virt 0.6.5 compiled from the source. The libvirt and qemu-kvm libraries are com-plied with the default parameters. The virtual machines will be running on the local disk of the physical machine. In our benchmark, the base image for the virtual machines are in "raw" format.

4 TOOLS & METHODOLOGY

For each of the performance testing, we perform 10 round per metrics and tak the average. Each of test tools have input parameter which significantly affect the outcoming results. Careful consideration of each parameter, here we list all the tools used in our benchmark test.

- CPU
    a. 7ZIP-Compression - http://www.7-zip.org/
- Memory
    a. RAMspeed - http://alasir.com/software/ramspeed
- Storage
    a. Iozone - www.iozone.org
    b. Tiobench - http://tiobench.sourceforge.net/ [11]
- Application
    a. Java-SciMark 2.0 - http://math.nist.gov/scimark2/ [12]
    b. Database - SQLite - http://www.sqlite.org/
- Network
    a. Netperf - http://netperf.org

5 RESULTS

5.1 *Overhead*

Here we present the overhead results. We present first the overhead occured for each server element and lastly we present application specific overhead. For the guest VM, we use the exact configuration number of memory, CPU cores etc of physical host. This will show any performance degradtion of host versus virtual machine.

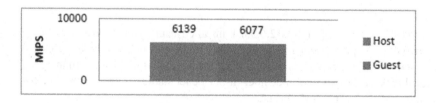

Fig. 2: CPU Host vs. Guest

CPU on guest machine is near to host-native performance with 1% overhead as shown in Figure 2.

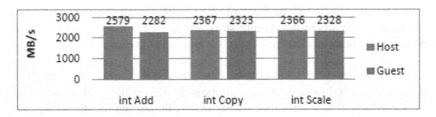

Fig. 3: Memory Host vs. Guest

We benchmark memory using RAMSpeed with 3 subtests. Memory shows low overhead as shown in Figure 3.

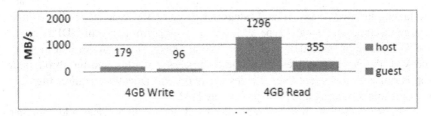

Fig. 4: IOZone Disk Host vs. Guest

Figure 4 shows read performance suffers more compared to write. Read perform-ance drop 72% while write drop to 46%. KVM I/O handling for disk adds signifi-cant performance penalty as compared to memory and CPU, which per-forms bet-ter.

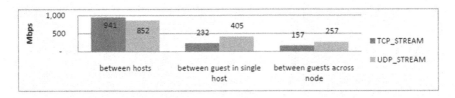

Fig. 5: Network Bulk Data Transfer Performance

Network throughput and latency test using netperf have different approach com-pared to other test. We measure the performance of throughput and latencies, between physical hosts, guests within the same host and between guests across physical host. These test reflects the actual performance differences of virtualization.

In bulk data transfer test (TCP_STREAM & UDP_STREAM), 4 common attribute may affect the performance indirectly. 1) **Network-bound** where speed is af-fected by the slowest link on the network, 2) **CPU-bound** The CPU utilization at the time of test where networking stack requires CPU cycle per KB of data trans-fer. 3) **Distance** of data needs to travel and 4) **Packet Lost** *(Care and Feeding of Netperf 2.4.X, 2007)*

Figure 5, shows the result of bulk data transfer performance. TCP overhead on VM guest compared to host machine dropped to 75% while UDP suffers 55% drop. Virtualization adds significant overhead over throughput results. While UDP seems to be better than TCP in virtualizes environment, the result is inconclusive. One plausible explanation could be TCP protocol is more expensive in terms of resource utilization it consumed as compared to UDP. TCP is, reliable, connection-oriented, sequenced, and requires acknowledgement on both sender and the re-ceiver[13]. On Virtual environment, these might amplify the usage where each of the entity, VM & host competes for the resources.

In a test done on Amazon EC2 infrastructure, the results of TCP & UDP are fluc-tuating in selected cases. EC2 categories its guest VM type by small, medium or large instances. In "small" type VM, the network performance of UDP is better than TCP while in "medium" type VM, TCP are better. It concludes that in small type VM, the guest machines are prone to processor sharing and the throughput drop is cause by this event. Nevertheless, network virtualization requires high degree of resource sharing and CPU processing [14].

Apart from the common attribute discussed earlier, hypervisor adds another layer of processing in order to emulate or virtualizes the network. To virtualize network, the outgoing network must be multiplexed together before sending out to the net-work and incoming be de-multiplexed before sending to designated VM guest. Second, VMM must protect the VMs from each other where VM cannot read or write to other network interfaces. [15] To enable resource sharing and enforce security it is at expense of performance drop and increases the complexity in managing network QoS.

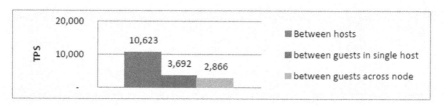

Fig. 6: Network Latency

Figure 6 shows the latency results. The measurement is in transaction per-seconds. The higher the value reflects lower latency or greater speed. Virtualization adds 65% performance overhead. Link between instances on different nodes add further latency, which drop 22% more.

Latency is typically incurred in processing of network data. Latency can be tem-porary which last for a few seconds or persistent which depends on the source of the delays.

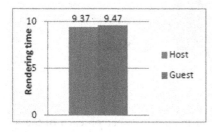

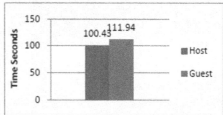

Fig. 7: Java Host vs. Guest   Fig. 8: SQLite Host vs. Guest

Figure 7, the performance overhead on guest is small with only 1.07% lower than physical. Figure 8 shows 11.46% SQLite performance drop for guest OS.

5.2 Variance & Isolation

Here we present the results of stressing out the physical hosts with compute, memory, read/write I/O of disk and the effects of network throughput.

CPU

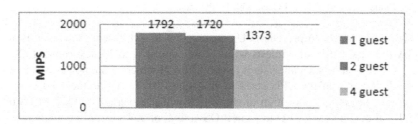

Fig. 9: CPU Variance Chart

Figure 9, we can see performance degradation by incrementally more VM in a single node. From the chart above, we can see the variance when more guests pre-sent. Performance varies between 1792 to 1373 MIPS or 20%.

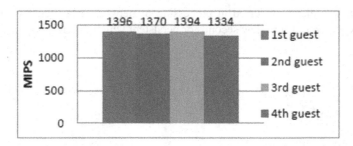

Fig. 10: CPU Fairness Chart

Figure 10, we would like to give insight of the performance on each of the 4 guests. Each of the guests have +/- 4% differences between each other. These results shows that, concurrent stressing the CPU, does not affect guests OS with significantly. We allocate each host CPU core to a single guest, thus no overselling test were conducted.

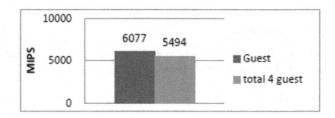

Fig. 11: 1 Guest with 4 CPU vs. 4 Guest with 1 CPU each

Figure 11, we try to present CPU consumption in a different view. We try to display the total MIPS of 4 guests with 1 core compared to 1 guest running all 4 cores. The reason of such analysis is to show how much compute power is wasted due to divisioning of the CPU cores to each guest. If we divide the 4 cores one each to the guests, the allocation of each guest will get average of 1373 MIPS or 22%. By allocating each CPU to a guest OS, a total of 9.6% lost of compute power as compared to assigning all cores to a single guest.

Memory

Host machine consist of 2 DIMMs of 4GB RAM and each guest have 512MB RAM. At the peak of the stress test, only 2GB RAM is utilize or 25% of actual RAM is utilize. Still the performance variance being affected greatly.

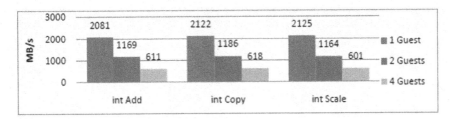

Fig. 12: RAMSpeed Memory Variance Chart

Figure 12, shows memory stress test. An average of 43% decreases in memory performance while running 2 guests. It suffers more with 70% performance drop while running 4 guest. Performance degradation occurs when more guest VM running on single machine. Performance varies between guest with value of 2081 – 611 Mb/s or 70%.

KVM does not manage the memory assigned to the VM. In the physical machine, libvirt API is used to create the VM and a user spaces emulator called qemu-kvm to provision the VM. The libvirt will initiate the VMs with the requested hard-ware such as number of CPU, memory size, disk etc. Qemu-kvm will prepare the VMs address space and I/O between the guest and the physical host. Each VM will run as separate qemu-kvm process with the memory size stated up front by libivirt. Therefore, the more VM launched in a physical host machine, the higher performance degradation we will notice.

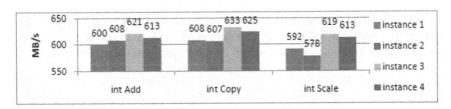

Fig. 13: RAMSpeed Memory Fairness Chart

Figure 13, shows good performance isolation of memory +/- 5% differences between guest. It shows good isolation or fairness of each VM even the variance differences is high.

Disk

For disk, we only perform maximum of 2 guest up concurrently. With 4 guest test, the guest OS will hang or become unresponsive due to the nature of the test.

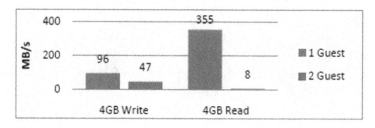

Fig. 14: IOZone Disk Variance Chart

Testing for performance variance on disk further worsen the case by comparing 1 guest with 2 guest as shown in **Figure 14:** IOZone Disk Variance Chart. For Iozone read test, the performance drop for 2 guests is 97% while write test suffers 52%.

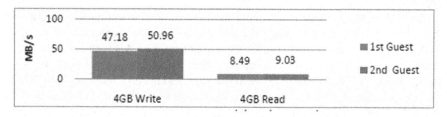

Fig. 15: IOZone Disk Fairness Chart

In Figure 15 both guest OS suffers almost the same degradtion. Even thou the performance drop caused by the total number of guest OS is significantly high, the perfromance of both guest OS's is almost divided equally show on IOZone test.

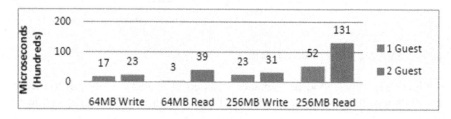

Fig. 16: Tiobench Disk Variance Chart

Tiobench perform more rigrous test compared to IOZone. Figure 16 shows the graph of performance variance, while Table 3 shows the percentage drop of such variance.

Table 3: Performance Variance

	Variance
WRITE 64	35%
WRITE 256	34%
READ 64	1200%
READ 256	150%

Table 4: Performance Fairness

Test	Fairness
WRITE 64	+/- 87%
WRITE 256	+/- 69%
READ 64	+/- 2400%
READ 256	+/- 236%

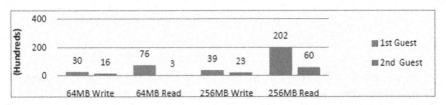

Fig. 17: Tiobench Disk Fairness Chart

Performance isolation test for tiobench as reflected on Figure 17 and Table 4 Multithread read/write shows bad distribution resource handling. With this results, it shows one guest have higher I/O compared to another. In tiobench, multiple I/O request is done with a total of 64 threads running at one time. This test shows more rigrous test as compared to iozone.From iozone and tiobench test, read variance is much more worst compared to write operation.

Application

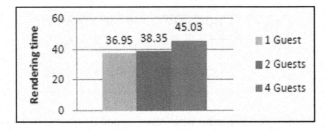

Fig. 18: Java Test

Figure 18 shows the results of Sunflow rendering on guests running concurrently. It shows 3.79% degradation when compared with 1 guest compared to 2 guest running. Another 20% drop when 4 guests running. Application benchmarking for Java does not reflect the performance drop as shown in CPU, memory and disk benchmarking. This test is analogous to CPU performance where the trend of performance drop is quite similar.

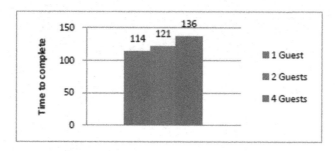

Fig. 19: SQLite Test

Figure 19 show the result of SQLite test to finish 125,000-query request. It shows performance variance of 21%. For performance isolation on SQLite it shows +/- 23%. For Java, the isolation value is 20%.

6 DISCUSSION

Table 3 shows the summary of overhead, variance and fairness of the server elements. CPU score good for all metrics. Memory on the other hand, shows bad variance.

Table 3: Overall Results

ELEMENTS	OVERHEAD		VARIANCE		FAIRNESS	
CPU	1%	GOOD	20%	GOOD	4%	GOOD
MEMORY	5%	GOOD	70%	BAD	5%	GOOD

For disk Iozone test, both read/write shows good distribution of fairness between competing guests. For tiobench it gives much more regression test as compared to Iozone. All three performances metrics show bad results.

In virtualization, the biggest complaint is sluggish disk I/O. VM disk will never perform like physical disk. In full virtualization, I/O channel specifically disk, will significantly degrades overall performance. To improve disk I/O, it is advisable to get high-performance disk, while waiting for the full virtualization maturing. For example, SCSI drive still outperforms even the highest-end IDE drives. Consid-eration on widest transfer rate, highest cache drives which IaaS provider could af-ford. Because of disk I/O overhead, High CPU core number or high memory will not be fully utilize. [16]

The performance shown in our test shows the worst case of each of the server elements couple together. Even memory shows bad variance and disk shows tremendous overhead, bad variance and no proper isolation, it still does not reflect on the SQLite and Java tests. The application test cases is also showing worst-case scenarios where each of the application servers being used fully on one node.

For network, we can see that UDP throughput is much better than TCP but we could not justify of such characteristic. There are suggestions to improve the network I/O throughput. For example, a dedicated NIC to VM might be advice able where highly network traffic dependent such as web server, application or terminal server. [16]

VMM introduce additional overhead on guest VM as compared to native due to either device emulation or types of virtualization (i.e. para-virtualization or full-virtualization). Another factor could be attributed to domain scheduling within VMM, which schedule the shared I/O devices. For example, even a single virtual machine is running on a single host, the sending or receiving network packets involves two domains; the driver and the guest. These domain must be scheduled and poor scheduling can result in increase of network latency. [15]

Further improvement on the virtual machine can be achieved from using Virtio (libvirt: Wiki : Virtio n.d.) devices. The Virtio drivers are optimized for KVM are provides performance for disk and network of theVM.

Choosing the right OS I/O scheduler for the host machine and virtual machine might improve the virtual machines performances. David Bouthcer n.d. have suggested the NOOP scheduler improves the throughput of the virtual machines. [17] From our studies, we have found several performance issues on the server elements. We know more dynamic deployment policy for cloud is needed in order to allocate guest resources more efficiently.

REFERENCES

[1] Jones, M. Tim. "Discover the Linux Kernel Virtual Machine-Learn the KVM architecture and advantages." IBM Developerworks. 18 April 2007.
http://www.ibm.com/developerworks/linux/library/l-linux-kvm/ (accessed October 25, 2009).
[2] VMWare Inc. Understanding Full Virtualization, Paravirtualization, and Hardware Assist. Palo Alto: VMWare Inc, 2007.

[3]   vmware. Technical Note-Networking Performance in Multiple Virtual Machine. VMware Inc., 2007.

[4]   Jones, M. Tim. "Discover the Linux Kernel Virtual Machine-Learn the KVM architecture and advantages." IBM Developerworks. 18 April 2007.
http://www.ibm.com/developerworks/linux/library/l-linux-kvm/ (accessed October 25, 2009).

[5]   QEMU disk image utility - Linux man page. http://linux.die.net/man/1/qemu-img (accessed November 19, 2009).

[6]   Why Virtualization. 08 04 2009. http://virt.kernelnewbies.org/WhyVirtualization (accessed 11 18, 2009).

[7]   Che Jianhua, He Qinming, Qinghua Goa, Dawei Huang. "Performance Measuring and Comparing of Virtual Machine Monitors." IEEE/IFIP International Conference on Embedded & Ubiquitous Computing. IEEE Computer Society, 2008. 381.

[8]   Gaurav Somani, Sanjay Chaudhary. "Application Performance Isolation in Virtualization." IEEE International Conference on Cloud Computing, 2009: 41-48.

[9]   IBM. "Quantitative Comparison of Xen and KVM." 2008 Xen Summit. Boston, June 23-24, 2008.

[10]   CentOS - Community Enterprise OS. 4 November 2009. http://www.centos.org/ (accessed November 18, 2009).

[11]   tiobench benchmark. 2 october 2002.
http://linuxperf.sourceforge.net/tiobench/tiobench.php.

[12]   Java SciMark 2.0. 31 3 2004 . http://math.nist.gov/scimark2/ (accessed 9 10, 2009).

[13]   Ghori. Asghar. Precio. HP Certified Systems Administrator 2nd Edition), 2007 Endeavor Technologies United States

[14]   Guohui Wang, T. S. Eugene Ng, "The Impact of Virtualization on Network Performance of Amazon EC2 Data Center", in IEEE INFOCOM'10, San Diego, CA, March 2010

[15]   Scott Rixner. "Network Virtualization Breaking the Performance Barrier" ACM Queue, January/Febuary 2008 edition.

[16]   Kenneth Hess, Amy Newman. Practical Virtualization Solutions. Pearson, 2009.

[17]   David Bouthcer, Abhishek Chandra. "Does Virtualization Make Disk Scheduling Passé?" Workshop on Hot Topics in Storage and File Systems (HotStorage'09). Montana.

Analyzing the Applicability of Airline Booking Systems for Cloud Computing Offerings

Johannes Watzl, Nils gentschen Felde and Dieter Kranzlmuller

MNM-Team, Ludwig-Maximilians-Universit at Munchen, Germany

Abstract   This paper introduces revenue management systems for Cloud computing offerings on the Infrastructure as a Service level. One of the main fields revenue management systems are deployed in is the airline industry. At the moment, the predominant part of the Cloud providers use static pricing models. In this work, a mapping of Cloud resources to flights in different categories and classes is presented together with a possible strategy to make use of these models in the emerging area of Cloud computing. The latter part of this work then describes a first step towards an inter-cloud brokering and trading platform by deriving requirements for a potential architectural design.

1 INTRODUCTION

Advance booking systems allow users to reserve Grid or Cloud resources in a certain timeframe or enable the booking of time slices of use for a Grid or Cloud service. This analysis describes the potential of utilizing a state of the art revenue management system used in the airline industry for the pricing of Cloud service offerings. Today, advance booking systems for Cloud services are introduced by several public and private Cloud providers. The pricing models used at the moment are strictly static. This means, there are predefined prices for the use of a resource or a given service for a certain time unit (i.e. CPU/hour of compute power, GB/month of storage).

Our analysis focuses on Infrastructure as a Service (IaaS) offerings as one of the three dominant domains of Cloud computing [1]. Our hypothesis is that a dynamic Cloud pricing model based on offer and demand can be mapped almost directly on booking systems utilized by the airline industry. The latter systems are based on dynamic pricing, revenue management and capacity planning models. Assuming an IaaS-provider is offering the hosting of virtual machines, the provider's datacenter can be mapped onto an airplane with seats in different service classes (i.e. economy, business, first class). For airplanes the differentiation might be for example legroom, special seats or meals and for (Cloud) services this could be parameters like guaranteed uptime or backups. Please note, that here the service class corresponds to a virtual machine's configuration, while the booking class may only give different service level assurances.

S.C. Lin and E. Yen (eds.), *Data Driven e-Science: Use Cases and Successful Applications of Distributed Computing Infrastructures (ISGC 2010)*, DOI 10.1007/978-1-4419-8014-4_26,

In the airline industry, the three basic service classes (economy, business, first class) are divided into booking classes. There is a minimum and a maximum price for seats allocated in the different categories on a plane or on the other hand space allocated for virtual machines in a datacenter. Booking classes allow the consideration of certain restrictions or discounts. They enable the handling of booking cancellation, no-shows, booking changes or refunding. In the field of Cloud services, booking classes can be used for similar objectives such as changing the time of reservations or the amount of resources, cancellation of reservations or refunding in case of not using the resources.

The main goal of this work is the introduction of a Cloud booking system using dynamic pricing, revenue management and capacity planning methods adapted from airline booking systems. Making use of revenue management systems for Cloud products enables maximized revenues and a better and more optimized utilization of the resources. In addition, this work marks a first step towards a trading and brokering platform for Cloud resources by deriving requirements for an architectural design of such a platform. The vision is to have a market place-like system, where Cloud service providers can offer their services and customers may choose from adequate offerings corresponding to their needs.

The remainder of the paper is structured as follows. Section 2 gives an overview about state of the art pricing methods taking the well-known Amazon Cloud as an example. Section 3 then applies airline booking methods for Cloud services and motivates the use of dynamic pricing by comparing a static with a dynamic pricing model. Afterwards, related work (also originating from Grid computing environments) is presented in Section 4. Together with Section 5, a first list of requirements towards a brokering and trading platform for Cloud resources is derived. Finally, Section 6 concludes the paper.

2   STATE OF THE ART OF CURRENT CLOUD PRICING MODELS

This section briefly describes the Amazon EC2 (Elastic Compute Cloud) pricing model as an example for the current state of the art pricing methods. Amazon offers a virtual machine hosting, managed using a web services interface. EC2 runs Amazon's Machine Images (AMI) which can be chosen from a pool of templates or customized for specific needs. Amazon offers three types of service, namely the Standard Instances, High-Memory Instances and High-CPU Instances. Each of which differs in CPU (number of cores and compute cycles), platform, memory size and virtual machine image size (storage). Whereas the platform, the memory size and the storage can be specified or measured easily, Amazon introduced the so-called Elastic Compute Unit (ECU) for gaining measurable and normalized CPU capacity. The ECU is defined by Amazon as "[. . .] the equivalent CPU capacity of a 1.0-1.2 GHz 2007 Opteron or 2007 Xeon processor." [2]

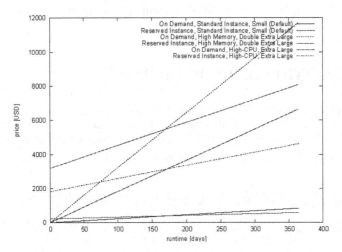

Fig. 1 Amazon AWS pricing – a comparison

2.1 Pricing Concept

At the moment, Amazon Web Services (AWS) offers three different concepts of pricing: *On-Demand Instances, Reserved Instances and Spot Instances.*

AWS have been introduced based on a static pay-per-use pricing model (On-Demand Instances). The price for a virtual appliance per hour (wall-clock time) of operation is composed of the type of image deployed (Linux or Windows), the amount of memory needed, the ECUs granted to the appliance and the location of the datacenter operating the appliance. The user is charged for the actual time of operation of the resources only.

The model of Reserved Instances features discounts in comparison to the On-Demand Instance prices. Paying a reservation fee for either one or three years ranging from app. 117 USD to 6370 USD (as of Feb. 2010) per year [2], gives the user discounts on the prices for a virtual machine's runtime. This type of service is thought for long-running virtual appliances as also shown in Figure 1. There, three exemplary AWS instances are compared in regard to their prices. The X-axis shows the actual runtime an appliance is online over a year, while the Y-axis represents the costs that arise there from. The breakeven in costs comparing the On-Demand and the Reserved Instances is between 170 and 173 days for all the examples shown. Data transfer and storage is not taken into account as the prices do not vary in regarding the offerings.

Taking offer and demand into account, Amazon AWS extended their pricing concepts introducing a spot market. Users can bid on unused EC2-instances giving their desired specification of the instances, the location and the maximum price they are willing to pay for. The instances are started at the very moment the criteria given by the customers are fulfilled and will be terminated automatically at the moment the spot price is over the given maximum.

3 APPLICATION ON CLOUD SERVICES

Before analyzing the applicability of airline booking systems for Cloud computing offerings, we show how the components and entities of airline booking systems can be mapped to Clouds. Section 3.2 then shows a comparison of the expected revenue generated using a static vs. a dynamic pricing model.

3.1 Mapping Flight Booking Systems to Cloud Offerings

In this section, the product and price differentiation for airline booking systems is mapped to Cloud offerings. In table 1, this mapping is summarized.

The different service classes from the airline industry (first, business, economy) can be mapped directly to the service levels (i.e. gold, silver, bronze) of Cloud computing offers. Each service class in the airline case contains a certain number of seats and for each of the service classes a number of booking classes is defined. For every booking class a price is determined. The Cloud resources needed or allocated for running virtual machines can be mapped to the seats. Introducing booking classes with different prices for the different service levels can be done similarly to systems adopted by the airline industry.

For defining the booking classes, airlines take into account certain criteria like the date of the booking, the type of flight route, the time between the out-and inbound flight, the number of hops and the level of flexibility customers wish to have. Most of these points can also be used for the price differentiation in the Cloud case, but some do not match well. The date of the booking is a good criteria in both cases. In the airline case the type of flight route and the time between out-and inbound flight play a major role, but can hardly be represented in Cloud offerings. As "type of flight", there are only "one-way flights" looking at Infrastructure as a Service offers. The time between out-and inbound flights cannot be mapped to Clouds, but in the case of Clouds, standing orders could be considered. In the field of Cloud computing, segmentation of the service delivery could be considered (suspend and resume virtual machines) instead of the number of hops. Flexibility in both cases is a very good criteria to be integrated into booking classes. The possibility of cancellation without paying the full price, the starting date and time and duration of service delivery as well as upgrading (or in case of Cloud computing up-and downgrading) represent adequate parameters for defining booking classes.

Table 1: Mapping flight bookings to Cloud offerings

Flight bookings	Cloud offerings
service class	service level
seat	virtual machine
booking class	booking class
price	price
price given by...	
service class	service class
booking class	booking class
date of booking	date of booking
type of flight route (One-Way vs. Go & Return etc.)	"one-way booking" only
time between out- and inbound flight	"standing order"
number of hops	segmentation of service delivery ...
	in time
	in location
flexibility	flexibility
cancellation	cancellation
date and/or time of flight	start time and duration of service delivery
upgrade of service class	up- & downgrade of resource capacities
	location of service delivery

In table 1, we introduce the mechanism of defining booking classes as a new concept. Service levels are already defined by the providers. In the future, comparable service level agreements (SLAs) are needed to be able to compare different providers' prices.

Having done the price and product differentiation, the mechanisms of capacity planning and overbooking can be applied to Cloud scenarios. A difference to airlines is the fact that in case of a flight, the plane is booked for the whole duration without dynamic changes in terms of seats used. The timeframe a product is offered in the Cloud case has to be discretized (hour, minute) to be able to represent this dynamic behavior. A very fine grained discretization leads to a computationally intensive task, dynamically determining the prices of the resources though.

To make consumers accept vendor lock-ins or even make them attractive, airline companies offer bonus programs for flying with a certain airline or a member of a group of airlines. In the future, bonus programs for Cloud resources could be interesting for both consumers and providers. The providers could benefit from binding customers to use their resources and the consumers could be rewarded with additional services, priorities or privileges.

3.2   Static Pricing versus Dynamic Pricing

The majority of providers makes use of static pricing models. Static pricing or fixed price models can be seen as a special case of dynamic pricing models, where all prices are to be assumed equal. For both customers and providers, static pricing models are easier to handle and especially for the customers the expected price for the resources is easier to calculate and more transparent.

In this section, we do assume a simple Cloud hosting scenario and compare the expected revenue from the provider's point of view. In this scenario, a provider can offer a maximum of 1000 virtual machines to his customers. He offers three different types of service, namely bronze, silver and gold. 50% of the virtual machines are bronze-class machines, 30% silver and 20% gold. Depending on the type of service granted, different prices are charged for one hour wall-clock time of a machine's operation. Table 2 summarizes the static pricing model assumed.

Table 2: The static pricing model and distribution of virtual machines assumed

type of service	price [USD per hour]	distribution
bronze	0.60	50%
silver	0.80	30%
gold	1.00	20%

On the other hand, we do assume the same provider making use of a dynamic pricing model. For each type of service, the provider does introduce three different booking classes. Each booking class does offer the same type of service for a different price, but in average the price equals the prices given in the static scenario (see Table 2). 50% of the machines of the same type of service do belong to the cheapest booking class III, 30% belong to booking class II and the remaining 20% do fit into the most expensive class I. III is assumed to be priced 70% of the price given in the static scenario, II costs exactly the same as compared to the previous scenario and thus booking class I has to be calculated as 175% the price in order to hold the same average price as before. Table 3 summarizes these assumptions.

Table 3: Distribution of booking classes and dynamic prices assumed weighted average

booking class	price [USD per hour]		
	bronze	silver	gold
III: 50%	0.42	0.56	0.70
II: 30%	0.60	0.80	1.00
I: 20%	1.05	1.40	1.75
weighted average	0.60	0.80	1.00

Taking the assumptions above into account and running a simulation [3] using the *Expected Marginal Seat Revenue* (EMSR) method [4, 5], Figure 2 shows the provider's expected revenue in relation to the average utilization of his entire resource pool (percentage of virtual machines "sold" to customers). In the simulation, the customers' requests follow a Poisson distribution. As input, the EMSR algorithm takes the number of booking classes, the prices for each booking class and the parameter of the normal distribution μ and $\sigma2$. With these two parameters, the Poisson distribution is approximated with the normal distribution.

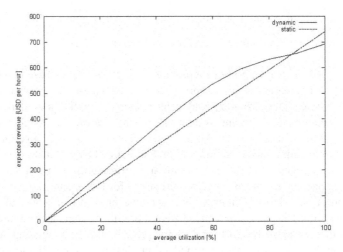

Fig. 2: Expected revenue of a static & dynamic pricing model – a comparison

Notably, the dynamic pricing model applied to Clouds from airline booking systems does create a greater revenue for not fully booked use cases. In the case that more than app. 85% of all the virtual machines available are "sold", the static prices do create more revenue though.

4 RELATED WORK

In the field of accounting and billing of Grid resources several works are published. In the German D-Grid, a brokering system is introduced for the billing of Grid services based on the Distributed Grid Accounting System (DGAS). The system enables both real (i.e. resource usage from industry) and virtual (i.e. science, funded on a national level) currency. To make the system work, the resources have to be monitored and the data gathered is fed into the accounting system [6, 7].

The requirements for a monitoring system in IaaS Clouds are to the ones found in Grid infrastructures. The Cloud resources provide space for the hosting of virtual machines which enables to gain useful monitoring data from the underlying virtualization layer. Requirements, a Cloud and Grid resource provider thus have to meet are as stated in [6, 7]:

- Determine the location of storing accounting data

- Define an appropriate unit for measuring the resource usage based on monitoring data

- Determine prices for the offered resources based on the measurement unit

- Define the architecture of an accounting and billing system

- Identify existing standards and solutions for a reasonable adoption

- Define service level agreements for the (different) offers

In his work, R. Buyya presents a pricing concept for Clouds based on a market model [8]. The intention for this approach is an exchange-based market for Cloud resources where Cloud providers may offer resources and the price is determined by offer and demand. A trading system like this allows users to request resources interacting with an additional brokering layer which will identify a service on the market place meeting the constraint and budget defined by the customer. This implies dynamic prices for the resources similar as offering these in conjunction with revenue management systems. The requirements for this scenario are a standardized resource description language, interoperable or convertible virtual machine image files, (live) migration between different providers, standardized image staging (in and out) and the support for dynamic prices either by integrating additional pricing concepts or relying on the providers' pricing models [8]. The following list summarizes the requirements for dynamic prices based on an exchange based market without claiming completeness:

- Standardized resource description language

- Interoperable or convertible virtual machine image files

- Migration (live) between different providers and data centers

- Standardized image staging (in and out)

- Support for dynamic prices

A. Caracas and J. Altmann have published a paper about "A Pricing Information Service for Grid Computing" [9]. In this work, they analyze different Grid middle-wares and the Amazon EC2 Cloud in regard to their billing and pricing capabilities. Different pricing schemes are presented and discussed and a general pricing scheme supporting various Grid middlewares is presented. The requirements stated in their work are as follows:

- Standardized description of the pricing schema and the resources

- Service level agreements which allow dynamic prices

- Decouple pricing from metering, accounting and payment

Clouds are always driven by a business model. Every Cloud provider needs to adopt a monitoring, accounting, and billing infrastructure for his business. Cloud providers have developed different models of accounting and billing their resources. Talking about Cloud computing, there is no general standardized unit for measuring compute power at the moment. For being able to compare different providers, especially taking into account the offering of resources with rapidly changing dynamic prices, a standard measure for compute power is required. Without the ability to compare offered resources, the federation of Clouds with transparent pricing is not possible.

One approach for a standardized unit for compute resources was introduced by the "Norddeutsche Verbund f'ur Hoch-und H'ochstleistungsrechnen" (HLRN) which has defined a unit for accounting the amount of compute resources used. This approach, adopted by data centers providing high performance computing resources is the Norddeutsche Parallelrechner Leistungseinheit (NPL) [10]. An NPL is defined as 1 hour wallclock time spent on an IBM p690 frame with 32 CPUs and 64 GByte physical memory. Therefore, this unit contains both the compute power and memory size of the compute nodes in a standardized way. Motivated by this NPL approach, a resource description language for Clouds has to be developed which enables standardized units and the comparing of resources. Such a description language has to meet certain prerequisites based on the demands of both users and providers. With the usage of this description language, trading arbitrary Cloud resources will be made possible.

Another approach of measuring compute power has already been described in Section 2. Amazon introduced the so-called Elastic Compute Unit (ECU) for gaining measurable and normalized CPU capacity. The ECU is defined by Amazon as "[. . .] the equivalent CPU capacity of a 1.0-1.2 GHz 2007 Opteron or 2007 Xeon processor." [2]

5   TECHNICAL REQUIREMENTS TO TRADE CLOUD RESOURCES

This section presents a first attempt to derive technical requirements in a use case-driven manner. The vision is to have a market place-like system, where Cloud service providers can offer their services and customers may choose from adequate offerings corresponding to their needs.

Even though this section does not provide a complete list of requirements, it presents first glance issues being faced during the construction process. Systematically, the derivation follows the concepts well-known from object oriented software development procedures as for example described in [11].

5.1 Use Case: Initially Buying an Adequate Appliance for the Lowest Price

Name: UseCase: buy

Short description: A customer wants to out-source some of his computational services and thinks about using Cloud computing resources. He himself is able to specify his resource demands in form of the technical specification his servers do come up with at the moment. Now, he is looking for an adequate appliance or a set of appliances that are capable of covering his demands. Having that, the customer wishes to choose the cheapest offer for his individual pattern of resource usage.

Prerequisite: A user wants to make use of Cloud services and is able to specify his ressure demands in terms of technical specifications.

Postcondition: The same user finds the offer that suits his demands best and is able to buy the resources of choice.

Requirements derived therefrom:

- Cloud resource description language (must be meaningful, all users' demands must be taken into account)
- Definition of semantics of units (e.g. for CPU power/usage)
- Comparability of resources described within a given resource description language
- Definition of resource demand "is satisfied"/"greater", "is not satisfied"/"less" and equality
- Quantization of usage over time (e.g. minutes or hours)
- Prizing of Cloud offerings per time unit

5.2   Use Case: Re-evaluating, If an Existing Offer Still Is "The Best" or Cheapest

Name: UseCase: re-evaluate

Short description: A customer is already using Cloud resources for his purposes for a longer period of time. Now, he wishes to re-evaluate, if he is still getting the best service out of his money or if alternatively the same service may be granted by another provider for a lower price. In case he does find a better offer, he wishes to transfer his running appliances to the cheaper or better provider. A short interrupt in service may be neglectable.

Prerequisite: A user is already making use of Cloud services for a certain period of time, but wants top re-evaluate his choice of Cloud service and/or provider.

Postcondition: The user does find the "best" or cheapest Cloud offering that satisfies his demands.

Requirements derived therefrom:
- Cloud resource description language (must be meaningful, all users' demands must be taken into account)
- Definition of semantics of units (e.g. for CPU power/usage)
- Comparability of resources described within a given resource description language
- Definition of resource demand "is satisfied"/"greater", "is not satisfied"/"less" and equality
- Quantization of usage over time (e.g. minutes or hours)
- Prizing of Cloud offerings per time unit
- Interoperability of different Cloud offerings
- Conversion of Cloud appliance formats used by different providers must be supported
- "Down & Upload" of virtual appliances must be given
- Optional: migration or even live migration between different providers must be supported

5.3   Use Case: Offer Ones Cloud Services at the Brokering Platform

Name: UseCase:offer

Short description: A provider wants to offer his Cloud services for trade at a brokering platform. He is able to technically describe his Cloud offerings and the service level agreement (SLA) he grants in a human readable manner. The pricing of his Cloud services depend on several different usage statistics (e.g. CPU-, main memory-and disk-consumption and/or network I/O etc.). Additionally, the provider uses dynamical pricing models, meaning the prices are subject of change over time.

Prerequisite: A Cloud service provider wants to offer his services at a brokering platform. He is able to technically describe his offerings as well as the price.

Postcondition: The offering can be listed at the brokering platform.
Requirements derived therefrom:

– Cloud resource description language (must be meaningful, all users' demands must be taken into account)
– Definition of semantics of units (e.g. for CPU power/usage)
– Quantization of usage over time (e.g. minutes or hours)
– Support of arbitrary pricing models
– Prizing of Cloud offerings per time unit in correspondence to quantization procedure (price may differ over time!)
– Description of arbitrary pricing models taking all providers' influencing attributes (e.g. CPU-, main memory-and disk-consumption and/or network I/O etc.) into account
– Need of a Cloud service level agreement (SLA) description language
– Interfacing the providers' Cloud management platforms from the brokering platform in order to trade resources fully automated

6   CONCLUSIONS AND OUTLOOK

This paper gives an overview of pricing models currently used for Cloud computing offerings which are mostly using static pricing models. For flight bookings, the airline industry is deploying revenue management systems which enable them to maximize their revenue and the capacity utilization. In this paper, the basic concepts of these systems are introduced together with presenting the idea of applying revenue management systems for Infrastructure as a Service Cloud offerings. It has been shown that Cloud offerings can be very well mapped on the models used by airlines together with pointing out the differences of flight booking systems and the proposed booking system for Clouds. A commonly used method in revenue management systems, the expected marginal seat revenue method, has been carried out showing the applicability. For a comparison of static and dynamic prices, the revenues created by the two approaches have been computed and illustrated in this work. Applying state of the art flight booking systems for selling IaaS Cloud resources seems promising particularly with an increasing demand of such resources.

Motivated by this increasing demand of Cloud resources and dynamic prices, related work dealing with models for the dynamic pricing of resources in the Grid, utility computing, and Cloud computing field are presented highlighting the requirements of these approaches. A use case analysis focusing on buying, selling, and re-evaluating points out the requirements.

The future work in this area will be focused on the federation of Clouds, both private and public. Enabling this, a standardized language for describing resources meeting the customers' and providers' needs has to be developed. With this description language, it will be possible to request resources from different providers over a broker in a standardized and comparable way. Increasing demands of Cloud resources naturally would lead to increasing price of resources and vice versa. The amount of Cloud resources seem infinite not taking into account the dynamics of demands when defining prices. Introducing a brokering system with the ability of handling and trading Cloud resources on an offer and demand base among autonomous providers is one of the important works we are focusing on in the future. From additional roles and use cases, additional requirements for dynamic pricing and brokering systems will be derived. A booking system deduced from this work could be integrated into a brokering infrastructure.

Acknowledgements The authors wish to thank the members of the Munich Network Management (MNM) Team for helpful discussions and valuable comments on previous versions of this paper. The MNM Team directed by Prof. Dr. Dieter Kranzlm¨uller and Prof. Dr. Heinz-Gerd Hegering is a group of researchers of the Ludwig-Maximilians-Universit¨at M¨unchen, the Technische Universit¨at M¨unchen, the Leibniz Supercomputing Center of the Bavarian Academy of Sciences, and the University of Federal Armed Forces in Neubiberg. See: http://www.mnm-team.org

REFERENCES

[1] Armbrust, M. et al.: Above the Clouds: A Berkley View of Cloud computing, 2009
[2] Amazon (Feb. 2010) Amazon Elastic Compute Cloud (Amazon EC2).
   http://aws.amazon.com/ec2/ (and sub-pages)
[3] Ivan, Paul and Ciblak, Abdil and Chavez, Abdil and Ngah, Elvis and de Nooij, Guido and Borgardijn, Majella (2005): Revenue Management DSS.
   http://www.math.vu.nl/ obpdss/revenue-management/revenue-management
[4] Belobaba, P. P.: Air travel demand and airline seat inventory management, Ph.D. thesis, Massachusetts Institute of Technology, Dept. of Aeronautics and Astronautics, 1987
[5] Shy, Oz: How to Price, Cambridge University Press, 2008
[6] Gohner, M. and R¨uckemann, C.-P.: Konzeption eines Grid-Accounting-Systems, 2006
[7] Falkner, J¨urgen et al.: Konzeption eines D-Grid-Billing-Frameworks, 2007
[8] Buyya, R. et al.: Market-Oriented Cloud Computing: Vision, Hype, and Reality for Delivering IT Services as Computing Utilities, High Performance Computing and Communications, HPCC '08 (2008)
[9] Caracas, A. and Altmann, J.: A Pricing Information Service for Grid Computing, 2007
[10] Kallies, B.: Allocations, Accounts, Policies, HLRN, 2008
   http://www.hlrn.de/doc/accounting/
[11] Bruegge, Bernd and Dutoit, Allen H.: Object-Oriented Software Engineering: Using UML, Patterns and Java, Second Edition. Prentice Hall (2003)

Part IX
Applications on High Energy Physics

Grid Computing Operations for the CMS Experiment at the GRIF Tier-2

A. Sartirana[1], P. Hennion[1], P. Mora de Freitas[1], I. Semenjuk[1], P. Busson[1], M. Jouvin[2], G. Philippon[2], C. Leroy[3], F. Schaer[3], P. Micout[3] and V. Mendoza[4]

1.LLR,E. Polytechnique,Palaiseau, French
2.LAL,U.Paris-Sud, Osay, French
3.IRFU, CEA, Saclay, French
4.LPNHE, U.Paris-7, Paris, French

Abstract CMS moved into LHC data taking mode on November 2009. In order to store, distribute, process and analyze the experiment data, the CMS collaboration relies on a Grid-based system of distributed computing resources. Such resources are organized in "Tiers" and, in particular, Tier-2' sareregional level centersdevoted to support Montecarlo production and Physics analysis. GRIF, a distributed Tier-2 built of 6 computing centers in the Paris region, is one of such CMS-supporting sites. The main focus of GRIF is to support the important Physics analysis activity brought by a very active local CMS community.

In this paper we describe the setup for CMS operation at GRIF, the lessons learned during the long commissioning period and the solutions adopted.We also present an over view of the CMS activities at the site both during the commissioning and the first data taking periods, pointing out successes and weaknesses.

1 INTRODUCTION

The Compact Muon Solenoid (CMS) is one out of two general purpose detectors hosted by the Large Hadron Collider (LHC) at CERN. The data-taking era started on November 2009 and CMS is expected to take data over a period of about ten years at a rate of several Peta Bytes (PB) per year. In order to cop with the demanding task of store, distribute, process and analyze this great amount of data, the experiment collaboration, during the last years, hasbuilt and commissioned itsown computing system. This is based on Grid services and resources provided by the Worldwide LHC Computing Grid (WLCG). Computing resources are worldwide distributed and organized in a hierarchic structure with "Tiers" having specific roles and responsibilities.

- Tier-0: Hosted at CERN. Gets data from the online experiment, performs realtime reconstruction, stores the samples in a primary tape archive and distribute them to theTier-1 centers.

S.C. Lin and E. Yen (eds.), *Data Driven e-Science: Use Cases and Successful Applications of Distributed Computing Infrastructures (ISGC 2010)*, DOI 10.1007/978-1-4419-8014-4_27,
© Springer Science+Business Media, LLC 2011

- Tier-1's: Seven national level centers. Each one gets a fraction of the experiment data from CERN, stores it in a secondary tape archive and takes care of its re-reconstruction and of the distribution of the required data at the Tier-2's. Moreover Tier-1's collect Montecarlo (MC) samples from the Tier-2's and archive them on tape.
- Tier-2's: About 50 regional level centers. Theyare resources for MC production and they are the place where end users can access and analyze data.

The GRIF (Grilleau Servicedela RechercheenIlede France) is oneoftheTier-2's supportingCMS.Itisadistributed centerbuiltby6sub-sitesall locatedintheregion of Paris, France. The main idea behind creating a distributed Tier-2, beyond the mere aggregation of resources, is togain high reliability leveraging on redundancy of services and sharing of manpower.AsaCMSsite, GRIF is mostly focusedonthe support of Physics analysis tasks. In particular, a rich analysis activity is brought at the site by a local CMS community heavily contributing to some of the main CMS analysis groups: Higgs, Exotica, Electron/Photon identification and reconstruction and Heavy Ions.

1.1   Plan of the Paper

In Sec.2 we will introduce the roles and responsibilities for a CMSTier-2 according to the CMS Computing Model (CMSCM). Sec.3 is an introduction to the GRIF Tier-2 in general and in particular (Sec. 3.1) for CMS. The CMS activity at the site will be discussed in more detail in Sec. 4, in particular for what concerns data hosting in Sec. 4.1, analysis activity in Sec. 4.2 and MC activity in Sec. 4.3. A summary is given in Sec. 5.

2   TIER-2 ROLE IN CMS COMPUTING MODEL

Tier-2 centers are official resources of the CMS collaboration. The CMS Computing Model establishes for them precise roles and responsibilities which are expressed in a Memorandumof Understanding thathastobe fulfilledbytheTier-2 sitesin delivering their services. The CMSCM also indicates some required resources for an average Tier-2 site (see Table 1), but this is to be considered a minimal and indicative requirement as actuallyTier-2 centers mayvarya lotin size.

Table 1: Minimal resources for a CMSTier-2 center.

Computing power	0.9MSI2k
Disk Space	200TB
NetworkWAN Connection	1Gb/s

Tier-2's are resources for MC production. They should be able to devote to this task the 50% of their overall computing power. Moreover they should be able to deliver30Tera Bytes (TB) of disk space for temporary store theMC data produced at the site before theyare uploaded to someTier-1 for archiving.

Tier-2's are also resources for Physics analysis and in particular for the analysis tasks performed by the official CMS Physics groups.For what concerns computing power, sites should guarantee roughly the 40% of their CPU capacity to this activity. Then, they are requiredtogive 50 TB of disk storage to be centrally managed by the Analysis Operation Team. This space is meant be used for placing at the sites MC samples of general interest or for performing some centrally managed skims of primary datasets. Moreover, eachTier-2, depending on itsavailabilityof resources, can support one or more Physics groups.For each of the supported groups the site is required to give 50 TB of disk storage.This space is used by the group analysts to place the data samples needed for analysis and the outcome of private MC productions or skims. What is left in term of storage and computing power can be devoted to the local community activity.

TheTier-2s, as all the CMS supporting sites, are also required to host and run CMS specific applications.

- PhEDEx: This system provides data placement and transfer. When a data set is requested at a given site, the system finds out all possible data sources and submit the transferstothe Grid FileTransfer Service.The central brain of the PhEDEx application is located at CERN with a database of all the replicas of the collaboration samples and central agents which take care of finding possible routes for transfers. Each site, then, host local agents which take care of submitting the transfers and check the replicas in interaction with the local storage.
- Squid Frontier: Each site is also required to host one or two squid cache proxy fortheCMS condition data base in such a way that jobs running at

the site can get the conditions directly from the cache without contacting the database located at CERN.

3   INTRODUCING THE GRIF TIER-2

GRIF is a distributed Tier-2 center built of six sub-sites all located in the Ile de France region (the region of Paris, France). In Table 2 are listed the sites, their locations and their resources.

Table 2: GRIF sub-sites locations and resources.

Subsite	Location	Job Slots	Disk
IRFU	CEA, Saclay	1700	650TB
LAL	U Paris-Sud, Orsay	1800	240TB
IPNO	U Paris-Sud, Orsay	400	35TB
LPHE	U Paris-7, Paris	250	165TB
APC	U Paris-7, Paris	60	32TB
LLR	E.Polytechnique, Palaiseau	850	300TB

The six sites are seen, from the point of view of the Grid, as a single Tier-2 , i.e. they have a single entry in the Grid BDII and in the GOCDB. This sums up to a considerable amount of resources with 11 farm clusters providing about 5000 job slots and 7 DPM storage instances serving about 1400 TB of disk. Moreover GRIF delivers many Grid services as top BDII, WMS, VOMS, LFC, etc.

GRIF supports more than 20 Virtual Organizations (VO), including the 4 LHC experiments, other High Energy Physics (HEP) experiments, like ILC, babar, dzero as well as non HEP organizations as biomed, fusion, etc. In Fig.1 are reported the graphs of the CPU usage between March 2009 and February 2010 by the 4 LHC VO's and the aggregateof the non-LHCVO's. One can see that CMS is the second VO, for what concerns the resource usage, after Atlas.

The backbone which connects the GRIF sub-sites is a 10 Gb/s (Giga bits per second) private network. Actually this network is to be completed to include LPNHE and APC. Moreover, from this private network, the GRIF sites can access a 5 Gb/s VLAN to Lyon, where the French Tier-1is located.

An important point to stress is that the main idea behind creating a distributed Tier-2is not merely to aggregate resources into a site of relevant size but rather to gain high reliability by redundancy of services and ease of management by sharing of manpower. Most of the Grid services hosted at GRIF run in multiple parallel instances: SRM, CE, etc. The services which are required to run in a single in stance, as the BDII, have a fall-back instance in a different sub-site. A centralized Nagios monitoring keeps all the administrators up to date with the status of theTier-2. Moreover the services configuration is managed centrally by a Quattor instance. This allows to share the working configurations and factorize the parts which are common to all sites so that the sub-sites administrators only have to deal with the peculiarities of theirown center. Expertiseis collected in an internal twiki and problems tracked by an internal ticketing system. Concluding, shifts are organized among the administrators to keep the site attended.

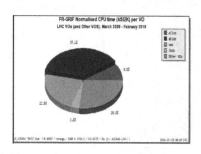
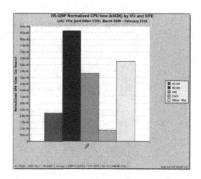

Fig. 1: CPU usage between March 2009 and February 2010 at GRIF for the 4 LHC experiments and the aggregateof all non-LHCVO's.

3.1 CMS Setup at GRIF

There are four out of the six GRIF sub-sites that support the CMS activity: IRFU, LAL, LLR, LPNHE. The CMS "data driven" computing model requires each CMS site to have only one storage element. In order to fit this requirement into the distributedsetupofGRIFitwas decided to organize the four sub-sites supporting CMS into two full CMS Tier-2's:

- T2 FR GRIF IRFU: composed by the IRFU and LPNHE, it includes the computing elements of both sites and the storage element of IRFU.
- T2 FR GRIF LLR: composed by the LLR and LAL, it includes the computing elements of both sites and the storage element of LLR.

From the point of view of CMS these are two completely independent Tier2's. They support four CMS analysis groups. Higgs, E-Gamma and Heavy Ions are supported by T2 FR GRIF LLR and Exotica is supported by T2 FR GRIF IRFU. Moreover T2 FR GRIF IRFU hosts the 50TB of storage which is to be centrally managed by the Analysis Operation Team. Each of the two sites hosts a squid proxy server. The two servers are configured to fall-back one on the other in case of failure. Moreover each site has a PhEDEx node and runs the corresponding agent.

This configuration with two couples of GRIF sub-sites building two independent CMSTier-2's has turned out to be the best solution which allows to match the requirements of CMS computing and keep on exploiting the advantage of having a distributed Tier-2. Of courseitbrings some technical complication as GRIF is a single site according to Grid operation but it pays in terms of site availability. Fig. 2 shows the CMS site availability of the two sites in the last year.

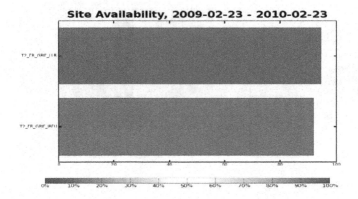

Fig. 2: CMS Site Availability of the two CMS GRIF Tier-2 centers from February 2009.

4   CMS ACTIVITY AT GRIF

In this section we will review the activity of CMS at GRIF focusing on three main aspects: data hosting and imports, analysis activity and MC activity.

4.1   Data Hosting and Imports

GRIF hosts 196 TB of CMS data which have different owners as shown in Table 3. The largest fraction comes from samples requested by the analysis groups (E-Gamma, Higgs, Exotica, Others) and by the Analysis Operation Team. There are then few TB of data needed for technical reasons, i.e. samples used for tests and monitoring (Other Operations). Then, there is an important fraction of data produced by users. These are about 60TB which are mostly outcomes of private MC productions performed by local users on behalf of CMS Physics groups. What should be stressedis that for the GRIFTier-2 thisis an important responsibility and an assurance of a good exploitation of the site as these samples are not replicated any where else and can be accessed only running jobs at the site.

Table 3: CMS data at GRIF split by own

Requestor/Owner	Size
E-Gamma	70TB
Higgs	21TB
Exotica	9TB
Other Groups	27TB
Analysis Ops.	6TB
Other Ops.	3TB
Users	60TB

Another important aspect connected with data hosting is the capability of the site to import and export data. When PhEDEx routes requested data to a site, it selects possible routes among a set of "commissioned" links. These are links between sites whichhave undergonea testandproved their capabilitytogain required transfer rates.For this reasonitisof great importancefora sitetohavethelargest number of links commissioned, or at least to commission links with all the sites with which it expects to exchange data. GRIF itself has up and down links commissioned with al lthe Tier-1's, with the other FrenchTier-2's and with the Tier-2's in the world that supports the same analysis groups.

To conclude, Fig.3 is a cumulative graph of the data import for the GRIF CMS sites in the last year.

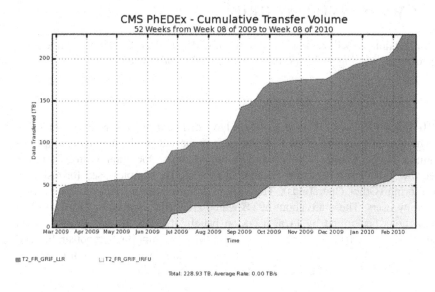

Fig. 3: Cumulative data import from March 2009.

4.2 Analysis Activity

Analysis activity is the main focusof the GRIFTier-2 for what concerns CMS. The site hosts an important local community of CMS Physicists which is very active in some of the major CMS analysis groups. Pushed by this, the site has an important and continuous analysis activity withanaverageof 100kjobs running on the farm each month. In the graph of Fig.4 are reported the terminated jobs between the 25 January and the25 February2010.The site runs about 5k jobs per day.In an average good day this brings the two GRIFTier-2's among the ten most used CMS sites for analysis.

Looking on a longer timescale, the graph in Fig.5 reportsthe terminated analysis jobs since September 2009 to February 2010. It is interesting to see how the activity evolved with the approach of first data taking (November 2009). From the graph one can see that there was no substantial increase in the volume of the activity which has, infact, rather changedin quality.Upto October2009the analysis activity was mainly performed by few power-users with well defined high-scale tasks. Such users were very skilled in exploiting computing resources and their request of support was very focused and easy to satisfy. In October 2009 CMS performed a first large scale analysis test and in this occasion the great part of the Physics community started to exploit regularly the Grid for performing its tasks. Therefore, since October 2009 the number of users has increased of a factor ten or more. This did not necessarily increased the load as these users submit smaller tasksbut this radically changed the request for support. How to manage the support of such a large and heterogeneous community of users actually turned out to be the major non-technical issue brought by the start of LHC activity.

Turning to technical aspects, the main issue pointed out by these first months of real activity was the data serving capacity of the site storage. In particular, it was observed that often, an high load brought by manyjobs reading files on the same server,may lead the server performances to drop to10% of the expected through put. This seemstobe caused by the factth at the DPM storage system does not manage any queue for the rfio file requests, therefore 1000 requests turn into 1000 rfio processes running and the file servers, having so many processes to manage in parallel, do not reach an optimal exploitation of their serving capacity. In the short term the only solution is to take care of distributing the files which are likely to be accessed together among different servers. In the longer term we are planning to test different storage access solutions to find a better setup.

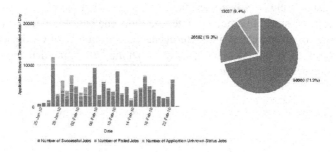

Fig. 4: Terminated analysis jobs at GRIF between January and February 2010.

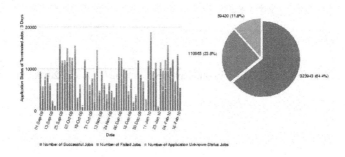

Fig. 5: Terminated analysis jobs at GRIF between September 2009 and February 2010.

4.3   Montecarlo Activity

GRIF also supports the official CMS MC Production. In the graph of Fig. 6 are reported the terminated MC jobs since September 2009. This activity brings much less load to the site with respect to analysis activity and general there are no main issues connected with it. This tasks is performed by a central team of experts and problems are rares and promptly addressed and solved.

5   SUMMARY

GRIF has a longstanding experience in supporting CMS computing activity within theframeworkofa distributedTier-2.Thesite contributesMC productionaswellas Physics analysis. In particular, an important and stable analysis activity is brought by very active local communities and it has been increasing and evolving since the start of LHC data-taking in November 2009. After these first months of real activity, few important issues have been pointed out. On one side the need to cop up with the support of an increased and heterogeneous community of Grid users. On the other the seek for a storage serving setup which may effort the demanding file access performances required by analysis.

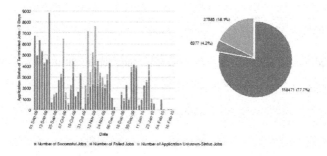

Fig. 6: Terminated MC jobs at GRIF between September 2009 and February 2010.

From the CMS Computing Experience in the WLCG STEP'09 Challenge to the First Data Taking of the LHC Era

D. Bonacorsi[1] and O. Gutsche[2]

1. University of Bologna, Physics Department, Italy
2. Fermilab, Chicago, USA

Abstract The Worldwide LHC Computing Grid (WLCG) project decided in March 2009 to perform scale tests of parts of its overall Grid infrastructure before the start of the LHC data taking. The "Scale Test for the Experiment Program" (STEP'09) was performed mainly in June 2009 -with more selected tests in September-October 2009 -and emphasized the simultaneous test of the computing systems of all 4 LHC experiments. CMS tested its Tier-0 tape writing and processing capabilities. The Tier-1 tape systems were stress tested using the complete range of Tier-1 work-flows: transfer from Tier-0 and custody of data on tape, processing and subsequent archival, redistribution of datasets amongst all Tier-1 sites as well as burst transfers of datasets to Tier-2 sites. The Tier-2 analysis capacity was tested using bulk analysis job submissions to backfill normal user activity. In this talk, we will report on the different performed tests and present their post-mortem analysis.

1   THE CMS PARTICIPATION IN THE STEP'09 CHALLENGE

The STEP'09 challenge was a WLCG [1, 2] multi-experiment exercise involving all 4 LHC experiments and many Grid sites worldwide on all levels of the multi-tiered computing infrastructure (Tier-0, Tier-1 and Tier-2 sites -T0, T1, T2 in the following, respectively). This infrastructure comes from the evolution of the hier-archical model of computing Tiers as proposed in the MONARC [3] working group and since the first Review of LHC Computing [4]). In this section we discuss the lessons learned in STEP'09 by the CMS [5] Computing project. STEP'09 was the end of a long roadmap of both WLCG computing challenges (see e.g. [6]) and CMS-specific challenges (see e.g. [7, 8, 9, 10]). The WLCG Common Computing Readiness Challenge in 2008 (CCRC'08) [11, 12] was the last complete WLCG computing exercise, in which CMS participated very successfully [13, 14]. The CMS Computing project operated STEP'09 as a series of tests rather than as a fully integrated WLCG challenge. In STEP09, CMS tested specific aspects of its

S.C. Lin and E. Yen (eds.), *Data Driven e-Science: Use Cases and Successful Applications of Distributed Computing Infrastructures (ISGC 2010)*, DOI 10.1007/978-1-4419-8014-4_28, © Springer Science+Business Media, LLC 2011

computing system while overlapping with other experiments, with emphasis on: i) Data recording to tape at the T0 level; ii) Pre-staging & rolling processing at the T1 level; iii) Transfer tests in T0-T1 routes, in T1-T1 routes and in T1-T2 routes; iv) Analysis tests at the T2 level. Some more details on each testing area are given in the following.

T0 level: In the current implementation of the CMS Computing Model [15] CMS stores a copy of recorded RAW+RECO data at T0 on tape. This "archival" copy is not meant to be accesses by processing and analysis workflows. The scope of this part of the challenge was to verify that CMS can archive data at the needed tape-writing rates, and to investigate possible effects when other experiments archive data at the same time. Specifically for STEP'09, CMS generated a realistic tape-writing load on Castor [16] at CERN. To maximize tape rates, the repacking/merging T0 workflow [17] was run in two test periods between Cosmic data taking runs. The CMS T0 tests were successful in both periods, as shown in Fig. 1. In the first period, CMS measured a tape writing peak at >1.4 GB/s for more than 8 hours with ATLAS writing at 450 MB/s at the same time. In the second period, CMS sustained >1 GB/s for about 3 days. No overlap with ATLAS was possible in this period. Some structure is visible in the first period due to problems in the CMS usage of the Castor disk pools at CERN. As a conclusion, in the STEP'09 tests at the T0, CMS collected no evidence of any destructive overlap with ATLAS while running simultaneously and was able to sustain a sufficiently high data rate to tape to support data taking.

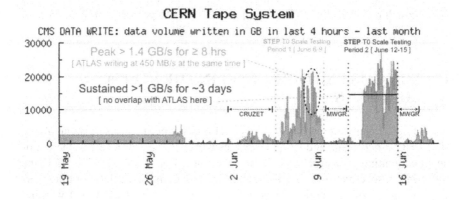

Fig. 1: CMS data volume written to Castor tapes at CERN in STEP'09 Tier-0 operational tests. From the sustained rates in excess of 1.4 GB/s for more than 8 hours in the first period and in excess of 1 GB/s for about 3 days in the second period, CMS collected no evidence of destructive overlaps with ATLAS and could demonstrate sufficiently high tape writing rates to support data taking.

T1 level: The CMS T1 sites have significant disk caches to buffer access to data on tape and allow high CPU efficiencies. At the start of the data taking period 2009-2010, CMS was able to keep all RAW and 1-2 RECO passes on disk and used the buffers as static disk caches. With increasing data sample sizes, CMS will have to use a dynamic disk cache management. To achieve high CPU efficiencies, data will have to be pre-staged from tape in larger parts and then processed. During STEP'09 CMS performed tests to investigate pre-staging rates and performed stability checks of the tape systems including a "rolling" re-reconstruction at the T1 sites. The pre-staging was performed at T1 sites using different techniques chosen by the T1 sites as CMS does not yet have a global pre-staging mechanism: i) a manual, "site-operated" pre-staging (adopted by FNAL, FZK, IN2P3); ii) a staging triggered centrally via a "SRM/gfal script" [18] (adopted by CNAF); iii) a pre-staging agent approach based on the PhEDEx experience in data management [19, 20, 21, 22] (adopted by ASGC, PIC, RAL). The rolling re-reconstruction consisted of dividing the datasets to be processed into 1 days-worth-of-processing parts according to the custodial fractions of the T1 sites, and of triggering pre-staging prior to submitting the re-reconstruction jobs. As shown in Fig. 2, the tape performance achieved in STEP'09 was very good at ASGC, CNAF, PIC, RAL; IN2P3 was in scheduled downtime during the first part of STEP'09; FZK had to declare a tape system unavailability and could only join the tests later; FNAL failed the goals during the first days, the problems got resolved promptly and good performance could be achieved for the remaining days of the challenge. The CPU efficiency -computed as the ratio of CPU processing time (CPT) to wall-clock time (WCT) -for the re-reconstruction jobs was measured on a daily basis during STEP'09 for all T1 sites. In general, mixed results were obtained: very good CPU efficiencies for FNAL, IN2P3, PIC, RAL; good efficiencies for ASGC, CNAF; a non-significant test for FZK which had to be repeated (see the section on post-STEP'09 tests).

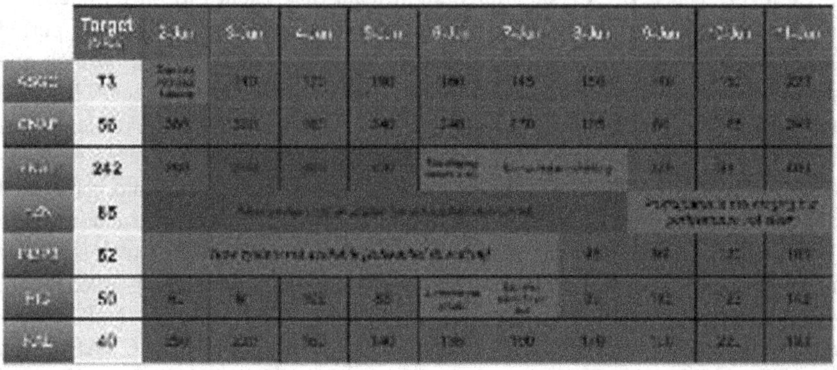

Fig. 2: Outcome of STEP'09 pre-staging tests at CMS Tier-1 sites. Most sites showed a very good tape performance; IN2P3 was unavailable in the first half of the challenge due to a long-scheduled downtime, FZK had to declare a tape system unavailability and FNAL had to solve some problems in the beginning but showed very good tape rates at the end of the challenge.

Transfers: The transfer sector of the CMS Computing Model was widely investigated by CMS in CCRC'08 on all possible route combinations (T0-T1, T1-T1, T1-T2, T2-T1). Additionally, CMS runs ad-hoc transfer links commissioning programs in daily operations, as the Debugging Data Transfer (DDT) program [23, 24], based on the PhEDEx LoadTest infrastructure [25]. In STEP'09, CMS defined only limited and very specific objectives, namely i) stress the tapes at T1 sites (with write and read load while measuring transfer latencies), and ii) investigate the AOD synchronization workflow in T1-T1 transfers. The AOD's can be produced during a re-reconstruction pass at a T1 site and have to be synchronized to all other T1 sites so that every T1 site has a complete copy. The workflow was simulated by initially populating the T1 sites with datasets whose size was determined from the custodial AOD fraction. These datasets were subscribed to all other T1 sites. The data flow was used to measure latencies and transfer patterns. The goal to completely redistribution the AOD sample (about 50 TB) to all T1 sites in 3 days would have required about 1 GB/s sustained network throughput. During STEP'09, the tests ran for almost 2 weeks and reached during the second week a total of 989 MB/s on a 3-day average without particular optimizations, down to a hourly resolution, thus demonstrating that the goal is definitely within reach. Concerning the transfer latencies in T1-T1 traffic, CMS observed in STEP'09 tests that most files reached their destination within few hours, but long tails were regularly observed for few blocks/files. CMS is currently working on improving this situation. An interesting observation in PhEDEx operations was an evident load sharing in the AOD replication pattern: the WAN transfers pattern was optimized by PhEDEx via files being routed from several already existing replicas instead of all from the original source, thus sensibly optimizing the overall distribution process. For examples, the replication pattern of one ASGC dataset to other CMS T1 centres was measured: at the beginning ASGC was the only source site for the files of that dataset, but at the end eventually about 52% of the files at the destination site did not originate from ASGC but from another T1 hosting replicas (see Fig. 3, plot 1). In general, by investigating the data traffic pattern down to a hourly resolution it is visible that all STEP'09 transfer tests on all possible route combinations showed smooth features without significant structures, not only in T0-T1 and T1-T1 routes, but also in T1-T2 traffic (see Fig. 3, plot 2).

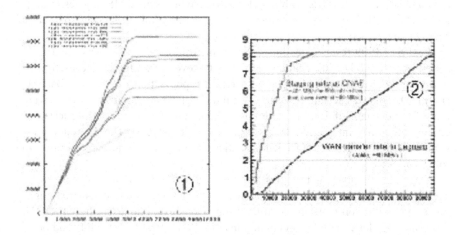

Fig. 3: Examples of STEP'09 transfer tests. (1) T1-T1 transfers pattern optimization by PhEDEx; (2) Data pre-staging from tapes at CNAF Tier-1 centre and simultaneous export to Legnaro Tier-2.

Analysis: The CMS model of Distributed Analysis is described elsewhere (see e.g. [26]). The goal of the analysis tests in STEP'09 was to assess the readiness of the global T2 infrastructure by increasing job scales to use most of the pledged analysis resources on the T2 level (close to 22k pledged slots, about 50% of which are for analysis), and by exploring data placement scenarios for analysis (measuring how much space granted to physics groups is used, investigating the replication of "hot" datasets and monitoring its effect on job success rates). The increase in the number of running jobs submitted via the CRAB tool [27] is well visible in the challenge period. STEP'09 more than doubled the average number of jobs on the T2 level: during the challenge, the average number of concurrently running jobs was higher than the analysis pledge (about 11k slots). Another interesting observation in STEP'09 is related to the T2 storage pledge utilization: before the challenge, very few T2 sites hosted dataset corresponding to more than 50% of the space they pledged and therefore were used less; through the submission of test analysis jobs to 49 T2 centres (and some T3 sites1), it was demonstrated that CMS is capable of using all pledged resources and will be able to store datasets at the majority of sites corresponding to their pledges and use them efficiently for analysis. Some caveats must be reminded for this analysis test. Firstly, several sites had at least one day downtime during STEP'09; secondly, the CMS submitters in STEP'09 did not queue jobs at all sites all the time; additionally, it must be noted that standard analysis jobs of realistic duration were run, reading data without remote stage-out of the analysis output. To fulfill all needs in the test phase, an ad-hoc Analysis Exercise (called "Oct-X") was run in October-November 2009, aimed to address such tests with a wider involvement of the CMS physics groups, and ran "realistic" analysis tasks (unpredictable pattern, full output stage-out, etc.). More on this in Sec. 4.

Post-STEP'09 tests: After June 2009, some test re-runs were performed as an appendix of the STEP'09 challenge. At the T0 level, scale tests were performed using special MC samples emulating a realistic population of Primary Datasets (PD) [17]. This was set-up to worth several days of T0 operations at a data taking rate of the detector of 300 Hz, by running bulk and express processing tests, including the newly introduced 48-hrs prompt conditions hold. The 48 hours delay is motivated by collecting sufficient statistics for prompt calibration workflows to finish and feed

The STEP'09 analysis test jobs also reached 8 additional Grid sites acting as Tier-3 supporting the CMS virtual organization back the newly calculated alignment and calibration constants into the prompt reconstruction. On the CERN T0 farm of 2300 slots, the bulk processing test used on average 1900 slots and demonstrated that CMS is able to sustain a repacking and prompt-reco load corresponding to a 250 HZ data taking rate at a 13% event duplication fraction due to the split in PDs. The express processing test showed that a 25 Hz express stream needed on average 120 slots. At the T1 level, re-processing tests were done to re-check the CPU efficiency measurements. They were performed in October 2009 at IN2P3, KIT (still due after June 2009) and at ASGC, CNAF (requested by sites). As highlights, CNAF successfully ran on a new and very promising storage set-up [28]; FZK tests were successful as well, peaking at 300 MB/s in reading (100-150 MB/s on average) and at 400 MB/s in writing.

2 FROM STEP'09 TO COLLISIONS IN 2009: THE T0 SYSTEM

The original planning expectations for late 2009 -early 2010 comprised a first da-ta-taking period in October-November 2009, followed by a second starting in April 2010. In the first one, the expectation was: to run 100 days at 20% live-time of the machine (20 days); to collect a total of 726M events (including a 40% over-lap between the different PDs); the size of RAW and RECO to be 1.5 MB/evt and 0.5 MB/evt respectively; to collect a total data volume of 1 PB of RAW and 359 TB of RECO; to collect a few tens of pb^{-1} of integrated luminosity; to measure an average data rate from P5 of 450 MB/s corresponding to a data taking rate of 300 Hz. In the end these expectations could not be met. The 2009 data taking period (till the end of March 2010) can be summarized as follows. CMS collected data worth nearly 16k lumi sections (93s) in the minimum-bias PD ('MinBias' in the following), corresponding to 17 days of running; 90M events had been collected, corresponding to a total of 2400 files of 2 GB average size; the total size of the MinBias dataset was 7.8 TB; the MinBias PD corresponded to 10 μb^{-1} of luminos-ity; if selecting only "good" runs usable in physics analysis, the dataset is reduced to 870 lumi sections, 22 hours of data taking, 6.8 M events, 1 TB of overall size. During data taking, the T0 workflows were put to the test with real collisions data. These rolling, fully automated workflows are: *i*) express processing, *ii*) bulk proc-essing and prompt reconstruction and *iii*) prompt skimming (executed at the T1 level, but scheduled by the T0 system). The CMS online system records events and stores them in binary files (streamer files, see also Fig. 4) grouped into streams. "Stream A" is the source of the physics PDs. For 2009, CMS expected data taking at a rate of 300 Hz for 16 hours per day with 8 hours of no collisions to catch-up with the processing therefore sustained at about 200 Hz data taking rate, for a total of 10 individual PDs. During 2009, CMS recorded collisions at 200 Hz data taking rate (with spikes of more than 1 kHz), corresponding to 730M events and a total size of 100 TB in Stream A. The events were stored in only 2 Physics PDs. "Stream B" was proposed before the run as an insurance to not miss any events. This stream was meant not to be reconstructed at the T0 and only stored on tape due to the trigger. It contained a very high rate stream of zero-bias data ('Ze-roBias' in the following) and was later restricted to an averaged rate of 1 kHz. The" Express" stream which provides access to reconstructed events within 1 hour was expected to correspond to a rate of about 40 Hz. During 2009, it generally stayed within 40-60 Hz, with occasional spikes to 3 kHz, corresponding to 80M events and a total size of about 12 TB. The T0 farm utilization at CERN is shown in Fig. 5. CMS used less than the available resources because of the nature of the recorded events (the reconstruction time for MinBias events is significantly less than for high energy collision events and the events are also significantly smaller in size). In general T0 job success/failure rates were irrelevant in terms of data us-ability for physics. The few observed reconstruction and express failures were dominated by trigger rate explosions in pre-collision Cosmic runs and data rates creating individual files too large to process (one lumi section has to be stored in an individual file for bookkeeping reasons). The overall efficiency of all processing jobs at the T0 in 2009 is beyond 98%, exceeding 99% if considering the collisions data taking period only. Interesting measurements of latencies in the T0 system were possible analyzing the 2009 data taking period. The latency from receiving first streamers of a run at the T0 (corresponding to run start) to first express files available for analysis on the CERN CMS Analysis Facility (CAF) [29] was on average 25 minutes (see Fig. 6, plot 1). The express stream is designed for a latency of 1 hour. The actual measured latency was less due to the nature of the recorded MinBias events which show a significantly lower multiplicity of recorded particles and therefore a much shorter reconstruction time. The latency from run end to RAW data arriving at the custodial T1 site was on average 6 hours (see Fig. 6, plot 2), with long tails due to administrative issues with the data transfer subscriptions. The latency from run start to the start of the first reconstruction job was on average 1.4 hours, with tails corresponding to runs with high rates; most runs started the reconstruction within a couple of hours from the run start. The latency from first reco job starting to first Reco data becoming available at T0 (post merge) averaged at 1.7 hours (see Fig. 6, plot 3); this means that first events for most runs were promptly recoed and available for analysis within a couple of hours from the reco start (note that no 48 hours conditions hold was applied here). The latency from run end to reconstruction files available at the custodial T1 site was on average 15 hours (see Fig. 6, plot 4), with long tails observed mostly due to transfer request approval latencies; most reconstruction files completed at T1 sites about 10 hours after the run ended.

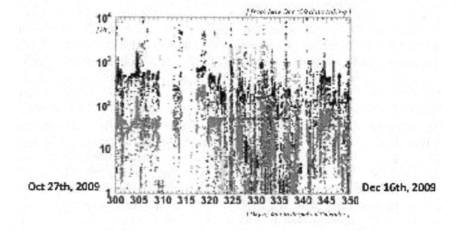

Fig. 4: Rates into streams from the CMS Online system. Black dots are "Stream A", green dots are "Stream B", red dots are "Express" stream, blu dots are buffered "Stream B" (manual injection of streamers). See text for a description of streams.

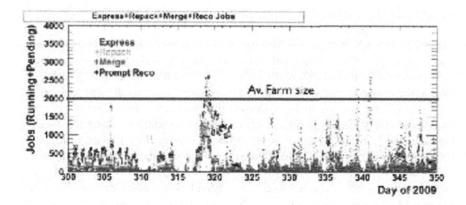

Fig. 5: Tier-0 farm queue utilization and jobs statistics during 2009 data processing. Each set of dots is cumulative. The two bigger spikes on the right correspond to reading ZeroBias buffers.

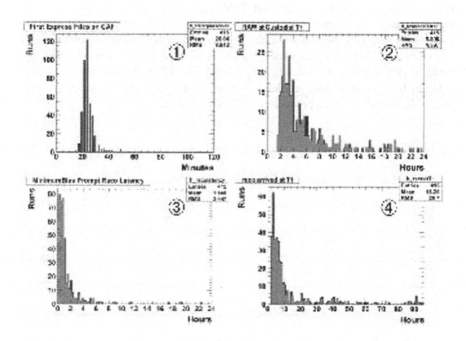

Fig. 6: Latencies measured in the T0 workflows with 2009 data: (1) latency of first express file available for analysis after run start; (2) latency of RAW data arriving at custodial T1 site after run end; (3) latency of start of prompt reconstruction after run start; (4) latency of reco arrival at T1 sites after run end. For a more detailed explanation, see text.

3   FROM STEP'09 TO COLLISIONS IN 2009: THE T1 SITES

The T1 sites readiness and stability has improved over time [30] and was very good during the 2009 collisions data taking period. The goal was to distribute multiple copies of individual PDs to T1 centres (plus one archival copy at CERN), as long as the resources permit in 2010. CMS replicated collision datasets to 6 out of 7 T1 sites (ASGC was not included due to tape problems). More than 0.9 PB were transferred out of CERN to T1 sites from November 2009 to March 2010. The high-demand MinBias dataset was sent to 4 T1 centres. Unfortunately, the total data volume was too small to investigate the behavior of the transfer system under high load, a more refined tuning will hopefully be possible in 2010. The T1 sites were involved in all scheduled workflows, namely i) re-reconstruction; ii) skimming; iii) MC production (mostly at T2 level -but low-latency requests were run at the T1 level as needed for details on this activity, see Sec. 4). Until early March 2010, a total of 9 re-reconstruction passes of a good run list had already been performed: a pass of the good run list on the MinBias PD re-reconstructed 22M events, corresponding to a total output data size of 2.3 TB; the corresponding ZeroBias re-reconstruction pass ran over 23M input events and produced a 2.2 TB output dataset. The average latency was 1-2 days. The CPU efficiency for reprocessing jobs was as high as 8090%. The re-reconstruction workflows were not resource limited. The total time used for a pass was dominated by long-running individual jobs with many events in single input file. The re-reconstruction passes suffered from bookkeeping problems and required significant debugging efforts due to shortcomings of the production tool infrastructure.

4   FROM STEP'09 TO COLLISIONS IN 2009: THE T2 SITES

The T2 site readiness has plateaued in late 2009 to about 40 usable T2 sites (see Fig. 7). Many structures are visible, related to holiday periods, problematic sites, or simply downtimes (one recent example: SL5 migration of all resources) for groups of sites at a time. But in general a clear trend to more sites being considered ready can be seen over time which is due to the significant effort of the CMS computing project to bring and keep the sites in a ready state [30]. The Monte Carlo production ('MC' in the following) at the T2 level continued in parallel to data taking, mostly producing MinBias MC samples for comparison with data. The jobs were submitted via the ProdAgent tool [31]. The baseline for CMS is to perform MC production at T2 centres, but some special high-priority MC requests were produced at T1 sites to use all available resources and to decrease the latency. In total 63 production workflows were executed at the T1 level, corresponding to 189 output datasets, for a total of 385M events (RAW, RECO, AOD about 1/3 each) of a total output size of 58 TB. The latency for MC production on the T1 level was approximately 2 days between request and sample available for analysis. This increased to approximately 4-5 days on the T2 level because of the necessary transfer back to the T1 level for archival. Additionally, the release validation ('RelVal' in the following) production was performed at FNAL T1 centre and at CERN: it sums up to about 235M events, corresponding to 32 TB of tape space in 2567 datasets for 17 CMSSW releases. The RelVal latency was measured to be roughly 24 hours (using a fixed number of slots at the T0 -it could be eventually faster at the FNAL T1 centre). Launched in 2009, a new Analysis Operations team of the CMS Computing project provides technical support for the analysis tool infrastructure, and manages the centrally controlled space at T2 sites by subscribing samples which are used by the whole collaboration and by replicating samples in high demand to distribute access over more resources. The total central space available for the Analysis Operations team is 50 TB of space at each of about 50 existing T2 centres. After the "Oct-X" exercise in October 2009, the team overviewed a consistent data flow of datasets needed for analysis, while the actual transfer troubleshooting and technical support was provided by the CMS Facilities Operations team. About 1.5 PB were transferred to CMS T2 sites as destinations in the December 2009 -February 2010 time window, and roughly 300 individuals on average submitted CMS analysis jobs on the distributed infrastructure in a given week (see Fig. 8 -plot 1). About 11k jobs slots are available for Analysis at T2 level, and CMS reached roughly a 75% utilization around the beginning of 2010 (see Fig. 8 -plot 2): in any given week 47±2 T2 sites ran CMS analysis jobs.

The analysis job success rate remained a persistent issue: CMS stabilized on average at around 80% success rate, hence with visible improvement over last year when CMS averaged about 65%. It was determined that roughly half of errors are

related to remote stage-out of produced output analysis files. This is still an area
with relatively large margins of possible improvements.

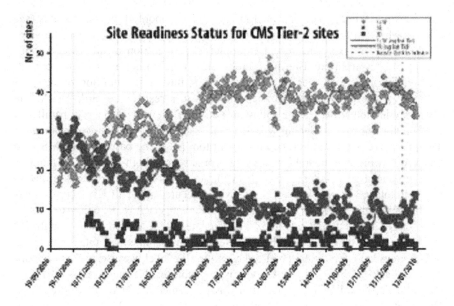

Fig. 7: Evolution in the number of CMS Tier-2 sites which are considered 'ready' for CMS
Computing operations, according to the metrics defined by the CMS Site Readiness program
[30].

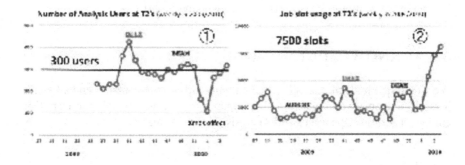

Fig. 8: (1) Number of CMS analysis users at the Tier-2 level; (2) Job slots usage at the Tier-2 level.

5   CONCLUSIONS

The STEP'09 exercises focussed on tests of specific key areas of the distributed computing infrastructure of CMS. They were an efficient approach to test and measure the tape system performance at T0 and T1 sites, several aspects of the transfer system, and the analysis performance at T2 centres at high scales. The WLCG sites profited from these exercises to further mature and tune their infrastructure. In particular, the T1 sites demonstrated that their MSS systems are commissioned and able to face the challenges of the LHC data taking in the future. With the experience gained during the last years and from STEP'09 as the very last computing challenge before the proton-proton collisions started, we entered the LHC era. The 2009 data taking gave us few collisions events but plenty of operational observations. The CMS T0 system was very stable during operations. A predominant part of the effort was spent on monitoring incoming data rates and on occasional modifications of thresholds to adapt to changing data taking conditions. The CMS Tier-1/2 sites have reached a remarkable operational maturity. In addition, the CMS operations team identified clearly the areas of potential fragility of the infrastructure and are operationally mitigating the associated dangers (e.g. CMS is currently working on on risk-assessment analyses for different crisis scenarios at T1 sites). The 2009 data taking period was successfully and smoothly handled by CMS Computing. New limitations might appear in 2010 collisions data taking though: CMS will have to constantly control increasing data volumes, and a more thorough planning and monitoring of data placement and WAN transfers will be needed and pursued. With this experience and lessons learned, CMS Computing is ready for the next round of data taking in 2010.

6   ACKNOWLEDGEMENTS

We would like to thank the WLCG community, all the site contacts, and all members of the teams working on CMS Computing operations, namely the Data Operations, Facilities Operations and Analysis Operations teams.

REFERENCES

[1]   The Worldwide LHC Computing Grid (WLCG) web portal: http://lcg.web.cern.ch/LCG

[2]   J. D. Shiers, "The Worldwide LHC Computing Grid (worldwide LCG)", Computer Physics Communications 177 (2007) 219–223, CERN, Switzerland

[3]   M. Aderholz et al., "Models of Networked Analysis at Regional Centres for LHC Experiments (MONARC), Phase 2 Report", CERN/LCB 2000-001 (2000)

[4]   S. Bethke et al., "Report of the Steering Group of the LHC Computing Review", CERN/LHCC 2001-004 (2001)

[5]   CMS Collaboration, "The CMS experiment at the CERN LHC", JINST 3 S08004 (2008) doi: 10.1088/1748-0221/3/08/S08004

[6]   D. Bonacorsi et al., "WLCG Service Challenges and Tiered architecture in the LHC era", IFAE, Pavia, April 2006

[7]   D. Bonacorsi et al., "Towards the operation of the INFN Tier-1 for CMS: lessons learned from CMS DC04", Proceedings of XI International Workshop on Advanced Computing and Analysis Techniques in Physics Research (ACAT'05), DESY, Zeuthen, 2005

[8]   I. Fisk, "CMS Experiences with Computing Software and Analysis Challenges", presented at Computing in High Energy and Nuclear Physics (CHEP'07), Victoria, BC, Canada, September 2007

[9]   O. Gutsche et al., "WLCG scale testing during CMS data challenges", J. Phys.: Conf. Ser. 119 062033 (2008) doi: 10.1088/1742-6596/119/6/062033

[10]   CMS CSA'07 twiki portal: https://twiki.cern.ch/twiki/bin/view/CMS/CSA07

[11]   WLCG CCRC'08 twiki portal: https://twiki.cern.ch/twiki/bin/view/LCG/ WLCGCommonComputingReadinessChallenges

[12]   J.D. Shiers et al., "The (WLCG) Common Computing Readiness Challenge(s) -CCRC'08", contribution N29-2, Grid Computing session -Nuclear Science Symposium, IEEE (Dresden), October 2008

[13]   CMS CCRC'08 twiki portal: https://twiki.cern.ch/twiki/bin/view/CMS/CMSCCRC08

[14]   L. Bauerdick and D. Bonacorsi, "CMS results in the Combined Computing Readiness Challenge (CCRC08)", 11th Topical Seminar on Innovative Particle and Radiation Detectors (IPRD'08), Siena, Italy, Jun 7-10, 2010

[15]   CMS Collaboration, "The CMS Computing Project Technical Design Report", CERN-LHCC2005-023

[16]   CASTOR project website: http://castor.web.cern.ch/castor

[17]   17. S. Chatrchyan et al., "CMS Data Processing Workflows during an Extended Cosmic Ray Run", J. Instrum. 5 T03006 (2009) arXiv: 0911.4842. CMS-CFT-09-007

[18]   Storage Resource Management (SRM) project website: http://sdm.lbl.gov/srm-wg

[19]   D. Bonacorsi, T. Barrass, J. Hernandez, J. Rehn, L. Tuura, J. Wu, I. Semeniouk, "PhEDEx high-throughput data transfer management system", CHEP06, Computing in High Energy and Nuclear Physics, T.I.F.R. Bombay, India, February 2006

[20]   T. Barrass et al, "Software agents in data and workflow management", Proc. CHEP04, Interlaken, 2004. See also http://www.pa.org

[21]   R. Egeland et al., "Data transfer infrastructure for CMS data taking", XIII International Workshop on Advanced Computing and Analysis Techniques in Physics Research (ACAT'08), Erice, Italy, Nov 3-7, 2008 -Proceedings of Science, PoS (ACAT08) 033 (2008)

[22]   L. Tuura et al., "Scaling CMS data transfer system for LHC start-up", presented at Computing in High Energy and Nuclear Physics (CHEP'07), Victoria, BC, Canada, September 2007 J. Phys.: Conf. Ser. 119 072030 (2008) doi: 10.1088/1742-6596/119/7/072030

[23]   Debugging Data Transfer program twiki portal: https://twiki.cern.ch/twiki/bin/view/CMS/ DebuggingDataTransfers

[24] N. Magini et al., "The CMS Data Transfer Test Environment in Preparation for LHC Data Taking", IEEE Nuclear Science Symposium, Dresden, Conference Record N67-2, Applied Computing Techniques session (2008)

[25] L. Tuura et al., "Scaling CMS data transfer system for LHC start-up", presented at Computing in High Energy and Nuclear Physics (CHEP'07), Victoria, BC, Canada, September 2007 J. Phys.: Conf. Ser. 119 072030 (2008)

[26] A. Fanfani et al., "Distributed Analysis in CMS", Journal of Grid Computing, Computer Science Collection, 1570-7873 (Print) 1572-9814 (Online), doi: 10.1007/s10723-010-9152-1, March 2010

[27] D. Spiga et al., "The CMS Remote Analysis Builder (CRAB)", Lect. Notes Comput. Sci. 4873, 580-586 (2007)

[28] D. Andreotti et al.,, "First experiences with CMS Data Storage on the GEMSS system at the INFN-CNAF Tier-1", International Symposium on Grid Computing 2010 (ISGC'10), Taipei, Taiwan, March 5-12, 2010

[29] P. Kreuzer et al., "The CMS CERN Analysis Facility (CAF)", presented at Computing in High Energy and Nuclear Physics (CHEP'09), Prague, Czech Republic, March 21-27, 2009 -to be published in J. Phys.: Conf. Ser.

[30] S. Belforte et al., "The commissioning of CMS Computing Centres in the WLCG Grid", XIII International Workshop on Advanced Computing and Analysis Techniques in Physics Research (ACAT'08), Erice, Italy, Nov 3-7, 2008 -Proceedings of Science, PoS (ACAT08) 043 (2008)

[31] D. Evans et al., "The CMS Monte Carlo production system: Development and Design", Nucl. Phys. Proc.Suppl. 177-178 285-286 (2008)

First Experiences with CMS Data Storage on the GEMSS System at the INFN-CNAF Tier-1

D. Andreotti[1], D. Bonacorsi[2], A. Cavalli[1], S. Dal Pra[1], L. dell'Agnello[1], Alberto Forti[1], C. Grandi[3], D. Gregori[1], L. Li Gioi[4], B. Martelli[1], A. Prosperini[1], P. P. Ricci[1], Elisabetta Ronchieri[1], V. Sapunenko[1], A. Sartirana[5], V. Vagnoni[3] and Riccardo Zappi[1]

1. INFN-CNAF, Bologna, Italy
2. University of Bologna, Physics Department and INFN-Bologna, Italy
3. INFN-Bologna, Italy
4. now at Laboratoire de Physique Corpusculaire (LPC), Clermont-Ferrand, France
   formerly at INFN-CNAF, Bologna, Italy
5. now at Laboratoire Leprince-Ringuer (LLR), Ecole Polytecnique, Palaiseau, France
   formerly at INFN-CNAF, Bologna, Italy

Abstract A brand new Mass Storage System solution called "Grid-Enabled Mass Storage System" (GEMSS) -based on the Storage Resource Manager (StoRM) developed by INFN, on the General Parallel File System by IBM and on the Tivoli Storage Manager by IBM -has been tested and deployed at the INFN-CNAF Tier-1 Computing Centre in Italy. After a successful stress test phase, the solution is now being used in production for the data custodiality of the CMS experiment at CNAF. All data previously recorded on the CASTOR system have been transferred to GEMSS. As final validation of the GEMSS system, some of the computing tests done in the context of the WLCG "Scale Test for the Experiment Program" (STEP'09) challenge were repeated in September-October 2009 and compared with the results previously obtained with CASTOR in June 2009. In this paper, the GEMSS system basics, the stress test activity and the deployment phase -as well as the reliability and performance of the system -are overviewed. The experiences in the use of GEMSS at CNAF in preparing for the first months of data taking of the CMS experiment at the Large Hadron Collider are also presented.

1 THE INFN-CNAF TIER-1 CENTRE

The INFN-CNAF computing centre [1], located in Bologna (Italy), is the central computing facility of INFN. The CNAF site, in the framework of the Worldwide LHC Computing Grid (WLCG) [2] and according to the hierarchical model of computing Tiers as proposed in the MONARC [3] working group and since the first Review of LHC Computing [4] -is one of the 11 computing sites that serve as "Tier-1" centres and offer computing resources to all four LHC experiments at CERN (ATLAS, ALICE, CMS, LHCb). CNAF is also one of the main processing facilities for many other non-LHC experiments, both at present and future accelerator facilities (BaBar, CDF, SuperB) and for astrophysics and space physics experiments (VIRGO, ARGO, AMS, PAMELA and MAGIC). In this paper, we will focus on the experience by the CMS experiment [5].

In early 2010, the CPU power installed at CNAF is about 42k HEPSPEC06 and the installed net disk capacity is nearly 2.3 PB. In the second quarter of 2010, CNAF is expected to increase the CPU power to about 67.8k HEPSPEC06, and to approximately triplicate the disk capacity. The CNAF tape library is a SUN SL8500 with 20 T1000B drives in production (1 TB/tape capacity and 120 MB/s bandwidth), delivering an actual overall capacity of 10 PB. In order to allow a broad flexibility and to increase the performances, all storage resources are organized in a Storage Area Network (SAN) with redundant interconnections between the disk systems and the approximately 200 disk-servers.

Among its major duties, a Tier-1 centre must provide the safekeeping of raw and reconstructed experimental data. This functionality is provided with a Mass Storage System (MSS). The traditional solution for the MSS at CNAF, used for all the Grid Virtual Organization since 2003, is CASTOR [6], a Hierarchical Storage Management (HSM) solution developed at CERN. Since 2003, the CMS experiment has been the main user of the CASTOR system at CNAF. At the end of September 2009,

CMS data on tapes at CNAF summed up to almost 1 PB of tape space (for the CPU and disk shares of the experiments at CNAF see Fig. 1). Since the beginning, a large variety of issues with CASTOR were experienced by the CNAF storage team, both at the system and users administration levels, mainly tied to the inner complexity of the system itself. On the other hand, even if stability problems frequently arose with CASTOR at CNAF, this storage system was kept online for production use, despite the sometimes large operational overheads. In particular, the CMS contacts at CNAF constantly helped the CNAF storage team to keep the system in production for the CMS experiment (see e.g. [7]), and for all other experiments relying on it.

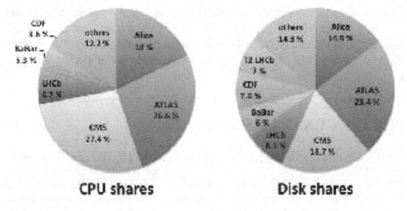

Fig. 1: Assigned shares of resources at INFN-CNAF Tier-1 for the year 2010.

In parallel to maintaining CASTOR in production, the CNAF storage team in 2006 started to search for a potentially more scalable, performing and robust solution. Several tests were performed, on parallel file-systems such as the General Parallel File System (GPFS) [8], a scalable, highly-available, high-performance file-system by IBM optimized for multi-petabyte storage management -as well as with Lustre [9] (currently from Oracle). The CNAF storage team concluded this phase in early 2007, with a stress test aiming to compare CASTOR, GPFS (Lustre had been excluded in a direct comparison with GPFS) together with dCache [10, 11] and xrootd [12]. As an outcome of those tests, GPFS qualified itself as the best solution both in terms of easiness of management and outstanding throughput performances (roughly a factor of 2 better with respect to dCache and xrootd) [13].

At the same time, StoRM [14, 15], an implementation of the Storage Resource Management (SRM) [16] interface for POSIX file-systems (including GPFS and Lustre) conforming to SRM 2.2 specifications, was being implemented at INFN. After another round of tests on StoRM itself, aiming to demonstrate the scalability and the robustness of such product [17], the CNAF storage team encouraged all experiments to progressively migrate from CASTOR to GPFS for the storage of data resident on disk (i.e. the so-called "D1T0" storage class: one copy on disk, no copy on tape). At the end of 2007, the StoRM/GPFS system was put into operations for ATLAS and LHCb. Both these experiments gained clear benefits from this migration, and the residual load on CASTOR (for the tape back-end storage) became smaller. On the other hand, CMS could not benefit from this change as much as other experiments supported at CNAF, since in the CMS main workflows at Tier-1 sites the disk is configured as a buffer in front of the tape system. Some experience was nevertheless gained in the CMS community, both with some specific workflows at the Tier-1 level (such as the 'un-merged' area of MonteCarlo production) and in using StoRM plus a parallel file-system at the Tier-2 level [18].

A complete MSS solution based on StoRM/GPFS was seeked after that. At the end of 2007, CNAF launched a project to realize a complete grid-enabled HSM solution, i.e. based on i) StoRM; ii) GPFS; iii) the Tivoli Storage Manager (TSM) [20, 21] by IBM. In this implementation, the GPFS specific features (available since version 3.2) were basically combined with TSM and StoRM. In particular, StoRM was extended to include the SRM methods required to manage data on tape, and -since not all the needed functionalities were provided out of the box -an ad-hoc interface between GPFS and TSM was implemented.

In the second quarter of 2008, a first implementation of the so-called "D1T1" storage class (i.e. enabling data replication to tape and keeping one copy of data on disk and another on tape) was put in production for LHCb. This was also used in the WLCG Common Computing Readiness Challenge in 2008 (CCRC'08) [22, 23], in which CMS also participated [24, 25]. In the third quarter of 2009, the fully integrated StoRM/GPFS/TSM system supporting a full HSM solution -called "Grid-Enabled Mass Storage System (GEMSS)" in the following -was released. A preproduction testbed was built to accommodate a test aimed to demonstrate if the system satisfies the scaling needs of CMS. After the test described in the following sections, in the end of third quarter of 2009 CMS at CNAF moved to fully use the GEMSS system.

2   THE GEMSS COMPONENTS AND INTERACTION

A pictorial view of the functional blocks of the GEMSS system is shown in Fig 2, while the layout of the actual current CNAF implementation of the GEMSS storage set-up for CMS can be found in Fig. 3.

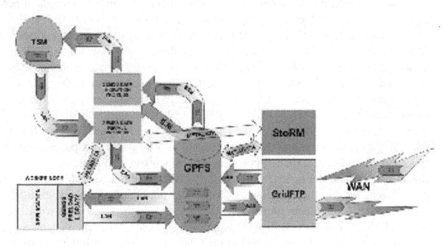

Fig. 2: Functional blocks of the GEMSS system.

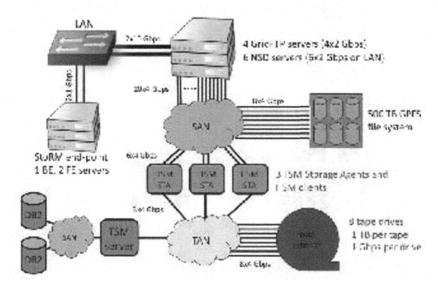

Fig. 3: Pre-production layout of the storage set-up for CMS at CNAF Tier-1

The interface to Grid is provided by the StoRM service (widely described elsewhere [14, 15]). In the CNAF implementation it has a layered architecture with two main components, a Front-End and a Back-End. The Front-End exposes the SRM service interface and manages user authentication. The Back-End is the StoRM core component, that executes all SRM requests, interacts with file-systems via a driver mechanism, publishes a Web Service to be used by external interfaces for implementing full HSM functionalities. A database component, called Request DB, is required to store SRM request data and StoRM internal metadata. The database does not hold any crucial information, and a backup plan is not necessary, since any accidental loss of the full database just leads to the failure of ongoing SRM requests only. The entry points for data are the gridftp servers (WAN access) and the NSDs (LAN access) directly connected to GPFS where the files are initially stored, while the archival is provided by TSM.

The main components of the TSM system (see also Fig. 4) are the Server, the Client Storage Agent and the HSM part. The Server is the core component of TSM: relying on a database to track the informations, provides the space management services to the clients. The Client Storage Agent enables LAN-free (i.e. over Fibre Channel, FC) data movement for client operations, greatly increasing the performances. The HSM component provides space management services: it automatically migrates files that are less frequently used to tapes, freeing space on disk.

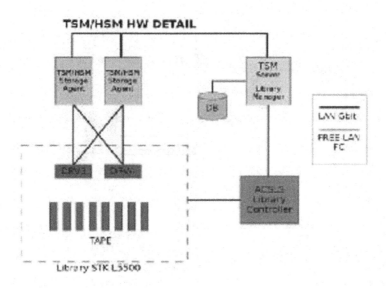

Fig. 4: Schematic layout of the TSM service.

In CNAF setup, GPFS and the HSM nodes are completely decoupled, hence enabling the nodes maintenance without any interruption in the file-system availability. Moreover, all components of the system have intrinsic redundancy (provided by the GPFS failover mechanisms) apart from the unique TSM server with the database, which, in the CNAF production environment, is replicated on disk and on tape to allow a fast recovery in case of problems. The interaction between GPFS and TSM is very tight: GPFS performs file-system metadata scans, according to a set of policies specified by the administrators, to identify the list of files to be migrated to tape; this list is passed to an external process running on the HSM nodes performing the migration to TSM (this part in particular has been implemented at CNAF). The recalls can be done passing to TSM a list of files, to be tape-ordered by TSM itself.

3   TESTS PERFORMED TO SUPPORT THE CMS EXPERIMENT

The CMS experiment contacts at CNAF have been supporting the usage of StoRM at the Tier-1 level by helping on its deployment and test on-site, and providing guidance to some CMS Tier-2 sites [18]. Recently, they found a synergy with the CNAF storage team to perform the first tests on TSM using local access (i.e. not through the StoRM layer) during the Summer 2009: both recalls from tape (with peak rates as high as almost 600 MB/s) and migration to tape (with peak rates of the order of 100 MB/s) were successfully tested (see Fig. 5). Local access to data on TSM from the batch farm nodes was recorded to be as speed as 400 MB/s. In the meantime, and in parallel to ongoing production activities, a global migration of all data from the old CASTOR system to the new TSM-based system was performed: about 1 PB of data in total were copied from Castor to TSM in roughly 1 month with no service interruption, and with CMS operations continuing unaffected on the Castor set-up throughout the copy process.

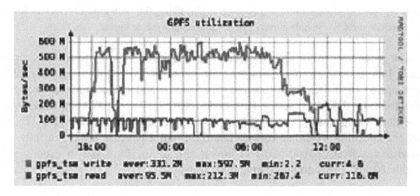

Fig. 5: TSM performance during tape writing and tape reading tests (see text).

At the beginning of the Fall 2009, CMS performed a validation of the new system through a complete round of tests of the most important CMS workflows, including a repetition of the STEP'09 tests [19]. During this test the complete production chain was checked with the inclusion of the StoRM layer. The total disk buffer used in these tests was roughly 450 TB, with 6 drives used for recalls and 2 drives for migrations. In the tests, partially concurrent activities were run: manual massive file recall from tape, recalls triggered by Wide Area Network (WAN) transfers, recalls triggered by jobs running on the batch farm, migration of new files produced locally on the farm or transferred to the site by WAN transfers. CMS performed a stress test of recall from tape: about 24 TB (corresponding to 8000 files) randomly spread over 100 tapes were recalled in 19 hours (see Fig. 6, plot 1). An average throughput of 400 MB/s was achieved, with a peak at 530 MB/s, achieving the 85% of nominal tape drive throughput (see Fig. 6, plot 2).

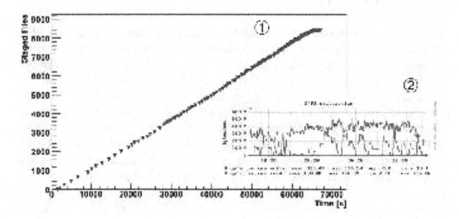

Fig. 6: (1) Number of staged files as a function of time during the CMS tests. (2) Net GPFS disk throughput on the GEMSS data movers as a function of time during the tests (see text).

The processing from the farm nodes was also tested. Data were accessed from nearly 1000 concurrent jobs, using the "file" protocol. These jobs triggered recalls from tape of 1930 files, with 100% job success rate and a throughput of up to 1.2 GB/s from the disk pools to the farm nodes (see Fig. 7). The WAN transfer tests were done using PhEDEx, the official CMS data management tool [26, 27, 28, 29], and profiting of the so-called "LoadTest" infrastructure [30]. The tests allowed to reach up to 160 MB/s in import and up to 300 MB/s in export, and roughly 80 MB/s background during other tests.

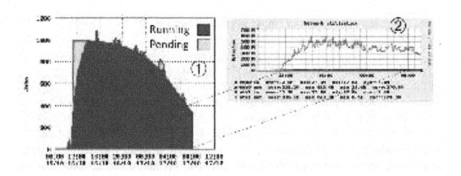

Fig. 7: (1) Running and pending jobs on the farm during the CMS tests. (2) Traffic on one of the two network cards of the GPFS server during the CMS tests (see text).

4   GEMSS IN PRODUCTION FOR CMS

The GEMSS system went in production for CMS in October 2009, without major changes with respect to the layout used for the tests. The main change was the upgrade of StoRM to include checksum verification and improved authorization. A good performance was achieved in transfer throughput, and a high use of the available bandwidth (up to 8 Gbps) was observed.

An example of usage in export transfers is shown in Fig. 8. Additionally, CMS performed some additional checks by verifying the output of the test jobs continuously submitted to the CMS sites to control their availability (JobRobot) in different periods and environmental conditions ("CASTOR storage on SL4 nodes" vs "TSM on SL4" vs "TSM on SL5"). In this way it was possible to observe that the efficiency of CMS workflows was not impacted by the change of storage system. As from the current experience, CMS can only give a very positive feedback on the new system, and a very good stability for production activities has been observed so far.

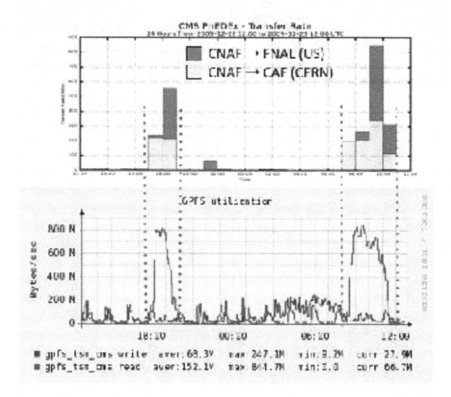

Fig. 8: CMS export transfers from CNAF with the GEMSS system in production on-site.

5   CONCLUSIONS

The CMS experiment has been using CASTOR at the INFN-CNAF Tier-1 Computing Centre for several years, being its main user. The rate of problems reported by the storage team and experienced by the experiment (not only CMS) contacts on-site has been high. This nevertheless did not stop CMS to use this storage solution in production for years. After a development phase by INFN, CMS accepted during the second half of 2009 to take part in a series of functional and stress tests of a new storage set-up, called GEMSS, that exploits and glues features by StoRM, GPFS and TSM. The CNAF storage team required the experiments contacts on-site to perform some tests to familiarize with the system and to eventually validate it as a complete substitute for CASTOR. CMS actively joined such tests. It must be remarked that on the D1T1 storage class the system had been already used in production from the LHCb experiment; additionally, a large expertise on the disk-only solution (D1T0 storage class) had been developed in the operations at CNAF with the ATLAS experiment; finally, the test described in this paper has been the first large scale (about 500 TB) implementation of the D0T1 storage class. Since the validation was successfully completed, CMS Computing at CNAF switched all operations to the new system in October 2009, with all the old data on CASTOR copied to TSM. The first 6 months of production so far -including the handling of LHC collisions data -have been very promising, both in terms of high performance and remarkable stability.

REFERENCES

[1]   INFN-CNAF Computing Centre web portal: http://www.cnaf.infn.it
[2]   WLCG web portal: http://lcg.web.cern.ch/LCG/public/
[3]   M. Aderholz et al., "Models of Networked Analysis at Regional Centres for LHC Experiments (MONARC), Phase 2 Report", CERN/LCB 2000-001 (2000)
[4]   S. Bethke et al., "Report of the Steering Group of the LHC Computing Review", CERN/LHCC 2001-004 (2001)
[5]   CMS Collaboration, "The CMS experiment at the CERN LHC", JINST 3 S08004 (2008) doi: 10.1088/1748-0221/3/08/S08004
[6]   CASTOR project website: http://castor.web.cern.ch/castor
[7]   G.LoReetal,"Storage resources management and access at CNAF Tier-1, Proceedings of XI International Workshop on Advanced Computing and Analysis Techniques in Physics Research (ACAT'05), DESY, Zeuthen, 2005 -Nucl. Instrum. Meth. NIM-A 559 62-66 (2006)
[8]   GPFS web page: http://www.ibm.com/systems/software/gpfs/
[9]   Lustre web page: http://www.lustre.org
[10] dCache web site: http://www.dcache.org
[11] The dCache Book: http://www.dcache.org/manuals/Book
[12] xrootd web portal: http://xrootd.slac.stanford.edu
[13] M. Bencivenni et al., "A comparison of Data-Access Platforms for the Computing of Large Hadron Collider Experiments", IEEE Transactions on Nuclear Science, Volume , Issue 3, Part 3, pp. 1621–1630 (June 2008) -ISSN: 0018-9499
[14] StoRM project website: http://storm.forge.cnaf.infn.it
[15] E. Corso, S. Cozzini, A. Forti, A. Ghiselli, L. Magnoni, A.Messina, A. Nobile, A. Terpin, V. Vagnoni, R. Zappi, "StoRM: A SRM Solution on Disk Based Storage System", Proceedings of the "Cracow Grid Workshop in 2006" (CGW2006), Cracow, Poland, October 15-18, 2006
[16] Storage Resource Management (SRM) project website: http://sdm.lbl.gov/srm-wg
[17] A. Carbone et al., "Performance studies of the StoRM Storage Resource Manager", Proceedings of "Third IEEE International Conference on e-Science and Grid Computing", December 10-13, 2007, pp. 423–430 -ISBN: 978-0-7695-3064-2
[18] A. Sartirana, D. Bonacorsi, I. Cabrillo Bartolom`alez Caballero, F. Matorras, "The e, I. Gonz`CMS experiment workflows on StoRM based storage at Tier-1 and Tier-2 centers", Computing in High Energy and Nuclear Physics (CHEP'09), Prague, March 30-27, 2009
[19] D. Bonacorsi, O. Gutsche, "CMS Computing experience from the WLCG STEP'09 challenge to the first data taking of the LHC era", International Symposium on Grid Computing 2010 (ISGC'10), Taipei, Taiwan, March 5-12, 2010
[20] The TSM web page: http://www.ibm.com/software/tivoli/products/storage-mgr
[21] Tivoli Storage Manager V6.1 Technical Guide, ISBN 0738433691, IBM Form Number SG247718-00, available online at
       http://www.redbooks.ibm.com/abstracts/SG247718.html?Open
[22] WLCG CCRC'08 twiki portal: https://twiki.cern.ch/twiki/bin/view/LCG/ WLCGCommonComputingReadinessChallenges
[23] J.D. Shiers et al., "The (WLCG) Common Computing Readiness Challenge(s) -CCRC'08", contribution N29-2, Grid Computing session -Nuclear Science Symposium, IEEE (Dresden), October 2008
[24] CMS CCRC'08 twiki portal: https://twiki.cern.ch/twiki/bin/view/CMS/CMSCCRC08
[25] L. Bauerdick and D. Bonacorsi, "CMS results in the Combined Computing Readiness Challenge (CCRC08)", 11th Topical Seminar on Innovative Particle and Radiation Detectors (IPRD'08), Siena, Italy, Jun 7-10, 2010
[26] D. Bonacorsi, T. Barrass, J. Hernandez, J. Rehn, L. Tuura, J. Wu, I. Semeniouk, "PhEDEx high-throughput data transfer management system", CHEP06, Computing in High Energy and Nuclear Physics, T.I.F.R. Bombay, India, February 2006

[27] T. Barrass et al, "Software agents in data and workflow management", Proc. CHEP04, Interlaken, 2004. See also http://www.pa.org

[28] R. Egeland et al., "Data transfer infrastructure for CMS data taking", XIII International Workshop on Advanced Computing and Analysis Techniques in Physics Research (ACAT'08), Erice, Italy, Nov 3-7, 2008 -Proceedings of Science, PoS (ACAT08) 033 (2008)

[29] L. Tuura et al., "Scaling CMS data transfer system for LHC start-up", presented at Computing in High Energy and Nuclear Physics (CHEP'07), Victoria, BC, Canada, September 2007 J. Phys.: Conf. Ser. 119 072030 (2008) doi: 10.1088/1742-6596/119/7/072030

[30] D. Bonacorsi et al., "The CMS LoadTest 2007: An Infrastructure to Exercise CMS Transfer Routes among WLCG Tiers", Computing in High Energy and Nuclear Physics (CHEP'07), Victoria B.C., Canada, September 2-9, 2007

Part X
Applications on Humanities and Social Sciences

GENESIS Social Simulation

Andy Turner

University of Leeds, UK

Abstract   GENESIS is a research project funded by the UK Economic and Social Research Council through the National Centre for e-Social Science research node program. Details of GENESIS can be found on-line via the following URL: http://www.geog.leeds.ac.uk/people/a.turner/projects/GENESIS/ One strand of GENESIS work aims to develop simulation models that represent individual humans and their organisations and how they change their location and influence over time. This chapter describes the development of two types of model that operate at different temporal resolutions over different time scales: Traffic Models work with time steps of a second; and Demographic Models work with time steps of a day. Both are computationally demanding and the chapter describes not just the development of the models, but also the work done to scale up from village scale with a thousand individuals, to produce simulation results at city scale with a million individuals.

1   INTRODUCTION

GENESIS is a research project funded by the UK Economic and Social Research Council through the National Centre for e-Social Science research node program[1]. Details of GENESIS can be found on-line via the following URL: http://www.geog.leeds.ac.uk/people/a.turner/projects/GENESIS/

One strand of GENESIS work aims to develop simulation models that represent individual humans and their organisations and how they change their location and influence over time. For this strand, the author is developing two types of model that operate at different temporal resolutions over different time scales. These models are implemented in the Java programming language and share a common code base (packages, classes and methods) which is released as open source on-line via the following URL: http://www.geog.leeds.ac.uk/people/a.turner/src/andyt/java/projects/GENESIS/

The types of models are: traffic models that work with time steps of a second and are aimed to be run for simulated time scales of days; and demographic models that work with time steps of a day and are aimed to be run for simulated time scales of years. Both are computationally demanding and much effort has gone into organising data and processing so as to scale up from village scale models with a thousand inhabitants residing in a region with a radius of a few kilometres, to

S.C. Lin and E. Yen (eds.), *Data Driven e-Science: Use Cases and Successful Applications of Distributed Computing Infrastructures (ISGC 2010)*, DOI 10.1007/978-1-4419-8014-4_30, © Springer Science+Business Media, LLC 2011

city scale models with a million inhabitants residing in a much larger region. A long term aim is to scale up further and run larger regional, national and even global scale simulations. Some background to this modelling work is provided in Section 1.2. More detailed descriptions of the traffic and demographic models and their development is provided in Section 1.3 and Section 1.4 respectively. Section 1.5 focusses on computationally scaling up. Section 1.6 considers further work. Section 1.7 provides a short summary and concluding remarks.

2   BACKGROUND

The dynamic simulation models described in Section 1.3 and Section 1.4 were developed from first principles, conceptually aiming to be as basic as possible in the first instance then develop incrementally by: factoring in constraints; incorporating less basic concepts; computational enhancements (i.e. improving scalability); enabling simulation control (stop and restart); and interfacing with some form of archive.

The first phase of development involved a sort of prototyping that evolved basic visual outputs from the two types of models. The second phase has focussed on scaling up so that simulations of the models would run for larger regions at higher spatial resolution and for larger populations of individually represented people. For the first phase, a basic demographic model was reasonably straightforward to develop, whereas a basic traffic model was more of a challenge and was developed in several steps.

As part of the EUAsiaGrid project [2] (funded via the European Commission), Alex Voss [3] implement a basic demographic model in Repast [4] based on a basic GENESIS demographic model. This was presented at specially arranged meetings at the Academia Sinica Centre for Survey Research during the International Symposium for Grid Computing 2009 [5] aiming to encourage EU-AsiaGrid collaboration and raise awareness of the GENESIS social simulation efforts. This pioneering work was progressed by Alex who with David Fergusson [6] developed materials for and organised a Social Simulation Tutorial which we ran together at the International Conference on e-Social Science 2009 [7]. An updated Social Simulation Tutorial developed by Alex, Rob Procter [8] and myself was run at the International Symposium for Grid Computing 2010 [9].

To begin to address the computational challenge of developing large scale social simulation models, the GENESIS models were evolved to take greater advantage of the usually relatively large persistent disk based memory of contemporary computer hardware to store data about a simulation. Methods were developed to control the swapping of simulation data from this large disk memory to and from the smaller, more volatile yet faster memory. The author had experience of implementing such memory management in the development of a raster data handling library called Grids [10] about which he made a presentation at FOSS4G2006 [11]. The development of Grids has been a singular effort funded indirectly under various research grants from the European Commission and UK research councils. It is a core library used in the traffic models which needed adapting to work in this context. The general solution for memory handling in Grids could be readily applied memory handling for the agent data for the GENESIS models. (This agent data currently representing individual humans in the models.) The generic code used in Grids and the GENESIS software was abstracted to another library called Generic [12].

Along side the GENESIS project, the author is working on the NeISS project [13] (funded via the UK Joint Information Systems Committee) to develop a national e-Infrastructure to support social simulation. NeISS aims to support GENESIS models and the hope is that a community of users will be established for these models. The e-Infrastructure should make the models more easy to use by allowing for Grid and Cloud based computational resources to be tapped and the results of running the models easier to archive and reproduce. Key to the NeISS work is making it easy for others to modify and run the simulation models and produce outputs they are interested in.

3   DEVELOPING A TRAFFIC MODEL

To model people movements on an individual level requires a way to store the location of each individual. A first model positioned people agents in a bounded region of a Euclidean 2D plane and moved these around randomly by repositioning them at each time tick. Movement was then constrained so these agents could only move a set distance at each time tick. A basic visualisation was developed which depicted agent movements as lines on an image. Next the concept of destinations was developed, so that rather than necessarily having a different destination at each time tick, an agent might be assigned a destination beyond its maximum range for movement in a time tick which it would gradually move to over successive ticks.

Models were generated with agent origins and destinations initialised in various ways and the output images were studied. None of the resulting images of these basic origin-destination models looked as 'road like' as random movement models. The agent routes were too direct and unique to appear collectively like a road network and so were somewhat unrealistic. Some form of agent-environment and/or agent-agent interaction can be used to encourage agents to share routes. Models were conceived with a small benefit to each agent of using an existing route or sharing journeys with other agents. In a way this implementing these models would be like modelling the emergence of a road network. Rather than do this, focus switched to route agents via an existing road network.

So, adding to the typology of models let us distinguish those that are entirely synthetically made up, and those which are seeded from available data. Also for those models seeded with available data there can be a distinction of those seeded from open use and publicly available data, and those seeded (at least in part) from data which is not.

Data about commuting journeys in the UK is captured by its Human Population Census that has been taking place every ten years. From the 2001 Census, Special Transport Statistics (STS) datasets are available for registered users via the Centre for Interaction Data Estimation and Research (CIDER) [14]. These provide a snapshot about where people lived and worked in the UK in 2001 and are available at a range of levels of spatial detail down to Output Areas which typically contain around 300 people. The STS data contain some details of commuting journey flows (breakdowns by mode of transport and job type variables), but there is no direct linkage to data about the usual times of work of the people represented in the flows. Although the STS data is incomplete and lacking many of the theoretically desirable details, it offers an opportunity to seed some UK traffic models which might be assumed to make them more realistic.

Commuting models for individual UK Local Authority Districts (LAD) were developed based on the STS data. These represented people moving from home to work locations and back again in a daily cycle. Initially, to keep the model simple, all people agents were given the same times (shift) to be at the work location and only the commuting journeys that both started and ended in any of the LAD were considered. As the distance to the work locations was variable, each agents journey would not necessarily start or end at the same time.

Let us consider a commute to work and the need to have an estimate of the time needed for the journey and how this might be calculated. An attempt can be made to compute this using data (such as the distance to be travelled) and it can be learned by timing the undertaken journey. In a basic model without constraints on the amount of traffic located in any place or the amount of traffic moving from one place to another, learning can be done in a single journey and agents can arrive at work on time at the start of their shift and arrive back at home at a predictable time. The unconstrained calculation (although perhaps idealistic and certainly unrealistic) is still of use as it indicates the minimum travel time if no agent got in another agents way. Anyway, despite being based on real-world data the visualisations of these models seemed as unrealistic as any made previously. This was mainly due to the aforementioned observation that agents were rarely sharing routes, but also because no capacity like constraints were being imposed to constrain movement. Additionally there was no other (non-commuter) traffic active which is likely to effect commuter traffic...

To constrain agent movements, two things were considered:

1. Restricting agent movements to a high resolution regular network
2. Routing agents along known transport infrastructure

Code was developed to restricting movements to a high resolution regular network. There are still plans to develop models for simulating the evolution of transport infrastructure through use with this, but little progress has been made...

Effort was focussed on constraining movement to existing transport infrastructure. For this two data options were considered:

1. OpenStreetMap [15] data which is publicly available for the entire world
2. UK Ordnance Survey [16] data available under an academic license via Edina [17]

The first option was made more attractive by the existence of the Traveling-Salesman routing API [18] [19]. TravelingSalesman provided a means to route Agents via the OpenStreetMap road network. Code was developed to route an agent using this, but a problem was encountered when trying to route many agents. The issue was that agents needed reference to the route they had planned for a journey and this was a reasonably large amount of data compared with simply knowing a destination location. Also the road network had to be loaded into the fast access memory for the routes to be obtained meaning there was less available memory for initialising agents. To scale up to something city size, a computational resource with a few hundred Gigabyte of fast access memory or some better way to handle the data was needed.

4   DEVELOPING A DEMOGRAPHIC MODEL

For GENESIS, Belinda Wu [20] and Mark Birkin [21] are developing dynamic demographic models that work with time steps of a year [22] whilst the author is developing similar models with time steps of a day. Many things happen day to day, most importantly in terms of a demographic model, people conceive, give birth and die on specific days. Variations in rates of these within a year could be important. Indeed, the timings of conceptions, births and deaths are more fine grained than days and this might also be important, but in terms of demographic modelling, it can be argued that a resolution of a day is perhaps best. Arguably it will depend on what the model is to be used for and at this stage GENESIS model development is not use case driven, so a day time step keeps options more open than any time step longer than a day. Also, people move house, get married and organise other activities on specific days; and, in many contemporary societies there are holidays when people generally may have very different activity patterns compared with other days. It is known that many activities are seasonal and relate to holidays and this is sure to have demographic consequences.

Explicit linkages between traffic and demographic models is also easier with a demographic model time step of a day. An example link between the models could be the journeys that many people make to a hospital for a birth, the timing of the birth can be given by the demographic model simulation, and the journey for the individuals can be simulated in the traffic model. A more complex feedback example, from the traffic model simulation to the demographic simulation model is to do with conception and the general need for partners to be together for this to happen.

One further reason for a daily time step is computational. There are a similar number of time steps running a model that works with time steps of a day and runs for years as there are for one that works with time steps of a second and runs for days. Even with a time step of a day, demographic models are probably less computationally demanding than traffic models with the same number of agents (depending on the level and complexity of agent movement).

Development of a basic demographic model focusses on the processes of death and birth. A more sophisticated model might include the notion of a home and migration. In the authors GENESIS code there are Male and Female classes extended from the People class representing males and females respectively. For simulating death at each time step, age and gender specific mortality probabilities are used. The next number in a pseudo-random sequence gets compared with the probability for each individual to determine if they become dead. If they become dead, they are no longer active in a basic model simulation and it is sensible to store the agents data on disk and delete it from the volatile fast access memory so this storage can be used to store other data.

For Female agents additional processing is done each time step. Firstly pregnancy (conception) is determined. For each Female that is not yet pregnant (and is of fertile age), their age specific fertility probability is obtained and compared with the next number in a pseudo-random sequence. Those that become pregnant are set a due date in 266 days time. Secondly, all pregnant Female agents are iterated over to determine if any miscarry. For a basic model the miscarriage probability is constant. Thirdly, birth is simulated. In a basic model, the due date is determined at conception and the birth occurs on this date unless the female dies or there is a miscarriage.

In reality conception is much more complex and fertility depends on other characteristics of the female (such as, day in a menstruation cycle, number of existing children, whether using birth control, whether they are in good health) and the fertility and availability of a male. Miscarriage is also variable over the stages of pregnancy and is also likely to be effected by environmental circumstance. The time of birth is also variable and some babies are born prematurely and some are born over term. The calculation of a due date is commonly used to induce birth in some societies. All these things may be taken into account in more complex models.

The basic model allows for the generation of population visualisations, such as Age Gender Plots showing counts of Male and Female Agents of different ages or with different birth dates within each year. Such plots are interesting graphical outputs which demographers commonly study. Automated procedures for generating these types of output using the JFreeChart library [23] were developed. These graphical outputs can be studied to see how a simulation settles into a steady state and seeded and compared with population data.

Much can be done to make basic models more realistic, and more fitting in terms of a real population being simulated. For instance, a contemporary demographic model for the population in mainland China where a one child policy is in place [24] should use a very different Female fertility, one that is more conditional such that if a Female already has one living child, they become much less likely to have another. Furthermore, the probability may depend upon the gender of the existing child. All probabilities used in the demographic models can be modified and different random number sequences can be used in the simulation resulting in different Age Gender Plots. The variation, tends and extremes in multiple simulation runs can then help to reveal some of the uncertainties in population forecasts based on current trends.

Probabilities for a basic model were adjusted so that for a given seed population and pseudo-random sequence, a gradually increasing population was obtained. This was then allowed to run for thousands of years. Providing a way to seed the population from any age and gender distribution allowed city and indeed national population scale simulations on a modest desktop computer.

Examining the distribution of births within a year revealed a major cohort effect as the basic models did not initialise pregnancies prior to the first tick of the simulation. The consequence is that a large number of pregnancies are simulated in the first few days and there is a high level of births 266 days or so after the model starts. It can take many iterations, indeed (depending on age based fertility rates) generations before the rate of births per day begins to average out. To begin a simulation with a more realistic pregnancy rate, one solution is to initialise pregnancies by running the simulation forward but only simulating pregnancy and miscarriage (not birth and death) for a year and then seed the pregnancy and due date back. This can be repeated and should gradually smooth out pregnancy and birth rate and result in start situation for the simulation in which Females may be simulated to give birth in the first iteration.

5   SCALING UP

Scaling up to run larger simulations with more agents and input data is partly an issue to do with accessing bigger and better computational resources with a greater amount of memory and processing power. It can also be achieved by using computational resources more effectively and improving efficiencies in the computation steps. It is probably not something that is best done by attempting translation of some part or all of the implementation into what may be perceived as a more efficient language.

For the initial basic GENESIS models it was evident that more use could be made of the slower access persistent disk memory of the computational resources being used, especially when the faster access volatile memory of a processing unit was becoming fully used and the programs failed with out of memory type error. Some form of this data handling is probably needed to run large scale traffic simulations even on the contemporary computers with the largest amounts of fast access memory. Access to such computer resources is also not readily available.

The key to good data handling and memory management for simulation modelling is knowing; what data is needed and in what order, and the approximate amounts of allocatable memory that can be used. If allocatable memory is about to run out, it is best that the model either takes steps to cope before there is a problem, or it fails or copes gracefully when one is encountered (so that if more resources become available, the simulation can be restarted from the point of failure rather than having to be re-run from a much earlier stage).

To phrase this another way: Suppose the fast access memory is running low during a simulation and a reasonably large amount of data is to be created or loaded from persistent memory (disk). Further assume that if nothing else is done, when trying to create or load the data an out of memory type error will be encountered. Furthermore, assume there is plenty of available disk. Now, this is the problem of memory management that I have addressed in GENESIS model development. There are two ways to proceed: One way is to calculate in advance and make more memory available in advance to prevent the error, the other is to try to create or load the data and catch the error when it happens and then swap data around and try again repeatedly. These two approaches are complimentary. There is an overhead in calculating in advance if memory is low and there is an overhead in the try and catch error handling. It is possible to have a concurrent thread keeping track of memory allocation so that a method does not have to wait long to know there is enough memory to continue, but still there is some overhead to this.

In the basic demographic models outlined in Section 1.4, the only data are agent data; whereas in the traffic models outlined in Section 1.3, there are agent, raster, vector and other data. So developing memory handling code for the demographic models was an easier task as well as being a step towards developing memory handling for the traffic models.

Swapping individual agents to disk and back again was found to be expensive computationally due to the overhead of opening and closing files. So, agents were organised into collections and it is these collections became the entities swapped to and from disk. This is similar to how Grids data is organised where data is swapped to and from disk in chunks. Anyway, an agent file store as well as an agent collection file store was wanted. The agent store was to store all data for agents by the end of the simulation and the agent collection store was like a cache extending the memory for a running simulation.

The file structure for agent and agent collection files is such that given a numerical identifier, and the location of the top level directory, the file location for storing the serialised Object and other data can be calculated. In other words the location of the files are implicit given some configuration parameters and an simple numeric identifier (ID). With most operating systems there is a maximum number of files it is sensible to store in a directory. Also, there is a maximum length of file name (including the directory path) it can cope with. Setting the maximum number of files to be stored per directory to be 100 is a reasonable compromise and it makes it relatively easy for a human to find a particular file. A million million files can be stored in directory structure with a depth of six directories branching by 100 each time. Consider this as follows:

```
1
100= 100 *1
10000 = 100 * 100
1000000 = 100 * 10000
100000000 = 100 * 1000000
10000000000 = 100 * 100000000
0= 100 * 10000000000
```

So, files for an agent with ID equal to zero would be stored in the directory that can be addressed as follows:

```
Agents/
000000000000-199999999999/
0000000000-0199999999/
00000000-01999999/
000000-019999/
0000-0099/
0/
```

Similarly, files for an agent collection with ID 123456789 would be stored in the directory that can be addressed as follows:

```
AgentCollections/
000000000000-199999999999/
0100000000-0199999999/
23000000-23999999/
450000-459999/
6700-6799/
89/
```

In attempting to create or retrieve data from disk, care is needed so memory handling operations do not get stuck in loops swapping to file the data that is required. Indeed, memory handling needs various sophistications to work well. For each of the library the author has developed that attempt memory handling, if that instance cannot cope with the memory handling using methods internal to the library, it throws the error or an exception to a higher level manager. Rather than detail any memory handling code here, readers that are interested are referred to the latest releases of the authors code which is openly available on-line [25]. Much optimisation has been implemented in this memory handling, but this is perhaps only a start to the work needed to generate spectacular city or larger scale simulation results. The next section outlines what is planned in terms of computational enhancement to the GENESIS modelling effort.

6   FURTHER WORK

GENESIS models can be developed in lots of ways, some have been suggested in the preceding sections. Simulations can be run for synthetic data under different scenarios for different parts of the world seeded with data about the local population and environment. The long term goal which is to integrate the traffic and demographic models requires a number of refinements in each model first.

The next steps for enhancing traffic models is to develop code to constrain traffic to specific densities on the networks and allow for queueing of traffic. With this implemented, a set of simulation results should be produced and examined. Some outputs that help identify where network congestion occurs in the models might be wanted and some comparison of the simulated results with what is known about traffic in reality might be of general interest. Next, for commute journeys code to allow agents to try alternative routes and also allow for dynamic re-routing around queues is wanted. For the UK models, more journeys including journeys to school and to places of entertainment might be modelled. For some of this work in the UK I hope to make use of the linked data being made available via the data.gov.uk initiative [26].

The next step for enhancing demographic models is to develop code to explicitly model male parentage and develop a process for partnering parents. People agents will hold references to collections of other agents that they have been close to and these will more likely be those that are partnered. A crucial next step is to evolve spatially explicit demographic models and begin to model the processes of migration. Many other things can then be considered, such as explicitly modelling change in health status, but there is much to do before this!

In terms of computation, one of the key challenges is to parallelise the models to exploit distributed resources. This is non-trivial and there are various options that need to be explored for partitioning the models. Similarly, with the multi-core nature of many compute resources, threading the processing should be considered not least in terms of memory management. Various technology (e.g. Virtual File System, database software and persistence frameworks) can be investigated in this respect.

Perhaps key to all future work is to build up a community of users to test code and get involved in developing and using models.

7   SUMMARY AND CONCLUDING REMARKS

Development of two different types of simulation models has been outlined: traffic models that operate on the scale of days with a second time step, and a demographic models that operate over the time scale of a number of years with a day time step. There is a long term goal to somehow integrate these into general geographical social simulation models and use these to study various socio-economic and environmental interactions. Basic traffic and demographic models have been developed separately and work has bee done to produce simulation outputs at a city scale of up to a million individual agents. The models share the same code base and less basic models are being worked on to produce more realistic outputs.

There are significant computational challenges in social simulation work. Running a model for the contemporary UK involves modelling and recording changes in the locations and other aspects of the state of agents representing approximately 60 million real people. The entire history of an agent in terms of the interactions it has with other agents and the environment could be massive and there is a challenge to resources the storage of these data if national level simulation models are wanted.

A generic data storage solution has been outlined and its use in memory handling for scaling simulation models described. The generic data storage solution is for storing data in files using a simple branching directory structure which allows for data to be stored in file locations that are implicit from a number used as the identifier for the data.

8   ACKNOWLEDGEMENTS

GENESIS is funded by the ESRC (RES-149-25-1078). The e-Research community; developers Paul Townend provided a method to get the total free memory available to the Java Virtual Machine [27] Alex Voss for taking an interest in social simulation and collaborating with me as a geographer. [3] Thanks to the reviewers of this work. An initial review in the context of the target publication

REFERENCES

[1]   Andy Turner's GENESIS Project Web Page
      http://www.geog.leeds.ac.uk/people/a.turner/projects/GENESIS. Cited 8 June 2010
[2]   The EUAsiaGrid Website http://www.euasiagrid.org/. Cited 8 June 2010
[3]   Alex Voss' University of St Andrews Web Page http://www.cs.st-andrews.ac.uk/~ avoss/.
      Cited 8 June 2010
[4]   Repast Sourceforge Web Page http://repast.sourceforge.net/. Cited 8 June 2010
[5]   Andy Turner's NCeSS Sakai Portal: My Workspace Worksite: Wiki: ISGC 2009 Page
      http://portal.ncess.ac.uk/access/wiki/site/%7Ea.g.d.turner%40leeds.ac.uk/isgc%202009.htm
      l. Cited 8 June 2010

[6]   David Fergusson's NeSC Web Page http://www.nesc.ac.uk/nesc/staff/dfergusson.html. Cited 8 June 2010

[7]   NCeSS Sakai Portal: SocSim Tutorial Worksite: Wiki: Social Simulation Tutorial at 5th International e-Social Science Conference 2009 Page
      http://portal.ncess.ac.uk/access/wiki/site/socsim/social%20simulation%20tutorial%20at%2 05th%20international%20esocial%20science%20conference%202009.html.
      Cited 8 June 2010

[8]   Rob Procter's MeRC Web Page http://www.merc.ac.uk/?q=Rob. Cited 8 June 2010

[9]   Alex Voss' ISGC 2010 Social Simulation Tutorial Wiki Page
      https://e-research.cs.st-andrews.ac.uk/site/bin/view/SocialSimulation/ISGC2010.
      Cited 8 June 2010

[10] Andy Turner's Grids Java Library Web Page
      http://www.geog.leeds.ac.uk/people/a.turner/src/andyt/java/grids/. Cited 8 June 2010

[11] FOSS4G2006 Conference Website http://www.foss4g2006.org. Cited 8 June 2010

[12] Andy Turner's Generic Java Library Web Page
      http://www.geog.leeds.ac.uk/people/a.turner/src/andyt/java/generic/. Cited 8 June 2010

[13] Andy Turner's NeISS Project Web Page
      http://www.geog.leeds.ac.uk/people/a.turner/projects/e-ISS. Cited 8 June 2010

[14] CIDER Website http://cider.census.ac.uk/. Cited 8 June 2010 Andy Turner

[15] OpenStreetMap Website http://www.openstreetmap.org/. Cited 8 June 2010

[16] Ordnance Survey Website http://www.ordnancesurvey.co.uk/. Cited 8 June 2010

[17] Edina Website http://www.edina.ac.uk. Cited 8 June 2010

[18] Sourceforge Traveling Salesman Wiki Main Page
      http://sourceforge.net/apps/mediawiki/travelingsales/. Cited 8 June 2010

[19] Sourceforge Traveling Salesman Project Web Page
      http://sourceforge.net/projects/travelingsales/. Cited 8 June 2010

[20] Belinda Wu's University of Leeds Web Page http://www.geog.leeds.ac.uk/people/b.wu.
      Cited 8 June 2010

[21] Mark Birkin's University of Leeds Web Page
      http://www.geog.leeds.ac.uk/people/m.birkin. Cited 8 June 2010

[22] Wu, B.M., Birkin, M.H. and Rees, P.H.: A spatial microsimulation model with student agents, Journal of Computers, Environment and Urban Systems (32) pp. 440-453 (2008) doi: 10.1016/j.compenvurbsys. 2008.09.013

[23] JFreeChart Web Page http://www.jfree.org/jfreechart/. Cited 8 June 2010

[24] Wikipedia One-child policy Page http://en.wikipedia.org/wiki/One-child policy.
      Cited 8 June 2010

[25] Andy Turner's Open Source Java Web Page
      http://www.geog.leeds.ac.uk/people/a.turner/src/andyt/java. Cited 8 June 2010

[26] data.gov.uk Website https://www.data.gov.uk/. Cited 8 June 2010

[27] Paul Townend's University of Leeds Web Page
      https://www.comp.leeds.ac.uk/people/staff/scspmt.html. Cited 8 June 2010

Part XI
Applications on Earth Sciences and Mitigation

A Grid Application on Climate Change in EUAsiaGrid

A.S. Cofiño[1], S. Boonya-aroonnet[2], Royol Chitradon[2], Simon C. Lin[3], Marco Paganoni[4], M. Petitdidier[5] and Eric Yen[3]

1. Dep. of Applied Mathematics and Computer Sciences, University of Cantabria, Spain
2. Hydro and Agro Informatics Institute; Ministry of Science and Technology, Thailand
3. Institute of Physics, Academia Sinica, Taiwan
4. University of Milan-Bicocca and INFN, Italy
5. Université Versailles St-Quentin; CNRS/INSU, LATMOS-IPSL, Guyancourt – France

1   INTRODUCTION

The most general definition of climate change is a change in the statistical proper-ties of the climate system when considered over periods of decades or longer, re-gardless of cause. However this change could be very different from one region to another. Glaciers are considered among the most sensitive indicators of climate change, advancing when climate cools and retreating when climate warms. Today, it is the case in Greenland and then a global increase of the sea level may occur that worries island population. More frequent violent meteorological events are many times related to this climate change. In order to understand the causes of this climate change and long trend issues, scientists all over the world have been work-ing on the evaluation of the risk of climate change caused by human activities; natural causes always playing a role in changing Earth's climate, but now being overwhelmed by human-induced changes. Global simulations are carried out on super computer and results have been gathered by the Intergovernmental Panel on Climate change (IPCC). The panel was established in 1988 by the World Meteoro-logical Organization (WMO) and the United Nations Environment Programme (UNEP), two organizations of the United Nations. The IPCC shared the 2007 No-bel Peace Prize with former Vice President of the United States, Al Gore. Based on the results provided by the scientists, the IPCC published its first assessment report in 1990, a supplementary report in 1992, a second assessment report (SAR) in 1995, and a third assessment report (TAR) in 2001. A fourth assessment report (AR4) was released in 2007 and a fifth report (AR5) is under preparation. Each country or region is more interested in its probable regional climate change. Then to fulfil this requirement CORDEX, a Coordinated Regional Downscaling Ex-periment, has been defined and its goal is to provide a set of Regional Climate Scenarios covering 1950-2100, for the majority of populated land-regions of the globe. The downscaled scenarios will derive boundary conditions from new Glob-al model scenarios and decadal prediction runs. Many countries interested in such studies cannot carry them out due to a lack of compute power. However the use of

S.C. Lin and E. Yen (eds.), *Data Driven e-Science: Use Cases and Successful Applications of Distributed Computing Infrastructures (ISGC 2010)*, DOI 10.1007/978-1-4419-8014-4_31,
© Springer Science+Business Media, LLC 2011

compute resources available on a Grid infrastructure is a solution for the regional scenarios.

The term "Grid computing" originated in the 1990s as a metaphor for making computer power as easy to access as an electric power grid [1]. Grid computing is in general considered as a solution for scaling up computing power and storage capacity by sharing resources among institutions. To be efficient Grid technology needs an internet network enough reliable and fast. Now there are grid infrastructures deployed over continents and/or regions. This infrastructure has permitted to some sites relatively isolated in their country to be linked to larger infrastructure. The Grid allows to run ensemble of jobs that improve the results by submitting this collection of jobs simultaneously in different sites . The focus of this paper is on a collaboration workplan between the virtual European ES Grid community and EUAsiaGrid partners. In particular the University of Cantabria, involved in the Latin America Grid projects, EELA and EELA2, has ported the CAM and WRF models on the EELA and EGEE Grid infrastructures for collaboration with EELA partners and for its own research within CORDEX. This achievement is proposed to be installed and used by EUAsiaGrid partners, in particular in Taiwan and Thailand.

The second part is focused on the interest of the partners of Taiwan and Thailand to carry out regional climate research. Then an overview of Grid infrastructure and characteristics are given with the involvement of the ES community in Europe and in Asia through the EUAsiaGrid. In the fourth part the status of some climate models already ported on Grid by the University of Cantabria is described with the advantages and limitations of this method. The fifth part is focused on the collaboration plans.

2   INTEREST OF CLIMATE CHANGE STUDIES BY EUASIAGRID PARTNERS

Introduction

In the Asian countries, observational records and climate projections provide abundant evidence of climate change. The extreme events, observed those last years and the possibility that they occur more frequently, and also long-term variations are stressing the population and their governments. For example, one very critical point concerns the freshwater resources that are vulnerable and have the potential to be strongly impacted by the climate change, with wide-ranging consequences for human societies and ecosystems. Climate change also aggravates the impact of other stresses on freshwater systems such as population growth, changing economic activity, changes in land use and urbanization. Globally, demand for water will grow in the coming decades, primarily due to population growth and increasing affluence; on a regional level, large changes in demand for irrigation water as a result of climate change are expected. Climate change may affect the function and operation of existing water infrastructure (reservoirs, flood defences, urban drainage and irrigation systems) as well as water management practices. Therefore, the provision of a water supply and sanitation, securing food for growing populations and maintaining ecosystems are all enormous challenges.

Thailand Case

Flood and drought are the main risks in water resource management in Thailand and they are associated with weather extremes. Traditionally statistics can be adequately used for quantifying and managing risks from these extremes. However, the climate change not only reduces efficiency of our existing systems or infrastructures to cope with weather extremes, but also makes the statistical approach becoming outdated to manage water resource. There is a tendency that climate change would cause more frequent and severe floods or droughts as well as more unusual meteorological events. Therefore, the new challenge is that weather forecast or climate projection should be more physically based and integrate interaction from local climate.

Taiwan Case

Taiwan lies in a complex tectonic area with unique geological structure and complex hydrological circumstances. Nearly 78% of the rain takes place during the wet months from May to October, although the annual mean rainfall is about 2.6 times the world annual average. Due to high mountains and limited flatland, rivers are short and steep leading to rapid drain of precipitation. Untypical or even strong fluctuation rainfall cases occur almost every year and cause serious flood and drought disasters side by side sometimes. According to the analysis of the World Bank in 2006 [2], Taiwan was categorized as the place on Earth most prone to natural hazards, with 73 percent of its land and population exposed to three or more disasters.

Meteorological researches in Taiwan mainly include the heavy rainfall system during the Mei-Yu season (typically in May and June), the typhoon, and the East Asian climate studies [3, 4]. Typhoons and heavy rainfall events are the most serious and threatening weather incidents among all natural disasters in Taiwan. Numerical weather prediction (NWP) system has been deployed and keeping on improving the accuracy and performance by the Central Weather Bureau (CWB) for more than 20 years.

3 GRID INFRASTRUCTURE

Grid in General

Grid computing consists of a network infrastructure comprising loosely coupled heterogeneous data storage and computing resources connected via the Internet and controlled for management and access by software (middleware) such as gLite, UNICORE, and Globus Toolkit. A grid system is based on long- term and dynamic collaboration among grid partners (resource providers and user communities) with a trust agreement to guarantee security and confidentiality. The most widely used is the Globus toolkit that has the largest range of higher level services and permits the users to easily build their own services, in particular interface with Web services. It is used currently by thousands of sites in Business and Academia but mostly not inter-connected. gLite is the middleware of the largest Grid deployment today, Enabling Grids for E-SciencE (EGEE[1]), that is also part of the Worldwide LHC Computing Grid (WLCG) for the analysis of the petabytes of data that will be produced by the European Organization for Nuclear Research's (CERN) Large Hadron Collider (LHC) experiment in Geneva. Access to EGEE is not restricted to high energy physics and is currently used by other scientific communities mainly in public research including bioinformatics, Earth Science, Astronomy & Astrophysics, Fusion and so forth. gLite middleware is also used in other geographical areas such as Latin America, Mediterranean countries, Asian countries and is interoperable with Open Science Grid (OSG) in USA, Naregi in Japan

Grid computing is in general considered as a solution for scaling up computing power and storage capacity by sharing resources among institutions. However Grid infrastructure could be also considered as an e-collaboration platform allowing scientific cooperation within a virtual team, i.e. sharing information, knowledge, application, data and resources [5].

ES Grid Activities in Europe

To face the data deluge and, more and more complex simulations, the Earth Science (ES) community has started to use new technologies like the Web and the Grid. The Web services were rapidly adopted and are the base of many international ES initiatives. In Europe, Earth Science partners have been involved in Grid activity since the first European Grid project, DataGrid, a feasibility study. During different projects, EGEE, SEEGrid[2], CYCLOPS[3], DEGREE[4], the ES community

---

[1] http://www.eu-egee.org/

[2] http://www.see-grid.org

[3] http://www.cyclops-project.eu

analyzed the environments commonly used by its scientific community, defined the missing functionalities to interface them in particular with the EGEE middleware, gLite, and provided those requirements to Grid developers; some gaps being fulfilled within the relevant projects. In the framework of the EU project DEGREE (Dissemination and Exploitation of Grids in Earth science) the proposed strategy consists of propagating grid technology to all ES disciplines, setting up interactive collaboration among the members of a virtual ES grid community, and stimulating the interest of stakeholders on the political level [6]. The EGEE ES team, called ES cluster, invested a significant amount of time and effort to evolve from the strategic discipline cluster in EGEE to a ES Grid community, by bridging different ES activities in Europe and related countries (a total of 22 countries), as well as in related projects such as EELA2, EUMEDGRID-support and EUAsia-Grid.

The penetration of Grid in the ES community is pointed out by the variety of applications, the number of countries in which ES applications are ported and an estimate of the number of users. Numerous applications in meteorology, seismology, hydrology, pollution, climate and biodiversity were deployed successfully on Grid [7, 8]. Teams, having participated to Grid project and application porting, belong to Albania, Armenia, Bulgaria, France, Germany, Greece, Italy, Netherlands, Portugal, Romania, Russia, Turkey, Spain, Switzerland, UK, Ukrainia and Taiwan. The users are spread in 7 Virtual Organizations (VO); their number is approximately 300.

In order to fulfil requirements of risk management (fire and flood) provided by the civil protection, several applications were deployed and used the OGC (Open Geospatial Consortium) components, implemented on top of Grid [9]. A large number of applications that heavily rely on the use of Earth remote sensing data from space have been deployed and concerned also risk management. This includes rapid flood mapping from satellite radar imagery for the United Nations Platform for Space-based Information for Disaster Management and Emergency Response (UN-SPIDER) and International Federation of Red Cross [10]. Activities in this area provide contribution to the development of the Global Earth Observation System of Systems (GEOSS) and Global Monitoring for Environment and Security (GMES)

Grid also penetrates into Companies within EGEE and other Grid projects. The Compagnie Générale de Géophysique Veritas achieved within EGEE project the implementation of its generic seismic platform software, based on Geocluster commercial software, and support academic teams using it.

---

[4] http://www.eu-degree.eu

EUAsiaGrid

Asia is a geographically large region, with diverse levels of adoption of Grid technologies to facilitate Science. The EUAsiaGrid project, funded in the frame of the EU Seventh Framework Program (FP7) – Research Infrastructures, promotes interoperation between the European and the Asian-Pacific Grids. The project, with a total number of 15 partners coordinated by INFN, started on April 1st 2008. It disseminates the knowledge about the EGEE Grid infrastructure, organizes specific training events and supports applications both within the scientific communities with an already long experience in the computing Grids (High Energy Physics, Computational Chemistry, Bioinformatics and Biomedics) and in the most recent ones (Social Sciences, Disaster Mitigation, Cultural Heritage). The main objective of the project is to attract user communities through explicit support of scientific applications in specific areas. Ultimately the EUAsiaGrid project will pave the way towards a common e-Infrastructure with the European and the Asian Grids.

4 CLIMATE MODEL ON GRID

To carry out studies on the climate change impacts under different scenarios for the coming century, one of the most useful tools are the Dynamical climate models. Dynamical climate models are mathematical models that solve the governing equations, the different physical processes of the atmosphere and other components of the climate system. This is usually done on a discrete grid of points. Global circulation models (GCM) solve the equations with horizontal resolutions ranging from 50km to 300km, depending on the application, while regional climate models solve the equations over a region with higher resolution than GCMs (5 to 50km). In order to propagate the solution forward in time, both families of models require a set of initial conditions at their starting time, t0, given by larger scale models and/or observations. Additionally, regional models also require boundary conditions (values of climate variables at the boundaries of the analyzed region for all time steps), which are usually taken from a GCM. In the next subsections a gridified version of a global and circulation models are presented.

CAM4G Model

In order to analyze the atmospheric part of the global climate system, the CAM model (Community Atmosphere Model) is selected; it is the latest one in a series of global atmosphere models developed at National Center for Atmospheric Research (NCAR) of the United States, for the weather and climate research communities [11]. CAM is used for short (hours, days) or long periods of time (decades, centuries) to investigate the present, past or future climate variability. As a first step, at University of Cantabria we ported the CAM model, an atmosphere-only model enabling a wide range of experiments and only requiring lower boundary conditions at the surface (sea surface temperature).

The model runs either in parallel (using MPI) or in serial mode. The single-process version has been deployed and run in the EELA testbed with an equivalent horizontal resolution of 2.5°: 128 longitude × 64 latitude and 27 vertical levels, i.e. 221184 points per integration time step. The model produces 32 3D and 56 2D variables over the lattice. As an example, a one year simulation takes approximately 48 hours of wall clock time on typical computer, then, 100 years would take around 7 months. The model produces 197 MB per time step, i.e. more than 720 GB per century. These figures increase when running the model at higher resolution, i.e. double the horizontal resolution (256x128 grid points) will increase the previous figures in one order of magnitude.

The application design aims to perform sensitivity experiments by running an ensemble of CAM simulations by perturbing the sea surface temperatures as boundary conditions [12].

WRF4G Model

WRF4G shares much of its design with the earlier port of the CAM4G [12]. Based on the previous experience, the porting methodology has been improved providing to the framework extra capabilities, tools and services helping the development and porting of applications to the Grid infrastructure.

The Weather Research and Forecasting (WRF) model is a state-of-the-art regional modelling tool developed at the NCAR. It has been designed to serve both operational forecasting and atmospheric research needs and it has a rapidly growing community of users all around the world.

WRF is a computationally intensive application that can run with different degrees of parallelism (single process, MPI, OpenMP, ...). It only requires as input 5x3D and 9x2D fields. A typical simulation includes 63x43x31, 89838 points with a time step of 1.5 min. One such simulation for a year would take 72 CPU hours and produce 15 GB (1.5TB per century). These numbers vary wildly with the size of the domain and the resolution.

Regardless the infrastructure used to run WRF (single computer, cluster or Grid), its execution is not a simple task. WRF workflow involves the execution of several pre-processors in order to prepare the input data and the boundary conditions (see Figure 1). Although several users run the WRF workflow manually, preparing the configuration file and data for each pre-processing (ungrib, metgrid, geogrid), it is advisable to create a customized set of scripts that execute all the pre-processing in the correct order. This set of scripts will download the input data and boundary conditions from the repository where they are located and manage all the intermediate steps, feeding finally the WRF core with the results of the previous operations.

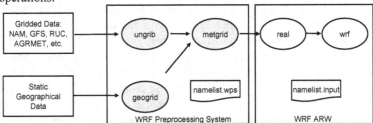

Fig. 1: WRF's execution flow.

Once all the data have been pre-processed and the WRF core itself has started to run, every certain number of simulation time steps, several output files are generated. Furthermore, as most experiments carried out with WRF need to be executed during long periods of time, WRF code is provided with the capability of generate restart data periodically in order to continue the simulation in case of system's failure.

In our port of WRF to Grid, we have tried to develop a tool that, apart from making possible the execution of the model in different Grid platforms, allows the users to carry out simulations using WRF with a minimum effort [12].

Porting CAM and WRF on Grid

Requirements

At a first stage, for both numerical models it has been provided a layered architecture separating three different roles:

- *Gridificator*: person in charge of porting the application to the Grid and hiding the complexity of the Grid to the application developer,
- *Application developer:* person in charge of adding new capabilities to the application itself. E.g. add a new pre-processor or postprocessor, add data assimilation support.
- *Application user:* This is an end-user of the application. It's only responsible setting the application configuration by making changes on configuration files for running different scientific experiments.

In order to hide the complexity of the Grid to the application developer, WRF4G includes several abstraction layers which encapsulate the routine task in generic function calls. These abstraction layers should support several protocols and platforms. This way the application developer does not have to know if the files are stored locally, in a GridFtp server or in a HTTP server. The same would happen with the execution management; with small changes in the configuration files the user can submit jobs to its local computer or to the Grid.

After the experience with the previous CAM porting to the Grid, it was decided that, apart from reusing the capabilities of the workflow management of the previous migration (simulation monitoring and restart management) [12], a different approach has been required to face problems related to the duration of the jobs (usually 48 hours). This has been solved by dividing the simulations into dependent chunks. Those chunks represent small parts of the complete long simulation, which take into account the CPU and wall time limitations in a particular compute element.

Regarding the data management, the final output data structure viewed by application user is hiding the complexity due to the existence of these chunks [13].

Advantages

Climate models are complex computer programs which require large amounts of cpu power. However, even if clusters are installed on Grid infrastructures, Grid is not efficient for high-parallel codes, such as most of the model ones. Apart from computer parallelism, climate science is recently making use of a large number of simulations, referred to as an "ensemble", of the same phenomenon in order to assess the uncertainty inherent to the simulation. Ensembles of simulations with varying parameters are also used for sensitivity experiments and many other applications. Each simulation in an ensemble is independent of the others and can be run asynchronously. In case of models, this kind of parametric jobs is well suited for the Grid, since each simulation can be carried out in different nodes and the results are made available as a uniform data set in the Logical File Catalogue (LFC), ready to be analyzed.

Unlike volunteer computing projects, such as climateprediction.net where the GCM needs to be simplified and most of the results thrown away to avoid the overloading of the volunteer hosts, the GRID allows running a full state-of-the-art model and store the regular output information.

Drawbacks & limitations

Current GRID technology is not completely well suited for the Earth Science community. Specifically, for climate models, it has several weaknesses such as a high failure rate and time simulation limits. The high failure rate is related to the fact that there is a large diversity of sites and failures may occur due to missing libraries, long waiting queue or temporary site malfunctioning. Then to improve this rate some tests or tools have to be set up before sending the ensemble of jobs; several solutions having been deployed in several ES applications i.e. black list of sites, survey of the jobs with re-submission to other sites...The time limitation (24h) of the proxy is a problem for long jobs and also long waiting queue with job duration around several hours. The proxy renewal is possible but failure of the compute element may occur. Other weaknesses are related to efficient access to external databases, priority of real-time jobs and specific environments.

In spite of these weaknesses, there are some fields in earth science, including recent trends in sensitivity studies or any other involving independent simulations, which could greatly benefit from the GRID.

Unlike in local clusters or supercomputers, where the applications running on those clusters are optimized for parallel running jobs based on MPI and OpenMP, the Grid is well suited for independent simulations where the application doesn't require a parallel code optimization and compilation.

Another important topic is the storage capacity; climate models manage huge amount datasets that need a lot of storage capacity. This issue is only solved by providing large storage installed on the Grid infrastructure or having agreement with other site managers.

5   WORKPLAN OF THE COLLABORATION

Current Status of WRF4G in EUAsiaGrid

Integration and continuous upgrade of observation facilities, data assimilation, right modelling and high performance computation capability provide the solid groundwork of NWP. The Very Short-Range Forecasting (VSRF) system of the climate variation and severe weather monitoring had been also established. In addition, quantitative precipitation estimation and the lightning data are included as part of VSRF system to support the alleviation of potential weather disasters. Active research communities focusing on physics of weather changes, weather systems and the modelling, and the close collaboration with CWB effectively upraise the governance of precision, timeliness, resolution, scale and the critical factors of potential risks.

The high-resolution Weather Research and Forecasting model (WRF) and Nonhydrostatic Forecast System (NFS) are currently the backbone of regional weather simulation and prediction applications in Taiwan. Many research groups also use the WRF for cutting-edge weather researches and to extend many local adapted atmospheric topics. This also expedites the interactions between research findings and daily operational models for better forecasts. With the newly confirmed model approved by WRF for the peculiar Morakot typhoon case, we learnt that the heavy amounts of rain over the southern portion of the island is due to persistent southwesterly flow associated with typhoon and it's circulation was able to draw up abundant amounts of moisture from the South China Sea into southern Taiwan where it was able to interact with the steep topography [14, 15, 16].

Environmental change is one of the target e-Science applications of ASGC to support the researches on climate physics, impact of climate change and also the regional weather systems, by cooperating with local user communities and partners from EUAsiaGrid and the world. Other than those research focus identified by the research groups, WRF regional weather simulation application is the best candidate for Grid as it is popularly adapted in Asia and it had been integrated into gLite [17]. Streamlining the workflow according to scientist requirements and make the system self-refined by new initial conditions from the previous simulation are the most essential issues identified for weather simulation by WRF on Grid. WRF4G platform is available at ASGC, topics such as impact of air pollution, long-range transport dust, urban heat island effects and the rainfall systems are potential candidates to be realized by e-Science paradigms on the world-wide Grid.

Need & Benefit of the Collaboration

What it is observed in the different Grid projects is the role of Grid technology to facilitate an interactive scientific and technical collaboration among the members due to its geographically distributed resources and teams. The resources are heterogeneous but as the middleware is the same then applications ported by one team may be used by another team.

Asian Grid partners want to run climate models for their country and/or region on EUAsiaGrid. Using the grid infrastructure permits to get more compute resources. Such models have been already ported on the EGEE middleware by the team of the University of Cantabria and used for regional climate studies

Then collaboration is proposed between this Spanish team from the University of Cantabria and EUAsiaGrid partners, especially the Thailand ones.

The main outlines of the workplan have been defined. The first one concerns the real need of the Thailand team; it is expressed in part 2. The second step is the organisation of a training period in Thailand, it is described below. A questionnaire has been prepared for the future participants in order to know their expectation and their level of climate expertise. The third step is the implementation of WRF4G in EUASIAGrid. One of the main points is the involvement of climate experts to parameterize it and interpret the results from the WRF4G model. This model has been made available to the ASGC during the ISGC workshop.

Once the application and the training to use it will be provided the application will be the focus of collaboration among climate scientists of the concerned area.

Training

The target audience for the training is the partners with mixed members, climate researchers and system administrators. In particular researchers are expected to be experienced to run and interpret results from the WRF or similar model.

This tutorial will be opened for those EUAsiaGrid partners that already have expressed their interest. These partners are from Thailand, Philippines, Vietnam, Malaysia and Taiwan.

The first tutorial is at first planned during 3 days in July 2010. The topics covered in this tutorial will consist in the installation and configuration of WRF4G, and will be organized following the plan:

- Day 1: Technical requirements, installation, configuration
- Day 2: Optimization and verification
- Day 3: Visualization and training summary

To carry on this tutorial is required the preparation of:

- GRID Computing facilities
- Setup of a experimental Data Set
- Tutors with experience in climate research using WRF and GRID (2 people)
- Training materials
- Budget for logistic, venue and accommodation.

Implementation of WRF4G

The tutorial will cover the use of WRF4G developed by the University of Cantabria team. The current version is the release candidate 1.0, which has been already deployed in the Earth-Science-Research Virtual Organization (ESR VO) of the EGEE Grid infrastructure and in the EELA-2 testbed. This version has already started to be tested inside EUAsiaGrid.

6 CONCLUSION

In this paper, shortly the worries of climate change from EUAsiaGrid partners are expressed. A difficulty to anticipate the climate change is not to have at their disposal any tool and compute resources to carry out those studies. Grid, which provides compute resources and facilitates collaboration among Grid projects and teams, is a way to fulfil this gap.

A proposal is setting up to implement the climate model, WRF4G, already working on Grid and ported by the University of Cantabria, first in Thailand and to train the scientists to use it.

The first step is to master the model, and interpret the results. Getting expertise by collaborating with other climate teams will permit to predict climate change in their region and participate to international programme.

7 ACKNOWLEDGMENTS

The porting of WRF4G and CAM4G applications has been supported by EELA-2 project, the Spanish e-Science Network, the EGEE VO Earth Science Research and by the Spanish Santander's Meteorology Group .

REFERENCES

[1] Foster, I., Kesselman, C.: The Grid: Blueprint for a new computing infrastructure. Morgan Kaufmann (1999)

[2] Dilley, M. et al.: Natural Disaster Hotspots: A Global Risk Analysis, World Bank Publications, Washington, D.C., (2005). ISBN 0-8213-5930-4.

[3] Wu, C-C., Kuo, H-C., Hsu, H-H., Jou, B. J-D.: Weather and Climate Research in Taiwan: Potential Application of GPS/MET Data. Terr. Atmos. Ocean. Sci., 11, 211-234, (2000).

[4] Shiao, C. H., and H. M. H. Juang:: Sensitivity Study of the Climate Simulation over East Asia with the CWB Regional Spectral Model. Terr. Atmos. Ocean. Sci., 17, 593- 612 (2006)

[5] Bourras, C, Giannaka, E, Tsiatos, E.: e-Collaboration Concepts, Systems and applications, in : Information Science Reference, E-Collaboration: Concepts, Methodologies, Tools, and applications- Vol1, Section I, Chap. 1.2 Ed. N. Kock. (2009)

[6]   Cossu R, Petitdidier M, Linford JL, Badoux V, Fusco L, Gotab B, Hluchy L, Lecca G, Murgia F, Plevier C, Renard P, Schwichtenberg H, Som de Cerff W, V. Tran, Vetois G.; A roadmap for a dedicated Earth Science Grid platform. Earth Science Informatics, (2010). doi: 10.1007/s12145-010-0045-4

[7]   Renard P, Badoux V, Petitdidier M, Cossu R.: Grid computing for Earth Sciences. Eos, 90, 14, 117&119, (7 April 2009).

[8]   Petitdidier M, Cossu R, Fox P, Schwichtenberg H, Som de Cerff W.: Grid in Earth Sciences.. Earth Science Informatics, (2009). doi: 10.1007/s12145-009-0028-5 (Editorial)

[9]   Mazzetti P, Nativi S, Angelini V, Verlato M, Fiorucci P; A Grid platform for the European Civil Protection e-Infrastructure: the Forest Fires use scenario. Earth Science Informatics, (2009). doi: 10.1007/s12145-009-002

[10] Kussul N., Shelestov A., Skakun S., Grid System for Flood Extent Extraction from Satellite Images. Earth Science Informatics, 1, 105-117 (2008).

[11] Collins, W. D., et al.: Description of the NCAR Comunity Atmospheric Model (CAM 3.0). Tech. Report Number NCAR/TN-464+STR. National Center for Atmospheric Research (2004).

[12] Fernandez-Quirelas V, Fernandez J, Baeza C, Cofino AS, Gutierrez JM, Execution management in the GRID for sensitivity studies of global climate simulations. Earth Science Informatics (2009a). doi: 10.1007/s12145-008-0018-z

[13] Fernández-Quiruelas et al.: WRF4G: enabling WRF on the Grid. Proceedings of the Second EELA-2 Conference, (2009b).

[14] Chien, FC, Liu YC, and Lee CS, Heavy Rainfall and Southwesterly Flow after the Leaving of Typhoon Mindulle (2004) from Taiwan. Journal of the Meteorological Society of Japan. Ser. II 86 (1), 17- 41 (2008).

[15] Hsu HH, et al.: Special Report on Typhoon Morakot (2009). International Workshop on Typhoon Morakot, Taiwan, (2009)..

[16] Lin, S.J.: Track and the Precipitation Predictions of Typhoon Morakot Using the GFDL High-Resolution Global Weather-Climate Model. International Workshop on Typhoon Morakot, Taiwan (2009).

[17] Fernández-Quiruelas et al.:Climate modelling on the GRID Experiences in the EU-project EELA. Proceedings of the Third EELA Conference, (2007). ISBN: 9788478345656

Lessons Learned in Thailand from 2004 Tsunami

Vorawit Meesuk[1], Royol Chitradon[2], Amnart Bali[3] and Wong K. Snidvongs[4]

1. HAII, Head of environmental observation and telemetry section
2. Director General, HAII
3. Director of Disaster Relief and Public Health, Thai Red Cross
4. Member of Executive Board of Directors, HAII

Foreword   This article is a result of cooperation between HAII, many Thai government agencies as well as the Thai Red Cross.

Information and data both domestic and international, both in printed and electronic forms were collected, analyzed and summarized to give an overall pictures of events unfolded on 26 December 2004 when a natural disaster of unprecedented scale in the region. Thailand's six provinces on the Andaman coast suffered severe damages both in human losses and economic damages which have just recovered five years after the event.

It is intended for readers to realize what happened during the fateful twelve hours from the quake of 9.2 magnitude near Sumatra Island, Indonesia which caused the most devastating tsunami on record in Asia Pacific region. It left a trail of human sufferings and property damages in several developing countries from Indonesia, in South East Asia to Tanzania in East Africa.

Several conclusions may be drawn but costly lessons learned are not intended to blame but to build on past shortcomings of the entire system of environmental monitoring network, data collection, and precise information leading to timely warning and public alert, leading to evacuation according to well laid out and rehearsed plans.

Contents   This article contains background information on quakes and tsunamis. Tsunamis' strength and damages they have caused.

Brief sequence of events on 26 December 2004 when a tsunami hit the Andaman coast of southern Thailand devastating areas in six provinces of Phuket, Pangnga, Krabi, Satun, Trang, and Ranong.

Damages and losses will be summarized. Monitoring systems, disaster preparedness and mitigation at the time and at the end of 2009 five years after the tragedy will be described.

1. Background information on quakes and tsunamis.
2. Tsunami's strength and damages caused in the past.
3. Events, damages and losses during 2004 tsunami
4. Monitoring systems, disaster preparedness and mitigation at the time and at end of 2009.
5. Lessons learned in Thailand.
6. Acknowledgements

S.C. Lin and E. Yen (eds.), *Data Driven e-Science: Use Cases and Successful Applications*   415
of Distributed Computing Infrastructures (ISGC 2010), DOI 10.1007/978-1-4419-8014-4_32,
© Springer Science+Business Media, LLC 2011

1   BACKGROUND INFORMATION ON QUAKES AND TSUNAMIS

Tsunami is Japanese for 'harbor wave' so named because of its devastating power on arrival at a harbor which is usually a quiet and safe place. Tsunami or seismic wave results from quakes of more than 7.2 magnitude caused by movements of continental and oceanic plates, 77% occurring in the Pacific 'Ring of Fire'.

Tsunami run up locations

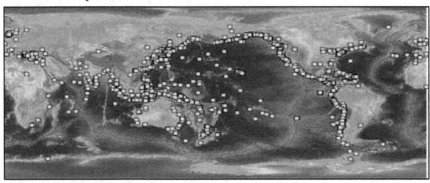

Events generating tsunami

Other causes of tsunamis include under ocean floor volcanic eruptions, subsidence of volcanic craters, underwater landslides or coastal subsidence, nuclear tests, and dam bursts. The rare meteorite hits in an ocean can also cause quakes and generate tsunamis. The resulting strong vertical separation of earth crusts force enormous amount of water to move upwards generating vast amount of energy propelling waves which can be as high as 40 meters when reaching shorelines.

Factors affecting strength of tsunamis and resulting damages, that should be included in disaster preparedness and mitigation for high risk areas, are coastal profiles and shore characteristics.

In deep sea, tsunami waves are only 0.3 to 0.6 meters high with crest intervals of 10-120 minutes but the length of waves can be more than 500 km. Nearing shores the waves become taller at narrow coastal inlets while wide inlets will see less tall waves.

Shallow coastal water reduces wave velocity. Contributing factors such as coral reefs, beach gradients and distance from the originating quake all contribute to speed and severity of devastation.

2   QUAKES' STRENGTHS AND DAMAGES CAUSED BY RESULTING TSUNAMIS

Between 1900 to end of 2004, eleven large quakes occurred both on land and in the sea. The area stretched from Tibet to Alaska. Magnitudes were between 8.5 to 9.5 as shown in table 1.

Table 1

	Location	Date UTC	Magnitude	Coordinates	
1.	Chile	1960 05 22	9.5	38.24 S	73.05 W
2.	Prince William Sound, Alaska	1964 03 28	9.2	61.02 N	147.65 W
3.	Andreanof Islands, Alaska	1957 03 09	9.1	51.56 N	175.39 W
4.	Kamchatka	1952 11 04	9.0	52.76 N	160.06 E
5.	Off the West Coast of Northern Sumatra	2004 12 26	9.0	3.30 N	95.78 E
6.	Off the Coast of Ecuador	1906 01 31	8.8	1.0 N	81.5 W
7.	Rat Islands, Alaska	1965 02 04	8.7	51.21 N	178.50 E
8.	Assam - Tibet	1950 08 15	8.6	28.5 N	96.5 E
9.	Kamchatka	1923 02 03	8.5	54.0 N	161.0 E
10.	Banda Sea, Indonesia	1938 02 01	8.5	5.05 S	131.62 E
11.	Kuril Islands	1963 10 13	8.5	44.9 N	149.6 E

Between 1900 and 1989, there were 946 tsunamis and 120 of them (14.5%) caused widespread destruction and heavy loss of lives. Between 1782 and 1994 approximate number of tsunamis related deaths ranged from 1,997 to 200,000 as shown in table 2. (slide 7 in power point)

Recent tsunamis between 1992 and 2001 which resulted in loss of lives occurred in the Pacific area. Magnitude of quakes ranged from 7.0 to 8.3 and three of those were measured Pacific wide. Maximum wave heights ranged from 5 meters to 30 meters. Number of people killed ranged from 11 to 2,000. Loss of lives did not appear to relate to magnitudes of quakes and heights of waves alone. Others factors such as distance from originating quakes, sea depths, shore characteristics, population density, types of communities as well as their preparedness must be taken into account as shown in table 2.

Table 2

Date UTC	Magnitude	Max Ht	Killed	Location	Comments
1992 09 02	7.2	10 m	170	Nicaragua	Measured Pacific-wide
1992 12 12	7.5	26 m	1000	Flores Island	
1993 07 12	7.6	30 m	200	Hokkaido	
1994 06 02	7.2	14 m	220	Java	
1994 10 04	8.1	11 m	11	Kuril Islands	Measured Pacific-wide
1994 11 14	7.1	7 m	70	Mindoro	
1996 02 21	7.5	5 m	12	Peru	
1998 07 17	7.0	15 m	2000	New Guinea	
2001 06 23	8.3	5 m	50	Peru	Measured Pacific-wide

Damages were not strictly related to one single factor such as quake's magnitude or wave heights.

Source events:

Tsunamis, Japanese for 'harbor waves' have occurred worldwide. Of the 1,700 tsunami events – 77% occurred in the Pacific Ocean, 7% in Mediterranean Sea, 5% in Indian Ocean, 5% in Caribbean Sea, 3% in Atlantic Ocean and 3% in Red Sea and Black Sea.

Run up locations:

Of 9,200 locations – 84% were in Pacific Ocean, 8% in Indian Ocean, 2% Atlantic Ocean, 3% Caribbean Sea, 2% Mediterranean Sea, Red Sea and Black Sea <1%.

Source distribution:

81% earthquakes including quakes generated landslides, 10% unknown, 5% volcanoes, 3% landslides, 1% combination.

Magnitude of quakes alone can not accurately predict tsunamis and their devastation. Height, velocity, length, of waves, shape of shore inlets, beach gradients, profiles of communities in target areas all have to be taken into account. Proper training, clear evacuation routes, full understanding of the population are vital to avoid panic.

3 EVENTS, DAMAGES AND LOSSES DURING 2004 TSUNAMI

Geographic background and seismic events

The Andaman coast of southern Thailand is known for its popular beach resorts of Phuket, Pangnga, Krabi, Ranong, Trang, and Satun. The area lies in South China Sea bordering the Indian Ocean and is in the region known as the 'Ring of Fire' for its movements of the earth crusts and volcanic eruptions.

The underwater quakes causing that tsunami resulted from collision of the Indian and Myanmar plates in the area adjoining the Australian plate. This is known as the Sunda Trench. The Indian plate which had been moving 6 cm. a year sank along this trench generating enormous accumulated pressure on the ocean floor which finally erupted. Part of the floor lifted and the other subsided causing a crack approximately 1,200 km. long parallel to the Sunda Trench from northwest of Sumatra Island reaching north to Andaman group of Islands. Series of after shocks followed the line of the adjoining two plates.

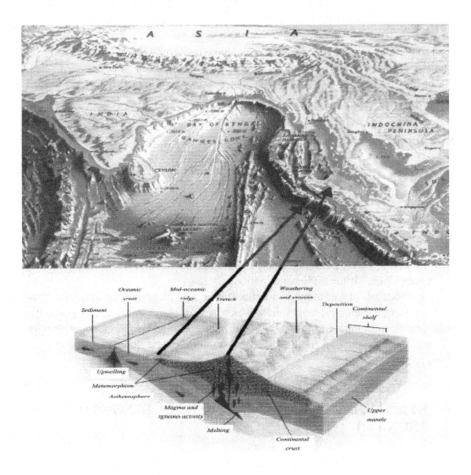

Sequence of events

(shown in Thailand time)

7.58 am: Undersea quake n/w of Sumatra Island, Indonesia. Magnitude 9.2 – 500 km. from Phuket on Andaman coast of southern Thailand.

9.35 am: The sea receded 500 meters from the beach.

9.55 am: First series of waves 2-3 meters high hit with continuous and sustained velocity. Those waves traveled 500 kilometers in two hours from source.

10.10am: Second series of waves 3- more than10 meters high arrived forming gigantic wall of water several kilometers long and very powerful destroying buildings, hurling cars and even police coastal patrol boat more than 50 meters in land, continuing for 20 minutes flooding area more than 1 kilometers in land.

10.20am: Third series of waves, 5 meters high arrived completing the devastation and causing widespread flooding for about one hour.

Summary of assistance

- Immediate response by local authorities.
- Disaster area in all six provinces declared.
- Food, water, shelter, clothing distribution in place and adequate within 12 hours.
- Field surgical teams from the Red Cross, university and armed forces hospitals in Bangkok deployed within 24 hours to help local hospitals.
- Search and identification of victims by forensic teams were difficult because of delay in recovering bodies as well as lack or loss of personal records.

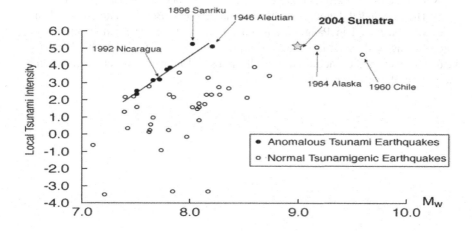

Second largest of the world tsunamigenic earthquakes record in history

Damages and losses incurred

Human suffering and loss from this natural disaster were unprecedented. 5,395 people both local Thai people and visiting foreigners died. 2,817 people remain missing and presumed dead. More than 8,400 were injured. Within four hours from the source event, northwest of Sumatra Island, Thailand experienced hitherto unimagined devastation in six provinces which were major tourist attractions along her Andaman coast.

Damage to private properties numbered over 4,800 homes in the six provinces devastated by the tsunami. Economic losses were considerable from tourism related businesses totaling 15 billion baht (USD 429 million) representing 87.7%, with loss from fishing industry amounting to 1.8 billion baht. 1,202 large fishing boats were damaged and 4,783 smaller ones severely damaged.

Damages to public utilities included shops, restaurants, roads, water supplies, drains, piers, excursion boats and other beach facilities. Government help was immediate and effective. Financial and technical help poured in both from domestic and international sources. Wholehearted participation by local population helped numb the pain endured by those who suffered personal losses.

Damages to and loss of marine and coastal resources were also considerable. More than 50% of coral reeves were damaged in some areas, especially in Pangnga, Surin and Similan groups of islands. As for mangrove forests on the coast, almost all of Pangnga 600 acres were destroyed by strong waves and resulting sand dunes further in land, making them inaccessible to sea water.

Rare species of marine creatures were found beached and subsequently rescued. These included dugongs, sea turtles and dolphins. Beaches and coastal damages were sustained in Pangnga and Phuket with entire resorts obliterated and headlands as well as estuaries disappearing under water. A nearby Prathong Island, however, gained additional beach almost all along its beaches from sand swept from the nearby mainland of Pangnga.

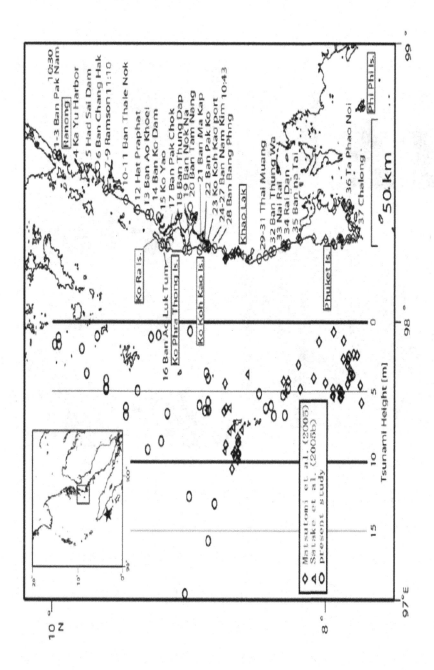

Tsunami heights measured at Andaman coast, Thailand

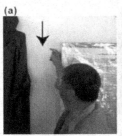

Photo 1.   (a) Water mark on the wall, and (b) that on the column at the office of Ramason National Park.

Photo 3.   Damaged house by the tsunami at Ban Ma Kap.

Photo 4.   Tsunami height at Ban Nam Kim.

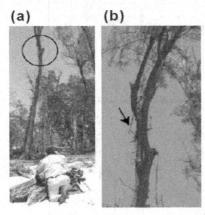

Photo 2.   (a) Broken branches due to the tsunami current at Ban Tung Dap, and (b) zoomed up of the circle.

Photo 5.   Broken clock at Ban Nam Kim.

Sea surface height from space

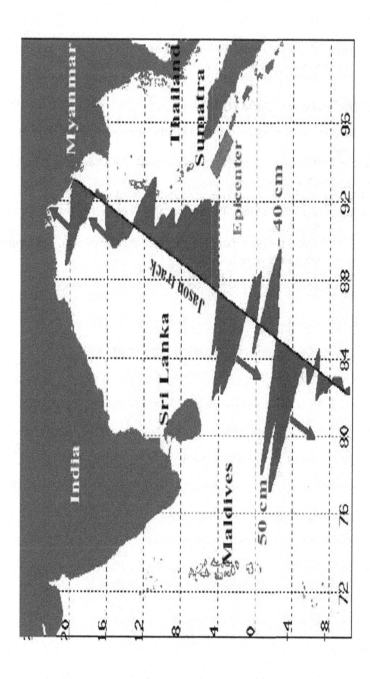

(12/26/04 US/France Jason, courtesy of NASA, EARTHQUAKES & TSUNAMIS Frequently
Asked Questions & 12/2004 Asian Event Ellen Prager, PhD StormCenter Communications, Inc.)

Path and run up time of tsunami from point of origin to its final destination in Tanzania more than 6,000 kilometers away are detailed below.

Sunday 26 December 2004 (GMT)

00.57 9.0 magnitude earthquake occurred on the seafloor near Aceh in northern Sumatra

01.10 Waves hit Sumatra coast (10-15 min.) Clock on Mosque in Banda Aceh stopped at 08.20 local time

02.30 Sri Lanka was hit by waves (reported at 8.30 local time)

02.45 Phuket, Coast of Thailand: The sea retracted before big waves hit around 10.00 a.m. local time.

04.00 Male, Maldives, Indian's eastern Coastline: about 9.00 a.m. the capital of Male and other parts were flooded

09.45 Tsunami hit Dar es Salam, Tanzania, East Africa.

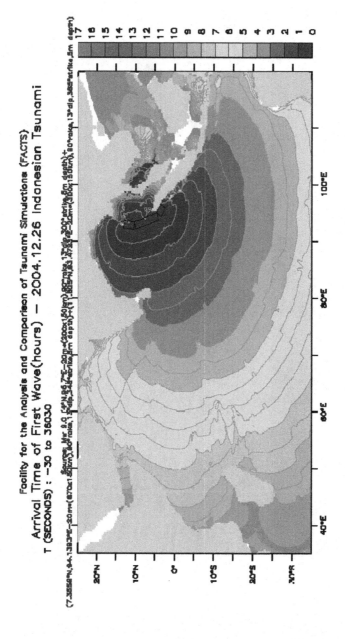

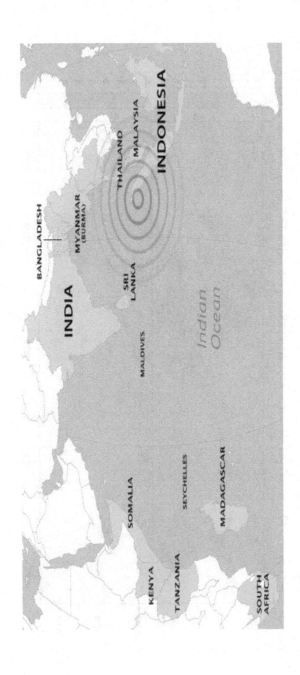

4 MONITORING SYSTEMS, DISASTER PREPAREDNESS AND MITIGATION AT THE TIME AND AT END OF 2009

Deployment of monitoring devices, information relay equipments as well as warning networks in the region and along tsunami's path may not have been up to expectation. Distances between source event and times it reached each target from Aceh, Thailand, Bangladesh, Sri Lanka, Maldives, India, and finally Tanzania are shown in the diagram below. The waves had traveled more than 6,000 kilometers in 9 hours.

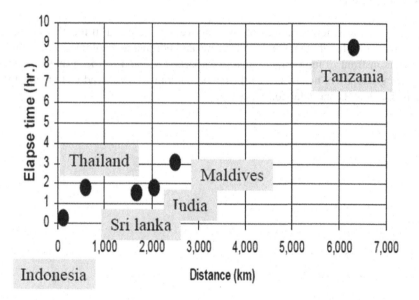

In this age of satellite imaging and electronic communication, data and information relays seemed to have been inadequate. Breakdowns must have occurred, information may not have been directed to relevant authorities, responses may not have been appropriate or timely. All these are open to questions and the answers will be lessons learned from the 2004 tsunami.

Possible EU Asia grid applications

Seismic Stations:

- PTCW global seismic network
- ISSE network
- Broadband seismic stations in Taiwan

- VIETNET seismic network in Vietnam
- Thailand Seismic Network
- Real-time sea level
    - PTWS network
    - UHSLC IOTWS network
    - Thailand Network

- Mooring buoys
    - DART mooring buoys

- NOAA weather radio
- Alarm towers

EU Asia grid application as outlined above may be useful if member countries are aware of what it means in human terms and not just technological ones. Junior officers in front of monitors are just as important as heads of departments, ministers or government heads. Over reliance on equipments will lead us to neglect the human elements and fatal complacency.

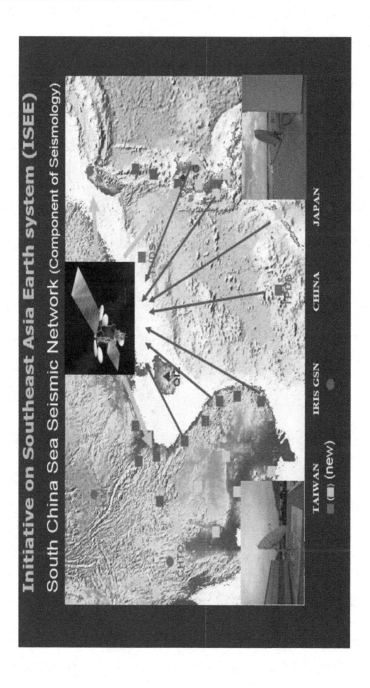

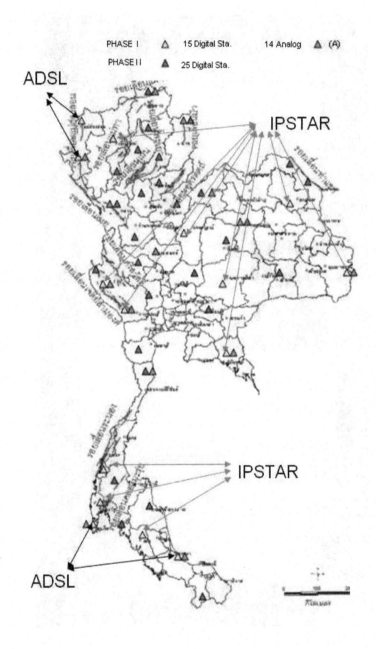

5 LESSONS LEARNED IN THAILAND

- Relay of data, formulated to information, timely warning, alert and evacuation orders seemed possible especially for targets beyond Thailand.
- Evacuation routes, practices and depots of supplies for the first 24 hours are essential mitigation measures.
- Specially trained search and rescue teams at village levels are vital. Back up medical teams at local hospitals.
- Efficient logistics for relief supplies and personnel needed for large scale disasters are very important.
- Search and identification of victims must be systematic, professional and of international standard.
- Communities' participation in relief operations helped console victims and relatives.
- Rehabilitation measures, both physical and mental, must be sustained.

Who knows when and where the next one will come?

Since 26 December 2004, there have been 10 quakes in Asia Pacific region of more than 7.7 magnitude, with various consequences as shown in the table below as shown in table 3. None resulted in a tsunami.

Table 3

Date	Location	Magnitude	Early Warning?	Fatalities
26 Dec 2004	Sumatra	9.2	No	Tsunami death~230,000
23 Mar 2005	Nias Island	8.7	Panic evacuation	Evacuation killed ~100
19 July 2005	North California	7.7	False alarm	No tsunami
27 Jan 2006	Benda Sea	7.6	?	No tsunami
3 May 2006	Tonga	8.0	False Alarm	No tsunami
19 July 2006	South Java	7.7	No	Tsunami death~730
15 Nov 2006	Kuril Islands	8.3	False alarm/alert	Small tsunami
13 Jan 2007	Kuril Islands	8.1	False alarm/alert	No tsunami
1 Apr 2007	Solomon Island	8.0	No	Tsunami death~54
15 Aug 2007	Central Peru	8.0	Alert	No tsunami
12 Sep 2007	South Sumatra	8.4	Alert	No tsunami

Discussion points

- Are we adequately equipped to accurately predict one? If not, what are our improvement priorities?
- The next one may be sooner than we think with all that climate changes and overexploitation of earth's resources bring. The next one might be worse!
- Do disaster preparedness and mitigation measures have negative impacts on tourism industry and deter investments on major public utilities such as building hydroelectric dams?

6   ACKNOWLEDGEMENTS

- Chulalongkorn University, Bangkok, Thailand
- Department of Disaster Prevention and Mitigation, Ministry of Interior
- Department of Hydrology, Royal Thai Navy
- Meteorological Department, Ministry of Transports
- National Centre for Disaster Warning, Ministry of Information Technology and Communications
- Department of Public Health and Disaster Relief, Thai Red Cross
- International sources of information as appeared in the article

Efficient Bulk Data Replication for the EarthSystem Grid

Alex Sim[1], Dan Gunter[1], Vijaya Natarajan[1], Arie Shoshani[1],
Dean Williams[2], Jeff Long[2], Jason Hick[3], Jason Lee[3] and Eli Dart[4]

1. Lawrence Berkeley National Laboratory
2. Lawrence Livermore National Laboratory
3. National Energy Research Scientific Computing Center
4. Energy Sciences Network

Abstract   The Earth System Grid (ESG) community faces the difficult challengeof managing the distribution of massive data sets to thousands of scientistsaround the world. To move data replicas efficiently, the ESG has developed a data transfer management tool called the Bulk Data Mover (BDM).We describe the performance results of the current system and plans towards extending the techniques developed so far for the upcoming project, in which the ESG will employ 100Gbps networks to move multi-TBdatasets with the ultimate goal of helping researchers understand climatechange and its potential impacts on world ecology and society.

Keywords   ESG, climate, BDM, data transfer, NetLogger

1   INTRODUCTION

The Earth System Grid (ESG) [1] community faces the difficult challenge of managing the distribution of massive data sets to thousands of scientists around the world. An important new collection of climate data sets, referred to as the "centralized data", is expected to comprise 0.6-1.2PBduring the Intergovernmental Panel on Climate Change (IPCC) FifthAssessment Report (AR5) in 2011. The new centralized data can only beefficiently served to researchers all over the world by replicating it to sitescloser to them. To move data replicas efficiently, the ESG has developed adata transfer management tool called the Bulk Data Mover (BDM) [2]. The BDM achieves high performance using a variety of techniques, including multi-threaded concurrent transfer connections, data channel caching, balanced transfer server connections, storage I/O prefetching, andautomatic transfer tuning. To optimize the BDM to use the full available full available network and storage bandwidth of multi-gigabit paths, monitoring information from the BDM and transfer servers is collected and analyzed in near-real time with the NetLogger toolkit. In the results from ESGdata replication on the current networks, NetLogger [4] analyses provided an intuitive view of time-varying patterns in the overlap between multiple concurrent transfers that proved invaluable for tuning the BDM concurrency algorithms. In future networks, it is expected that tuning anddebugging concurrent performance will become even more difficult. Asdata volume grows super-linearly and network and storage bandwidth increase, more concurrency will be needed for data transfers, the volume ofmonitoring data will increase, and disparities between components will beexacerbated. We describe the performance results of the current systemand plans towards extending the techniques developed so far for the upcoming project, in which the ESG will employ 100Gbps networks to movemulti-TB datasets with the ultimate goal of helping researchers understandclimate change and its potential impacts on world ecology and society.

2   EARTH SYSTEM GRID

As the climate community makes its first steps towards building a "science gateway"—a data access and analysis system open to everyone —the*Earth System Grid" (ESG)* is central to the current and future infrastructure that enables the large federated enterprise system for the dissemination and management of extreme scale climate resources. ESG provides climate resources such as data, information, models, analysis and visualization tools, and other computational capabilities for data management anddiagnosis. The ESG project's goals are (1) to make data more useful to climate researchers by developing Grid technology that enhances data usability; (2) to meet specific needs which national and international climateprojects have for distributed database, data access, and data movement; (3)to provide a universal and secure web-based data access portal for broad-based multi-model data collections; and (4) to provide a wide-range ofGrid-enabled climate data analysis tools and diagnostic methods to climate communities [3]. Thus, ESG is working to integrate distributed data andcomputers, high-bandwidth wide-area networks, and remote computing using climate data analysis tools in a highly collaborative problem-solvingenvironment.

Since production began in 2004, the ESG has hosted and distributedsignificant and often very large data collections for many well-known efforts in climate science. As of February 2010, the ESG production systemhas over 16,000 registered users. ESG manages approximately 270 TB of model data, comprising the contents of archives at five sites around theUS. ESG users have downloaded more than 1PB of data.

3   BULK DATA MOVER

The Bulk Data Mover (BDM) is responsible for the successful replication of large datasets. Climate datasets are characterized by large numbersof small files; to handle this issue the ESG uses the BDM software as ahigher-level data transfer management component to manage the file transfers with optimized transfer queue and concurrency management algorithms.

The BDM can accept a request composed of multiple files or an entiredirectory. The files or directory are described as Universal Resource Locators (URLs) that indicate the source sites that contain the files. The request also contains the target site and directory where the replicated fileswill reside. If a directory is provided at the source, then the BDM will replicate the structure of the source directory at the target site. The BDM is capable of transferring multiples files concurrently as well as using parallelTCP streams. The optimal level of concurrency or parallel streams is dependent on the bandwidth capacity of the storage systems at both ends ofthe transfer as well as achievable bandwidth on the wide-area-network (WAN). Setting up the level of concurrency correctly is an important issue, especially in climate datasets, because of the small files. Concurrency thatis too high becomes ineffective (high overheads and increased congestion),and concurrency that is too low will not take advantage of available bandwidth. A similar phenomenon was observed when setting up the level ofparallel streams.

The BDM is designed to work in a "pull mode", where the BDM runs asa client at the target site. This choice is made because of practical securityaspects: site managers usually prefer to be in charge of pulling data, ratherthan having data pushed at them. However, the BDM could also be designed to operate in a "push mode", or as an independent third-party service. Because a large scale data replication can take a long time (frommany minutes to hours and even days) the BDM must be an asynchronousservice. That means that when a replication request is launched, a "requesttoken" is returned to the client. The client should be able to use that request token to check the status of the request execution at any time. Another obvious implication to the long lasting nature of large scale replication is the need for automatic monitoring and recovery from any transientfailures, which is an important part of the BDM's design.

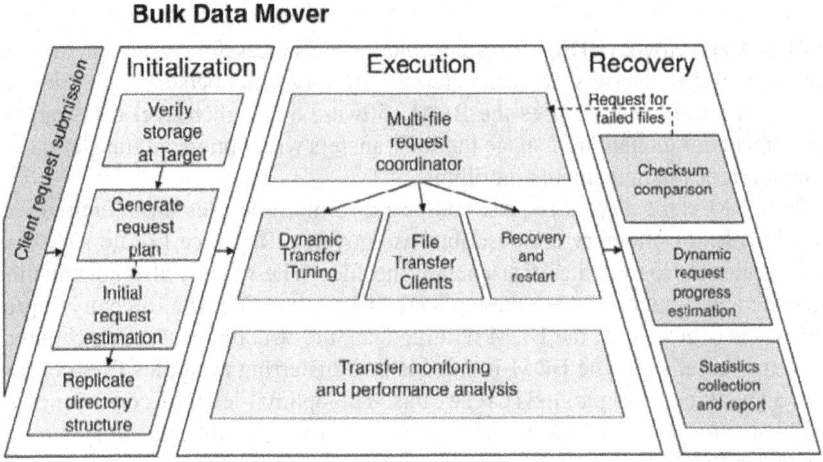

Bulk Data Mover

Fig. 1: The design of the Bulk Data Mover (BDM)

3.1   Multi-phase Transfer Request Management

The tasks that the BDM performs to accomplish a successful replicationare organized into three phases, as shown in Figure 1. The initializationphase plans and prepares file replications from the data source to the localtarget storage. It includes the following tasks: 1) Storage allocation verification at the target site; this requires collecting the total data size from thesource site. 2) Generating a request plan. The plan includes the initiallevel of concurrency, number of parallel streams, and buffer size for therequest. 3) Returning an initial request estimation to the client. 4) Mirroring the directory structure of the source at the target site. It then generatesan execution plan that includes pair-wise source-to-target URLs for all thefiles to be replicated. This is used by the execution phase.

The Execution phase transfers the requested files, while monitoring and analyzing transfer performance for dynamic adjustment on the transferproperties. It consists of four modules. 1) The Multi-File Request Coordinator uses the information from the "execution plan" and transfer properties including the concurrency level, and accordingly instantiates the file transfer client. 2) The File Transfer Client can support any transfer protocols or services preferred by the virtual organization. Supported transferprotocol could be GridFTP, HTTPS, SCP, SFTP, etc. 3) The Recoveryand Restart module continuously monitors the health of the system and thefiles being transferred. If a transient error occurs it waits for the system torecover and depending on the transfer protocol used, either removes thepartial files transferred and reschedules the transfer or continues the transfers from the point of interruption. For example, GridFTP allows partial transfers to be resumed.

4) The module responsible for monitoring and adjusting concurrency collects dynamic transfer performance, and if significant discrepancies from the estimated performance are noticed, it adjuststhe number of concurrency and parallel streams.

The Recovery phase interacts dynamically with the components of theexecution phase to validate the completed request by collecting statistics,generating dynamic progress estimation on-demand, and validating transferred files at the end of the request. It has three functions. 1) It collectsstatistics from the execution of the replication request. 2) It generates dynamic progress estimation on-demand when a client asks for request progress status. This module needs the information on file transfers that completed, are in-progress, or are pending, as well as bandwidth usage statistics and estimation. 3) The file validation module can be running assoon as files are transferred, or at the end of the request, depending on thesite preference. The reason for preferring file validation by checksumcomparison after all transfers complete is that calculating checksums iscomputationally intensive and may perturb the running transfers. This module is also responsible for resubmitting files whose checksums indicated data corruption.

3.2   Transfer Queue Management and Balanced Concurrency

The BDM achieves high performance using a variety of techniques, including multi-threaded concurrent transfer connection management, transfer queue management and single control channel management for multiple data transfers, while the GridFTP library supports data channel cachingand pipelining.

Transfer queue management and concurrency management contribute tomore transfer throughput, including both network and storage. When thereare many small files in the dataset, continuous data flow from the storage into the network can be achieved by pre-fetching data from storage on tothe transfer queue of each concurrent transfer connection. This overlappingof storage I/O with the network I/O helps improve the performance.

Figure 2 shows the file size distribution from a dataset in IPCC CMIP-3 with 300GB of total dataset size. In this figure, most of the data files haveless than 200MB of file size, and among those smaller files, 10-20MB filesize range has the biggest portion. So, in most climate datasets, about onethird of a dataset has less than 20MB in file size. As in Figure 3, BDMmanages a DB queue for balanced access to DB from the concurrent transfer connections, and also manages the transfer queues for concurrent filetransfers. Each transfer queue checks a configurable threshold for thequeued total files size and gets more files to transfer from the DB queue when the queued total files size goes below the configured threshold. Default threshold is set to 200MB based on the file size distribution as in Figure 2. Figure 4 shows the results from the effect of transfer queue and concurrency management. When the transfer queue and concurrency arewell managed (shown in the bottom left plot of the figure), the number ofconcurrent data transfers shows consistent over time, compared to the ill ornon-managed data transfers (shown in the top left plot of the figure), and it contributes to the higher overall throughput performance (shown in thebottom right of the figure).

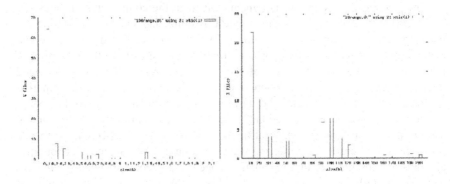

Fig. 2: Typical file size distribution of a climate dataset in IPCC CMIP-3, showing majority of dataset file sizes less than 200MB (shown left), and majority of smaller files are around 10-20MB range (shown right)

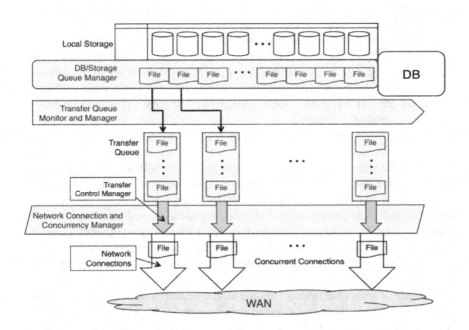

Fig. 3: Transfer Queue Management and Concurrency in the BDM

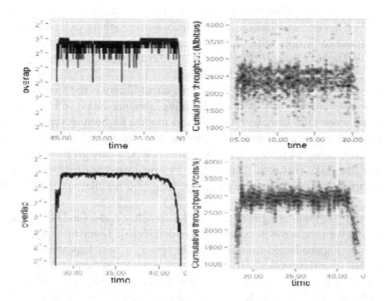

Fig. 4: Results from transfer queue and concurrency management in BDM, showing ill or non-managed queue and concurrency on the top row and optimized queue and concurrency on the bottom row, for the number of overlapping concurrent transfers on the left and the transfer throughput over time on the right.

For further optimization in the transfer queue management, the order ofthe transfer files based on file sizes is considered in concurrent transfer connections. Also, the concurrent transfers are balanced across multiplesource transfer servers, when multiple transfer servers are available at thedata source. In the future, network delay will be considered in the calculation of concurrency and parallelism in BDM file transfers.

4   NETLOGGER AND MONITORING

The NetLogger Toolkit [4] implements a comprehensive end-to-endmonitoring framework for performance analysis and troubleshooting ofdistributed applications. It includes the following components:
-   *NetLogger methodology*: A methodology, summarized in the "Logging Best Practices" document [5], for analyzing distributedsystems, which includes a simple, common message format for allmonitoring events that includes high-precision timestamps.

- *NetLogger storage and retrieval tools*: Tools for distributed logcollection, normalization, and storage in a relational database.
- *NetLogger visualization and analysis tools*: Python, SQL and R programs to flexibly retrieve, visualize, and analyze NetLoggerlogs.
- *NetLogger client API library*: C/C++, Java, Python, Perl languagebindings for source code instrumentation.

A unique feature of the NetLogger toolkit's client library is the "*log summarization*" module, which can perform adaptive summarization ofhigh-volume events. In previous joint work with Globus, this module hasbeen incorporated into GridFTP software to provide an online non-intrusive "*bottleneck detection*" capability for determining whether thetransfer bottleneck is, at any given point during the transfer, the disk ornetwork. The NetLogger storage and retrieval tools can ingest and correlate this information with logs from grid middleware and applications.

The goal of the monitoring is to track and help debug end-to-end performance. The tools that we used are NetLogger and Syslog-NG [6]. Themonitoring is based upon GridFTP logs collected from the transfer servers. These logs are forwarded, by Syslog-NG, to a designated host, where Net-Logger loads them into a database. A web interface provides a menu ofplots that displays the combined information in the database. The end-toend latency for the monitoring data, i.e. the time from the logging of thetransfer by GridFTP to the visualization of the transfer performance in anonline plot, is on the order of a few seconds. NetLogger analyses on filetransfers provided valuable information on time-varying patterns in theoverlap between multiple concurrent transfers for tuning the BDM queueand concurrency management algorithms.

5   TESTBED

The Green Data Oasis (GDO) [7] at LLNL has over 600 TB of spinning disk and serves 45 TB of CMIP-3 multimodel data. Three GridFTP server nodes with Solaris 10 running ZFS on AMD-64 hardware were used with access to the 10 Gbps ESnet network. Two NERSC Data Transfer Nodes [8] were used to transfer data located on NERSC storage units based onGPFS. A 10 Gbps SDN through OSCARS could be reserved throughESnet between NERSC and LLNL.

In this test setup, randomly selected a few climate datasets from CMIP3 were replicated for test runs under different transfer conditions. Datasetsizes range from 40 GB to 5 TB.

6   RESULTS

Fig. 5: shows a sample NetLogger graph from a series of short testruns run between NERSC and LLNL, at different times of day. The X-axis is time in seconds
since the start of each transfer, and the Y-axis shows MB/s of all currently over-
lapped transfers, which we call "cumulative MB/s". The cumulative MB/s is not a
raw value: it is derived from theGridFTP "transfer" logs, which contain the time,
duration and size of eachtransfer, by modeling each transfer as proceeding at the
average bandwidthfrom start to finish. Every time a transfer starts, its average
bandwidth isadded, and every time one ends, it is subtracted. The resulting step
function is actually a more accurate estimate of the transfer's throughput(goodput)
than the router packet counters because it does not include retransmitted packets.

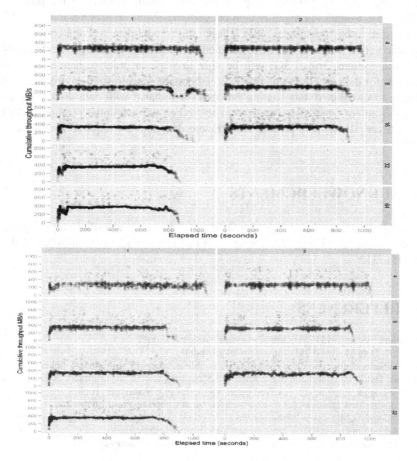

Fig. 5: Test results showing cumulative throughput in MB/sec for different concurrency level and
parallelism. Multiple tests were done at different time of the day and days.

For this path, the average bandwidth tended to improve at over 16 concurrent transfers and was consistently near the best at 32 streams. However, more tests need to be run across different network paths, storage systems, TCP stacks, etc., before we can create reliable heuristics for predicting optimal levels of concurrency and parallelism.

7   SUMMARY

The climate community faces the difficult challenges of managing the distribution of massive datasets and accessing and analyzing them. TheIPCC Coupled Model Intercomparison Project, phase 3 (CMIP-3) holds over 35 terabytes (TB) of data at the LLNL site. The IPCC Coupled ModelIntercomparison Project, phase 5 (CMIP-5) is assembling together themost comprehensive archive yet today, and it is projected to be 10petabytes (PB). These multi-model data sets and corresponding observation data sets will be distributed at many sites spanning six continents. TheEarth System Grid (ESG) will be able to scale in order to handle increasingneeds for data access in this highly collaborative decentralized environment, in relation to distributed data sharing processes associated with data discovery, access, movement, analysis, visualization and other computational resources. Bulk Data Mover (BDM) is to provide the efficient data delivery required for this scalability.

8   ACKNOWLEDGMENTS

This work was funded in part by the Office of Advanced ScientificComputing Research, Office of Science, U.S. Department of Energy, under contracts DE-AC02-05CH11231.

9   REFERENCES

[1]   Earth System Grid (ESG), http://www.earthsystemgrid.org/
[2]   Bulk Data Mover (BDM), http://sdm.lbl.gov/bdm/
[3]   Williams et al., "The Earth System Grid: Enabling Access to Multimodel Climate Simulation Data", in the Bulletin of the American Meteorological Society, February 2009.
[4]   NetLogger, http://acs.lbl.gov/NetLoggerWiki/index.php/NetLogger_Toolkit
[5]   Logging Best Practices, http://www.cedps.net/index.php/LoggingBestPractices
[6]   Syslog-NG, http://www.balabit.com/network-security/syslog-ng/opensourcelogging-system
[7]   Green Data Oasis (GDO), https://computing.llnl.gov/resources/gdo/
[8]   Data Transfer Node (DTN), http://www.nersc.gov/nusers/systems/datatran/

Grid Computing for Disaster Mitigation

Hock Lye Koh[1], Su Yean Teh[2], Taksiah A. Majid[1] and Hamidi Abdul Aziz[1]

1. Disaster Research Nexus, School of Civil Engineering, Engineering Campus, Universiti Sains Malaysia, Malaysia
2. School of Mathematical Sciences, Universiti Sains Malaysia, Malaysia

Abstract The infamous 2004 Andaman tsunami has highlighted the need to be prepared and to be resilient to such disasters. Further, recent episodes of infectious disease epidemics worldwide underline the urgency to control and manage infectious diseases. Universiti Sains Malaysia (USM) has recently formed the Disaster Research Nexus (DRN) within the School of Civil Engineering to spearhead research and development in natural disaster mitigation programs to mitigate the adverse effects of natural disasters. This paper presents a brief exposition on the aspirations of DRN towards achieving resilience in communities affected by these natural disasters. A brief review of the simulations of the 2004 Andaman tsunami, with grid application is presented. Finally, the application of grid technology in large scale simulations of disease transmission dynamics is discussed.

Keywords Tsunami, disease, grid simulation, high performance computing

1 INTRODUCTION TO DRN

Giving due consideration to society perception of safety and experience of past natural disasters, the newly established Disaster Research Nexus (DRN) will develop long-term sustainable research methodology for comprehensive disaster management, focusing on disaster resilient living spaces and communities. Scientific analyses and predictions of disaster processes within the context of societal development and sophistication will be conducted based on technologies and methodologies well established for disaster mitigation design and planning. Community disaster management will be developed, taking into consideration cultural aspirations, sustainable development, community safety and comfort. Theories and practices of disaster mitigation policy that accommodate land use redevelopment, conservation of environment, and preservation of community harmony and safety will be established. DRN will co-ordinate the development of science and technology, human resources, education and community awareness to better understand, monitor, model and manage the risks associated with natural disasters. DRN will pursue its goal in advancing and communicating useful knowledge regarding natural disasters and community preparedness, response and recovery for effective

S.C. Lin and E. Yen (eds.), *Data Driven e-Science: Use Cases and Successful Applications of Distributed Computing Infrastructures (ISGC 2010)*, DOI 10.1007/978-1-4419-8014-4_34, © Springer Science+Business Media, LLC 2011

mitigation. Using an interdisciplinary framework, DRN fosters information sharing and promotes integration of activities among researchers, practitioners and policy makers; supports and conducts relevant research; and provides educational opportunities for the next generation of natural hazard scholars and professionals. The prime objectives consist of conducting fundamentally sound research of deep scientific interest, producing results which are reliable, accurate, and of practical use to society and community. The Mission of DRN is to:

1. Coordinate the development of technology and expertise to deal with a broad spectrum of issues arising from natural disasters;
2. Conduct rigorous and cutting-edge research on natural disasters, damage monitoring and risk assessment;
3. Collaborate with other research centers and institutes to extend the research to a broad social, economic and financial context;
4. Provide resources and support services to national and international projects that require natural disasters considerations.

2   METHODOLOGY

The sophistication of urban social structures contributes to increasing disaster vulnerability. Developing countries in particular face intensive progression of disaster vulnerability caused by population increase, adverse economic conditions, as well as social-environmental problems. DRN promotes research on integrated programs for disaster reduction, which encompass all phases of the disaster management cycle, focusing on the following domains: hazard prediction, community preparedness and education; reliable and timely information and intelligence dissemination leading to appropriate societal response in time of emergency. Collaborative research with natural scientists, social scientists, engineers, NGOs and practitioners will be conducted to accomplish DRN mission. Recognizing that disaster management is as much science as arts, DRN will integrate arts and sciences towards disaster resilience. Education, community awareness and preparedness will be a focus of this approach. DRN works to strengthen communication between the hazard academic scientists and on-site application communities to improve the implementation of hazards prediction, preparedness and mitigation leading to effective emergency management programs. DRN will be a recognized resource center for researchers and practitioners who wish to obtain the most current scientific knowledge and best practices available to solve hazards-related problems. DRN accomplishes its work through four major activities: information dissemination and services, regular training workshops, basic scientific research and dedicated consultancy services. DRN will host annual events for people interested in learning about and contributing to the education and research programs. High school students are particular targets as they form the future foundation of society.

3   RESEARCH AREAS

There are several areas of research interest that are within the scope of DRN including atmospheric and hydrospheric disasters for risk reduction. Research areas
include flood, hydrology, hydraulics and coastal engineering at various spatial and
temporal scales. Typhoons, tsunamis and monsoons are some of the typical processes that might lead to severe storm surges, high waves and associated coastal
disasters. Further, heavy precipitations could give rise to severe flash floods, particularly under the scenarios of sea level rise and climate change. Wetlands and
mangroves serve several important ecosystem functions, the demise of which may
lead to major natural disasters. Hence, a systematic and quantitative study by
means of physically based models and monitoring is essential to protect and enhance their ecological functions. Only two fields relating to the simulations of tsunami evolution and infectious disease transmission dynamics are discussed in this
paper. Tsunamis are large, potentially destructive sea waves, most of which are
formed as a result of submarine earthquakes. But tsunami may also result from the
eruption or collapse of island or coastal volcanoes and from the formation of giant
marine landslides. Tsunami can potentially be very destructive; hence methods for
mitigation are needed to protect vulnerable coastal regions and communities. In
the recent past, several infectious disease epidemics have occurred in many parts
of the world. These diseases include H1N1, SARS and dengue, which have the potential of causing global havoc. The simulations of the transmission dynamics of
these diseases provide a means to suggest control measures to reduce their impacts. However, these types of simulations often involve large computational resources, for which grid technology may be applied to enhance the simulation efficiency. We will demonstrate how these two types of simulations are performed in
the traditional nongrid environment. Then we will show how grid computing may
be used to enhance computational efficiency.

4   SIMULATION OF TSUNAMI EVOLUTION

A good mathematical description of tsunami propagation may be given by the so-
called Shallow Water Equations (1) to (3) as follows.

$$\frac{\partial \eta}{\partial t} + \frac{\partial M}{\partial x} + \frac{\partial N}{\partial y} = 0 \tag{1}$$

$$\frac{\partial M}{\partial t} + \frac{\partial}{\partial x}\left(\frac{M^2}{D}\right) + \frac{\partial}{\partial y}\left(\frac{MN}{D}\right) + gD\frac{\partial \eta}{\partial x} + \frac{gn^2}{D^{7/3}}M\sqrt{M^2 + N^2} = 0 \tag{2}$$

$$\frac{\partial N}{\partial t} + \frac{\partial}{\partial x}\left(\frac{MN}{D}\right) + \frac{\partial}{\partial y}\left(\frac{N^2}{D}\right) + gD\frac{\partial \eta}{\partial y} + \frac{gn^2}{D^{7/3}}N\sqrt{M^2 + N^2} = 0 \tag{3}$$

$$\Delta t \le \frac{\Delta x}{\sqrt{2gh}} \tag{4}$$

Here, discharge fluxes (M, N) in the x- and y- directions are related to velocities u and v by the expressions $M=u(h+\eta)=uD$, $N=v(h+\eta)=vD$, where h is the sea depth and η is the water elevation above mean sea level. The staggered explicit finite difference method is employed to solve the Shallow Water Equations, as the scheme is known to perform well, provided that the time step Δt fulfils the Courant stability criterion (Equation 4). Details regarding this numerical scheme used in the in-house tsunami simulation model TUNA developed by the authors are available elsewhere (Koh et al. 2009a, b; Teh et al. 2009) and hence will be omitted. An initial vertical lifting of the seabed due to the 2004 Andaman earthquake is represented by a five-segment fault, resulting in a leading depression tsunami wave propagating towards Thailand and Malaysia. Figure 1 (first frame from left) clearly demonstrates the initial waves splitting into two halves, one propagating eastwards, the other westwards. The tsunami waves reach the offshore of Phuket of Thailand after a travel time of about 2 hours (Figure 1, second frame). Subsequently the waves propagate towards Malaysia, arriving offshore of Langkawi (Figure 1, third frame) after 3 hours. The final snapshot (Figure 1, fourth frame) shows the waves propagating through the Straits of Malacca, having moved pass Penang. The computational time used for one simulation is about 8 hours on a regular lower end PC, with a scheme consisting of more than 10 million computational nodes. For community disaster mitigation, we need to perform thousands of simulations in order to generate a large database of tsunami propagation scenarios to permit adequate assessment of vulnerability and to prepare risk maps for affected coastal regions. Hence, the need to reduce computational time is obvious. Through careful analysis and reorganization of the finite difference scheme, we are able to shorten the computational time to 2 hours, without loss of accuracy and reliability of the simulation results on a similar PC. First, the nonlinear terms consisting of the friction terms can be removed as friction terms contribute insignificantly towards the simulation results in deep water. Then we use optimization methods to improve computational performance, such as loop interchange, loop unrolling, loop fusion/fission and floating point division, as briefly shown in Figure 2. Finally, a higher end PC reduces the computational time to 1 hour.

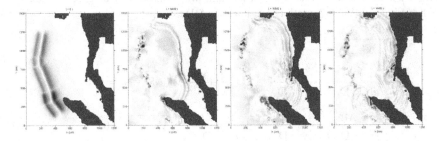

Fig. 1: Tsunami propagation snapshots for Andaman tsunami source with a five-segment fault

5 SIMULATION OF VECTOR-BORNE DISEASE

Mosquitoes are vectors that transmit diseases such as dengue, encephalitis and malaria to humans and animals. The authors have developed a set of spatial-temporal simulation models code-named DEER (Dengue and Encephalitis Eradication Routines) that provide simulation tools for fundamental understanding of the transmission dynamics of mosquito-borne diseases. Mosquitoes disperse in the form of traveling waves, with characteristics that can be determined from observations and from simulations of the model DEER. Numerical simulations and theoretical estimation may be performed to assess the wave front velocity, mosquito density distribution patterns and the disease prevalence. The results of these simulations provide the scientific basis for assessing the effectiveness of mosquito and associated disease containment strategy.

Loop Unrolling

- Replicate loop body;
- Perform several array elements during each iteration;
- Can be done automatically by compiler.

```
DO J = 1, N
    C(J) = A(J) + B(J)
ENDDO
```

```
DO J = 1, N, 4
    C(J) = A(J) + B(J)
    C(J+1) = A(J+1) + B(J+1)
    C(J+2) = A(J+2) + B(J+2)
    C(J+3) = A(J+3) + B(J+3)
ENDDO
```

Loop Interchanges

- Change the order of the loop in a nested loop;
- Better memory access patterns;
- Elimination of data dependencies;
- Fortran stores "column-wise".

Access Order == Storage Order

```
DO J = 1, 4
    DO I = 1, 4
        C(I,J) = A(I,J) + B(I,J)
    ENDDO
ENDDO
```

Loop Fusion/Fission

- Fusion: Merge multiple loops into one;
  - Dependent operations in separate loops

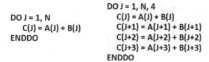

- Fission: Split one loop into multiple loops
  - Independent operations in a single loop

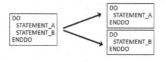

Floating Point Division

- Floating point division is an expensive operation;
- Replace a division with multiplication;
- Done automatically by most compilers at higher levels of optimization.

```
DO J = 1, N
    C(J) = A(J)/B(J)
ENDDO
```

```
DO J = 1, N
    TEMP = 1.0/ B(J)
    C(J) = A(J)*TEMP
ENDDO
```

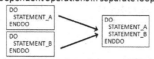

Fig. 2: Code Optimization consisting of loop unrolling, loop interchange, loop fusion/fission and floating point division

5.1   The Model MOS

We first describe a temporal model MOS for simulating mosquito density within a small homogenous environment, without diffusion and without advection of mosquitoes. We divide the mosquito population into two groups, namely the adult wing mosquito and the aquatic form (Focks et al. 1993). Let $W=W(t)$ be the density of adult wing mosquito and $A=A(t)$ be the density of the aquatic form (including eggs, larvae and pupae). The mathematical model can be formulated as Equation (5), with definitions and units of the model parameters given in Table 1.

$$\frac{dV}{dt} = \begin{cases} \dfrac{dW}{dt} = -\alpha_w W + \gamma A \\ \dfrac{dA}{dt} = \beta W - (\alpha_A + \gamma) A \end{cases} \quad \text{where } \gamma = \frac{1}{L_A} \text{ and } \beta = \frac{b}{L_w} \tag{5}$$

Table 1: List of symbols, variables and units used in MOS

Symbol	Variables	Explanation	Unit
α_W	ALPHAW	Mortality rate of wing mosquito	day^{-1}
α_A	ALPHAA	Mortality rate of aquatic form	day^{-1}
b	EGGS	Number of eggs per oviposition	eggs mos^{-1}
β	BETA	Oviposition rate of wing female mosquito	eggs mos^{-1} d^{-1}
γ	GAMMA	Development rate of aquatic form	day^{-1}
L_W	WLD	Number of days of wing reproductive cycle	day
L_A	ALD	Number of days of aquatic form	day

5.2 The Model MOSVIRUS

Secondly, the 2x2 system of equations for MOS can be readily modified to simulate transmission of dengue virus between mosquitoes and human (Esteva & Vargas 1998; Derouich & Boutayeb 2006; Yang & Ferreira 2007; Tan et al. 2009) in a homogenous environment as shown in Equation (6). Details regarding the variables and associated parameter values are given in Table 2. Figure 3 shows the input interface for the software MOSVIRUS, with default values as indicated therein.

$$\frac{\partial WI}{\partial t} = -ALPHAW \times WI + \left(\frac{DIS \times BITR}{HN + AHOST}\right) \times WS \times HI$$

$$\frac{\partial WS}{\partial t} = CONV \times A \times \left(1 - \frac{W}{CCW}\right) - ALPHAW \times WS - \left(\frac{DIS \times BITR}{HN + AHOST}\right) \times WS \times HI$$

$$\frac{\partial A}{\partial t} = BETA \times W \times \left(1 - \frac{A}{CCA}\right) - ALPHAA \times A - CONV \times A$$

$$\frac{\partial HI}{\partial t} = \left(\frac{HDIS \times BITR}{HN + AHOST}\right) \times HS \times WI - REMV \times HI - ALPHAH \times HI$$

$$\frac{\partial HS}{\partial t} = ALPHAH \times HN - ALPHAH \times HS - \left(\frac{HDIS \times BITR}{HN + AHOST}\right) \times HS \times WI$$

$$\frac{\partial HR}{\partial t} = REMV \times HI - ALPHAH \times HR \tag{6}$$

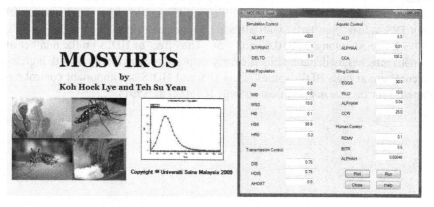

Fig. 3: MOSVIRUS input interface

5.3   Simulation Results

Then we simulate mosquito population and disease transmission by means of
MOS and MOSVIRUS to ensure that both models are properly formulated and
coded. Comparison between simulation results for both models and analytical solutions indicate proper performance of both models. It is widely known that mosquito populations are sensitive to temperature (Schoofield et al. 1981; Rueda et al.
1990). Hence, we simulate the impact of temperature variations on mosquito populations as shown in Figure 4. With cold temperature between 4 and 6 degree Cel-
sius (°C) in Case 1, both adult and aquatic forms quickly crash as the cold temperature causes high mortality and low reproduction. At higher temperature
between 8 and 12 °C for Case 2, both aquatic and adult forms manage to survive
at low density. However, at favorable temperature between 15 and 21 °C, both
forms respond favorably to achieve high density. We have chosen the temperature
to vary within short intervals to illustrate that mosquitoes can respond to temperature quickly due to their fast growth and reproduction cycles, implying that quick
response to temperature is indeed possible within a confined environment. However the real concern is the potential impact of climate change on mosquito population distribution over large spatial and temporal scales, and the associated health
risk (Patz et al. 1998; Reiter 2001; Hopp & Foley 2003), the simulation of which
can be facilitated by the application of grid computing.

Figures 5 and 6 summarize the effects of human-mosquito transmission probability DIS and HDIS on the incidence of dengue infections in human, subject to
MOSVIRUS parameter values given by Table 2. DIS is the transmission probability of dengue virus from infected human to susceptible mosquitoes; while HDIS is
the transmission probability of dengue virus from infected mosquitoes to susceptible human. With all other parameter values fixed as in Table 2, DIS is varied
among 0.60, 0.40 and 0.20. Figure 5 clearly demonstrates the effects of DIS on the
number of humans been infected with dengue virus, with high incidence rate at
high DIS values. Similarly, with all other parameter values fixed as in Table 2,
HDIS is varied among 0.70, 0.60 and 0.50. The effect of HDIS on the number of
humans infected by dengue virus is clearly demonstrated in Figure 6, with high incidence rate at high HDIS values. Thus DIS and HDIS are important control parameters for dengue management strategy (Gratz et al. 1991).

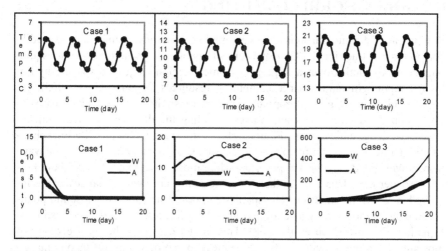

Fig. 4: Mosquito population subject to temperature variations

Table 2: Parameter values for MOSVIRUS

Variable	ALPHAA	ALD	CCA	EGGS	CONV	ALPHAW	WLD	CCW
Value	0.01	5	100	30.0	0.2	0.04	10	25
Variable	BETA	REMV	ALPHAH	DIS	HDIS	BITR	AHOST	
Value	3.0	0.1	0.0	0.75	0.75	0.5	0.00	

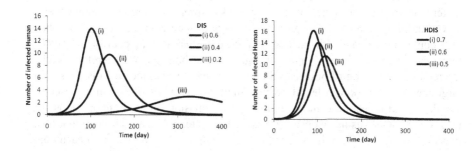

Right side Fig. 5: Infected humans when DIS is (i) 0.20, (ii) 0.40, and (iii) 0.60
Left side   Fig. 6: Infected humans when HDIS is (i) 0.50, (ii) 0.60, and (iii) 0.70

6   ROLE OF GRID COMPUTING

Simulation of dengue transmission over small geographical domain can be readily performed by traditional PC. However, simulations of swamp water mosquito population dynamics over a large geographical region subject to varying hydrological input will require large computing resources (Shaman et al. 2005), for which grid computing is appropriate. Further, mosquito can transmit diseases to other animals, such as birds and horses, enabling the diseases to spread quickly over large geographical areas. Figure 7 shows the spread of West Nile Encephalitis (WNE) in USA over a period of three years, starting at 1999, indicating a wave front travel speed of 1000 km per year, while mosquitoes can only fly about tens of meter per day. This implies that two time scales and two spatial scales are involved in WNE transmission. The spatial-temporal distribution of mosquito population may be modeled by a set of partial differential equations PDE consisting of Equations 7 and 8 (Koh et al. 2008). This model describes the local ecology of mosquito populations without disease subject to reproduction, diffusion and advective transport, over a heterogeneous region. The dynamics of disease transmission can then be incorporated into this model, using MOSVIRUS as a template.

$$\frac{\partial}{\partial t} W(x,t) = D \frac{\partial^2}{\partial x^2} W(x,t) - \frac{\partial}{\partial x} \left(v\ W(x,t)\ \right)$$

$$+ \gamma\ A\ (x,t) \left(1 - \frac{W(x,t)}{k_1} \right) - \mu_1\ W(x,t) \tag{7}$$

$$\frac{\partial}{\partial t} A\ (x,t) = r \left(1 - \frac{A\ (x,t)}{k_2} \right) W(x,t) - \left(\mu_2 + \gamma \right) A\ (x,t) \tag{8}$$

For WNE transmission, the process involves birds that fly over long distances of tens of km over a matter of days or weeks, spreading diseases among themselves and to mosquitoes. The birds will infect other birds in the same areas when they come into contact with each other. Figure 8 illustrates the pathways of WNE transmission among birds, horses, mosquitoes and humans. We therefore model the regional migration of birds and the regional spread of associated diseases with large meshes of 10 km in length, while smaller mesh sizes of 100 m are used to simulate local mosquito ecology and local transmission of WNE among mosquitoes and humans, using MOSVIRUS as a template. Hence, each computational mesh of 10 km by 10 km is assigned to a core computational grid, with each core performing the internal simulations of local mosquito-human transmission via MOSVIRUS formulation. This approach may be modified for simulations of other infectious diseases involving birds, animals and humans, such as the avian flu H5N1, which may be transmitted over large distances by migratory birds. Further, the surface protein structure of these viruses may be simulated by grid computing for the purpose of searching for effective drug.

Fig. 7: Spread of West Nile Encephalitis   Fig. 8: Transmission method of WNE

7 CONCLUSION

This paper presents a brief exposition on the newly established Disaster Research Nexus in USM regarding its objectives, missions and methodology in achieving its goals. Then a concise description of two types of large scale simulations on tsunami propagation and disease transmission dynamics is provided. Finally, the role of grid computing in improving computational efficiency is discussed. It is hoped that fruitful international research collaboration on grid application to large scale simulations for natural disaster mitigation could be established among grid community.

8 ACKNOWLEDGEMENT

Financial support provided by Grants 1001/PMATHS/817024, 1001/PMATHS /817025, 1001/PMATHS/811093, 305/PMATHS/613131, 302/PMATHS/611897 and 1001/PPTM/817006 is gratefully acknowledged.

REFERENCES

[1] Derouich, M. & Boutayeb, A. (2006). Dengue fever: Mathematical modeling and computer simulation. Applied Mathematics and Computation 177, 528-544.
[2] Esteva, L. & Vargas, C. (1998). Analysis of a dengue disease transmission model. Mathematical Biosciences 150, 131-151.
[3] Focks, D. A., Haile, D. C., Daniels, E. & Moun, G. A. (1993). Dynamics life table model for Aedes Aegypti: Analysis of the literature and model development. Journal of Medical Entomology 30, 1003-1018.

[4] Gratz, N. G. (1991). Emergency control of Aedes aegypti as a disease vector in urban areas. Journal of the American Mosquito Control Association 7, 353-365.

[5] Hopp, M. J. & Foley, J. A. (2003). Worldwide fluctuations in dengue fever cases related to climate variability. Climate Research 25, 85-94.

[6] Koh, H.L., Teh, S.Y., Izani, A.M.I. & DeAngelis, D.L. (2008). Modeling Biological Invasion: The Case of Dengue and Mangrove. Invited Lecture in International Conference on Mathematical Biology – ICMB07. American Institute of Physics Conference Proceedings, Volume 971, New York, p. 11-18.

[7] Koh, H.L., Teh, S.Y., Liu, P.L.-F., Izani, A.M.I. & Lee, H.L. (2009a). Simulation of Andaman 2004 Tsunami for Assessing Impact on Malaysia. Journal of Asian Earth Sciences 36, 74-83.

[8] Koh, H.L., Teh, S.Y., Izani, A.M.I., Lee, H.L. & Kew, L.M. (2009b). Simulation of Future Andaman Tsunami into Straits of Malacca by TUNA. Journal of Earthquakes and Tsunamis 3 (2), 89-100.

[9] Patz, J. A., Martens, W.J.M., Focks, D. A. & Jetten, T. H. (1998). Dengue Fever Epidemic Potential as Projected by General Circulation Models of Global Climate Change. Environmental Health Perspective 106(3), 147-153.

[10] Reiter, P. (2001). Climate Change and Mosquito-Borne Disease. Environmental Health Perspectives 109, 141-161.

[11] Rueda, L. M. Patel, K. J., Axtell, R. C. & Stinner, R. E. (1990). Temperature-dependent development and survival rates of culex quinquefasciatus and aedes aegypti (diptera: Culicidae). Journal of Medical Entomology 27, 892-898.

[12] Schoofield, R. M., Sharpe, P. J. H. & Magnuson, C. E. (1981). Non-linear regression of biological temperature-dependent rate models based on an absolute reaction-rate theory. Journal of Theoretical Biology 88, 719-731.

[13] Shaman, J., Spiegelman, M., Cane, M. & Stieglitz, M. (2005). A hydrologically driven model of swamp water mosquito population dynamics. Ecological Modelling 194, 395-404.

[14] Tan, K.B., Koh, H.L. & Teh, S.Y. (2009). Modeling Dengue Fever Subject to Temperature Change. Proceedings of the 6th International Conference on Fuzzy Systems and Knowledge Discovery (FSKD'09), Volume 5, 14-16 August 2009, Tianjin, China. The Institute of Electrical and Electronics Engineers (IEEE), USA, p. 61-65.

[15] Teh, S.Y., Koh, H.L., Liu, P.L.-F., Izani, A.M.I. & Lee, H.L. (2009). Analytical and Numerical Simulation of Tsunami Mitigation by Mangroves in Penang, Malaysia. Journal of Asian Earth Sciences 36, 38-46.

[16] Yang, H. M. & Ferreira, C. P. (2007). Assessing the effects of vector control on dengue transmission. Applied Mathematics and Computation 198, 401-413

Part XII
Applications on Biomedicine and Life Sciences

Applicability of Free Energy Calculations Using High–Throughput Grid Approach

Jan Kmunicek[1], Petr Kulhanek[2] and Zora Strelcova[2]

1. CESNET, Czech Republic
2. National Centre for Biomolecular Research, Masaryk University, Czech Republic

Abstract   Free energy calculations tightly bind together experimental observations and computer–aided design through corresponding simulations at atomic level. Nowadays, free energy calculations represent a cornerstone for obtaining deeper insight into any biomolecular system, its molecular structure and especially dynamic behaviour. Despite this fact, several challenges have to be considered before routine utilization of this type of calculations. At first one has to deal properly with so–called sampling problem. Secondly, the appropriate way how to treat their extreme time demands has to be applied for obtaining converged and reliable data comparable with the experimental ones. Here we present the experience obtained through design, implementation and subsequent application of Multiple Walkers Approach (MWA) connected with Adaptive Biasing Force (ABF) and corresponding advantages and added values of MWA ABF run within distributed, heterogeneous grid environment under the EUAsia virtual organization (VO).

Keywords   grid, distributed computing, virtual organization, Enabling Grids in E–SciencE, EUAsia VO, Multiple Walkers Approach, Adaptive Biasing Force

1   INTRODUCTION

Nowadays, the grid phenomenon has influenced nearly any research area trying to tackle computationally demanding tasks and challenges. The origin of grid activities lies in the high-throughput approach used primarily for the purposes of large, international high energy physics experiments. However, there are a lot of other promising areas and application domains utilizing the available grid environment through their own high-throughput computations. One of such promising areas is free energy calculations within the computational chemistry domain. Here we describe our implementation of Multiple Walkers Approach (MWA) connected with Adaptive Biasing Force (ABF) used to estimate free energy for supramolecular chemical systems.

A generic overview of grid technologies currently available is provided in Chapter 2. Next section – Chapter 3 – is dedicated to description of methods used

S.C. Lin and E. Yen (eds.), *Data Driven e-Science: Use Cases and Successful Applications of Distributed Computing Infrastructures (ISGC 2010)*, DOI 10.1007/978-1-4419-8014-4_35,
© Springer Science+Business Media, LLC 2011

for estimation of free energy and a molecular system studied. Chapter 4 is devoted to detail the achieved results and in Chapter 5 we summarize the observations and derive plans for future research in this area.

2   GRID TECHNOLOGIES

The most promising technology emerging from the mature utilization of advanced high-speed networks is the grid [1]. Grid environments represent a central layer built on the network ubiquitous infrastructure and providing an access to desired network of worldwide scientific knowledge. During last few years the grid technology moved from experimental and prototype (testing) version into a unique, worldwide production service for thousands of users performing global scientific tasks. Nowadays, Grids are considered to be a base of global e-Infrastructures providing an easier access for small and distributed research groups interconnecting scientists from many different fields to completely new technologies thus allowing them to produce, store, access and manipulate massive amounts of data, to utilize large amounts of CPUs to their maximal computational potential and to access high-end facilities (i.e. supercomputers). Moreover, grids brought a set of previously unknown added values in facilitating distributed collaborations as well as in provisioning of new ways of community building through remote resource sharing across different administrative domains.

The term grid can be defined as a large, distributed system [2] composed of computational and storage capacities (eventually together with further instruments) of distinct owners interconnected by high-speed network. These resources create an illusion of uniform, computational and storage space without perception of boundaries [3] formed by proprietary or administrative relations.

Basically, several different types of grid environments can be recognized according to its primary function. Originally, at the very first were the computational grids trying to fulfil ever-growing request for computational power with low cost of activation barrier in their utilization. The computational grid is expected to provide a computational service (i.e. provide secured services pro running applications at distributed computational resources). Generally speaking, it represents a "virtual distributed computer" for solving computationally demanding tasks as it dynamically aggregates computational capacity of huge number of individual computers. Simultaneously with computational grids one could expect needs to manage all the data produced during massive computation campaigns and challenges. This led to huge effort investments into forming a logical extension of computational environments – data grids – serving for remote management and transparent access to millions of files. Data grids basically represent a processing of large datasets using the services of computational grids. The data grid can be characterized by sharing of vast amounts of data, by provision of secure access to those data and allowing their subsequent management (solved using the form of replicated data catalogs creating of an illusion of uniform mass data storage). On the top of this hierarchy stays the third type of grid environments that is represented by informational/knowledge grids often also called as collaborative and/or application grids. This is an ultimate extension of grid approach into global sharing of resources of any kind at all. The knowledge grids are characterized by extension of data grid approach possibilities with provision of data categorization, ontology, knowledge sharing and workflow development. The collaborative added values including special cutting-edge services as the access to remote instruments, sensors and devices, smooth community/virtual laboratories building etc. are also standard part of the knowledge grids.

The principles driving the grid environment utilization can be summarized into following simple scheme: users should accept from the grid resources (CPUs or their power, respectively; disc space; transfer capacity of networks; special hardware) that they need, when they need and exactly where they need them. Grid is expected to provide unified access, security and reliable services on one hand and the necessary accounting on the other hand.

2.1 Worldwide Production Grid

Currently, all European grid computing projects are dominated by the Enabling Grids for E-sciencE (EGEE) [4] leading the way by providing a computing support infrastructure for over thousands of researchers from many distinct domains. The EGEE project brings together experts from more than 50 countries with the common aim of building on recent advances in Grid technology and developing a service Grid infrastructure which is available to scientists 24 hours-a-day (see infrastructure details in Table 1). The project provides researchers in academia and business with access to a production level Grid infrastructure, independent of their geographic location. The EGEE project also focuses on attracting a wide range of new users to the Grid. The main focus of the project is to expand and optimize Europe's largest production Grid infrastructure by continuous operation of the infrastructure, support for more user communities, and addition of further computational and data resources.

Table 1: EGEE infrastructure statistics.

Number of sites connected	260+
Number of countries connected	55
Number of CPUs available	24/7 cca 150 000
Storage capacity available	cca 28 PB disc space

Presently, EGEE worldwide production environment support quite a number of distinct application domains ranging from archaeology, astronomy and astrophysics, biotechnology, bioinformatics and biomedical sciences, civil protection, computational chemistry, computer science, earth sciences, finances, fusion, geo-physics, high-energy physics, life sciences up to multimedia and material sciences (Table 2). The end user work within EGEE is organized through appropriate sets of virtual organizations (VOs). The concept of virtual organization has been firstly introduced by I. Foster and C. Kesselman [1] defining the grid computing as "co-ordinated resource sharing and problem solving in dynamic, multi institutional vir-tual organizations". The virtual organization can be therefore defined as a sum of resources and persons usually spanning multiple administrative domains and even countries working on a joint project allowing seamless resource sharing and creat-ing an abstraction of the user community (set of users and resources with a com-mon goal in other words). Considerable number of EGEE virtual organizations (at least in the inital phase of EGEE project during which the appropriate user com-munities started to be engaged through formation and management of correspond-ing virtual organizations) have been set up and built as so-called catch-all virtual organizations. The catch-all virtual organizations represent an effective way for users to use grid environments. Catch-all VOs are provided as a service to users communities as part of user support activities of several projects. Catch-all VOs tie together resource providers and different end user communities, thus forming a crucial step towards routine production way of worldwide grid platform, which is easily available to users. Decreasing the entrance barrier is especially important for various regions with high heterogeneity and different grid knowledge of in-volved parties. Crucial advantages of catch-all VOs are especially their open envi-ronment nature (from the point of user access, application deployment, and high-level tools installation). The routine catch-all VO management is performed by dedicated administrators. In addition, the new user communities willing to test the grid environment are completely free from establishing their own VO before try-ing a Grid as the catch-all VO provide the initial outsourcing of all critical VO services. The suitable examples of such successes catch-all VO fulfilling regional needs are the Virtual Organization for Central Europe (VOCE) or EUAsia VO.

Table 2: EGEE end users statistics.

Number of VOs using EGEE	~200
Number of registered VOs	~140
Number of registered users	~14 000
Number of jobs	~330k jobs/day

3   FREE ENERGY CALCULATIONS

The free energy is a thermodynamical quantity that uniquely describes the state of chemical system. As it is a state function, its change is intimately connected with kinetics and equilibrium of chemical processes. Thus its knowledge can be helpful in computer aided rational drug design or in description of processes, which cannot be directly studied by experimental means. For such outstanding features, free energy calculations by computer simulations have attracted a lot of interest in the past. Quite huge effort was put to the development of the Potential of Mean Force (PMF) methods [5] because they are able to describe kinetics of studied systems. Popular methods that belongs to PMF group are constrained dynamics [6], umbrella sampling [7], metadynamics [8] and Adaptive Biasing Force (ABF) method [9]. All of them bias studied system along prescribed set of Collective Variables (CVs) (also called reaction coordinates) in such a way that the free energy of unbiased system can be easily recovered either directly from underlying simulations or during post-processing of their results. Despite achieved success in this area, very long simulations are usually necessary to obtain converged and reliable results. To overcome this problem, several techniques were recently suggested and used on the top of mentioned PMF methods. Promising methods are replica exchange molecular dynamics [10], string method [11], and Multiple Walkers Approach (MWA) [12]. Their common feature is parallel simulation of several replicas of studied system. Since communication overhead among replicas is usually very small, all of these methods are suitable for large scale calculations. In this work, we will demonstrate the utilization of ABF method accelerated by MWA in the grid environment. Both methods were tested on the study of a molecular switch from a pseudorotaxane family [13, 14].

Adaptive Biasing Force Method. [9, 15] The method will be briefly reviewed in this section. As mentioned above, the success of every PMF method lies in proper way of system biasing. In ABF method, the system potential V is biased by underlying free energy A in such a way that a motion in the space of collective variables is barrier-free. In other words, this motion is solely govern by diffusive motion, which guarantee that the system visits all places in CV space in reasonable time. The aim of ABF method is the calculation of free energy thus a simple question arises. How such unknown free energy can be applied? The answer is in adaptive application of continuously refined PMF. At the beginning, the molecular dynamics is started without any bias and PMF is calculated. Whenever the number of samples in any bin reaches predefined threshold, the calculated PMF is applied to the system. Such perturbed system has then tendency to visit places in CV space further from the starting point. As the number of samples in every bin increases, PMF is more precise and the barrier-free motion in an entire CV space is achieved very soon. The free energy is not direct outcome of ABF simulation but its derivative is. Thus the resulting free energy has to be obtained by numerical integration of PMF.

Multiple Walkers Approach. This idea was firstly used with metadynamics [12]. The utilization of MWA together with ABF is also very simple. The approach employs N independent molecular dynamic simulations biased by ABF (so called walkers) that feel the estimated PMF accumulated from all walkers. With this approach, the sampling of CV space is N-times faster than in conventional ABF run. A key essence of MWA is independence of the individual walkers. This condition is easily fulfilled, for example, when walkers start from entirely different configurations (reactants, product, and intermediates). But even, if these different starting configurations are not known in advance, one can start from the same configuration with different starting velocities. In this case, all walkers become incoherent very soon. ABF is not the only method that can be accelerated by MWA.

3.1 Pseudorotaxane Based Molecular Switch

Pseudorotaxanes [16] are supramolecular complexes which are formed by a cyclic molecule (wheel) threaded on a string molecule (axle). A key property of such complexes is a limited motion of both components to each other but without prohibition of complex dissociation. Pseudorotaxanes have several unique properties therefore they are intensively studied both experimentally [13, 14] and theoretically [17-19]. In our work, pseudorotaxane complexes composed of cucurbit[7]uril and 4,4'-bipyridinium based axle (1,1'-bis(4-carboxybutyl)-4,4'-bipyridinium) molecules (Fig. 1) were studied.

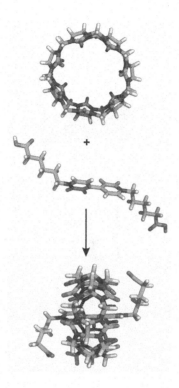

Fig. 1: Schematic representation of pseudorotaxane formation: (top) cucurbit[7]uril; (middle) axle component; (bottom) formed pseudorotaxane complex.

Since both axle terminals bear carboxylic groups, their protonation states can be changed by different pH conditions. At low pH (~3), both terminals are protonated (COOH) and the axle has +2 charge, which originates from the viologen core (State I). On contrary, at high pH (~9), both terminals loose two protons (COO-) and the axle then becomes electro neutral (State II). According to reported NMR, thermodynamic, and kinetic studies [13, 14] it was found that both states differ in the wheel position on the axle. The wheel prefers to bind to aliphatic sidearm (side position A and A') of the axle in State I rather than around the nucleus of the axle (central position B) in State II (see Fig. 2).

This pseudorotaxane system can be considered as a molecular switch, which is switched on and off by different pH conditions. Unfortunately, the molecular basis of this process is not fully understood. Thus, we used the free energy calculations to obtain more information about this interesting phenomenon.

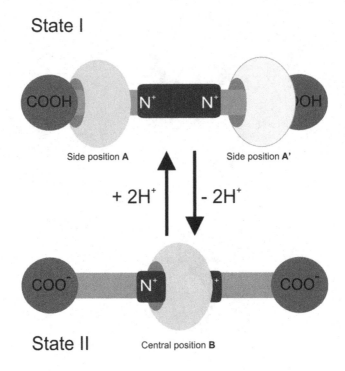

Fig. 2. Principle of molecular switch based on pseudorotaxane complex.

4   RESULTS AND DISCUSSION

Two distinct approaches accelerating free energy calculations employing ABF method were tested. One relies on the utilization of MPI parallel version of pmemd program. The second one uses MWA. Their comparison towards simple sequential run is shown in Fig. 3.

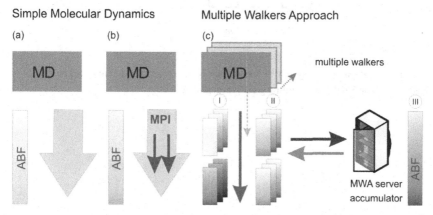

Fig. 3: Tested variants of ABF method: (a) simple ABF run; (b) MPI parallelized ABF run; and (c) MWA accelerated ABF run.

From profiling of modified pmemd program, it follows that almost 95 % of execution time is spent by the computation of potential of V(x). The rest is spent by integrating equations of motions, computing PMF, and constraining bonds including hydrogen atoms (via SHAKE procedure [20]). Thus it is straightforward to speed up an entire calculation by parallel computation of potential of V(x). Luckily, pmemd was already parallelized using MPI and used MPI implementation was not in conflict with our code modification due to ABF method.

We tested scaling of the MPI code on SMP (symmetric multiprocessing) system containing two Intel Quad-Core Xeon processors (E5472) clocked at 3 GHz (Fig. 4). Reasonable scaling was achieved in the range of 1 to 4 CPUs. For higher number of CPUs, the scaling drops down rapidly. This bad behaviour is probably due to very small size of simulated system (about 21 000 atoms), because significantly better scaling results were reported for larger systems [21]. Thus our results indicate that the free energy calculation acceleration by MPI parallelization is only moderate and reasonable only on SMP systems. To achieve higher acceleration a different strategy was tested. It is called Multiple Walkers Approach and its implementation will be described in detail in the following section.

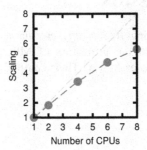

Fig. 4: (dark, red) Parallel scaling of MPI version of modified pmemd program tested on dual Intel Quad-Core Xeon SMP system; (gray, green) ideal scaling.

4.1 MWA Implementation

As it was mentioned in the introduction, MWA employs N independent molecular dynamic simulations so-called walkers that feel the estimated PMF accumulated from all walkers. This behavior can be achieved by simple client-server architecture. In our implementation, a client (a single walker) keeps two PMF accumulators. One accumulator (Fig. 3c – I) contains full set of PMF data, which are used to bias the system, and the other one (Fig. 3c – II) contains only those PMF data that were collected from the last data exchange with MWA server. Every accumulator is composed of three arrays. One array contains numbers of samples in every bin. Two other arrays contain sums and sums of squares of derivative part. Two first arrays are used to calculate PMF in every bin. The last array is only used to express basic statistical characterization of PMF such as standard deviation and error.

Data flow between clients and the server is as follows. Every specified period, which is 250 time steps in our case, newly accumulated data from accumulator II are sent by a client to MWA server. Received data are added by MWA server to its PMF accumulator III. Whole transaction is ended by sending accumulator III back to a client. Finally, received data are put by a client to accumulator I (previous data are discarded) and accumulator II is reset. From this moment, a client feels the PMF accumulated by all walkers so far plus newly accumulated data, which will be sent to the server during the next transaction. An advantage of our implementation is that the constant amount of data is sent back and forth between a client and the server. In the study presented here, it is about 35 kB.

MWA server is entirely written in C++ and is fully multithreaded using POSIX threads. Clients are written partially in Fortran 90 and partially in C++. The part responsible for communication with MWA server is written in C++. Data are transmitted in binary form over simple TCP/IP connection. This simplification was only used to test the MWA concept. For real application in the grid environment, it will be necessary to use secure connection and other than binary format to avoid possible problems arising from the utilizations of clients executed on different CPU architectures (little/big endian, different real number representation). Since the communication with the server is not necessarily required to be synchronized it is possible to run clients on machines with different CPU speed. Thus MWA approach is well suited for grid environments, which are usually highly heterogeneous from this point of view. Moreover, clients can also be run in parallel as described above. This speeds up further the entire free energy calculations.

4.2 Molecular Shuttle

The ABF MWA method was used to investigate in atomistic details a technologically important chemical problem – the evaluation of the free energy profile of the molecular shuttle process in the pseudorotaxane complexes. To be able to perform desired computations using ABF method, CVs have to be defined properly. Their appropriate selection is crucial for the free energy results accuracy and the ability to describe the system correctly from the free energy point of view. The selection of CVs has to be done in such a way that they allow maximal sampling of the conformation space while in parallel they are defined in accordance with the specific reaction mechanism.

In our case, one CV (ξ_1 was specified as the distance from the central plane of the wheel (formed by carbon atoms only), and the centre of mass of axle bipyridinium core. Since the system showed the unfavorable bending of the axle, the system was stacked in some states and the whole conformational space was not sampled properly. Consequently, we were forced to add the second CV (ξ_2) to ensure the sampling of all available system conformations. The second CV is defined as the angle between carboxyl group on the axle terminus, and the centers of both pyridinium rings given by their heavy atoms. Generally speaking, the utilization of multidimensional CVs requires an extensive usage of computational resources. The necessity to use 2D CVs during our exploration was a key motivating factor for trying to exploit advantages of current grid technologies enabling to solve challenging, computationally-demanding tasks in fast and reliable way.

The ABF MWA simulations were performed in two different environments – water and NaCl solution. Obtained results from both sets of the free energy calculations are presented in the form of 2D plots (Fig. 5 and 6), where x and y axes represent the used CVs (ξ_1 and ξ_2). The resulted plots show the complete free energy surface. Simultaneously, they indicate the most important points on the surface – the energy minima and the transition states. Knowledge of these points enables the definition of the reaction pathways and evaluation of the final free energy profiles.

In water media (Fig. 5), both studied systems (State I and State II, see Fig. 2) showed two energy minima: the first one (position A, see Fig. 2) in the central position of the axle and the second (central position B, see Fig. 2) in the distance about 6.1 Å (protonated system), 6.5 Å (neutral system) respectively. These two systems, (Fig. 5a and 5b) differ in the global energy minima position which is located on the axle terminus in the protonated system (State I), whereas this minimum lies in the central position in neutral system (State II). Since the global energy minimum represents the favorable system state, we can conclude that in State I the wheel is preferably located on the axle terminus while the central position will be the preferred one in State II.

Same sets of calculations were performed using the same systems in NaCl solution, which better represents the experimental conditions. Obtained free energy profiles show important differences in comparison with water environment. On one hand the protonated system (State I) contains two equal minima in the same positions as in water environment while the neutral complex (State II) shows only one global minimum in the axle centre. The free energy barrier which has to be overcome to exchange between two equal minima in the protonated system is about 8 kcal/mol. Such barrier is reasonably low to allow the fast interchanging between these two states. The difference in both states corresponds well to the previously experimentally suggested shuttle mechanism. In the neutral complex the central position seems to be clearly preferred.

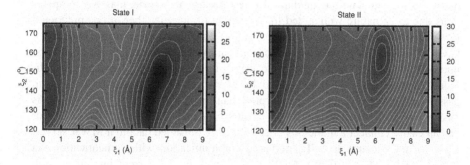

Fig. 5: Free energy profiles (in kcal/mol) for state I and II in water.

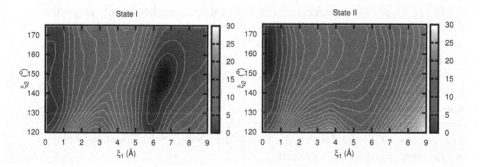

Fig. 6: Free energy profiles (in kcal/mol) for state I and II in NaCl solution (c(NaCl) ~ 0.1 M).

5   CONCLUSIONS AND FUTURE PERSPECTIVES

We successfully performed the free energy calculations of the molecular shuttle process using the Adaptive Biasing Force method accelerated by the Multiple Walkers Approach in two different grid computational environments: EUAsia VO and VOCE. The results were obtained nearly 40 times faster compared to a conventional run due to employing 40 independent walkers utilized for every single job. Currently, we are applying this approach to various complexes differed by cucurbit[n]uril sizes and axle lengths.

Our implementation of Adaptive Biasing Force method using Multiple Walkers Approach clearly indicated that grid environments - EGEE worldwide Grid in particular - create a unique medium for performing large scale, massive computations due to its nature well suited for execution of huge number of computational jobs. This evaluation study further motivates us to improve the current implementation of MWA. There are several issues in current implementation that need to be improved. Generally speaking, the security of communication between the individual clients and the server should be corrected. Current utilization of plain password authentication and unencrypted data transfer in the grid environment is clearly very risky, because potential intruder can easily change transferred data or he can easily connect a malicious client injecting poisoned data to a MWA server. Thus we plan to use an SSL encrypted communication with authentication via X.509 user proxy certificate. Another bottleneck of the current implementation lies in the utilization of the only server. If this server fails due to work node malfunction or communication problems, all accumulated data would be lost. To prevent such undesired behaviour we plan to utilize more mutually interconnected servers. We expect that this approach can potentially bring several benefits. Firstly, the required communication bandwidth will be smaller as only proportion of the clients will communicate with one of the servers. Secondly, this approach should minimize the risk of data loss as the accumulated data will be duplicated among the servers.

In conclusion, our study showed the applicability and usability of the worldwide grid environments represented by EGEE Grid. Taking into account suggested improvements and new planned features of currently tested and implemented approach one can expect in near future more intensive usage and wider acceptance of EGEE Grid within the field of free energy calculations and computational chemistry domain in general.

6 ACKNOWLEDGEMENTS.

The presented work is supported by following grants: The Ministry of Education of the Czech Republic (contracts LC06030, MSM0021622413 and MSM6383917201) and by EGEE III project funded by European Commission (contract number INFSO–RI–222667). The research leading to these results has also received funding from the European Community's Seventh Framework Programme under grant agreement n° 205872.

REFERENCES

[1]   Foster, I., Kesselman, C.: Computational grids – Invited talk (Reprinted from The Grid: Blueprint for a new computing infrastructure, 1998). Vector and Parallel Processing – Vecpar. 1981, 3–37 (2001)

[2]   Foster, I.: The anatomy of the grid: Enabling scalable virtual organizations. First Ieee/Acm International Symposium on Cluster Computing and The Grid. 6–7 (2001)

[3]   Foster, I., Kesselman, C., Nick, J.M., Tuecke, S.: The Physiology of the Grid: An Open Grid Services Architecture for Distributed Systems Integration. Available via http://citeseerx.ist.psu.edu/viewdoc/summary?doi=10.1.1.14.8105.

[4]   EGEE Portal: Enabling Grids for E–sciencE. Available via http://eu–egee.org/

[5]   Kirkwood, J.: Statistical mechanics of fluid mixtures. J. Chem. Phys. 300–313 (1935)

[6]   Mulders, T., Kruger, P., Swegat, W., Schlitter, J.: Free energy as the potential of mean constraint force. J. Chem. Phys. 104, 4869-4870 (1996)

[7]   Torrie, G., Valleau, J.: Non-physical sampling distributions in monte-carlo free-energy estimation - umbrella sampling. J. Comput. Phys. 23, 187-199 (1977)

[8]   Laio, A., Parrinello, M.: Escaping free-energy minima. P. Natl. Acad. Sci. USA 99, 12562-12566 (2002)

[9]   Darve, E., Pohorille, A.: Calculating free energies using average force. J. Chem. Phys. 115, 9169-9183 (2001)

[10] Sugita, Y., Okamoto, Y.: Replica-exchange molecular dynamics method for protein folding. Chem. Phys. Lett. 314, 141-151 (1999)

[11] E, W., Ren, W., Vanden-Eijnden, E.: String method for the study of rare events. Phys. Rev. B 66, 052301 (2002)

[12] Raiteri, P., Laio, A., Gervasio, F., Micheletti, C., Parrinello, M.: Efficient reconstruction of complex free energy landscapes by multiple walkers metadynamics. J. Phys. Chem. B 110, 3533-3539 (2006)

[13] Sindelar, V., Silvi, S., Kaifer, A.E.: Switching a molecular shuttle on and off: simple, pH-controlled pseudorotaxanes based on cucurbit[7]uril. Chem. Commun. 2185–2187 (2006).

[14] Sindelar, V., Silvi, S., Parker, S.E., Sobransingh, D., Kaifer, A.E.: Proton and electron transfer control of the position of cucurbit[n]uril wheels in pseudorotaxanes. Adv. Funct. Mater. 17, 694–701 (2007)

[15] Darve, E., Rodriguez-Gomez, D., Pohorille, A.: Adaptive biasing force method for scalar and vector free energy calculations. J. Chem. Phys. 128, 144120 (2008)

[16] Kim, K.: Mechanically interlocked molecules incorporating cucurbituril and their supramolecular assemblies. Chem. Soc. Rev. 31, 96-107 (2002)

[17] Grabuleda, X., Ivanov, P., Jaime, C.: Computational studies on pseudorotaxanes by molecular dynamics and free energy perturbation simulations. J. Org. Chem. 68, 1539-1547 (2003)

[18] Grabuleda, X., Jaime, C.: Molecular shuttles. A computational study (MM and MD) on the translational isomerism in some [2]rotaxanes. J. Org. Chem. 63, 9635-9643 (1998)

[19] Grabuleda, X., Ivanov, P., Jaime, C.: Shuttling process in [2]rotaxanes. Modeling by molecular dynamics and free energy perturbation simulations. J. Phys. Chem. B 107, 7582-7588 (2003)

[20] Ryckaert, J.P., Ciccotti, G., Berendsen, H.J.C.: Numerical-integration of cartesian equations of motion of a system with constraints - molecular-dynamics of n-alkanes. J. Comput. Phys. 23, 327–341 (1977)

[21] Duke, B.: PMEMD benchmarks for Amber 9. Available via http://ambermd.org/amber9.bench2.html Cited 2 Aug 2009

Grid Computing for Bioinformatics: An Implementation of a User-Friendly Web Portal for ASTI's In Silico Laboratory

Rey Vincent P. Babilonia, Marilyn V. Rey, Emmanuel D. Aldea and Urizza Marie L. Sarte

Research and Development Division, Advanced Science and Technology Institute, Department of Science and Technology, UP Technology Park Complex, Philippines

Abstract   Bioinformatics is an important discipline that is fast emerging in academic research and industrial applications, and thereby, one of the areas identified to benefit from Grid and cluster computing. Bioinformatics research can be significantly boosted by utilizing a computing Grid shared across multiple academic and research institutions. However, the setback in accessing Grid resources is the interface. The interface between the researcher and the technology is commonly done through a command line.

Hence, the Advanced Science and Technology Institute (ASTI) developed a web-based interface to enable a user-friendly way to access the Philippine e-Science Grid and the Banyuhay cluster of the ASTI high-performance computing (HPC) facility. ASTI deployed the OGCE Web portal. It comes with pre-existing portlets which we complemented with custom JSR 168-based portlets for searching the GenBank and for running applications using the Torque/OpenPBS job scheduler. Given that scientific tools can be difficult to install, it is particularly helpful for the researchers to be able to use these tools through a Web-based user interface. This paper highlights the existing applications available on ASTI's HPC facility with a Web-based interface.

Keywords   Grid, cluster, portal, portlet, bioinformatics, Torque, GenBank, UniProt, JSch

1   INTRODUCTION

Major advances in the field of molecular biology, coupled with advances in genomic technologies, have led to an explosive growth in the biological information generated by the scientific community. This large number of genomic information has, in turn, led to an absolute requirement for computerized databases to store, organize, and index the data, and for specialized tools to view and analyze the data [1].

S.C. Lin and E. Yen (eds.), *Data Driven e-Science: Use Cases and Successful Applications of Distributed Computing Infrastructures (ISGC 2010)*, DOI 10.1007/978-1-4419-8014-4_36, © Springer Science+Business Media, LLC 2011

In response to the increasing need for: greater computing power; diverse bioinformatics tools; and updated bioinformatics data, ASTI developed a user-friendly Web-based interface and set up a web-hosting service for bioinformatics software. This paper aims to present ASTI's implementation of a Web portal that aims to enhance the availability of bioinformatics applications locally and give local researchers access to (1) popular bioinformatics software which run on the computing Grid, cluster, or FPGA board; and (2) bioinformatics databases like GenBank and UniProt from Bio-Mirror, while hiding all the complexities of high-performance computing.

2   TARGET USERS

The local bioinformatics experts and researchers are targeted to benefit from this Web Portal. This initiative is part of a project that aims to enhance the local availability of bioinformatics services, and facilitate rapid access to large bioinformatics data sets. By developing the needed applications and tools, and making these locally accessible, we hope to contribute in improving research output of local bioinformatics experts.

3   WEB PORTAL

The development team assessed various open source portals to determine which among these will suit the specifications we wanted for the Web Portal. The requirements we wanted for the Web Portal included:

- easy to install and has quite a few or no dependencies at all;
- java-based Grid portal;
- no need to learn complex concepts or to install sophisticated software requirements;
- open source portal which comes with full support from the developers; and
- available to all operating system such as Windows, Linux, Unix, or Mac OS X.

Below, we describe the portals and their technology components, and our assessment of these.

3.1   Grid Engine Portal

The Grid Engine Portal (GEP, formerly known as Sun Technical Computing Portal -TCP) project provides a Java based capability for enabling the users to securely access and execute applications via a transparent interface to Grid Engine [2].

Grid Engine Portal, however, involves complex installation and configuration of various services like the Sun Java Enterprise System prior to the actual portal installation. GEP installation complains about missing packages like OpenInstaller and PortalServer and there aren't many tutorials out there describing the solution. ASTI's cluster is not using the Sun Grid Engine job scheduler.

3.2 GridPort

GridPort is a toolkit for developing Web-based portals and applications for computational science on top of underlying distributed and grid computing infrastructure [3]. GridPort aggregates grid services from popular grid software packages and provides additional grid capabilities, while presenting a simple, consistent API for portal and applications developers.

However, GridPort has been dormant since 2006. It uses GridSphere 2.0 even if the latest version is 3.1 and Maven 1.0 even if the latest version is 2.0. GridPort is now integrated into the Open Grid Computing Environments (OGCE) Portal and Gateway Toolkit.

3.3 P-GRADE

P-GRADE provides a unique and complete solution for development and execution of parallel applications on supercomputers, clusters, and Grid systems [4].

But P-GRADE Portal requires gLite User Interface component to be able to proceed with the installation process, which is not our primary goal for this Web portal. However, ASTI can set up this portal as an alternative to the command line user interface when submitting jobs to the EUAsiaGrid VO.

3.4 GridSphere

The GridSphere portal framework provides an open source portlet-based Web portal [5]. The GridSphere portal allows users to customize their workspace by adding and removing portlets as needed. In addition to standard window states like minimized or maximized, portlets can also provide various "modes" such as view, edit, configure and help. GridSphere allows developers to create custom portlets through its own application programming interface.

Though we did not adopt the GridSphere portal because OGCE portal download includes GridSphere 2.1 to get started with building a Java-based Grid portal, we were able to use its grid authentication module to perform grid authentication upon logging in to the portal, and also its tag library module to develop user interface of bioinformatics tools and integrate them to the Torque portlet.

3.5   OGCE Portal

Open Grid Computing Environments (OGCE) Portal is an open source project that comprises several portlets aimed to be used in Web portals for science purposes. It is a bundled set of JSR 168 compatible portlets and services for building Grid portals or science gateways [6].

OGCE Portal is easy to install and comes with many portlets and functionalities, such as: grid credential management, secure remote file management, secure remote code execution, views of grid information services (machine load, usage, and queue wait time) and workflow composers (Xbaya).

The Renaissance Computing Institute (RENCI) uses this for their Bioportal.

4   PORTLETS

Since a Web portal can accommodate various Java portlets, the team picked the most useful bundled portlets and added our in-house developments.

4.1   GenBank Entry Retrieval System (GenBankERS) Portlet

The GenBankERS portlet allows local bioinformatics researchers to view and download DNA sequences in GenBank and FASTA formats. It is connected to a MySQL database with the BioSQL schema and uses Hibernate and BioJava to query the database and display the results.

It is designed to provide access to the most up-to-date and comprehensive DNA sequence information.

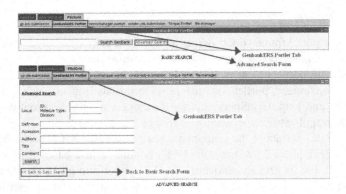

Fig. 1: GenBankERS Portlet

4.2   Grid Job Submission Portlet

The Grid Resource Allocation Manager (GRAM) Batch Job Submission Portlet enables users to submit batch jobs to remote resources. It currently supports pre-webservice Globus version 2.4, 3.2.1, and 4.x [7]. The portlet allows a user to specify job parameters, submit the job and view job status information. This portlet requires a working GRAM server or Globus gatekeeper running on port 2119 on the remote resources with which the users will interact.

Fig. 2: Grid Job Submissions Portlet

4.3   Torque Job Submission Portlet

The Torque/OpenPBS Job Submission portlet allows users to submit custom batch jobs or predefined bioinformatics tools to the Banyuhay cluster. This portlet is the Java equivalent of PBSWeb which was designed as an aid to the Portable batch System (PBS) job scheduler. It is responsible for scheduling jobs on high-performance machines so as to ensure far access to resources. However, many users find PBS hard to use as it requires users to write scripts containing complex directives and options, and so many potential users avoid using PBS and the machine upon which it is installed. PBSWeb simplifies the task of creating these scripts by allowing the user to specify these directives and options through the use of HTML forms [8].

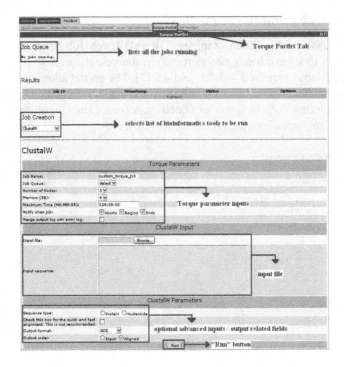

Fig. 3: Torque Job Submission Portlet

Currently the applications that have been made operational in the Torque Job Submission Portlet include the following:

- ClustalW ClustalW is a general purpose multiple sequence alignment program for DNA or proteins. All sequences are compared to each other and lines them up so that the identities, similarities and differences can be seen. It can align either nucleotide or protein sequences [9].
- HMMER HMMER is an implementation of profile HMM methods for sensitive database searches using multiple sequence alignments as queries. Basically, you give HMMER a multiple sequence alignment as input; it builds a statistical model called a "hidden Markov model" which you can then use as a query into a sequence database to find (and/or align) additional homologues of the sequence family [10].

Presently, the Development Team is doing a user-testing of some of the above-mentioned applications. Results of this user-testing will enable us to make the necessary improvements in the tool. Likewise, the following applications are intended to be made operational:

- FASTA Compares a DNA sequence to a protein sequence database, translating the DNA sequence in three forward (or reverse) frames and allowing frame shifts. This program achieves a high level of sensitivity for similarity searching at high speed. This is achieved by performing optimised searches for local alignments using a substitution matrix. The high speed of this program is achieved by using the observed pattern of word hits to identify potential matches before attempting the more time consuming optimised search [11].
- GLIMMER A system for finding genes in microbial DNA, especially the genomes of bacteria, archaea, and viruses. Glimmer (Gene Locator and Interpolated Markov ModelER) uses interpolated Markov models (IMMs) to identify the coding regions and distinguish them from noncoding DNA [12].
- GroMaCS GroMaCS (Groningen MAchine for Chemical Simulation) is an engine to perform molecular dynamics simulations and energy minimization [13].
- mpiBLAST mpiBLAST is a freely available, open-source, parallel implementation of NCBI BLAST. mpiBLAST takes advantage of distributed computational resources, i.e., a cluster, through explicit MPI communication and thereby utilizes all available resources unlike standard NCBI BLAST which can only take advantage of shared-memory multi-processors (SMPs) [14].
- MrBayes MrBayes is a program for the Bayesian estimation of phylogeny. Bayesian inference of phylogeny is based upon a quantity called the posterior probability distribution of trees, which is the probability of a tree conditioned on the observations. The conditioning is accomplished using Bayes's theorem. The posterior probability distribution of trees is impossible to calculate analytically; instead, MrBayes uses a simulation technique called Markov chain Monte Carlo (or MCMC) to approximate the posterior probabilities of trees [15].
- NCBI BLAST BLAST, or Basic Local Alignment Search Tool, is a collection of tools that are used to search for and find regions of local similarity between sequences. The program compares nucleotide or protein sequences to sequence databases, and calculates the statistical significance of the matches [16]. This software suite has been released free to the public by the National Centre for Biotechnology Information.
- Phylip PHYLIP, the Phylogeny Inference Package, is a free package of programs for inferring phylogenies.

It is available as source code in C, and also as executables for some common computer systems. It can infer phylogenies by parsimony, compatibility, distance matrix methods, and likelihood. It can also compute consensus trees, compute distances between trees, draw trees, resample data sets by bootstrapping or jackknifing, edit trees, and compute distance matrices. It can handle data that are nucleotide sequences, protein sequences, gene frequencies, restriction sites, restriction fragments, distances, discrete characters, and continuous characters [17].

- T_Coffee T-Coffee is a multiple sequence alignment program: given a set of sequences previously gathered using database search programs like BLAST,

FASTA or Smith and Waterman, T-Coffee will produce a multiple sequence alignment. To use T-Coffee you must already have your sequences ready [18].

- GMAP A standalone program for mapping and aligning cDNA sequences to a genome. The program maps and aligns a single sequence with minimal startup time and memory requirements, and provides fast batch processing of large sequence sets. The program generates accurate gene structures, even in the presence of substantial polymorphisms and sequence errors, without using probabilistic splice site models. Methodology underlying the program includes a minimal sampling strategy fro genomic mapping, oligomer chaining for approximate alignment, sandwich DP for splice site detection, and microexon identification with statistical testing [19].

- MSA A multiple sequence alignment (MSA) is a sequence alignment of three or more biological sequences, generally protein, DNA or RNA. In many cases, the input set of query sequences are assumed to have an evolutionary relationship by which they share a lineage and are descended from a common ancestor. From the resulting MSA, sequence homology can be inferred and phylogenetic analysis can be conducted to assess the sequences' shared evolutionary origins. Multiple sequence alignment is often used to assess sequence conservation of protein domains, tertiary and secondary structures, and even individual amino acids or nucleotides [20].

- PSA Pairwise Sequence Alignment methods are used to find the best-matching piecewise (local) or global alignments of two query sequences. Pairwise alignments can only be used between two sequences at a time, but they are efficient to calculate and are often used for methods that do not require extreme precision (such as searching a database for sequences with high homology to a query). The three primary methods of producing pairwise alignments are dot-matrix methods, dynamic programming, and word methods; however, multiple sequence alignment techniques can also align pairs of sequences [21].

Global alignments, which attempt to align every residue in every sequence, are most useful when the sequences in the query set are similar and of roughly equal size. (This does not mean global alignments cannot end in gaps.) A general global alignment technique is the Needleman-Wunsch algorithm, which is based on dynamic programming. Local alignments are more useful for dissimilar sequences that are suspected to contain regions of similarity or similar sequence motifs within their larger sequence context. The Smith-Waterman algorithm is a general local alignment method also based on dynamic programming. With sufficiently similar sequences, there is no difference between local and global alignments [22].

And the other default portlets are Proxy Manager Portlet, File Manager Portlet and Condor Job Submission Portlet.

4.4 Proxy Manager Portlet

The Proxy Manager Portlet enables a user to retrieve a grid proxy credential from a MyProxy server [23]. Proxy credentials can be stored temporarily in the user's session context. So if a user logs out of their portal or the portal server is restarted, the proxy credential will be deleted.

The certificate or a public key certificate (also known as a digital certificate or identity certificate) is an electronic document which uses a digital signature to bind together a public key with an identity — information such as the name of a person or an organization, their address, and so forth. The certificate can be used to verify that a public key belongs to an individual and is essential in order to utilize portal applications. This will be issued to Web Portal users by the Academia Sinica Grid Computing Certification Authority (ASGCCA) upon request.

Fig. 4: Proxy Manager Portlet

4.5 File Manager Portlet

The File Manager portlet allows the user to upload data files and scripts to the storage element for processing and executing the job.

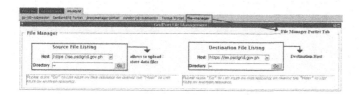

Fig. 5: File Manager Portlet

4.6 *Condor Job Submission Portlet*

The portlet uses Condor to submit batch jobs to remote resources on your flock via the Condor Central Manager [24]. This is the machine that runs the Collector and Negotiator daemons which is, in our case, the frontend. The Condor Roll is not yet upgraded for Rocks 5.2. This was, however, tested on Rocks 5.1.

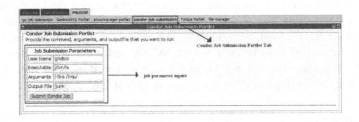

Fig. 6: Condor Job Submission Portlet

5 GRID INFRASTRUCTURE

ASTI has set up a high-performance computing (HPC) facility with installed applications for bioinformatics, seismology, and meteorology. The Banyuhay cluster is where the applications for bioinformatics are installed. The discussion below provides details on the capacity of the Banyuhay cluster, as well as the tool we use to manage our proxy and storage element.

5.1 Banyuhay Cluster

1. Specifications: The Banyuhay cluster comprises eight (8) computing nodes with eight (8) cores running at 2GHz, 500GB of disk space and 16GB of RAM per node. The nodes are connected via a gigabit ethernet switch.
2. Rocks Distribution: Banyuhay is running Rocks 5.2.2 from http:\\www.rocksclusters.org. It is an open-source Linux cluster distribution aimed at building and maintaining computational clusters easily.
3. gLite Middleware: Grid Middleware allows users to submit requests to execute jobs on the Grid. The gLite Middleware, initiated by the Enabling Grid for E-science (EGEE) Project, is used in building Grid computing systems and in enabling resource sharing.
4. Torque Roll: Torque Roll contains Torque and Maui job queueing system and was packaged by the HPC Group of the University of Tromso, Norway.
5. Bio Roll: Bio Roll contains open-source bioinformatics tools such as ClustalW; FASTA; GMAP; HMMER; MrBayes; PHYLIP; EMBOSS; Glimmer; GROMACS; mpiBLAST; NCBI; T-Coffee.
6. BioBoost: BioBoost contains hardware-accelerated algorithms from Progeniq Pte Ltd. Such as hardware-accelerated multiple sequence alignment (ClustalW); hardware-accelerated pairwise sequence alignment (Smith-Waterman).

5.2 gLite Proxy:

gLite Proxy is the gLite distribution of the MyProxy server. MyProxy is a stand-alone server which manages proxy renewal to avoid the need for long-lived proxies [25].

5.3 gLite Storage Element:

ASTI's storage element uses the Disk Pool Manager which is a lightweight solution for managing disk storage [26].

6   ACCESSING THE BANYUHAY CLUSTER

In order for users to access the applications installed in the Banyuhay cluster, i.e., BioBoost and BioRoll, ASTI implements the Java Secure Channel (Jsch). It is a pure Java implementation of SSH2 that allows users to: (1) connect to an sshd server and use port forwarding, X11 forwarding file transfer, etc.; and (2) integrate its functionality into the user's own Java programs. Jsch is licensed under BSD style license [27].

The JSSH library used was designed as a reusable software component that can be embedded in larger Java applications to provide secure shell client functionality.

7   SYSTEM ARCHITECTURE

7.1   Portal Perspective

There are three (3) portlets that will run together with the default portlets. The Torque portlet will contain a list of clusters (Banyuhay, Buhawi, Dalubhasaan and Unos) capable of running test jobs, bioinformatics tools and FPGA algorithms. The GenBank Entry Retrieval System (GenBankERS) portlet allows the extraction of matching GenBank records. The Grid portlet allows job submission to the Philippine e-Science Grid and international collaborations like EUAsiaGrid and eventually, the Pacific Rim Applications and Grid Middleware Assembly (PRAGMA).

7.2   Portal Features and Functions

The Web Portal provides a user-friendly web interface in using bioinformatics tools. To access the portal, a user certificate is needed which will be given to the users during account creation and will be validated every time they log in. Inside the portal, the users are allowed to manage their profile and the portlets they want to access.

The portal also provides user account, theme/layout, user group, and messaging service management utility for the administrators.

The following figures illustrate the features and functions of the portal.

Users of the Web portal are categorized into four (4), namely: Guest, User, Admin and Superadmin. The Guest is only allowed to create an account and browse the portal (Figure 7). The User can access the portal provided that he/she has an authentic certificate. Moreover, he/she can manage profile and customize the layout (Figure 9). Figure 8 explains the set of activities of the Admin which is a subset of Superadmin's activities (Figure 10).

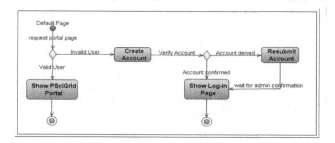

Fig. 7: Guest Activity Diagram

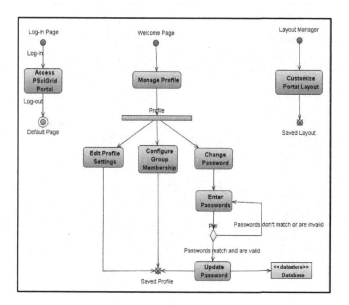

Fig. 8: Administrator Activity

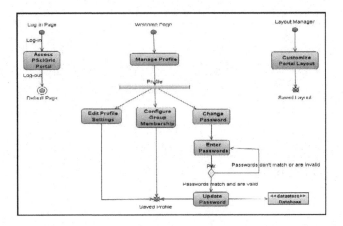

Fig. 9: User Activity Diagram

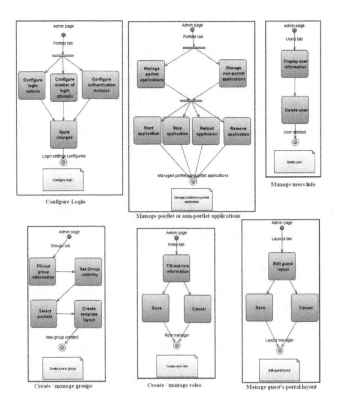

Fig. 10: Super Administrator Activity Diagram

Aside from account management, Figure 10 also illustrates the administrative actions available in the portal which include portlets, users, groups, roles, layouts and messaging service management.

7.3   User classes and Characteristics

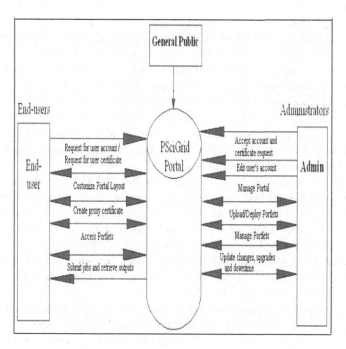

Fig. 11 Web Portal Context Diagram

Shown on Figure 11 are the pertinent characteristics of each user class: the end-user is the local bioinformatics researcher who will define and run Grid services and bioinformatics applications through submitting jobs in portlets. They should be able to run bioanalyses through a web interface without installing anything locally. The end-user may access these services on the portal by way of requesting a portal account and certificate to secure grid management. After the account verification, the end-user can customize its portal layout and manage their own profile. The portlets that the end-user can access are the GenBankERS, Grid-Port Job Submission, Torque Job Submission Portlets and any other default portlets. The end-user may also receive updates from the administrators regarding the implemented changes on the portal.

The administrator is responsible for all the services and maintenance of the Web Portal. He/She verifies user accounts and provides user certificates. The administrator provides an integrated access to the portal, as well as tools to manage job results and combine analyses to the local researchers.

8   CONCLUSION

Bioinformatics is one of the areas that stands to benefit from Grid and cluster computing. Research in this field can be significantly boosted by utilizing a computing Grid shared across multiple academic and research institutions. However, access to Grid resources is commonly carried out through a command line, which can be a hindrance for researchers. In order to address this concern, the ASTI developed a Web-based interface to enable a user-friendly way for local bioinformatics researchers to access the Philippine e-Science Grid (PSciGrid) and the Banyuhay cluster of ASTI's high performance computing (HPC) facility. The Web portal was designed to provide a flexible and usable Web environment for defining and running bioinformatics application without the user having to learn complex concepts or to install sophisticated software.

The team has successfully integrated custom JSR 168 portlets into the OGCE portal. GenBankERS has been converted into a portlet. Its biodatabase resides in the same MySQL server as the portal. The Torque portlet has a flexible and user-friendly Web interface for using bioinformatics tools and, with the help of JSch, can submit jobs to the 8-node Banyuhay cluster. The hardware-accelerated bioinformatics tools can also be accessed from the portlet. GenBank and UniProt databases from the Bio-Mirror can now be searched as well. The Condor portlet has been tested to work with Condor Roll 5.1.

The team was also able to connect the portal to some of the Grid services. The File Manager portlet allows users to upload files to PSciGrid's storage element. The Proxy Manager portlet makes use of PSciGrid's MyProxy server for retrieving long-term proxy credentials.

9   RECOMMENDATIONS

The development team intends to add more bioinformatics applications in the Torque job submission portlet. The team is also looking into adding meteorological applications to the portal. Likewise, the team is currently evaluating if the GENIUS portal can be deployed. This will give users access to PSciGrid and EU-AsiaGrid virtual organizations. Future work also includes utilizing the user certificate stored in the Web browser for logging into the portal.

10 ACKNOWLEDGMENT

The Web Portal was developed as part of the project entitled "Boosting Social and Technological Capabilities for Bioinformatics Research", which was funded by the Department of Science and Technology's Grants-in-Aid (DOST-GIA) Program. The development team wishes to extend their gratitude to the following: (1) the Department of Science and Technology; (2) the Philippine Council for Advanced Science and Technology Research and Development (PCASTRD); (3) the Advanced Science and Technology Institute (ASTI); (4) the PSciGrid Program Team, which the development team is part of; and (5) the Research and Development Division of ASTI.

REFERENCES

[1] Just the Facts: A Basic Introduction to the Science Underlying NCBI Resources. [Online].
     Available: http://www.ncbi.nlm.nih.gov/About/primer/bioinf ormatics.html
[2] Grid Engine Portal.[Online].Available:http://gridengine.sunsource.net/gep/GEP_Intro.html
[3] Grid Portal Toolkit 3.0 (GridPort). [Online].
     Available:http://www.computer.org/portal/web/csdl/doi/10. 1109/HPDC.2004.19
[4] P-GRADE Portal. [Online]. Available: http://portal.p-grade.hu/
[5] GridSphere Portal Framework. [Online].
     Available: http://www.gridsphere.org/gridsphere/gridsphere/ guest/home/r/
[6] The Open Grid Computing Environments Portal and Gateway Toolkit. [Online].
     Available: http://www.collab-ogce.org/ogce/index.php/Main_Page
[7] Job submission. [Online].
     Available: http://wiki.pscigrid.gov.ph/index.php/Batch_Job_Submission
[8] Introduction to PBSWeb. [Online].
     Available: http://www.cs.ualberta.ca/~pinchak/PBSWeb
[9] ClustalW Web Interface. Rob Edwards. [Online].
     Available:http://bioinformatics.utmem.edu/clustal/clustalw.html
[10] HMMER. [Online].
     Available: http://www.psc.edu/general/software/packages/hmme r/manual/node1.html
[11] FASTA @ EBI. [Online]. Available: http://www.ebi.ac.uk/Tools/fasta/index.html
[12] Microbial Genome Annotation Tools. [Online].
     Available: http://www.ncbi.nlm.nih.gov/genomes/MICROBES/g limmer_3.cgi
[13] David van der Spoel et al., GROMACS User Manual Version 4.0. [Online].
     Available:http://www.gromacs.org/@api/deki/files/82/=gromacs4_manual.pdf
[14] mpiBLAST: Open-Source Parallel BLAST. [Online].
     Available: http://www.mpiblast.org/About/Overview
[15] MrBayes: Bayesian Inference of Phylogeny. [Online].
     Available: http://mrbayes.csit.fsu.edu
[16] NCBI/BLAST Home. [Online]. Available: http://www.ncbi.nlm.nih.gov
[17] PHYLIP. [Online]. Available:http://evolution.gs.washington.edu/phylip/general.html
[18] C. Notredame et al., T-Coffee: A Consistency Based Multiple Alignment Method Multiple
     Alignments.
[19] GMAP: a genomic mapping and alignment program for mRNA and EST sequences.
     [Online]. Available:http://bioinformatics.oxfordjournals.org/cgi/content/full/21/9/1859
[20] Multiple Sequence Alignment. [Online].
     Available: http://en.wikipedia.org/wiki/Multiple_sequence_align ment

[21] Sequence Alignment. [Online].
     Available: http://en.wikipedia.org/wiki/Sequence_alignment#Pairwise_alignment
[22] Global and local alignments [Online].
     Available: http://en.wikipedia.org/wiki/Sequence_alignment
[23] ProxyManager. [Online].
     Available: http://www.collab-ogce.org/ogce/index.php/ProxyManager
[24] Condor. [Online]. Available: http://www.collabogce.org/ogce/index.php/Condor
[25] glite-PX. [Online]. Available: https://twiki.cern.ch/twiki/bin/view/EGEE/GlitePX
[26] DPM General Description. [Online].
     Available: https://twiki.cern.ch/twiki/bin/view/LCG/DpmGeneralDescription
[27] JCraft. [Online]. Available: http://www.jcraft.com/jsch

Grid Computing Technology and the Recurrence Quantification Analysis to Predict Seizure Occurrence in Patients Affected by Drug-Resistant Epilepsy

Roberto Barbera[1,2], **Giuseppe La Rocca**[1,2] **and Massimo Rizzi**[3]

1. Italian National Institute of Nuclear Physics, Division of Catania, Italy
2. Department of Physics and Astronomy of the University of Catania, Italy
3. ARCEM - Associazione Italiana per la Ricerca sulle Patologie Cerebrali e del Midollo Spinale, Italy

Abstract Nowadays, a hot topic in the field of epilepsy research is the detection of any reliable marker, embedded in the electroencephalograms (EEGs), that can be exploited to predict the seizure with a sufficient advance notice. A useful analytical tool which may help epileptologists to unveil significant patterns in EEGs of people suffering from epilepsy is the Recurrence Quantification Analysis (RQA). This technique can be easily exploited by researchers since RQA software applications and related source codes are freely available. Nevertheless, the analysis of extensive EEGs can be considerably CPU-time-consuming so researchers are often obliged to strongly reduce the amount of data RQA is applied to. High throughput computing appears as the best solution to solve this problem. In this paper we present the preliminary results of the RQA performed on the EEGs of four epileptic patients who underwent pre-surgical evaluation for the resection of epileptic foci. In this study, EEGs were segmented in epochs of proper length each one analysed independently from the others using a Grid computing infrastructure.

1   INTRODUCTION

Epilepsy is an illness as old as human kind and it is one of the most documented pathologies in the history of medicine. The Greek word from which the term epilepsy comes from, epilambanein, (to seize upon – to attack unexpectedly) describes well the main feature of this neurological disorder. Epilepsy is a disease that causes seizures. A seizure (from the Latin sacire – to take possession of) is the macroscopic manifestation of an abnormal synchronization of the electrical activities of vast populations of nerve cells broadly distributed inside the brain. From a clinical perspective, seizures can last from a few seconds to a few minutes and are associated with a variety of manifestations, spanning from auras to behavioural convulsions, often accompanied by a loss of consciousness, depending on which cerebral areas (and to what extent) are involved. Epilepsy represents one of the most common neurological disorders affecting about 50 million people world-

S.C. Lin and E. Yen (eds.), *Data Driven e-Science: Use Cases and Successful Applications of Distributed Computing Infrastructures (ISGC 2010)*, DOI 10.1007/978-1-4419-8014-4_37, © Springer Science+Business Media, LLC 2011

wide, with almost 90% of these people living in developing countries. It can arise at any age and the mechanisms leading to the development of this neurological disorder are still largely unknown. Often, aetiologies are well-determined such as stroke, tumors, head injury, hypoxia, and birth injuries but in a high percentage of cases the origin of epilepsy is still elusive. It is worth mentioning that, strictly speaking, the singular term epilepsy is inappropriate as there are over 40 types of epilepsy [1] each one with its own unique combination of seizure type, age of onset, electroencephalographic correlate and medical treatment.

2   THERAPEUTIC TREATMENT OF EPILEPSY

Despite a proliferating literature proposing multitudes of mechanisms possibly involved in seizure generation as well as interesting hypothesis potentially useful for new pharmacological treatments [2], from the point of view of medical sciences epilepsy still remains an unresolved issue. Indeed, notwithstanding the improvement of pharmacological intervention in the last decades, medical treatment is still symptomatic in that, for the majority of patients, epilepsy is usually controlled by drugs but can not be definitively healed. Therefore, withdrawal of drugs usually results in a worsening of seizure occurrence. Unfortunately, about 25% of patients are refractory to conventional anti-epileptic drugs treatment [3]. For many individuals of this group the frequency and the severity of seizures can seriously impair their daily life. Additionally, several brain areas of these patients may be damaged by the intensive seizing activity which may lead to the death of selected populations of neurons. At young ages, despite an enhanced capability of brain to resist to neuronal cells loss as compared to adults, an intense seizing activity may significantly impair the development of cognitive functions. In all these clinical cases, whether the risks/benefits ratio is considered acceptable, surgery aimed to remove the portion of brain tissue from which seizures originate is usually adopted. However, it is worth stressing that, in the majority of cases (80%), operated patients do not become really seizure-free but they only reach an acceptable level of responsiveness to common anti-epileptic drugs, thus keeping seizures under a pharmacological control which was impossible to achieve without surgery. However, total or partial resection of some cerebral areas is often associated to side-effects which can be severe and permanent [4, 5].

3   THE ELECTROENCEPHALOGRAM (EEG) AS A DIAGNOSTIC TOOL OF EPILEPSY

The EEG is the most important neurophysiological tool for the diagnosis, prognosis, and treatment of epilepsy. EEG depicts the global electrical activity of brain cells. EEG is usually recorded from multiple electrodes placed on the scalp where the electrical field generated by similarly oriented brain cells is detected. However, EEG can also be obtained from electrodes specifically positioned inside the brain (intracranial EEG recording). This latter procedure is accomplished during pre-surgical evaluation of patients refractory to conventional anti-epileptic drugs (see previous section) in order to identify the epileptogenic brain area to be surgically removed (focus epilepticus). Generally, the onset of a seizure is associated to a rapid build-up of 4 to 10 Hz rhythmic activity of the EEG (fig. 1).

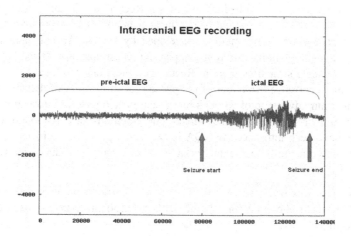

Fig. 1: Intracranial EEG recording collected from a patient who underwent pre-surgical evaluation for resection of the brain area from which seizures originate. The onset of a seizure is generally associated to a rapid increase of rhythmic EEG activity within the range 4 to 10 Hz.

In order to make further reading of this paper easier, we define here the terminology adopted in the next sections and related to EEG patterns:

- ictal EEG - EEG recording of electrical activity during a seizure;
- pre-ictal EEG - EEG recording of electrical activity immediately preceding a seizure;
- post-ictal EEG - EEG recording of electrical activity immediately following a seizure;
- inter-ictal EEG - EEG recording devoid of and sufficiently far from a seizure, hence excluding both pre-ictal and post-ictal EEGs.

Intracranial EEG recordings are particularly useful in the contest of detailed analysis of brain dynamics because they are much less affected by spurious signals as compared to scalp EEG recordings. A hot topic in epilepsy research is the detailed mathematical analysis of intracranial EEG recordings aimed to detect patterns of electrical activity forecasting the incoming seizures with a sufficient notice. An efficient algorithm would greatly improve the effectiveness of conventional anti-epileptic drugs as well as the investigation of novel therapeutic strategies.

4   THE RECURRENCE QUANTIFICATION ANALYSIS IN A NUTSHELL

A useful analytical tool which may help epileptologists to unveil significant patterns of electrical activity embedded in EEGs is Recurrence Quantification Analysis (RQA). The RQA is a method of nonlinear data analysis for the investigation of dynamical systems. This method, developed by Charles Webber and Joseph Zbilut [6], aims to quantify differently appearing recurrence plots (RPs) [7] based on the small-scale structures therein. Recurrence plots are graphical tools which visualise the recurrence behaviour of the phase space trajectory of dynamical systems. The main advantage of RQA is that it can provide useful information even for short and non-stationary data where other methods fail. Although several measures have been introduced in RQA in the recent past [8], we focused our attention mainly on the fundamental variables as originally introduced by Webber and Zbilut:

1. *Recurrence Rate (RR)*, which is the density of recurrence points in a recurrence plot. The recurrence rate corresponds with the probability that a specific state will recur;

$$RR = \frac{1}{N^2} \sum_{i,j=1}^{N} R(i,j)$$

2. *Determinism (DET)*, which is the fraction of recurrence points forming diagonal lines. Diagonal lines represent epochs of similar time evolution of states of the system. Therefore, DET is related with the determinism of the system;

$$DET = \frac{\sum_{l=l_{min}}^{N} lP(l)}{\sum_{i,j}^{N} R_{i,j}}$$

3. *Longest Diagonal Line (LMAX)*, which is a measure of the dynamical stability
of the system, being inversely related to the largest Lyapunov exponent;

$$L_{\max} = \max(\{l_i; L = 1...N_l\})$$

4. *Shannon Entropy (ENTR)* of the distribution of the line lengths, which is a
measure of the complexity of the recurrence structure:

$$ENTR = -\sum_{l=l_{\min}}^{N} p(l)l_n p(l)$$

It should be noted, however, that a proper measurement of RQA variables relies on the preliminary choice of fundamental parameters related to the theoretical
framework of nonlinear time-series analysis [9, 10]. Technically, two points of a
time-series (such as an EEG) are considered recurrent when their Euclidean distance is within a predetermined distance (called radius). The term "point" is not
referred to any single point in the time-series. Instead, the Euclidean distance is
calculated between pairs of vectors whose components are from properly selected
points of the time-series. The number of points chosen as components of vectors is
referred to as the embedding dimension of the time-series while the number of
points in the time-series which are to be skipped away between two consecutive
components is known as the time delay. The application of RQA to EEGs is accomplished in three steps:
- preliminary determination of the embedding dimension, time delay and
  radius necessary to measure the RQA variables;
- measurement of variables;
- statistical validation of measured variables.

All the above mentioned steps are markedly CPU-time consuming. This is a
significant constraint for the epileptologists since EEG recordings usually span
over a time scale of hours/days. Removal of this constraint is the preliminary condition for an efficient investigation aimed to seizure prediction by EEG analysis.

5   PERFORM RECURRENCE QUANTIFICATION
ANALYSIS IN GRID INFRASTRUCTURES

In this section we will describe how the geographically-distributed computational
resources of a Grid infrastructure have been used in order to allow epileptologists

to perform RQA of EEGs recorded from four epileptic patients who underwent pre-surgical evaluation for the resection of epileptic foci. All these patients were refractory to any conventional anti-epileptic drug treatment. The configuration and the set up of the Grid infrastructure to conduct EEG analyses at a large scale has been carried out by INFN in close synergy with ARCEM. As first step of the gridification process, the main software packages of the RQA method (ver. 13.1), were ported on Linux to be then used in the Grid environment. This was made possible thanks to the courtesy of Prof. Charles Webber who kindly provided the source code. The software package, developed in C, has been successfully compiled without any specific problems and executed in the e-Infrastructure developed by the EGEE project (http://www.eu-egee.org/), the Europe's leading grid computing project co-founded by the EU in the context of the 6th and 7th Framework Programme. The project aims at providing researchers with access to a geographically distributed computing Grid Infrastructure available around the clock. In this scenario the gLite middleware (http://glite.web.cern.ch/glite/), which allows scientific communities to develop applications to be executed on distributed computational and storage resources across the Internet, has been adopted for this use case. Since the dimension of the whole package is quite small (less than 10 MB), the software has not been deployed on the Grid sites. On the contrary, the software package needed for the EEGs analysis was sent using the InputSandbox attribute of the Grid job. At first, the analysis of EEGs, segmented in epochs of proper length, was conducted by creating and submitting a parametric jobs to the Workload Management System (WMS) of the Grid Infrastructure. The job description file created for this purpose is shown here:

```
JobType="Parametric";
Parameters=9;
ParameterStart=1;
ParameterStep=1;
Executable="start_rqh2.sh";
Arguments="eeg9.txt surr_par9";
StdOutput="eeg9_surr_PARAM__rqh.txt";
StdError="eeg9_surr_PARAM__err.txt";
InputSandbox={"start_rqh2.sh","rqh2.exe","eeg9.txt","surr_par9"};
OutputSandbox={"eeg9_surr_PARAM__rqh.txt","eeg9_surr_PARAM__err.txt"};
MyProxyServer="myproxy.ct.infn.it";
Requirements=(other.GlueCEPolicyMaxCPUTime>720);
Rank=(other.GlueCEStateWaitingJobs==0 ? other.GlueCEStateFreeCPUs : -
other.GlueCEStateWaitingJobs);
```

Unfortunately, the complexity of protocols and command line interfaces exposed to end users by the Grid middleware make the human interaction with this new technology particularly complicated and not straightforward especially for non-experts. There is a gap that users have to overcome before starting to obtain some benefits from the adoption of the Grid paradigm. In order to make this new technology easy to use also for epilepsy researchers, INFN has developed a web-based interface on top of the GENIUS Grid portal [11, 12]. This Grid portal, powered by EnginFrame (www.nice-software.com/web/nice/products/enginframe), provides the end-user with a transparent abstraction layer to access the distributed services and resources of a typical Grid infrastructure. Using a simple web browser, epileptologists can now access a Grid infrastructure and use the distributed computational resources available from anywhere they are located speeding up considerably the analysis of EEGs. EnginFrame is a Web-based technology, developed by the Italian company NICE, (www.nice-software.com/web/nice/home) that allows the access and the exploitation of Grid-enabled applications and infrastructures directly from the web. It allows users, grouped within a Virtual Organization (VO), to exploit the whole power of a Grid infrastructure hiding all its complexity and providing an abstraction layer to the Grid middleware services. EnginFrame is also well known in the Grid research world for being the technology which GENIUS (Grid Enable web eNvironment for site Independent User job Submission), one of the most known and used Grid portals of the European project EGEE, is based on. Due to the modularity and flexibility of EnginFrame, the GENIUS portal can be easily customized to interact with several Grid components and/or VOs allowing scientists to access, execute and monitor their own applications only by using a simple web browser. In fig. 2 are shown some snapshots of the dedicated services deployed on the portal.

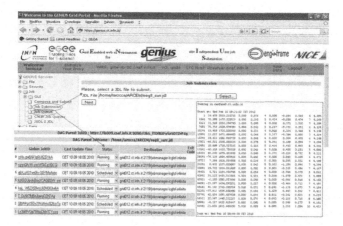

Fig. 2: Performing the RQA through the GENIUS grid portal enabled by EnginFrame

In the upper part of figure 2, the epileptologist selects and submits the file describing the job to be executed in order to perform the RQA of EEGs. In the lower part of the figure the monitoring of the EEG analysis is shown. Once the process is finished, users can download and use the output data to produce preliminary results. A first data challenge has been successful submitted to the INFN Grid infrastructure (https://grid.infn.it/) with a total of about 8,000 submitted jobs, corresponding to the analysis of approximately 225,000 EEG epochs. This amount of jobs required less than two weeks to be accomplished by the Grid infrastructure whereas the same calculation on a single computer would have been performed in approximately six months. The results collected from this data challenge produced the preliminary results described in the next session.

6   RESULTS

Although several methods are often proposed for the preliminary determination of
the embedding dimension, time delay and radius (see section 4), it is important to
notice that some techniques may not be appropriate for the analysis of time-series
of biological origin [6]. This is particularly true for the EEG which is intrinsically
non-stationary and affected by noise. We have chosen the strategy suggested by
Webber [13] and implemented by the Recurrence Quantification Scaling (RQS)
software, included in the RQA software package. Thus, for any given time-series
(e.g., the EEG), the RQA variables are calculated for all the combinations of embedding dimension, time delay and radius, letting these parameters to vary within
a broad range. For this study, we used intracranial ictal EEGs from four epileptic
patients who underwent pre-surgical evaluation for epilepsy surgery. For each
EEG we analysed 2 to 3 consecutive seizures and the analysis was also extended
over the EEG preceding each ictal activity (pre-ictal EEG). All recordings were
segmented in 10-second epochs (2248 epochs, 2560 points each) and parametric
jobs were submitted to the Grid infrastructure as described in the previous section.
Results from this preliminary step highlighted how the common attitude of choosing a fixed radius and then to determine the RQA variables [14] may not be the
most appropriate method for the analysis of EEGs recorded from patients affected
by epilepsy. In order to embrace the full pattern of variation of RQA variables
ranging from pre-ictal to ictal/post-ictal, we observed that it is useful to treat the
radius as it were a variable and the recurrence rate (RR) as a fixed parameter. Interestingly, this preliminary analysis showed a sensitivity of RQA variables to the
changing patterns of EEGs (see fig. 3). RQA variables are sensitive to different
patterns of EEG activity. Each panel is made of three graphs depicting the patterns
of variation of RR vs. radius, RR vs. DET and the original epoch from which
RQA variables were measured. Each coloured strip is related to a different embedding dimension (red to purple, 8 to 15, respectively) where the thickness of
each coloured strip is composed by different time delays (from left to right, 10 to
30 points, respectively).

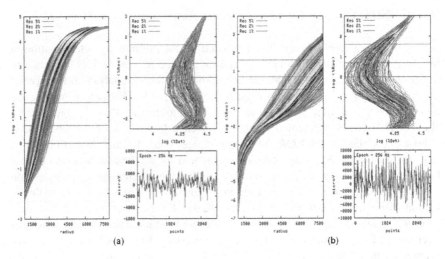

Fig. 3: The figure 3 (a) shows the variation of RQA variables calculated from 10-second epochs of pre-ictal EEG. The figure 3 (b) shows how RQA variable patterns look differently when calculated from 10-second epochs of ictal EEG.

In particular, it has been shown how the radius required for a fixed RR to be preserved changes as a function of the EEG pattern. This was especially evident following the pattern of variation of the radius from the onset of a seizure to its end. Indeed, the radius broadly expands and suddenly collapses, in association with the beginning and the end of the seizure. This preliminary analysis suggested parameters for the subsequent elaboration to be set as follows:

- embedding dimension: 10;
- time delay: 20;
- recurrence rate (RR): fixed, set to 5%;
- radius: variable, to be determined in order to meet 5% RR.

Next, the calculation of RQA variables was accomplished. It is relevant to notice that nonlinearities embedded in a time-series may also arise from random processes. Hence, RQA applied to the original EEG epochs is not sufficient per se to establish whether the pattern of variation of RQA variables has to be exclusively ascribed to a nonlinear dynamical system. To circumvent this problem, the statistical validation of RQA performed on the original time-series is made by the method of surrogate data [15]. Practically, the points of each original epoch are randomly shuffled and calculation of RQA variables is newly accomplished with the same operating parameters set as for the RQA of the original epochs. We randomly shuffled each original epoch 100 times, hence constructing 100 surrogate epochs for each original epoch. Hence, a total amount of 224,800 surrogate epochs was built. Grid computing was fundamental to allow and to manage the calculation of RQA variables for such a massive amount of time-series within eight days. Also in this case, the calculation load was distributed over several computing elements of the Grid infrastructure. We focused our attention to the four main variables returned from calculations (being RR fixed), i.e. radius, DET, LMAX and ENTR. For each group of 100 surrogate epochs, the mean and the standard deviation (SD) of these RQA variables were determined. Then, for each original epoch, we considered as acceptable the values of the four variables if they were larger than 3 times the SD of the mean of the same variables as calculated in the corresponding group of 100 surrogate epochs. This constraint ensured a statistical significance equivalent to $p < 0.01$ [15, 16].

As also noted by other investigators, DET, LMAX and ENTR are sensitive to the EEG patterns. In particular, the values of DET, LMAX and ENTR decrease when they are calculated from an ictal EEG. Nevertheless, the common method of letting the recurrence rate to vary whereas the radius is fixed, may not embrace properly the full range of EEG patterns and may yield a high variability of RQA measurements.

Supported by our preliminary analysis that suggested the setting of the radius as a variable and RR as a fixed parameter, and differently from other investigators who considered the temporal profile of RQA variables singularly, we have introduced the Dynamic Index (DI) defined as follows:

$$DI = \frac{radius}{DET \cdot LMAX \cdot ENTR}$$

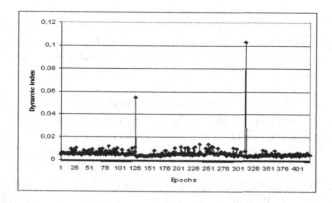

Fig. 4: The full (421 epochs, 4210 seconds) intracranial pre-ictal and ictal EEG of a patient has been commutated in the temporal profile of the Dynamic Index (see text). This parameter easily detects epochs of ictal EEG activity. Indeed, two peaks clearly denote two distinct seizures occurring at the EEG time of the corresponding epochs.

As depicted in fig. 4, DI revealed particularly useful in tracking seizures and, in our opinion, this feature may be exploited for off-line automated seizure detection.

However, we have focused our attention beyond the immediate usefulness of DI as ictal activity tracker. Indeed, we were interested in the full representation of EEG patterns by DI in order to test the sensitivity of this parameter to the dynamical changes of EEG. To this aim, we exploited the graphical representation known as delay plot which can efficiently depict on a plane the full dynamical behaviour of a system. For each temporal profile of DI (as represented in fig. 4), we reported on both the x- and y-axis the values of DI and plotted the points with coordinates (DIj, DIj+1), that is, DI at epoch j vs. DI at the next epoch (j+1).

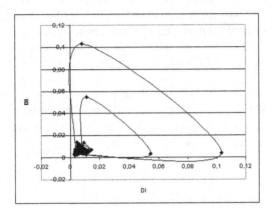

Fig. 5: Delay plot of the full temporal profile of the Dynamic Index (DI) reported in fig. 4. With this graphical representation ictal EEG activities are represented as broad excursions of DI trajectories departing from and returning to the mass of points confined in the small left-end area of the graph.

As shown in fig. 5, DI could fully depict the dynamical pattern of EEG. It is immediately evident how ictal activity corresponds to a broad excursion of DI, departing from a mass of DI values towards which, in any case, DI returns at the end of ictal activity. However, intriguing patterns emerge when one depicts the DI dynamical behaviour on separate delay plots for EEG activity preceding a seizure. This procedure operated as a magnifier lens of EEG dynamics which appeared as a compact mass of DI values in the delay plot when referring to the full temporal profile (fig. 5). The visual inspection of fig. 6 highlights how the compact mass is made of points non-uniformly distributed. Indeed, several points enter and exit a smaller aggregate of points, wandering in the plane of the delay plot for a limited time. Interestingly, one notices that delay plots of DI of pre-ictal activities (panels A and C) are qualitatively similar.

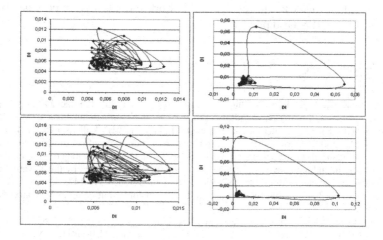

Fig. 6: Interesting patterns emerge when behaviours of pre-ictal DI and ictal DI are plotted separately. The full DI pattern as in fig. 5 was decomposed so that panels A represent the pre-ictal activity preceding ictal activity shown in panel B, whereas panels C represent the pre-ictal activity preceding ictal activity depicted in panel D. The compact mass shown in fig. 5 is only apparent. The visual inspection of panels A and C highlight how the compact mass is made of points non-uniformly distributed. Several points exit a smaller aggregate of points, wander in the plane of the delay plot for a limited time and then return to the same cluster. This pattern may represent a hallmark of the dynamical instability characterizing pre-ictal states. Referring to the temporal profile of DI as shown in fig. 4, plot in panel A embraces epochs from 1 to 91, in panel B from 92 to 188, in panel C from 189 to 284 and in panel D from 285 to 374.

At the present step of the investigation, we speculate that wandering patterns of DI values, as seen in delay plots associated to pre-ictal EEG, may represent a hallmark of dynamical instability characterising pre-ictal states. Interestingly, this observation raises the possibility to exploit this finding for incoming seizure prediction. Nevertheless, for a definitive word, RQA has to be performed also on inter-ictal EEG recordings of sufficient duration in order to check for significant differences with the respect to the present findings. This step of the investigation has already started, here again with the fundamental support of Grid computing technology which makes the analysis of a huge amount of epochs doable in an acceptable time.

7   ACKNOWLEDGEMENTS

We gratefully acknowledge all the people who supported this work contributing with ideas, requirements and feedback. Authors thank in particular Prof. Charles Webber who kindly provided the source code of the RQA application which has been ported on Linux in the context of this work and the support provided by the EGEE-III and INFN Grid projects.

REFERENCES

[1]   Fisher R, van Emde Boas W, Blume W, Elger C, Genton P, Lee P, Engel J (2005). "Epileptic seizures and epilepsy: definitions proposed by the International League Against Epilepsy (ILAE) and the International Bureau for Epilepsy (IBE)". Epilepsia 46 (4): 470–472.

[2]   Rizzi M (2009) "During a systemic inflammatory response, the effect of non-steroidal anti-inflammatory drugs on seizure susceptibility in the immature brain may depend on the proconvulsant and anticonvulsant mechanisms simultaneously induced by the elevation of parenchymal prostaglandin E2 levels". Biosci. Hypotheses 2 (3):143-147.

[3]   Sisodiya S (2003) "Drug resistance in epilepsy: not futile, but complex?". Lancet Neurol 2(6):331.

[4]   Engel J Jr (1996). "Surgery for seizures". New Eng. J. Med. 334 (10): 647–652.

[5]   Paglioli E, Palmini A, Paglioli E, da Costa JC, Portuguez M, Martinez JV, Calcagnotto ME, Hoefel JR, Raupp S, Barbosa-Coutinho L (2004) "Survival analysis of the surgical outcome of temporal lobe epilepsy due to hippocampal sclerosis". Epilepsia 45(11):1383-1391.

[6]   Webber CL Jr, Zbilut JP (1994) "Dynamical assessment of physiological systems and states using recurrence plot strategies". J. Appl. Physiol 76:965-973.

[7]   Eckmann JP, Kamphorst SO, Ruelle D (1987) „Recurrence plots of dynamical systems". Europhys. Lett. 5:973-977.

[8]   Marwan N, Romano RC, Thiel M, Kurths J (2007) "Recurrence plots for the analysis of complex systems". Phys. Rep. 438:237-329.

[9]   Takens F (1981) "Detecting strange attractors in turbulence". In: Rand DA, Young LS, editors. "Dynamical systems and turbulence". Lecture Notes in Mathematics 898, Springer: 336.

[10]   Kantz H, Schreiber T (2004) "Nonlinear time-series analysis". Cambridge.

[11]   Andronico, G. et al. (2003). GENIUS: a web portal for the grid. Nuclear Instruments and Methods in Physics Research, A 502, 433-436.

[12]   Barbera, R. et al. (2007). The GENIUS Grid Portal : Its Architecture, Improvements of Features ,and New Implementations about Authentication and Authorization. Paper presented at the meeting Enabling Technologies: Infrastructure for Collaborative Enterprises. 16th IEEE International Workshops on. doi: 10.1109/WETICE.2007.4407171

[13]   Webber CL Jr (2005) "Recurrence Quantification Analysis of Nonlinear Dynamical Systems". In Riley MA, Van Orden GC, editors. "Tutorials in contemporary nonlinear methods for the behavioural sciences". 27-94.

[14]   Li X, Ouyang G, Yao X, Guan X (2004) "Dynamical characteristics of the pre-epileptic seizures in rats with recurrence quantification analysis". Phys. Lett. A 333:164-171.

[15]   Theiler J, Eubank S, Longtin A, Galrikian B, Farmer J (1992) "Testing for nonlinearity in time series: the method of surrogate data". Physica D 58:77-94.

[16]   Schreiber T, Schmitz A (2000) "Surrogate time series". Physica D 142:346-382.

Construction of the Platform for Phylogenetic Analysis

Zhen Meng[1], Xiaoguang Lin[1], Xing He[1], Yanping Gao[1], Hongmei Liu[2],
Yong Liu[1], Yuanchun Zhou[1], Jianhui Li[1], Zhiduan Chen[3], Shouzhou Zhang[2]
and Yong Li[2]

1. Scientific Data Center, Computer Network Information Center, Chinese Academy of Sciences, China
2. Fairylake Botanical Garden, Chinese Academy of Sciences, China
3. State Key Laboratory of Systematic and Evolutionary botany, Institute of Botany, Chinese Academy of Sciences, China

Abstract   Based on discussing the history of advancement to building the tree of life using genetic and genomic information, effective strategies and methods for the construction of the tree of life, this paper carried out business process analysis and application design. It implements a phylogenetic analysis platform for the land plants based on this analysis. The platform extracts molecular data from the international public databases in batch, which is automated acquisition, cleaning function for users to understand the situation of peer data. The process of phylogenetic reconstruction includes several public modes and tools, such as batch extraction, multiple sequence alignment, cleaning & editing, tree reconstruction, phylogeny evaluation and visualization. All these procedures demand a number of interactive interfaces for phylogenetic tree automatic generation and decision-making aids experiment.

Keywords   **Phylogeny, Tree of life, Batch extraction, Tree reconstruction, PALPP**

1   INTRODUCTION

The Tree of Life (TOL) is to bring all living species, including existing and extinct, linked to a phylogenetic tree with the huge amount of information, which can be used to clarify the origin of life, biological evolution pattern, categories of biological evolution and phylogenetic relationships, and the survival of biodiversity patterns and dynamics of change in the law. Construction of the tree of life and to fully exploit and to take advantage of the information is another challenge facing the life sciences. The United States of America was officially launched a 15-year-TOL national research projects in 2002. European countries have also been many rounds of discussion and will soon launch its TOL program, held four meetings to discuss Europe's TOL projects [1], from Kew center in the United Kingdom to Patras, Paris, London and Brussels since 2002. In recent years, Chi-

S.C. Lin and E. Yen (eds.), *Data Driven e-Science: Use Cases and Successful Applications of Distributed Computing Infrastructures (ISGC 2010)*, DOI 10.1007/978-1-4419-8014-4_38,
© Springer Science+Business Media, LLC 2011

nese scholars believe that TOL project to undertake in China is absolutely necessary after many discussions, and it is very timely and feasible. In the October 2003
meeting held in Xiangshan, Chinese and foreign scholars from various fields of
micro-organisms, plants, animals, and evolutionary biology have discussed the details of our implementation of the scheme. Since then, via further discussion, a
"life Trees - China National Action Plan Outline" is intended to gradually promote
the process in China.

Speaking from the research accumulated, rapid accumulation of genetic and
genomic information for the construction of the tree of life, laid an important data
base over the past 20 years. However, there are a lot of technical problems, which
is automatic in the DNA data collection and screening, data integration, large tree
(Supertree) to build, and information for further excavation and sharing, etc.
Countries are looking for valid strategies and methods to build the tree of life from
genetic and genomic information [2]. To build Super tree, there are two different
ways: (1) based on the overlap of two or several smaller trees, integrating a number of trees to synthetic large tree; (2) directly on the super - data matrix for analysis, building the tree of life. But no matter which way to choose, there are currently facing the same problems, how to make use of public databases of DNA
sequence information, existing? How to effectively filter the information? How to
quickly auto-generate the tree of life which reflects the evolutionary history of different biological taxa? How to fully exploit and utilize the tree of life implied in
the great information?

In this paper, Phylogenetic Analysis of Land Plants Platform (PALPP), a phylogenetic platform based on web, which integrates some useful toolkits, is introduced. It is initiated and compiled collaboratively by Computer Network Information Center, Chinese Academy of Sciences (CNIC, CAS), Institute of Botany,
Chinese Academy of Sciences (IB, CAS) and ShenZhen Fairylake Botanical Garden, Chinese Academy of Sciences (FBG,CAS). From the starting of development
of phylogenetic framework of the Chinese land plant, it promotes to solve the
technical problems of tree of life in the build process, explores the strategies and
methods of using of genetic and genomic information to build the tree of life,
studies and develops technology of automatic collection of DNA sequence information and automatic reconstruction of the tree of life. It plans to establish information platform for the TOL and form the utilization mechanisms of it, in order to
start up and implicate national plans, to prepare conditions for the eventual establishment of database with information of species (Species Bank) of international
influence, compatible with species classification, morphological traits, fossil information, as well as the DNA database in China. Core scientific component of
PALPP is from biologists, experts in particular groups of organisms, informatics
and computer researchers. The goals of PALPP are to provide automatically work
environment for data gathering and phylogenetic analysis for scientific research,
and furthermore, to share information with other databases, and to link the information from other databases through phylogeny.

The remainder of this paper is organized as follows. Part 2 introduces the application design of PALPP. Part 3 introduces some examples of the usage in PALPP. Part 4 shows the application effectiveness and points out the future work.

2 APPLICATION DESIGN

PALPP in accordance with the "unified planning, unified standards, focused, step by step" principle, which is constructed from the following aspects:

The data integration technology of DNA sequence information with other information and the framework model of Species Bank; Life Tree Auto-generation technology and strategy for the assembly of large trees; DNA sequence information of the automatic acquisition, assessment and marking; Marker Gene screening, and Data Matrix automatic assembly; information mining of the tree of life, and analysis system construction. The business process, PALPP followed, is shown in Figure 1.

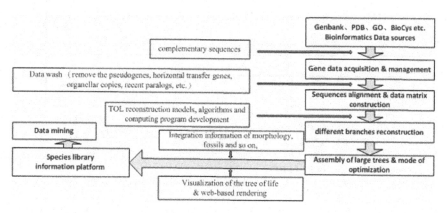

Fig. 1: Business process of PALPP

2.1 *Business Process*

The business process of PALPP is as follows. Firstly, it obtains basic data through the analysis of public bioinformatics resource databases, such as GeneBank [3], Gene Ontology (Gene Ontology Consortium, 2004), etc. and then biologists select species to get complementary sequences according to peer research status. Secondly, they do a data wash, as the analysis and evaluation of the sequences, to remove the pseudogenes, horizontal transfer genes, organellar copies, recent paralogs, etc. ; and then, multiple sequence alignment and data matrix construction, different branches reconstruction, assembly of large trees and mode of optimization are carried out. In the final, the working platform for the green plants is being formed by integration information of morphology, fossils and so on, visualization of the tree of life, and web-based rendering.

PALPP focus on achievements of the building models, algorithms and computing procedures for application and development of accumulation. In the Platform, the user can simply visit the related data and analysis.

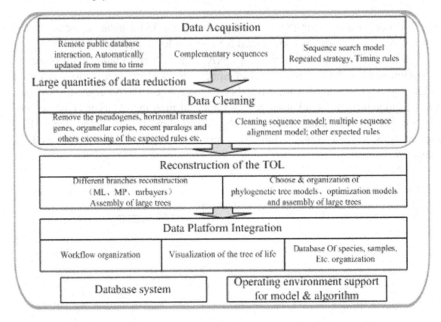

Fig. 2: Overall framework of PALPP

2.2 Building Framework

The overall framework of PALPP is shown in Figure 2, which includes database system design, operating environment with special model algorithm building, the starting large amounts of data collation, data acquisition, data cleansing, tree of life reconstruction and data platform integration, a total of seven aspects. The platform integrates BioEdit [4], ClustalW [5], modeltest [6], mrbayers [7], phyml [8], as well as the ncbi-sequin (version 5.26, 2004), ATV [9] and other tool package features.

It is well designed in MVC pattern using the Spring Framework, one of the most popular lightweight J2EE frameworks. JSP (Java Server Page), JSTL (JSP Standard Tag library) and Java Applet technology are used in the view layer of the MVC architecture. The AbstractWizardFormController of Spring Framework is used to manage the multiple-step wizard process. And, the Quartz Scheduler, an open-source enterprise job scheduler, is used to schedule the one-click process.

There are too many third-party applications called during the process of the phygenetic tree's generation. How to deal with these applications is a tough problem. In our solution, the Java object Process is introduced. The executable scripts of these third-party applications are transmitted to CMD (in Windows OS) or Shell (in Linux OS) to execute by the Process object. The details of each process's logs are written down in operating the input stream of Process object. According to these, a powerful middleware has been developed with the general features and good-definition interface to call these applications.

Some functions of BioEdit (Applet) are extended to upload the revised sequences data to web server in Data Editing & Cleaning using the socket programming.

A cluster with several high performance servers is built to do some parallel work using some applications implemented by MPI (Message Passing Interface), especially the ClustalW-MPI[10] and the mrBayes-MPI[11].

3   USAGE

PALPP is a web based platform, accessible using any modern web browser, like IE, Firefox, Opera. Figure 3 shows PALPP's user interface and an example tree.

Fig. 3: PALPP 's user interface and an example tree.

At present, PALPP extracts molecular data of rbcL, atpB and other genes or sequences, from the international public databases (GeneBank, DDBJ, and EMBL) in batch, which is automated acquisition, cleaning function for users to understand the situation of peer data. It also has the function of private data management to ensure that the data mining before publishing.

In PALPP, common users, privileged users and managing users as well as super user can visit it through the page (http://phylo.csdb.cn:8080/palpp/index.jsp), according to the relevant authority to conduct such as data update, data mining, workflow Custom, and modular analysis, etc. It is an example shown in Figure 4, that common users customized the workflow and data analysis.

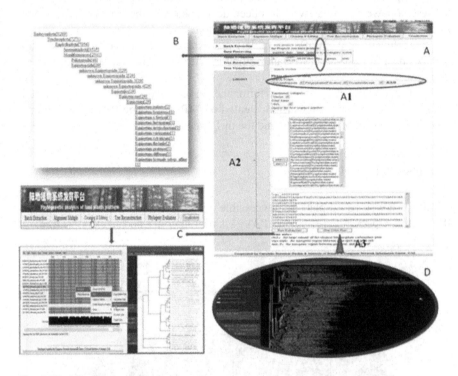

Fig. 4: Workflow & data analysis of common user

- "A" stands for customize options for the data; "B" stands for view the customized data due to category system chosen; "C" stands for an example of modular analysis; "D" stands for visualization of the tree file.
- "A" to "B" as shown in the process is that users customize the range of data and see peer status related to their study.
- "A" shows the analysis of user's operations: "A1" stands for selecting the existing data, "A2" stands for selecting the appropriate parameters (gene name, taxon, published sequence data, adding private sequence data); if you select the button, "One Click Run" (shown as "A3"), analysis results (shown as "D") are obtained as well as documents in middle analysis phases are retained (shown as "C"); if you select the button, "start wizard run" (shown as "A3"), the detailed analysis in accordance with the analysis phase of batch extraction, multiple se-

quence alignment, cleaning & editing, tree reconstruction, phylogeny evaluation and visualization (shown as "C") is carried out.

4 DISCUSSION AND FUTURE WORK

In our solution, a mass of useful software are integrated to do the phygenetic tree's generation. And, due to the huge advantage of hardware resource of CNIC, CAS, this solution is providing powerful one-stop service to molecular biologists. PALPP, the web implementation based on web of this solution, provides researchers a well-designed web interface to use. The distributed environment and some software based-on MPI and Map-Reduce strengthen the analysis ability of PALPP, and shorten the processing time.

Progressively, the platform is expanding scope of application from land plants to the entire plants, and then to be working platform for the entire life. It is open so that users can customize the existing range of data; can also submit the scope of the study species, the required genes, data sources and other parameters to scheduled data; users can use the exiting application, can also customize their own algorithms workflow.

As traction of the requirement from the experts, diversity of data types, promotion of data exchange, strengthening of data management, the platform will be the roles of both scientific data sharing and working platform and to achieve the target that a phylogenetic scholar can complete all of the data management and data mining work just via the internet.

At the same time, in the framework of the TOL, TOL Plan's general objective is to rebuild the evolutionary history of all living species, or that it is to let all of the biological organisms to find their place in the tree of life. When the tree of life eventually includes all kinds of levels of biological organisms, perhaps, the identification of biology organisms can be conducted by bar coding. By that time, people can identify species ever named or discover new species by sequence one or several gene using handhold species analyzer at once. Although this is just a fantasy at present, that it show a bright future in theory and practical implementation of the pathway under the TOL research programs.

5 ACKNOWLEDGMENT

We would like to acknowledge the staff of State Key Laboratory of Systematic and Evolutionary botany, Institute of Botany, CAS, Shenzhen Fairylake Botanical Garden, CAS and Scientific Data Center, Computer Network Information Center, CAS, for their good idea and helpful suggestions and discussions. This work was supported by data applications and services, environmental construction (0846061372, 0846061108 & 0846061208) in "tenth five-year plan" of Chinese Academy of Science.

REFERENCES

[1] Benton, M. J. and Ayala, F. J. Dating the tree of life. Science. 300(5626): 1698--1700 (2003)

[2] Ciccarelli, F. D., Doerks, T., von Mering, C., Creevey, C. J., Snel, B., and Bork, P. Toward automatic reconstruction of a highly resolved tree of life. Science. 311(5765): 1283--287 (2006)

[3] DA Benson, MS Boguski, DJ Lipman, J Ostell, and BF Ouellette. GenBank. Nucl. Acids Res. 27(1):12--17 (1999)

[4] TA Hill, BioEdit: a user-friendly biological sequence alignment editor for Windows 95/98/NT Nucleic Acids Symp. 41(1999):95--98 (1999)

[5] Julie D.Thompson et al. CLUSTAL W: improving the sensitivity of progressive multiple sequence alignment through sequence weighting, position-specific gap penalties and weight matrix choice. Nucleic Acids Research. 22(22): 4673--4680 (1994)

[6] Posada D., Crandall KA. Modeltest: testing the model of DNA substitution. Bioinformatics. 14(9): 817-818 (1998)

[7] John P. Huelsenbeck, Fredrik Ronquist. MRBAYES : Bayesian interface of phylogenetic trees. Bioinformatics. 17(8):754-755 (2001)

[8] Guindon S., Gascuel O. A simple, fast and accurate algorithm to estimate large phylogenies by maximum likelihood. Systematic Biology. 52(5):696-704 (2003)

[9] Zmasek C.M., Eddy S.R. ATV: display and manipulation of annotated phylogenetic trees. Bioinformatics. Apr;17(4):383-384 (2001)

[10] Kuo-Bin Li. ClustalW-MPI: ClustalW Analysis Using Distributed and Parallel Computing. Bioinformatics. 19(12): 1585-1586 (2003)

[11] Altekar, G., S. Dwarkadas, J. P. Huelsenbeck, and F. Ronquist. parallel Metropolis-coupled Markov chain Monte Carlo for Bayesian phylogenetic inference. Bioinformatics. 20:407-415 (2004)

Author Index

S.C. Lin and E. Yen (eds.), *Data Driven e-Science: Use Cases and Successful Applications of Distributed Computing Infrastructures (ISGC 2010)*, DOI 10.1007/978-1-4419-8014-4, © Springer Science+Business Media, LLC 2011